YOU'RE READING THE **WRONG WAY!**

PLATINUM END reads from right to left, starting in the upper-right corner. Japanese is read from right to left, meaning that action, sound effects and word-balloon order are completely reversed from English order.

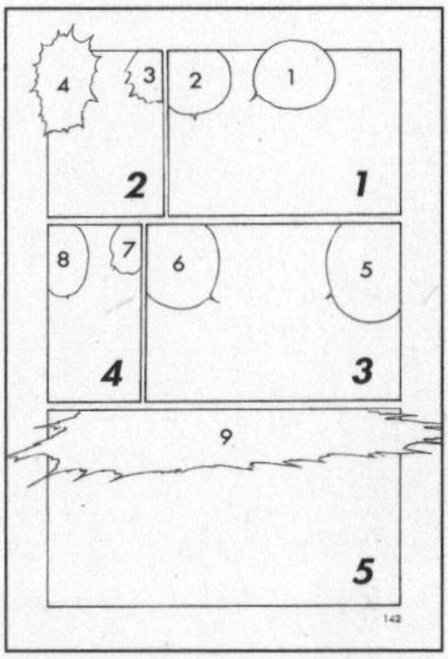

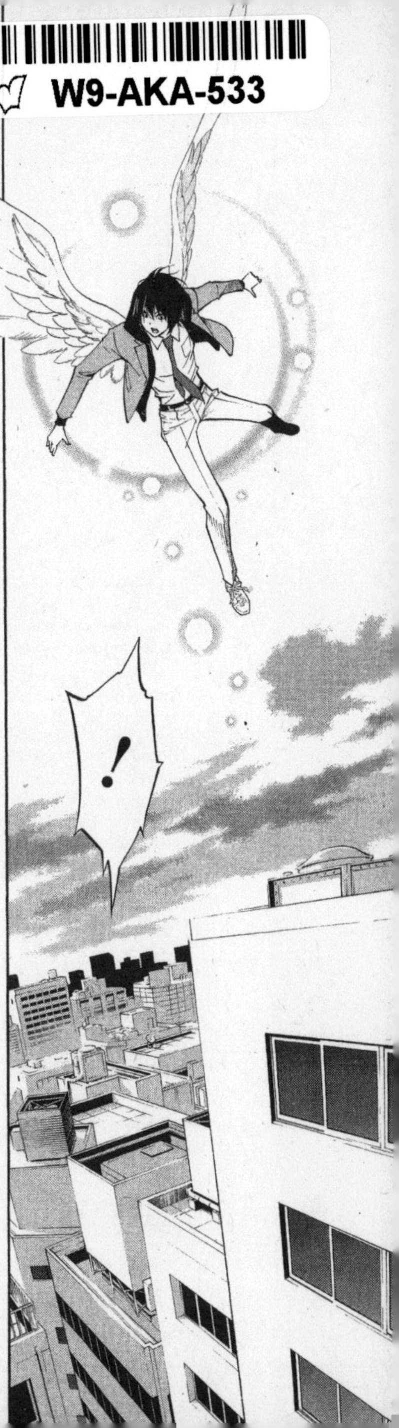
!

PLATINUM END

VOLUME 9
SHONEN JUMP Manga Edition

○

STORY **Tsugumi Ohba**
ART Takeshi Obata

○

TRANSLATION Stephen Paul
TOUCH-UP ART & LETTERING James Gaubatz
DESIGN Shawn Carrico
EDITOR Alexis Kirsch

○

ORIGINAL COVER DESIGN Narumi Noriko

○

Printed in the U.S.A.

Published by VIZ Media, LLC
P.O. Box 77010
San Francisco, CA 94107

○

10 9 8 7 6 5 4 3 2 1
First printing, July 2019

viz.com

shonenjump.com

PARENTAL ADVISORY
PLATINUM END is rated M for Mature
and is recommended for mature readers.
This volume contains suggestive themes.

CHARACTERS

Kanade

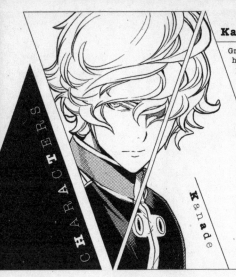

Kanade Uryu

Grandson of the Joso Academy headmaster, son of the Joso Industries president. He assumes the form of the Metropoliman character and purges the other god candidates until Mirai's group puts an end to him.

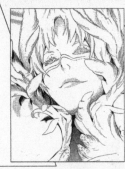

Meyza

The special-rank angel who chose Kanade. For unknown reasons she was elevated from rankless to the top special rank.

????

A god candidate who pierced Kanade with a red arrow. He gained all of the arrows and wings in Kanade's possession.

????

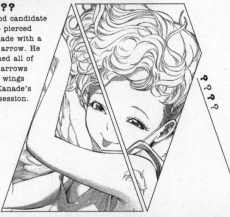

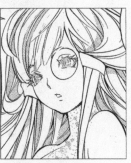

Baret

The first-rank angel who chose Mukaido. Possesses great knowledge about the celestial world.

Story

AFTER PARTING

Sadness prevails at Mukaido's death, even though it brought the end of Metropoliman. Meanwhile, the other god candidates spring into action...

PROOF OF LIFE

Mukaido points a gun at Metropoliman. He pulls the trigger at the cost of his life—for the sake of family.

NARROWING DISTANCE

During a one-on-one duel with Metropoliman, Mirai catches him off guard. He and Saki capture Metropoliman.

CONTENTS

9

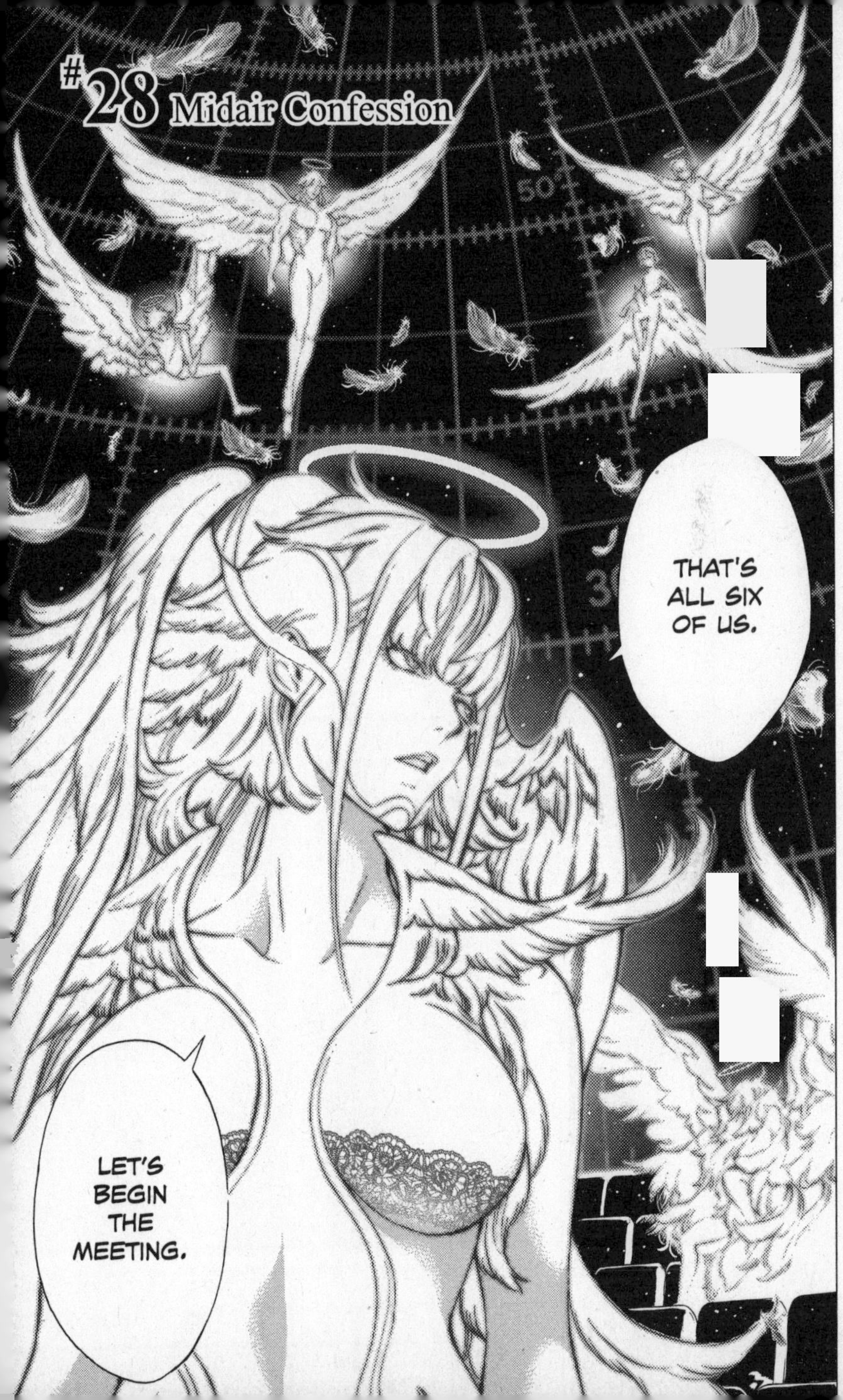
#28 Midair Confession
THAT'S ALL SIX OF US.
LET'S BEGIN THE MEETING.

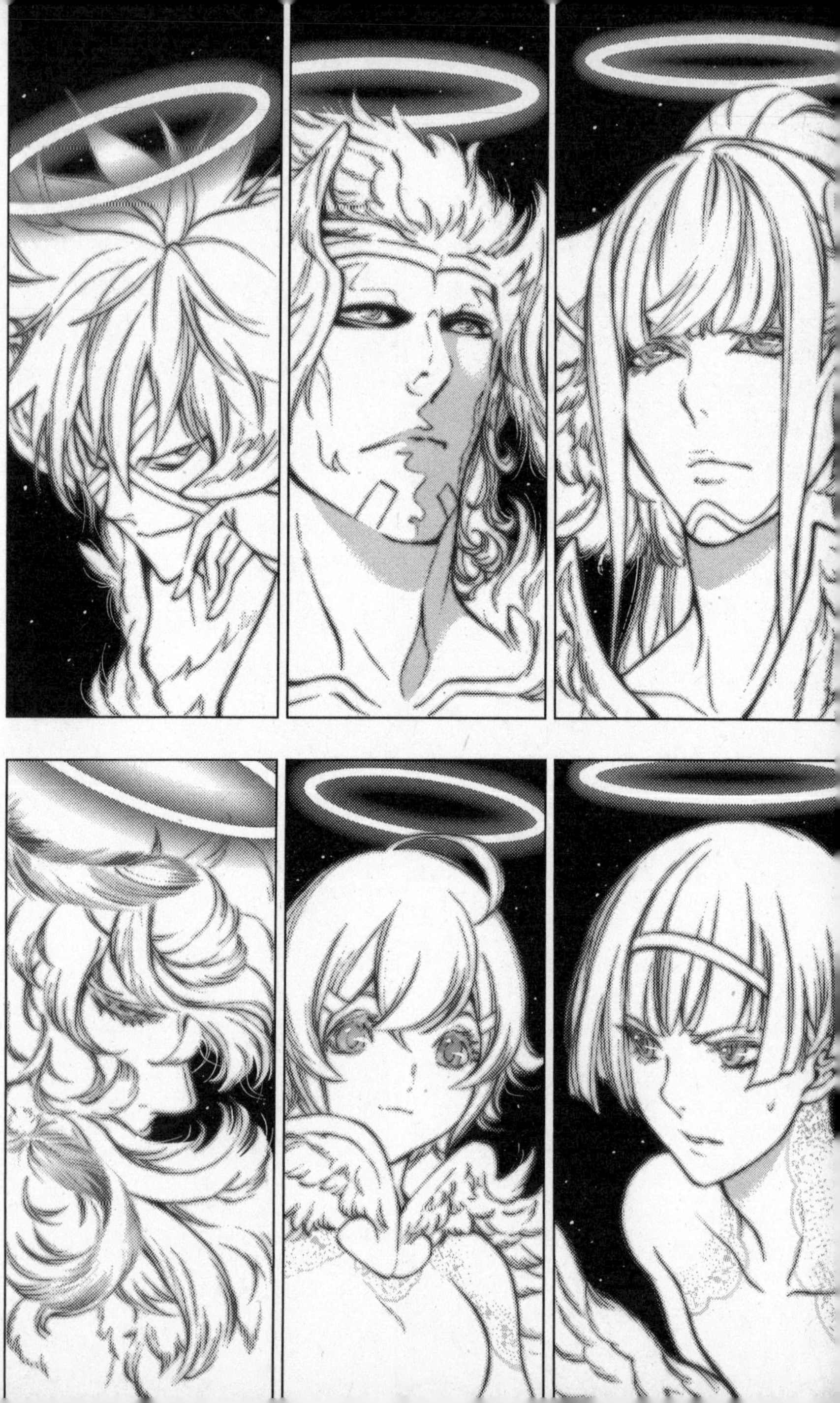

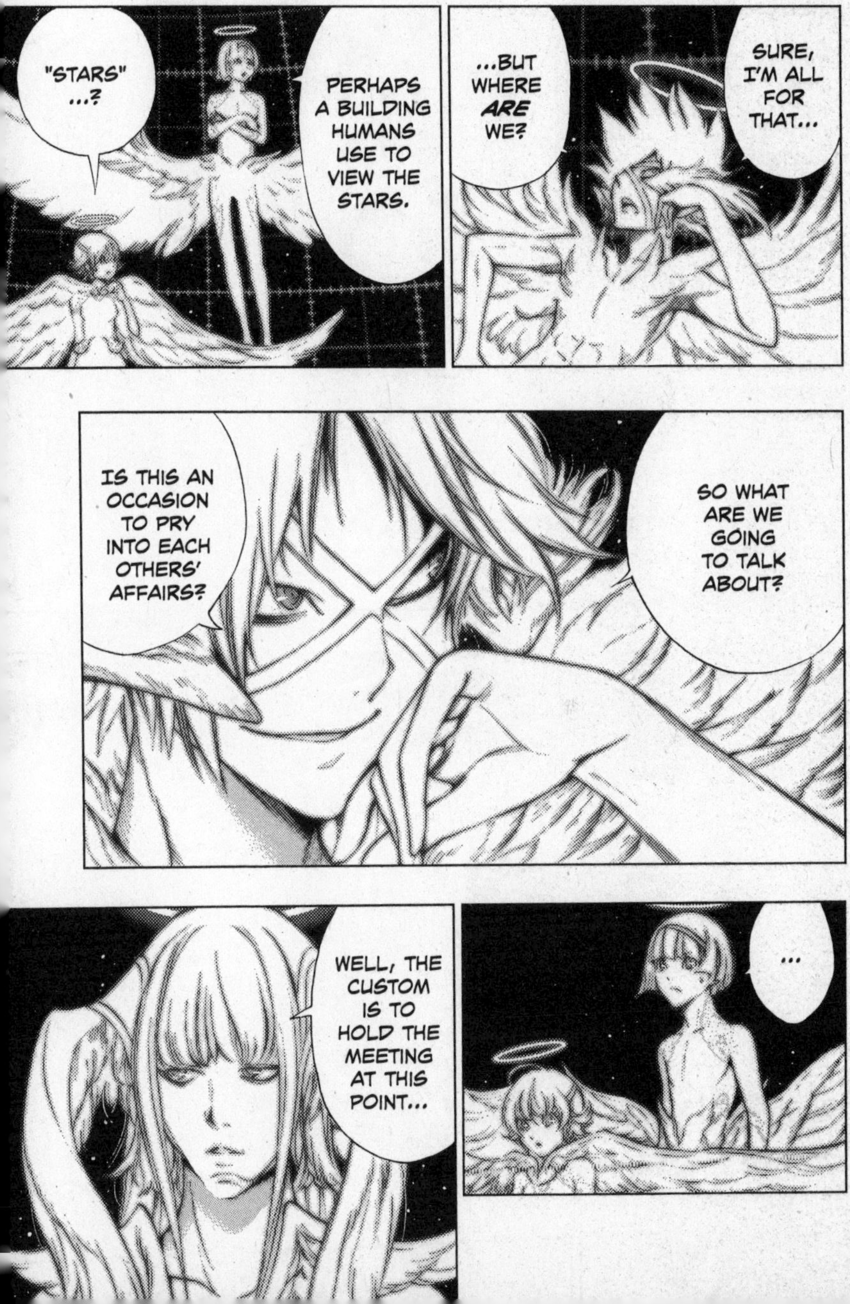
SURE, I'M ALL FOR THAT...
...BUT WHERE *ARE* WE?
PERHAPS A BUILDING HUMANS USE TO VIEW THE STARS.
"STARS" ...?
SO WHAT ARE WE GOING TO TALK ABOUT?
IS THIS AN OCCASION TO PRY INTO EACH OTHERS' AFFAIRS?
...
WELL, THE CUSTOM IS TO HOLD THE MEETING AT THIS POINT...

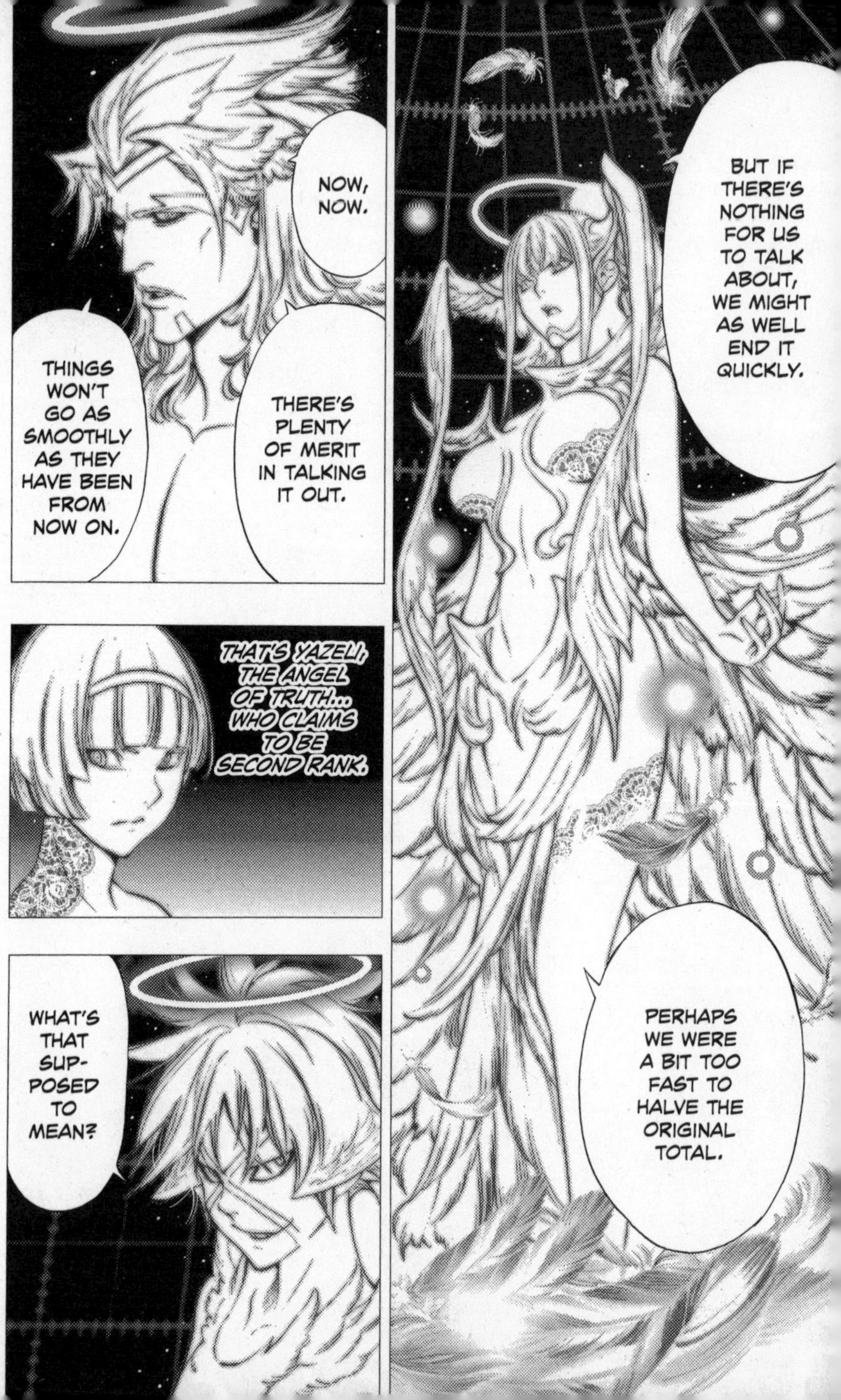
BUT IF THERE'S NOTHING FOR US TO TALK ABOUT, WE MIGHT AS WELL END IT QUICKLY.
PERHAPS WE WERE A BIT TOO FAST TO HALVE THE ORIGINAL TOTAL.
NOW, NOW.
THERE'S PLENTY OF MERIT IN TALKING IT OUT.
THINGS WON'T GO AS SMOOTHLY AS THEY HAVE BEEN FROM NOW ON.
THAT'S YAZELI, THE ANGEL OF TRUTH... WHO CLAIMS TO BE SECOND RANK.
WHAT'S THAT SUP-POSED TO MEAN?

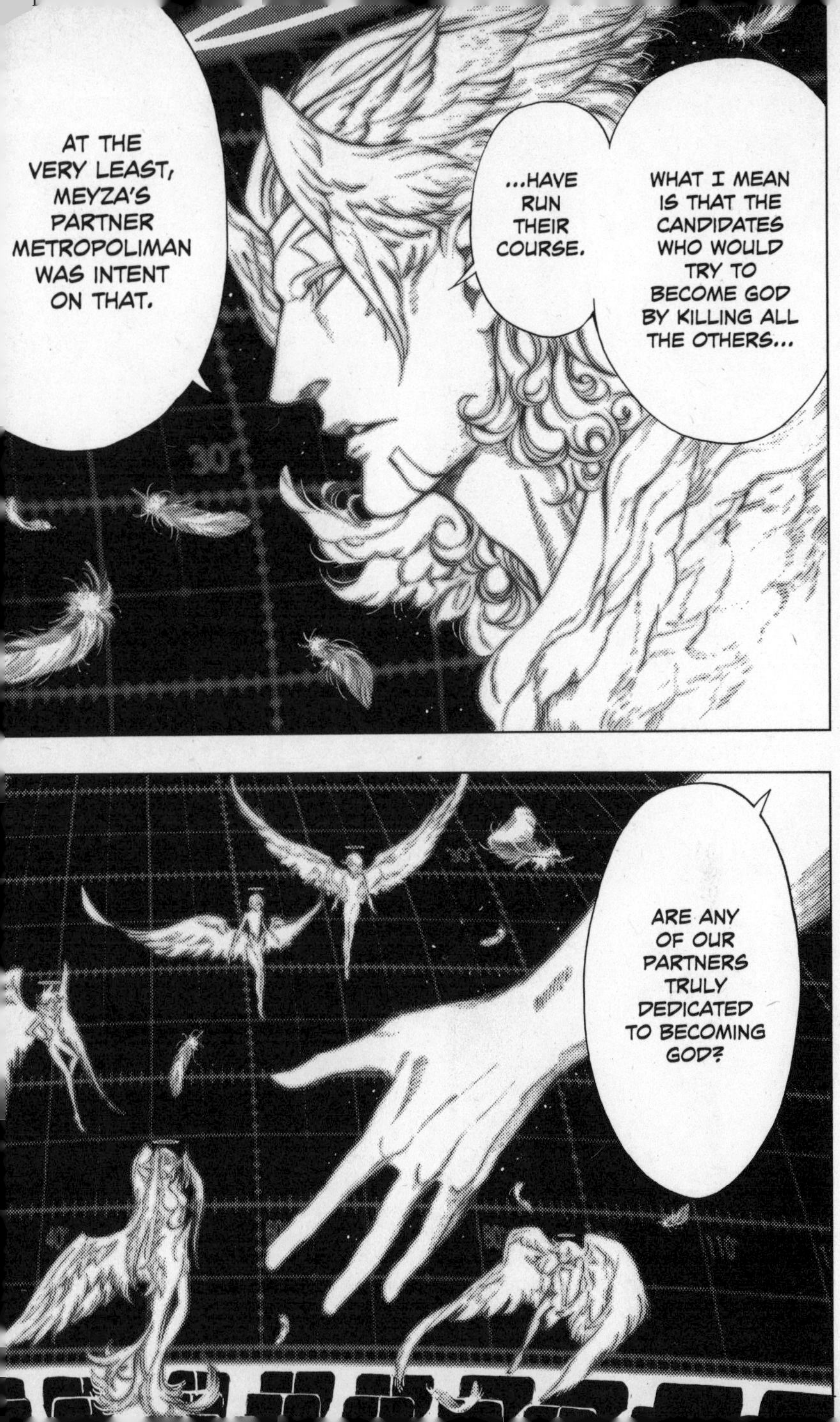
WHAT I MEAN IS THAT THE CANDIDATES WHO WOULD TRY TO BECOME GOD BY KILLING ALL THE OTHERS...
...HAVE RUN THEIR COURSE.
AT THE VERY LEAST, MEYZA'S PARTNER METROPOLIMAN WAS INTENT ON THAT.
ARE ANY OF OUR PARTNERS TRULY DEDICATED TO BECOMING GOD?

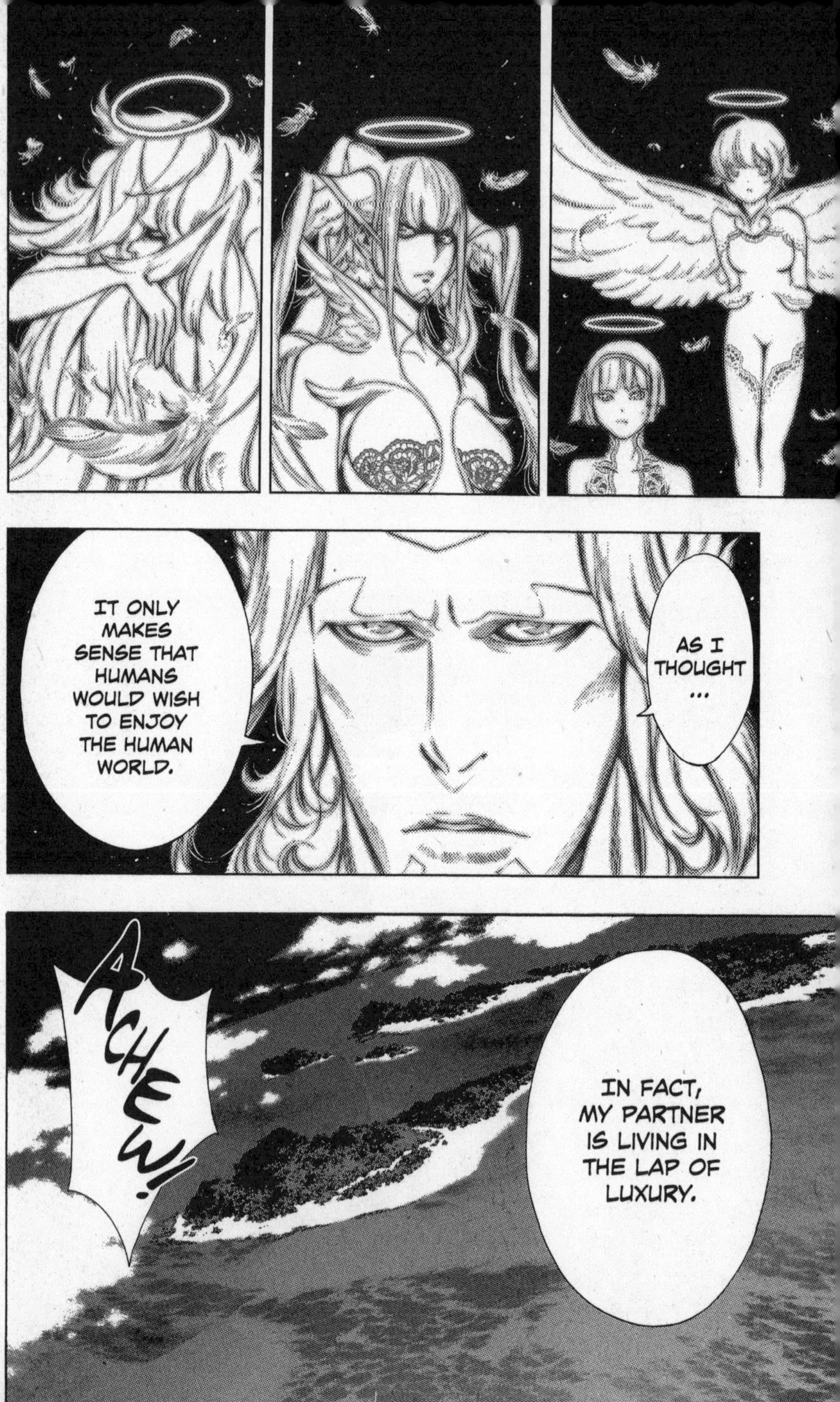
AS I THOUGHT ...
IT ONLY MAKES SENSE THAT HUMANS WOULD WISH TO ENJOY THE HUMAN WORLD.
IN FACT, MY PARTNER IS LIVING IN THE LAP OF LUXURY.
ACHEW!!

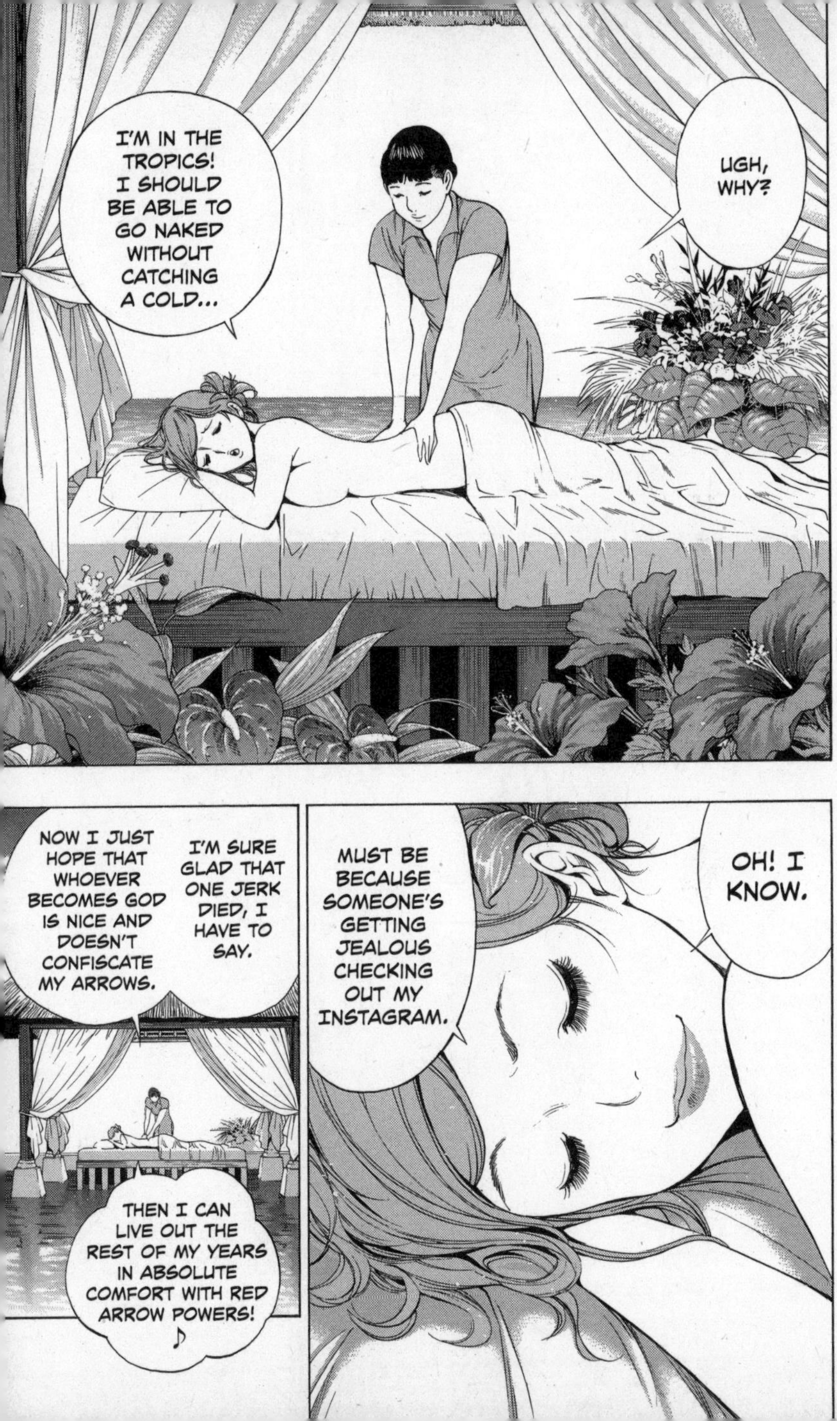
UGH, WHY?
I'M IN THE TROPICS! I SHOULD BE ABLE TO GO NAKED WITHOUT CATCHING A COLD...
OH! I KNOW.
MUST BE BECAUSE SOMEONE'S GETTING JEALOUS CHECKING OUT MY INSTAGRAM.
I'M SURE GLAD THAT ONE JERK DIED, I HAVE TO SAY.
NOW I JUST HOPE THAT WHOEVER BECOMES GOD IS NICE AND DOESN'T CONFISCATE MY ARROWS.
THEN I CAN LIVE OUT THE REST OF MY YEARS IN ABSOLUTE COMFORT WITH RED ARROW POWERS! ♪

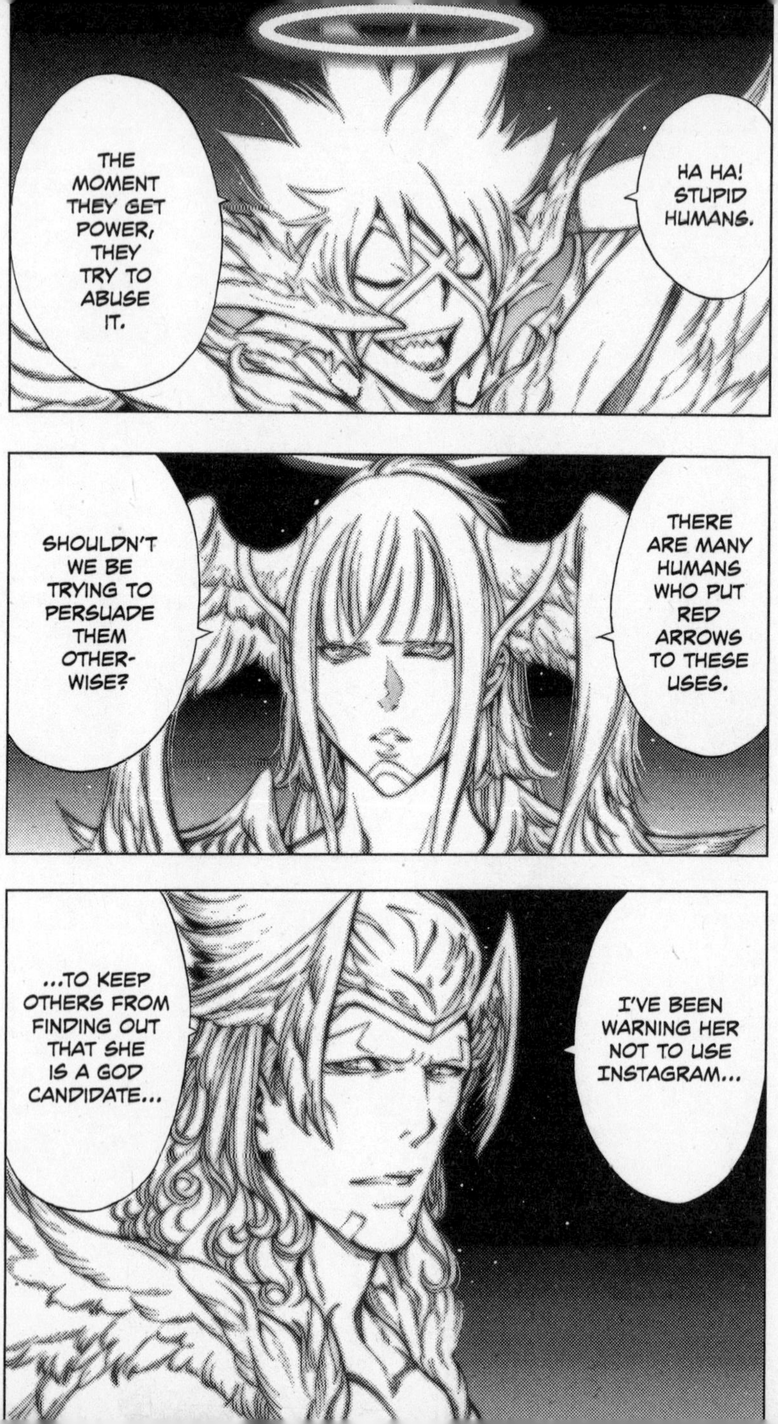
HA HA! STUPID HUMANS.
THE MOMENT THEY GET POWER, THEY TRY TO ABUSE IT.
THERE ARE MANY HUMANS WHO PUT RED ARROWS TO THESE USES.
SHOULDN'T WE BE TRYING TO PERSUADE THEM OTHER-WISE?
I'VE BEEN WARNING HER NOT TO USE INSTAGRAM...
...TO KEEP OTHERS FROM FINDING OUT THAT SHE IS A GOD CANDIDATE...

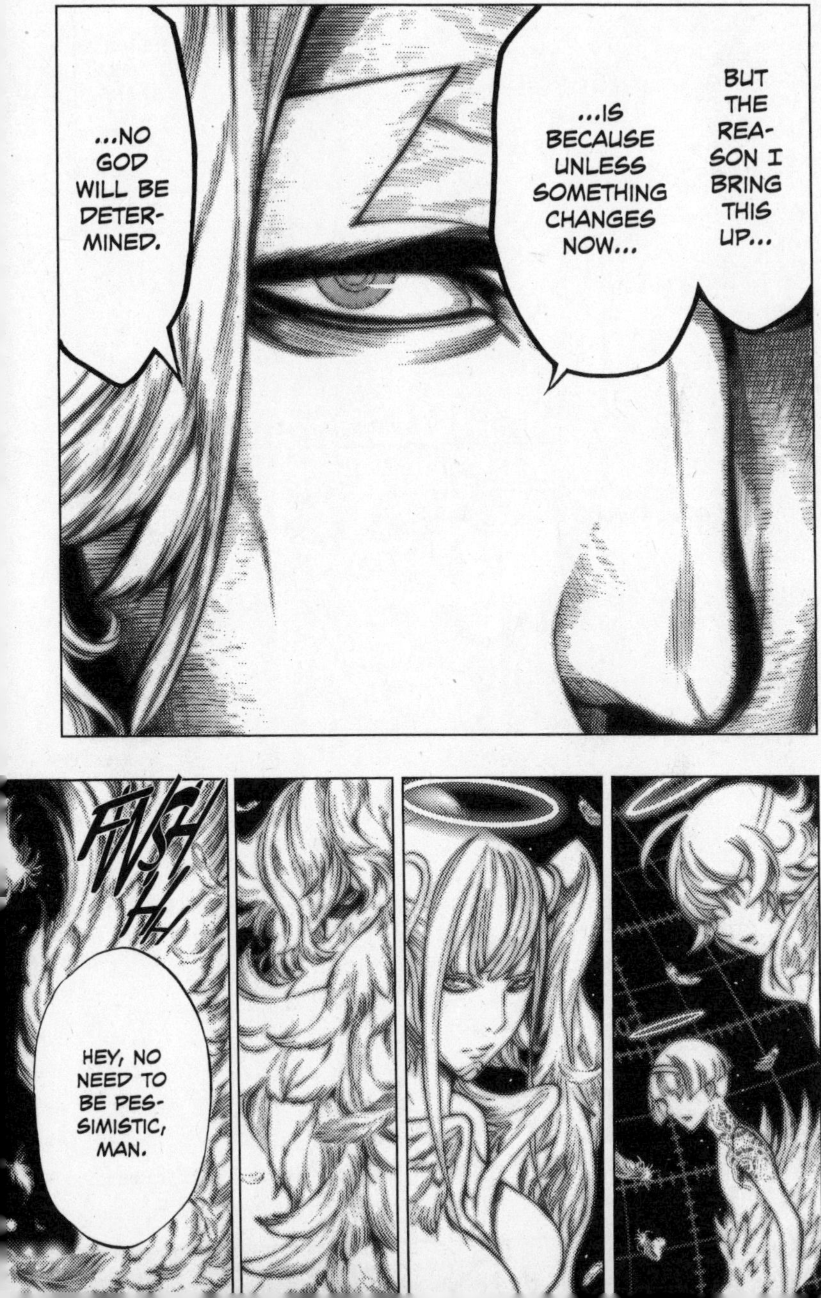
BUT THE REASON I BRING THIS UP...
...IS BECAUSE UNLESS SOMETHING CHANGES NOW...
...NO GOD WILL BE DETERMINED.
FWSHHH
HEY, NO NEED TO BE PESSIMISTIC, MAN.

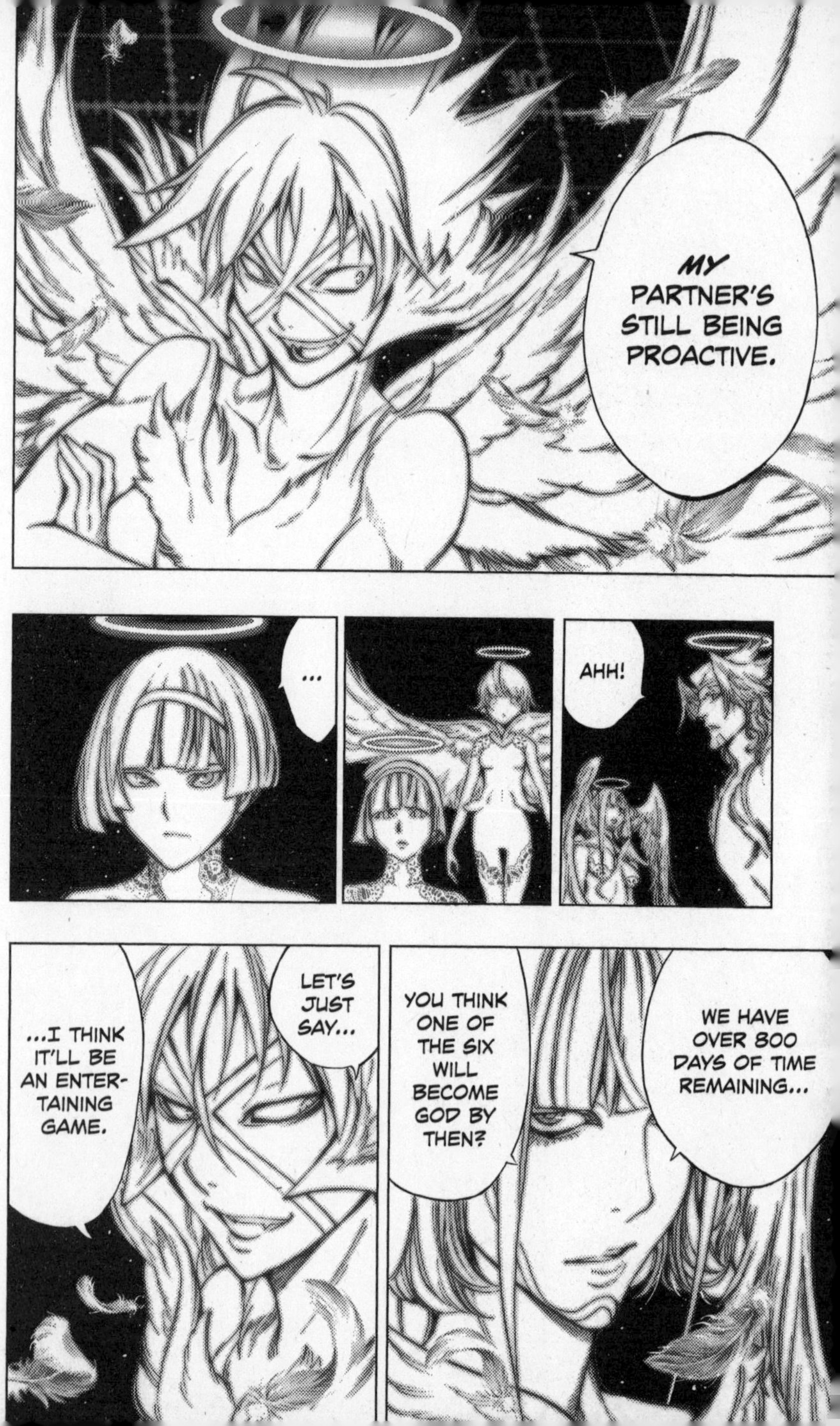
MY PARTNER'S STILL BEING PROACTIVE.
AHH!
...
WE HAVE OVER 800 DAYS OF TIME REMAINING...
YOU THINK ONE OF THE SIX WILL BECOME GOD BY THEN?
LET'S JUST SAY...
...I THINK IT'LL BE AN ENTERTAINING GAME.

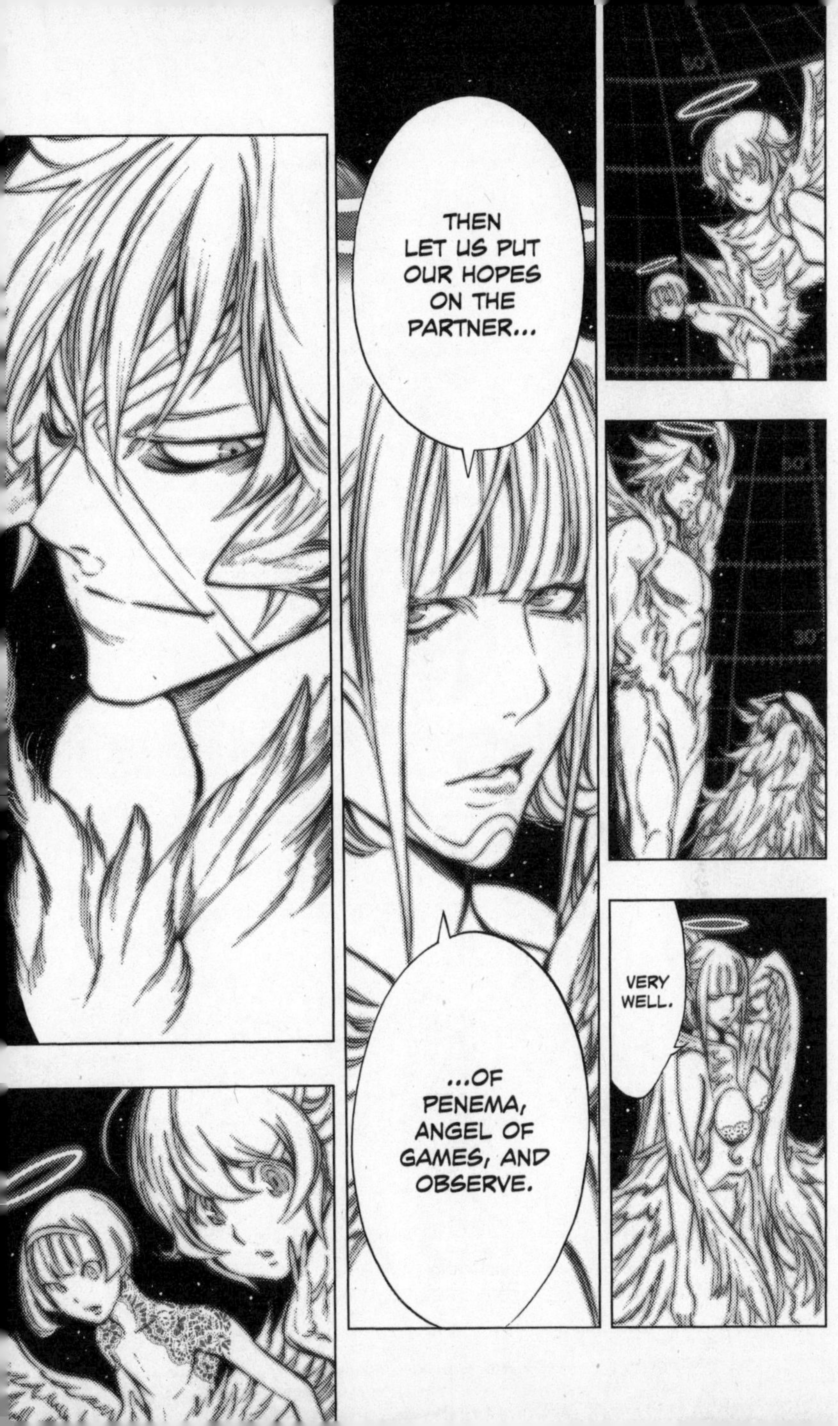
VERY WELL.
THEN LET US PUT OUR HOPES ON THE PARTNER...
...OF PENEMA, ANGEL OF GAMES, AND OBSERVE.

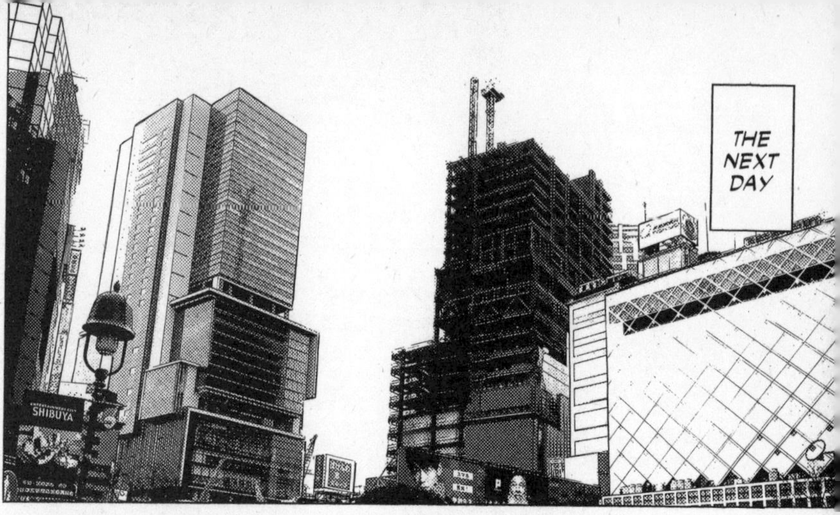
THE NEXT DAY
SHIBUYA

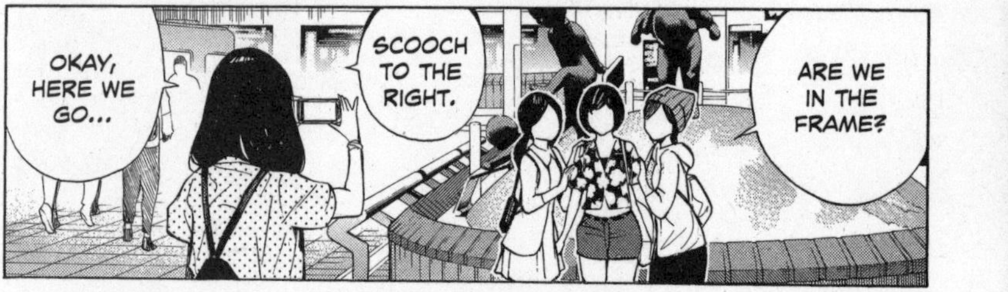
ARE WE IN THE FRAME?
SCOOCH TO THE RIGHT.
OKAY, HERE WE GO...

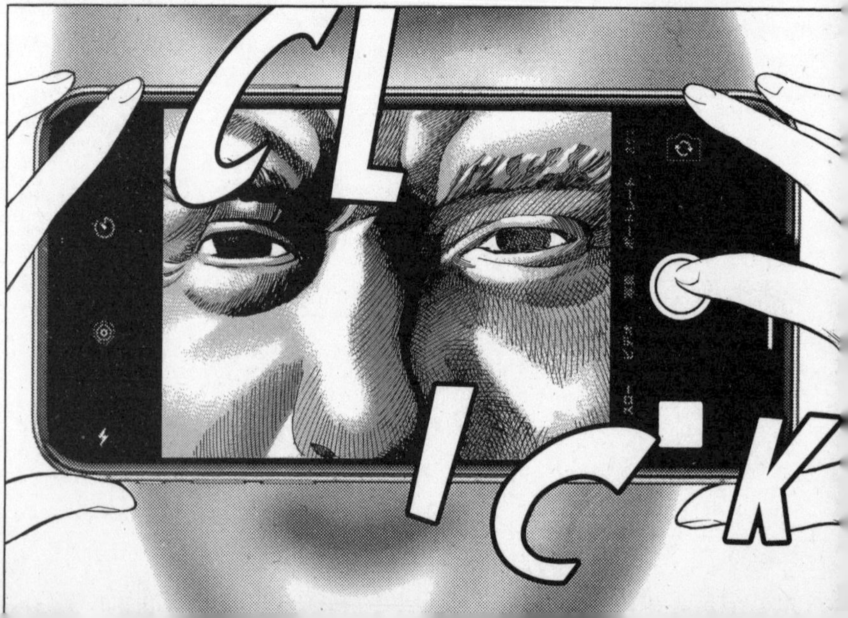
CLICK

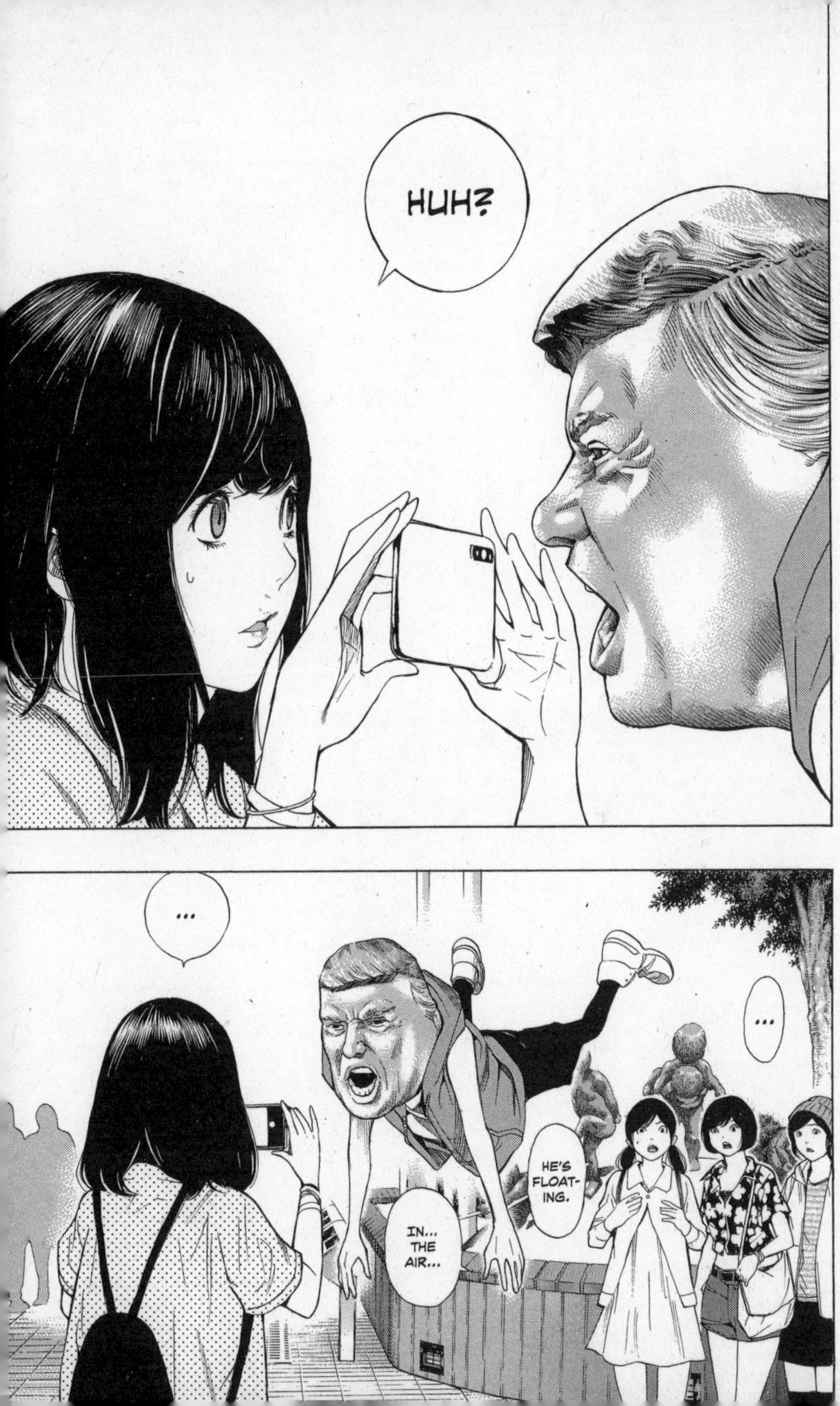
HUH?
...
...
HE'S FLOAT-ING.
IN... THE AIR...

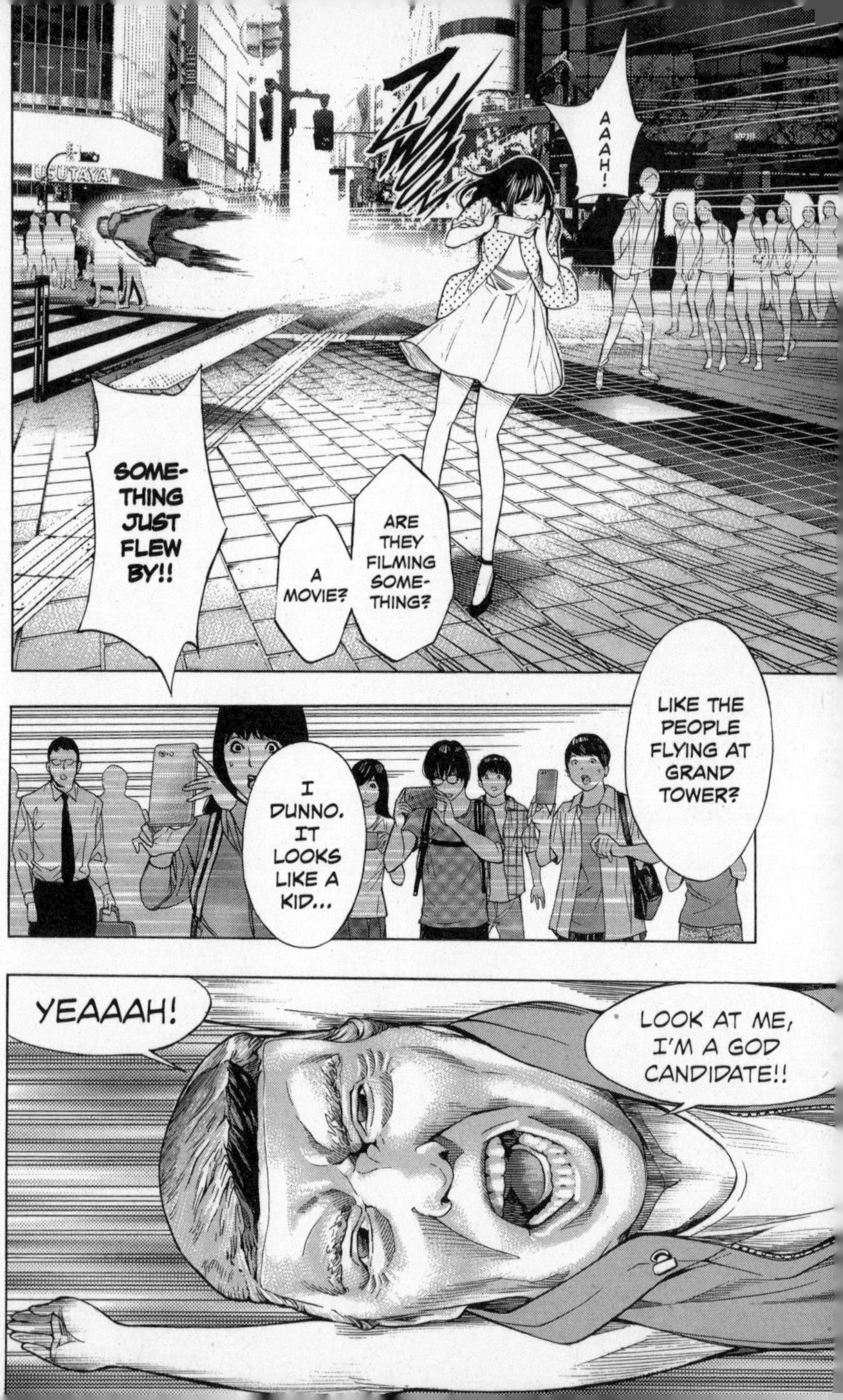
TSUTAYA
AAAH!
ARE THEY FILMING SOME-THING?
A MOVIE?
SOME-THING JUST FLEW BY!!
LIKE THE PEOPLE FLYING AT GRAND TOWER?
I DUNNO. IT LOOKS LIKE A KID...
LOOK AT ME, I'M A GOD CANDIDATE!!
YEAAAH!

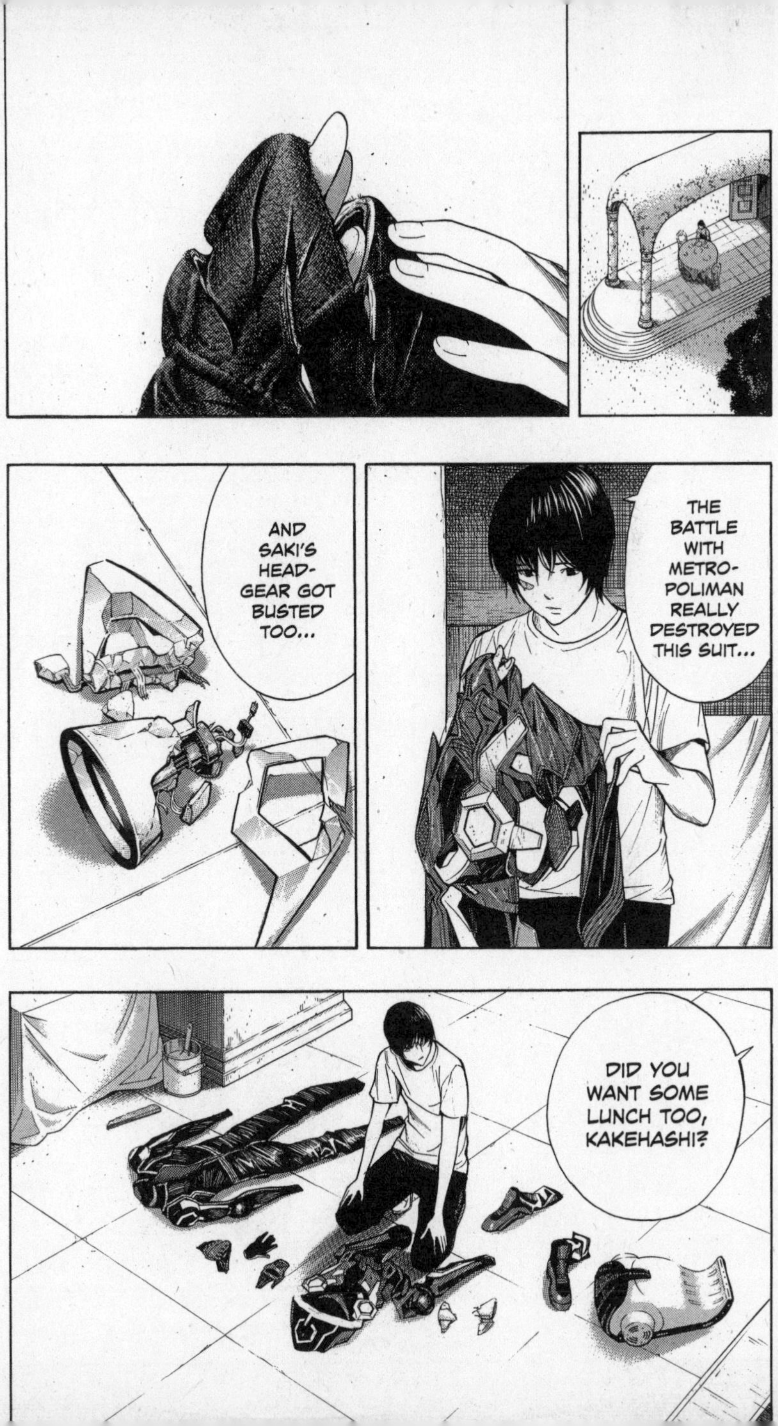
THE BATTLE WITH METRO-POLIMAN REALLY DESTROYED THIS SUIT...
AND SAKI'S HEAD-GEAR GOT BUSTED TOO...
DID YOU WANT SOME LUNCH TOO, KAKEHASHI?

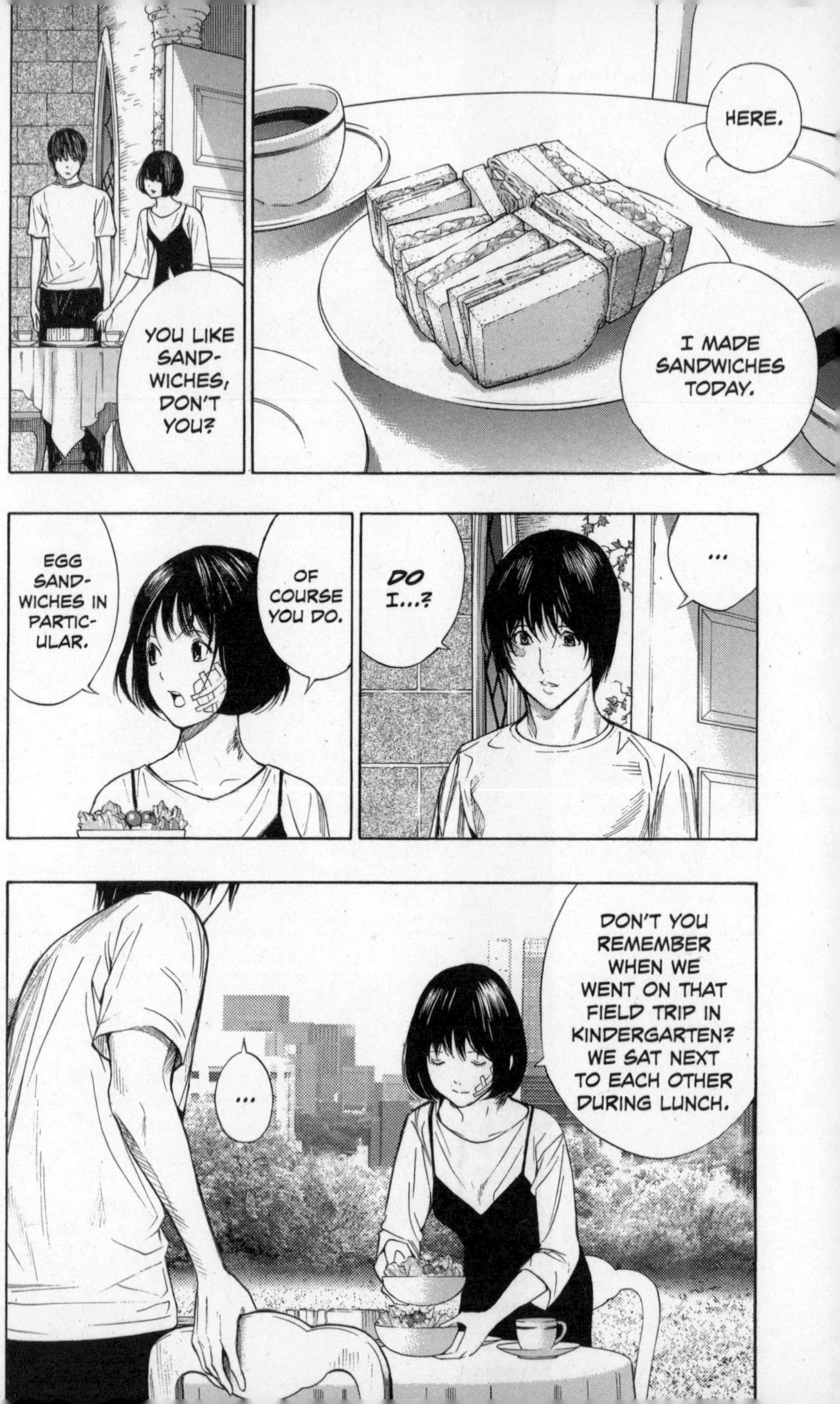
HERE.
I MADE SANDWICHES TODAY.
YOU LIKE SAND-WICHES, DON'T YOU?
...
DO I...?
OF COURSE YOU DO.
EGG SAND-WICHES IN PARTIC-ULAR.
DON'T YOU REMEMBER WHEN WE WENT ON THAT FIELD TRIP IN KINDERGARTEN? WE SAT NEXT TO EACH OTHER DURING LUNCH.
...

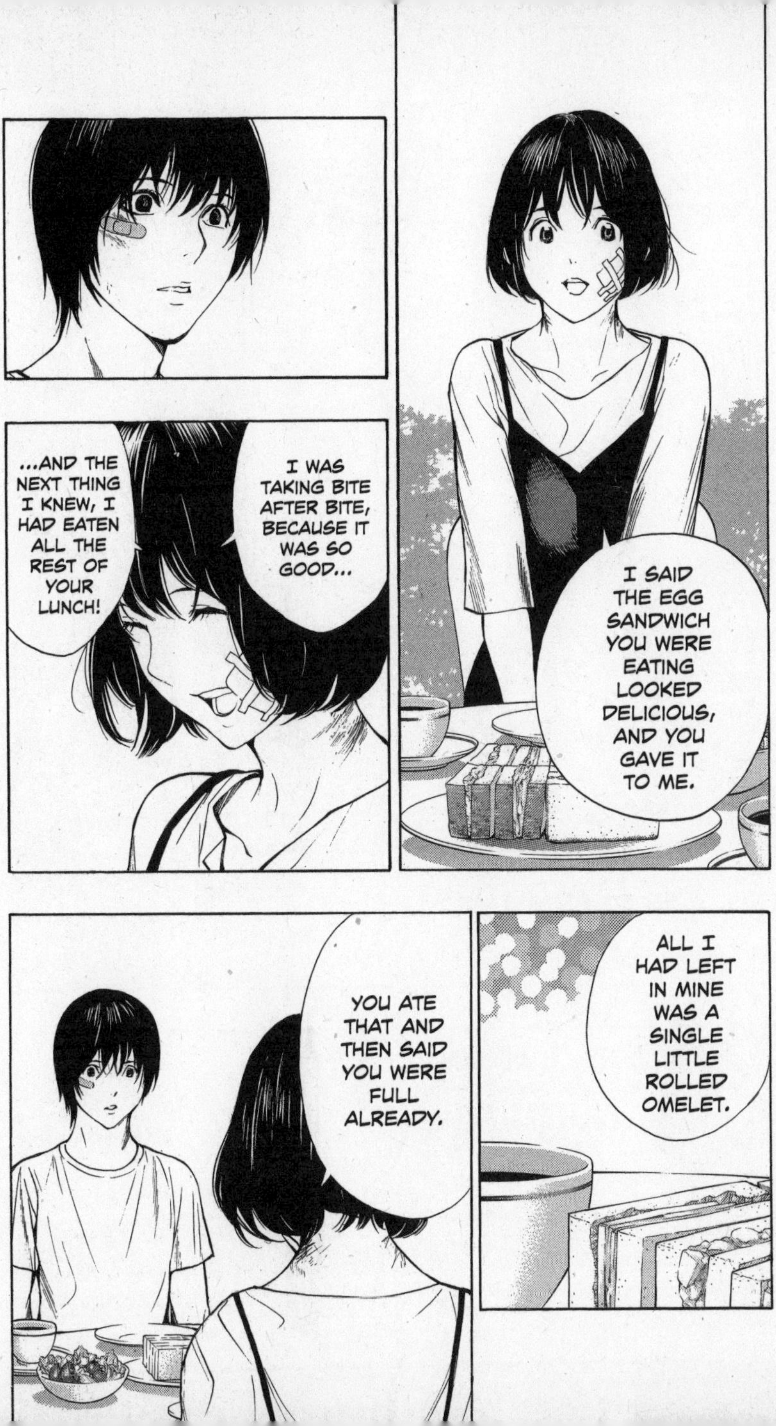
I SAID THE EGG SANDWICH YOU WERE EATING LOOKED DELICIOUS, AND YOU GAVE IT TO ME.
I WAS TAKING BITE AFTER BITE, BECAUSE IT WAS SO GOOD...
...AND THE NEXT THING I KNEW, I HAD EATEN ALL THE REST OF YOUR LUNCH!
ALL I HAD LEFT IN MINE WAS A SINGLE LITTLE ROLLED OMELET.
YOU ATE THAT AND THEN SAID YOU WERE FULL ALREADY.

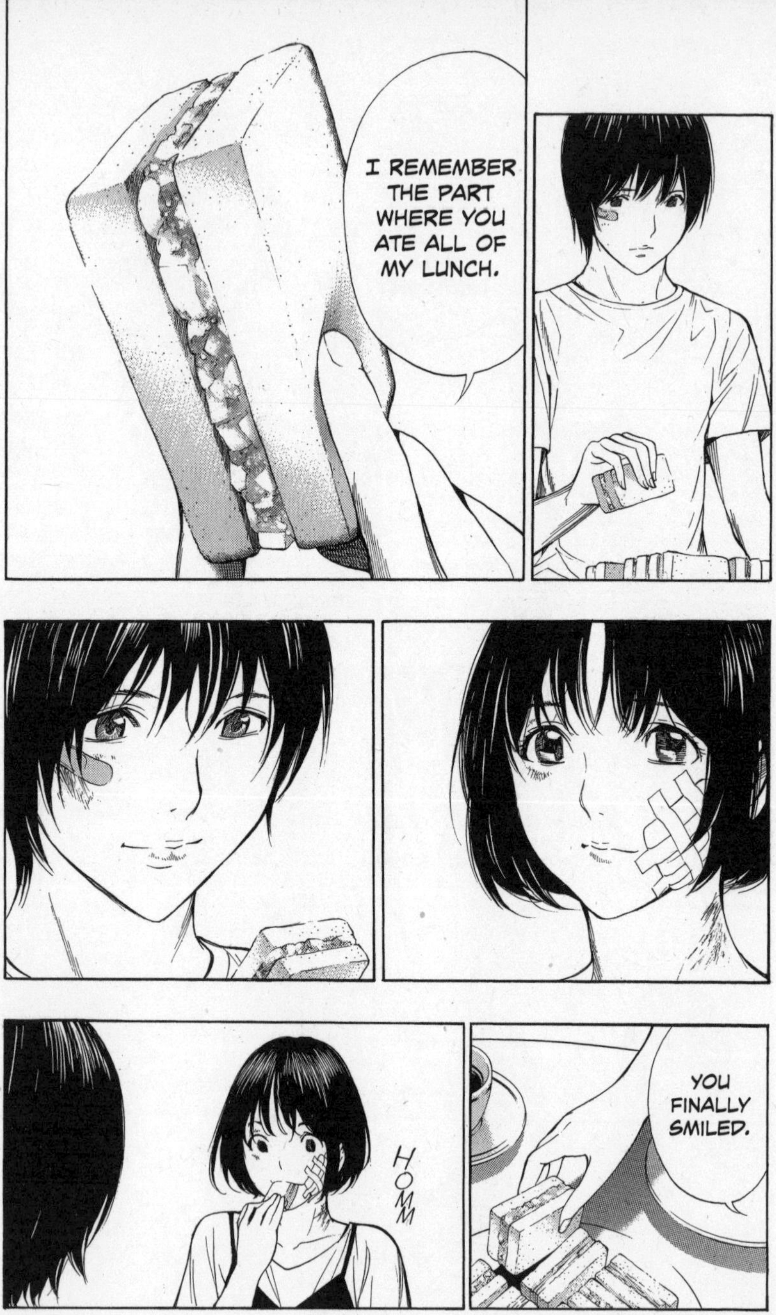
I REMEMBER THE PART WHERE YOU ATE ALL OF MY LUNCH.
YOU FINALLY SMILED.
HOMM

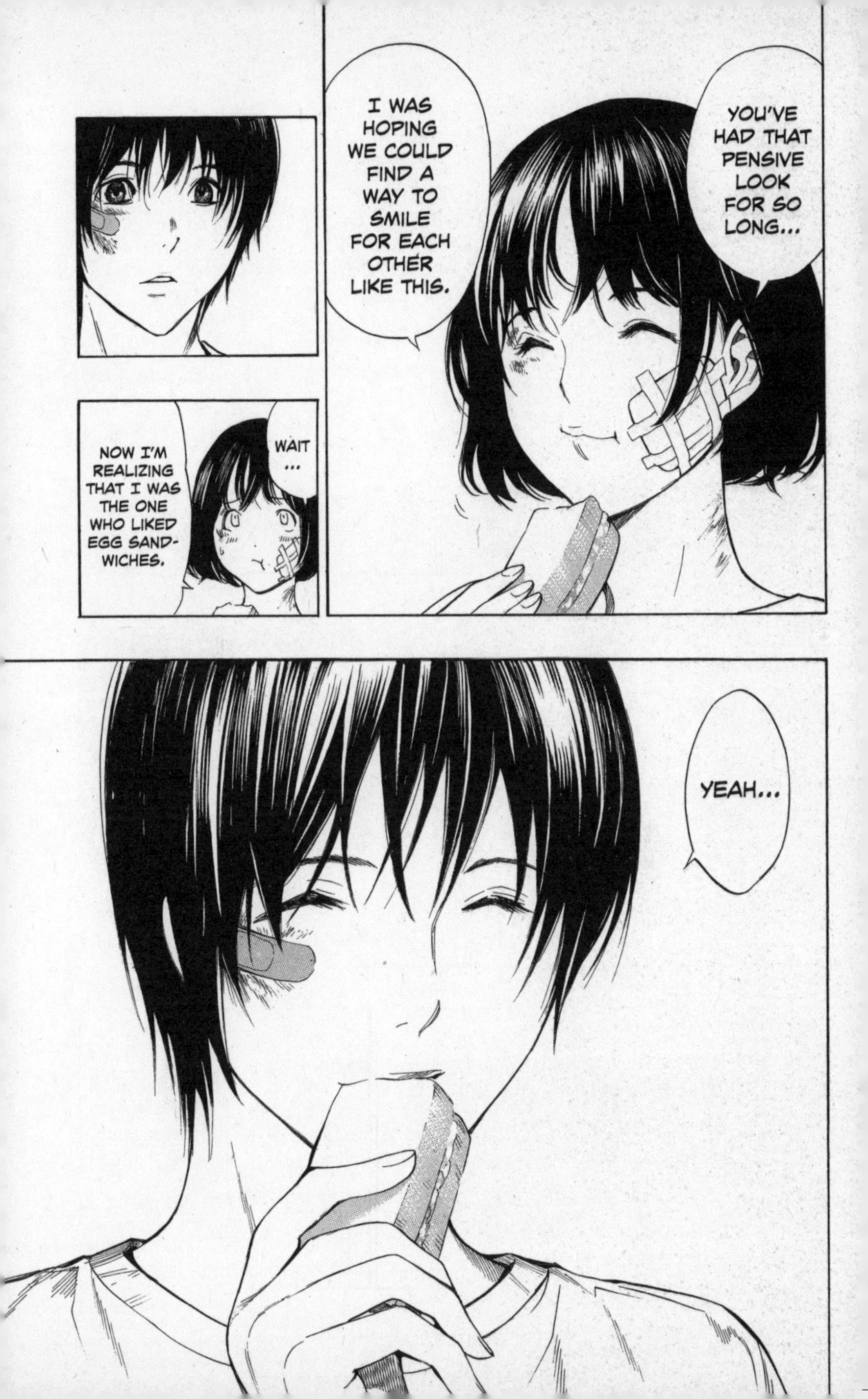
YOU'VE HAD THAT PENSIVE LOOK FOR SO LONG...
I WAS HOPING WE COULD FIND A WAY TO SMILE FOR EACH OTHER LIKE THIS.
WAIT...
NOW I'M REALIZING THAT I WAS THE ONE WHO LIKED EGG SAND-WICHES.
YEAH...

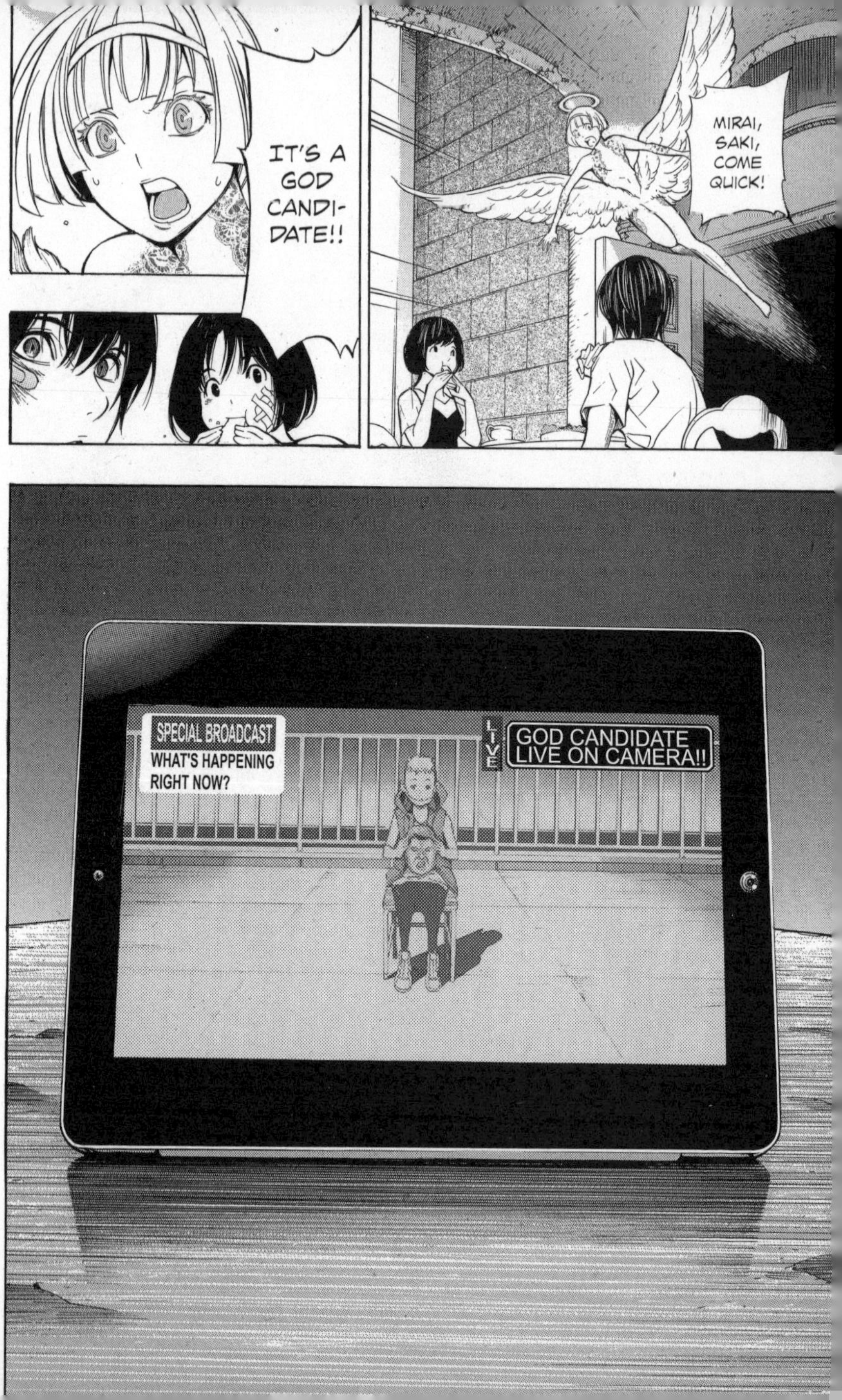
MIRAI, SAKI, COME QUICK!
IT'S A GOD CANDI-DATE!!
SPECIAL BROADCAST
WHAT'S HAPPENING RIGHT NOW?
LIVE
GOD CANDIDATE LIVE ON CAMERA!!

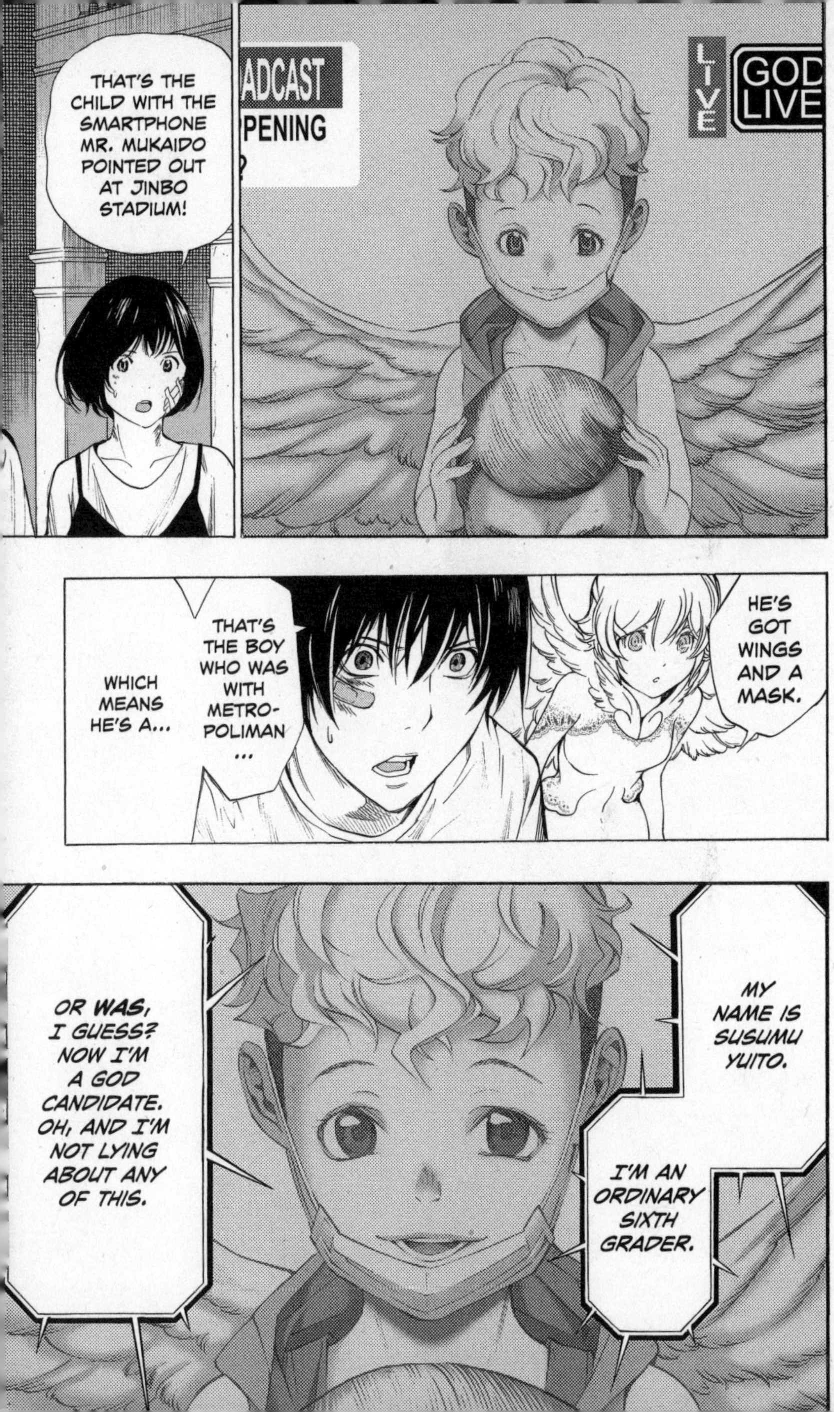
LIVE
GOD LIVE
ADCAST
PPENING
THAT'S THE CHILD WITH THE SMARTPHONE MR. MUKAIDO POINTED OUT AT JINBO STADIUM!
HE'S GOT WINGS AND A MASK.
THAT'S THE BOY WHO WAS WITH METRO-POLIMAN ...
WHICH MEANS HE'S A...
MY NAME IS SUSUMU YUITO.
I'M AN ORDINARY SIXTH GRADER.
OR WAS, I GUESS? NOW I'M A GOD CANDIDATE. OH, AND I'M NOT LYING ABOUT ANY OF THIS.

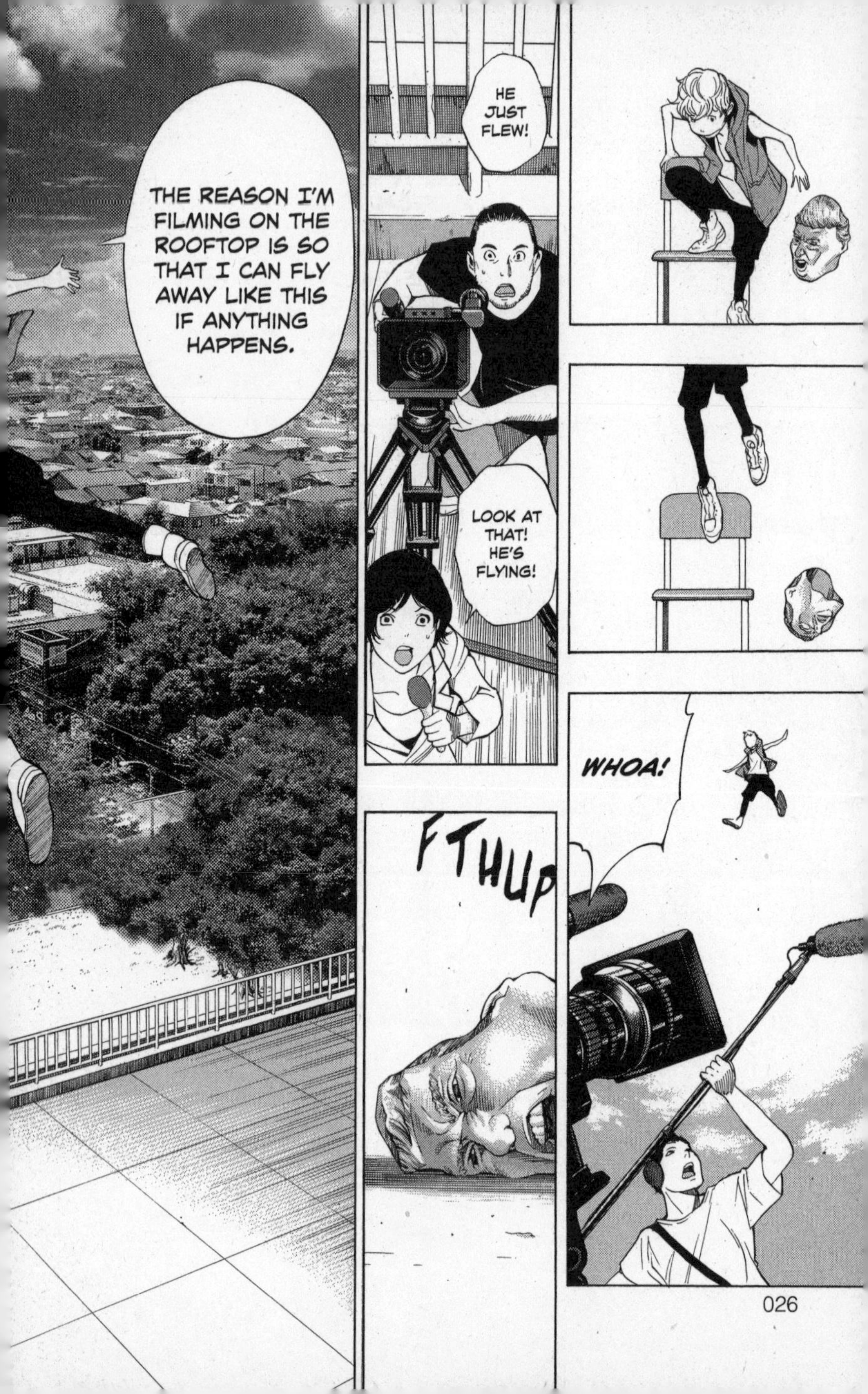
HE JUST FLEW!
LOOK AT THAT! HE'S FLYING!
WHOA!
FTHUP
THE REASON I'M FILMING ON THE ROOFTOP IS SO THAT I CAN FLY AWAY LIKE THIS IF ANYTHING HAPPENS.

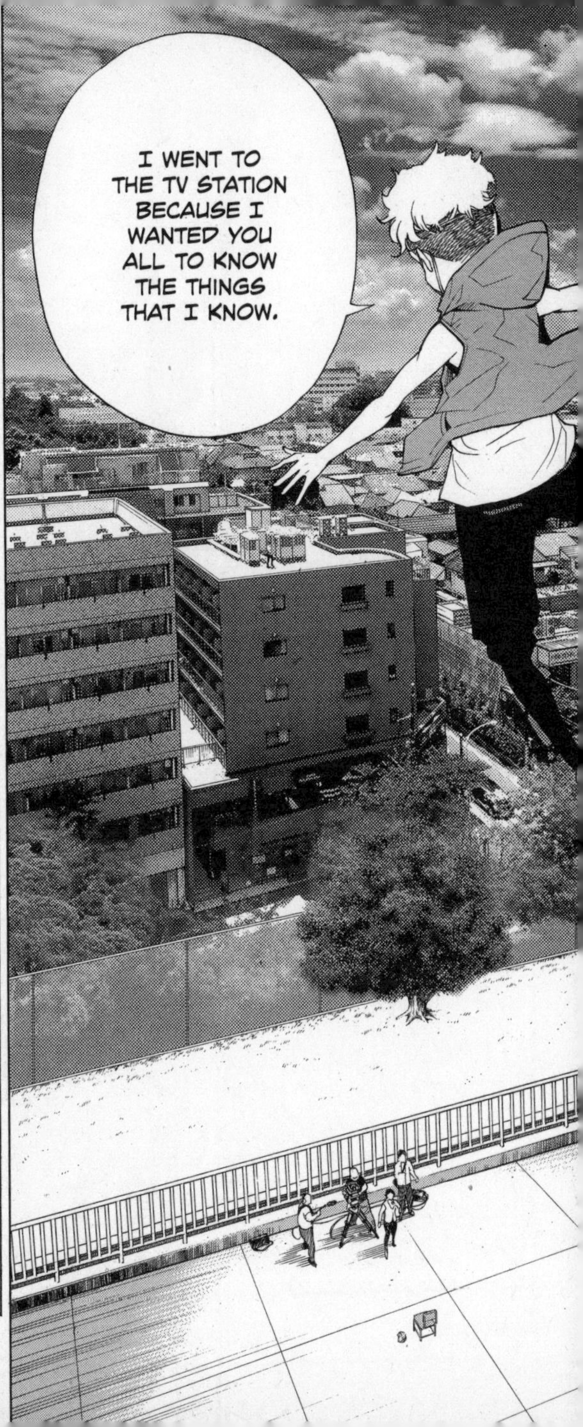
I WENT TO THE TV STATION BECAUSE I WANTED YOU ALL TO KNOW THE THINGS THAT I KNOW.

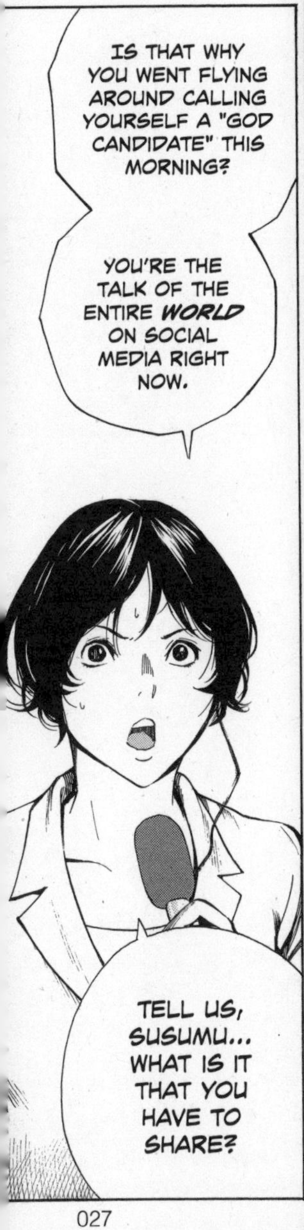
IS THAT WHY YOU WENT FLYING AROUND CALLING YOURSELF A "GOD CANDIDATE" THIS MORNING?
YOU'RE THE TALK OF THE ENTIRE *WORLD* ON SOCIAL MEDIA RIGHT NOW.
TELL US, SUSUMU... WHAT IS IT THAT YOU HAVE TO SHARE?

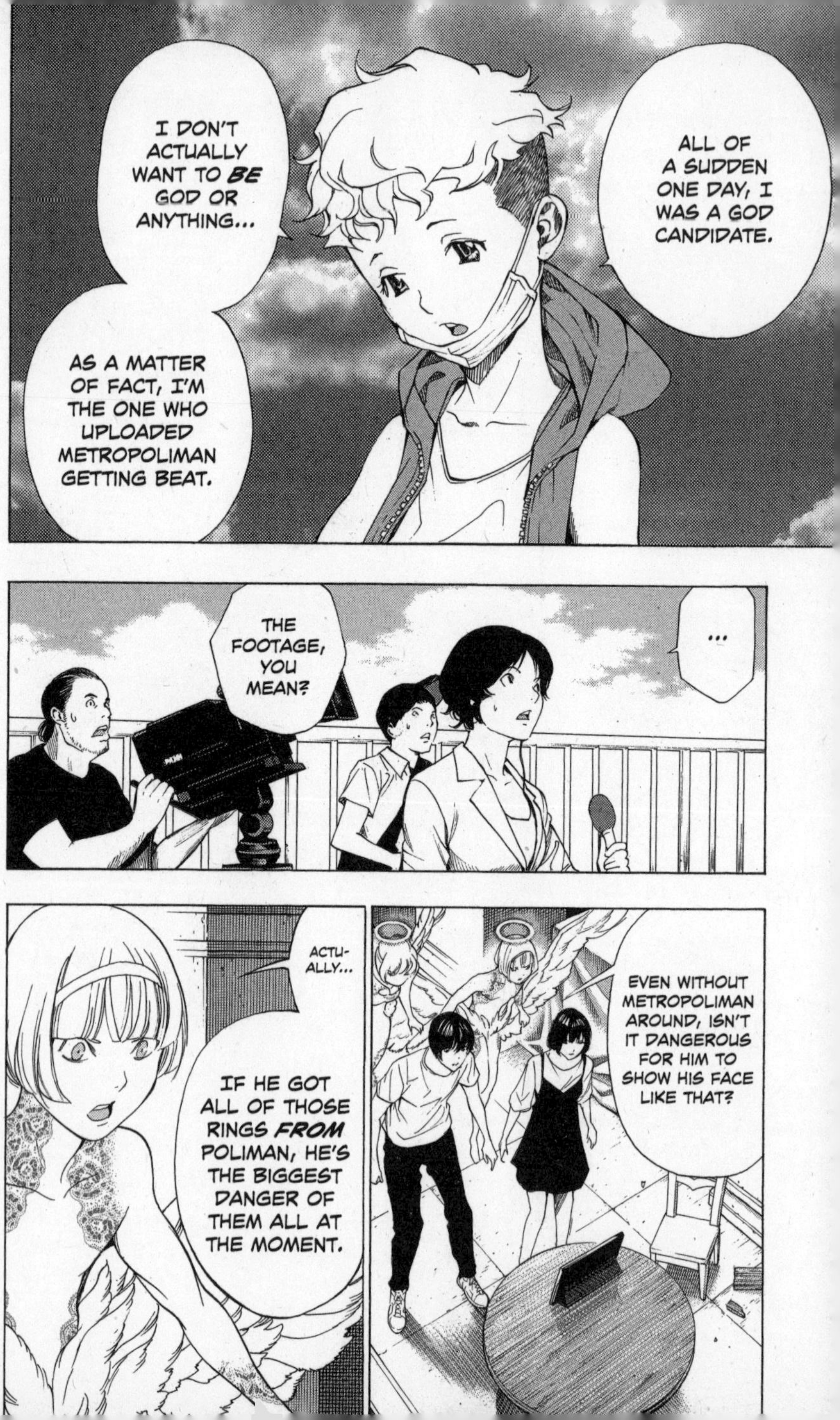
ALL OF A SUDDEN ONE DAY, I WAS A GOD CANDIDATE.
I DON'T ACTUALLY WANT TO *BE* GOD OR ANYTHING...
AS A MATTER OF FACT, I'M THE ONE WHO UPLOADED METROPOLIMAN GETTING BEAT.
...
THE FOOTAGE, YOU MEAN?
EVEN WITHOUT METROPOLIMAN AROUND, ISN'T IT DANGEROUS FOR HIM TO SHOW HIS FACE LIKE THAT?
ACTU-ALLY...
IF HE GOT ALL OF THOSE RINGS *FROM* POLIMAN, HE'S THE BIGGEST DANGER OF THEM ALL AT THE MOMENT.

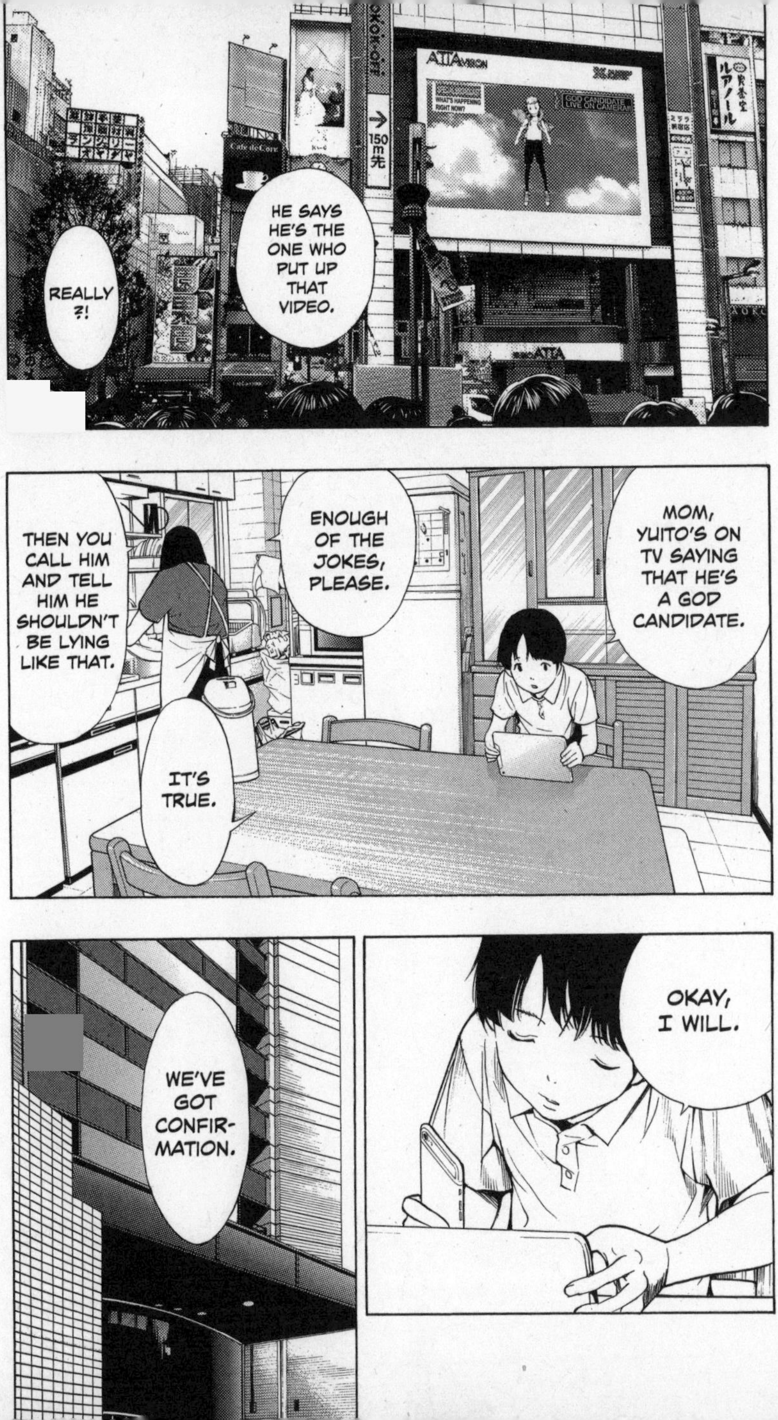
GOD CANDIDATE LIVE ON CAMERA!!
WHAT'S HAPPENING RIGHT NOW?
HE SAYS HE'S THE ONE WHO PUT UP THAT VIDEO.
REALLY ?!
MOM, YUITO'S ON TV SAYING THAT HE'S A GOD CANDIDATE.
ENOUGH OF THE JOKES, PLEASE.
THEN YOU CALL HIM AND TELL HIM HE SHOULDN'T BE LYING LIKE THAT.
IT'S TRUE.
OKAY, I WILL.
WE'VE GOT CONFIRMATION.

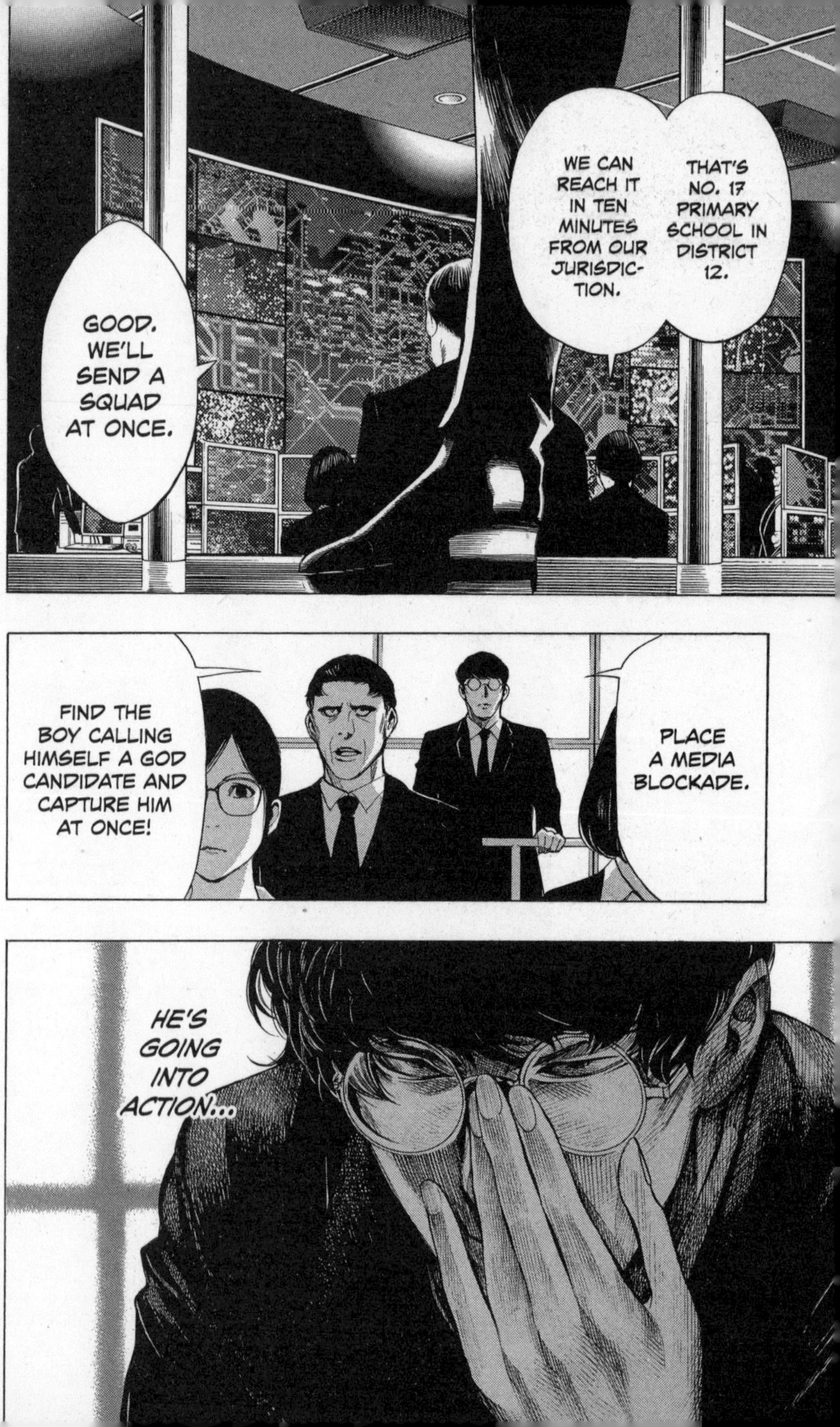
THAT'S NO. 17 PRIMARY SCHOOL IN DISTRICT 12.
WE CAN REACH IT IN TEN MINUTES FROM OUR JURISDICTION.
GOOD. WE'LL SEND A SQUAD AT ONCE.
PLACE A MEDIA BLOCKADE.
FIND THE BOY CALLING HIMSELF A GOD CANDIDATE AND CAPTURE HIM AT ONCE!
HE'S GOING INTO ACTION...

HUH?

SUSUMU, CAN YOU EXPLAIN EXACTLY WHAT A GOD CANDIDATE IS FOR US?

HMMM...

...AND *ARROWS.*

...AND *WINGS*...

AND IN ADDITION...

ANGELS AND *GOD...*

ALL OF THESE TERMS ARE TRENDING RAPIDLY ON SOCIAL MEDIA ALONG WITH "GOD CANDIDATE"!

SORRY, I FORGOT TO TURN OFF MY PHONE.

BEEP

IT'S FROM IIDA.

OH!

B L I N G K !

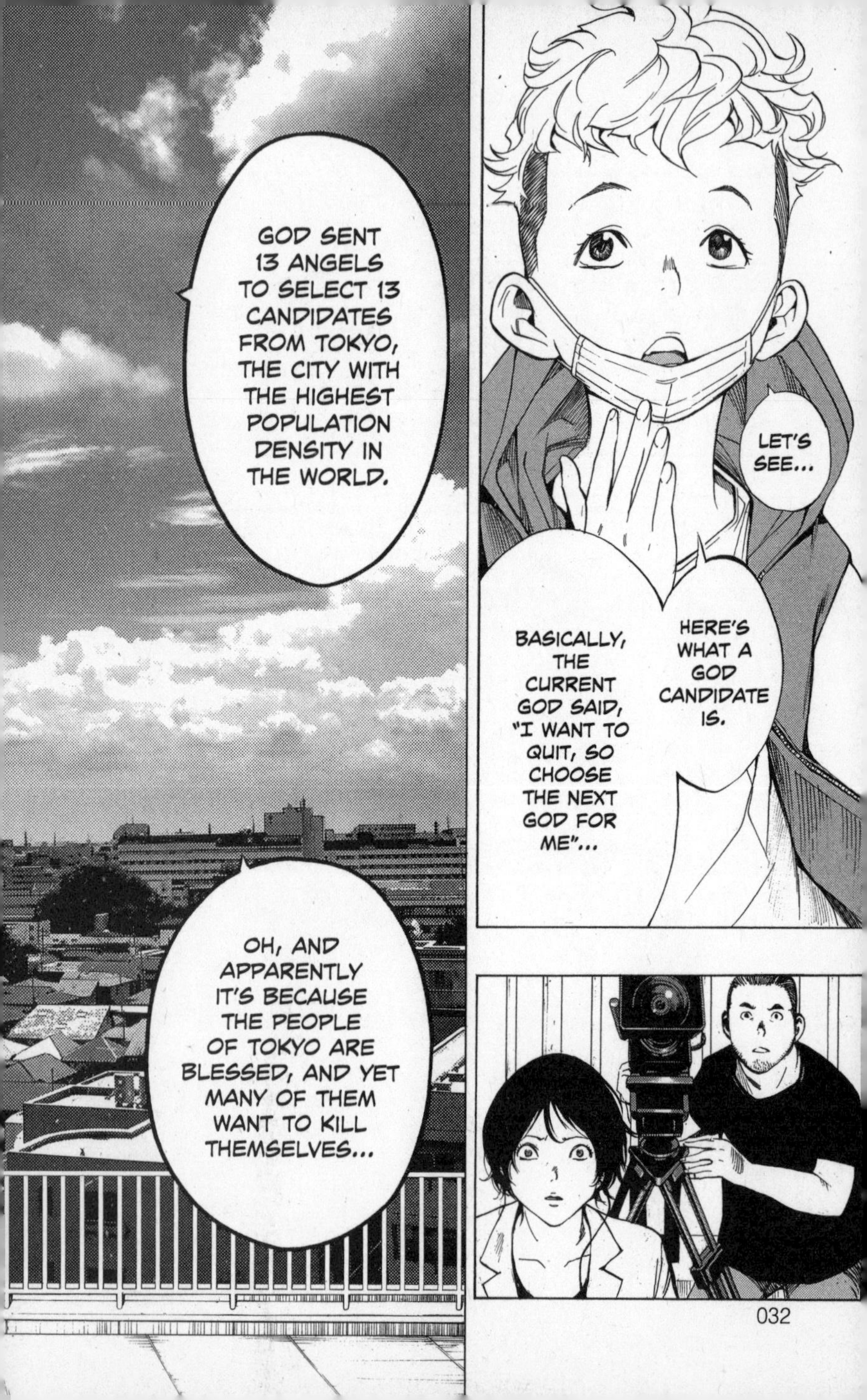
LET'S SEE...
HERE'S WHAT A GOD CANDIDATE IS.
BASICALLY, THE CURRENT GOD SAID, "I WANT TO QUIT, SO CHOOSE THE NEXT GOD FOR ME"...
GOD SENT 13 ANGELS TO SELECT 13 CANDIDATES FROM TOKYO, THE CITY WITH THE HIGHEST POPULATION DENSITY IN THE WORLD.
OH, AND APPARENTLY IT'S BECAUSE THE PEOPLE OF TOKYO ARE BLESSED, AND YET MANY OF THEM WANT TO KILL THEMSELVES...

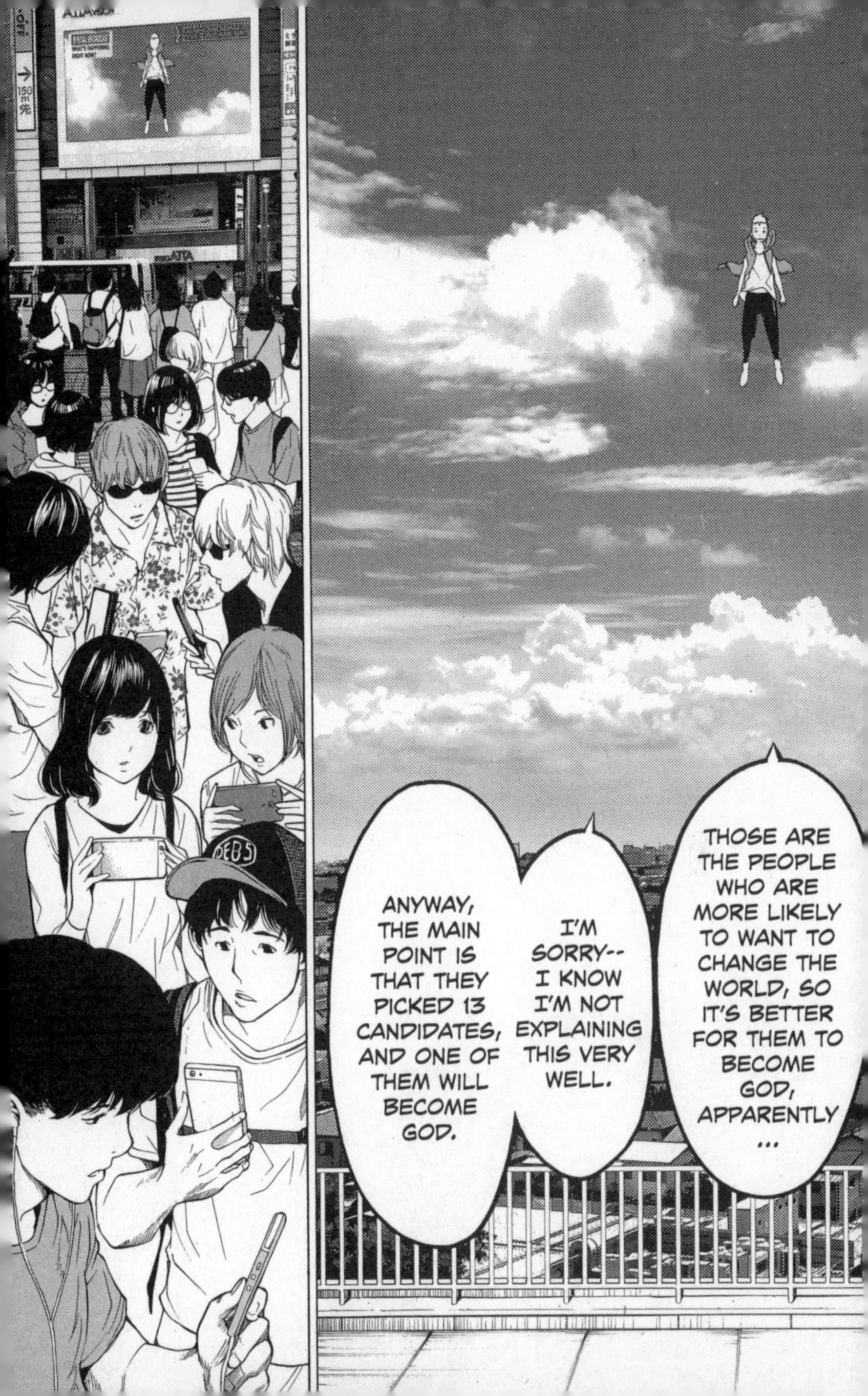
THOSE ARE THE PEOPLE WHO ARE MORE LIKELY TO WANT TO CHANGE THE WORLD, SO IT'S BETTER FOR THEM TO BECOME GOD, APPARENTLY...
I'M SORRY-- I KNOW I'M NOT EXPLAINING THIS VERY WELL.
ANYWAY, THE MAIN POINT IS THAT THEY PICKED 13 CANDIDATES, AND ONE OF THEM WILL BECOME GOD.

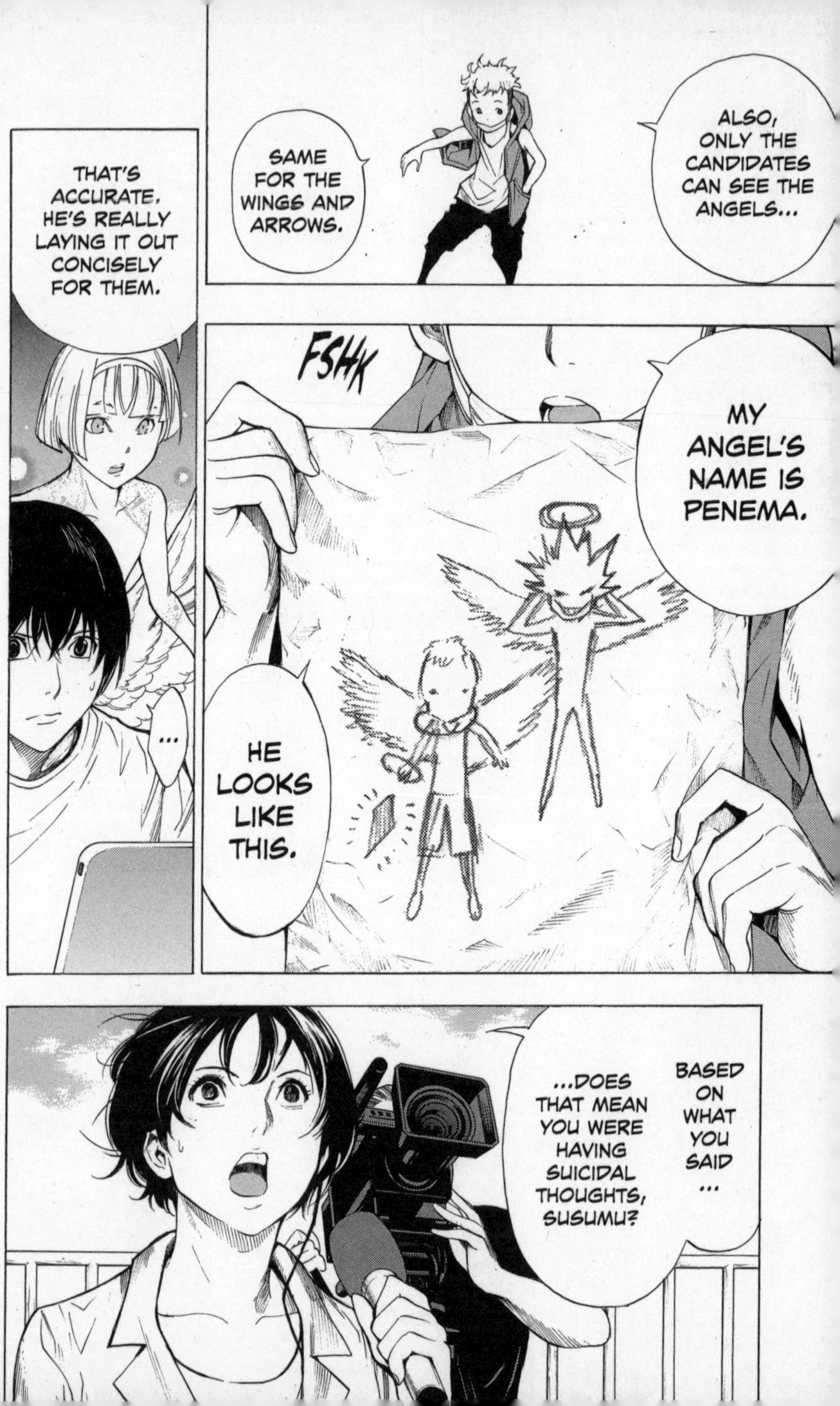
ALSO, ONLY THE CANDIDATES CAN SEE THE ANGELS...
SAME FOR THE WINGS AND ARROWS.
FSHK
MY ANGEL'S NAME IS PENEMA.
HE LOOKS LIKE THIS.
THAT'S ACCURATE. HE'S REALLY LAYING IT OUT CONCISELY FOR THEM.
...
BASED ON WHAT YOU SAID...
...DOES THAT MEAN YOU WERE HAVING SUICIDAL THOUGHTS, SUSUMU?

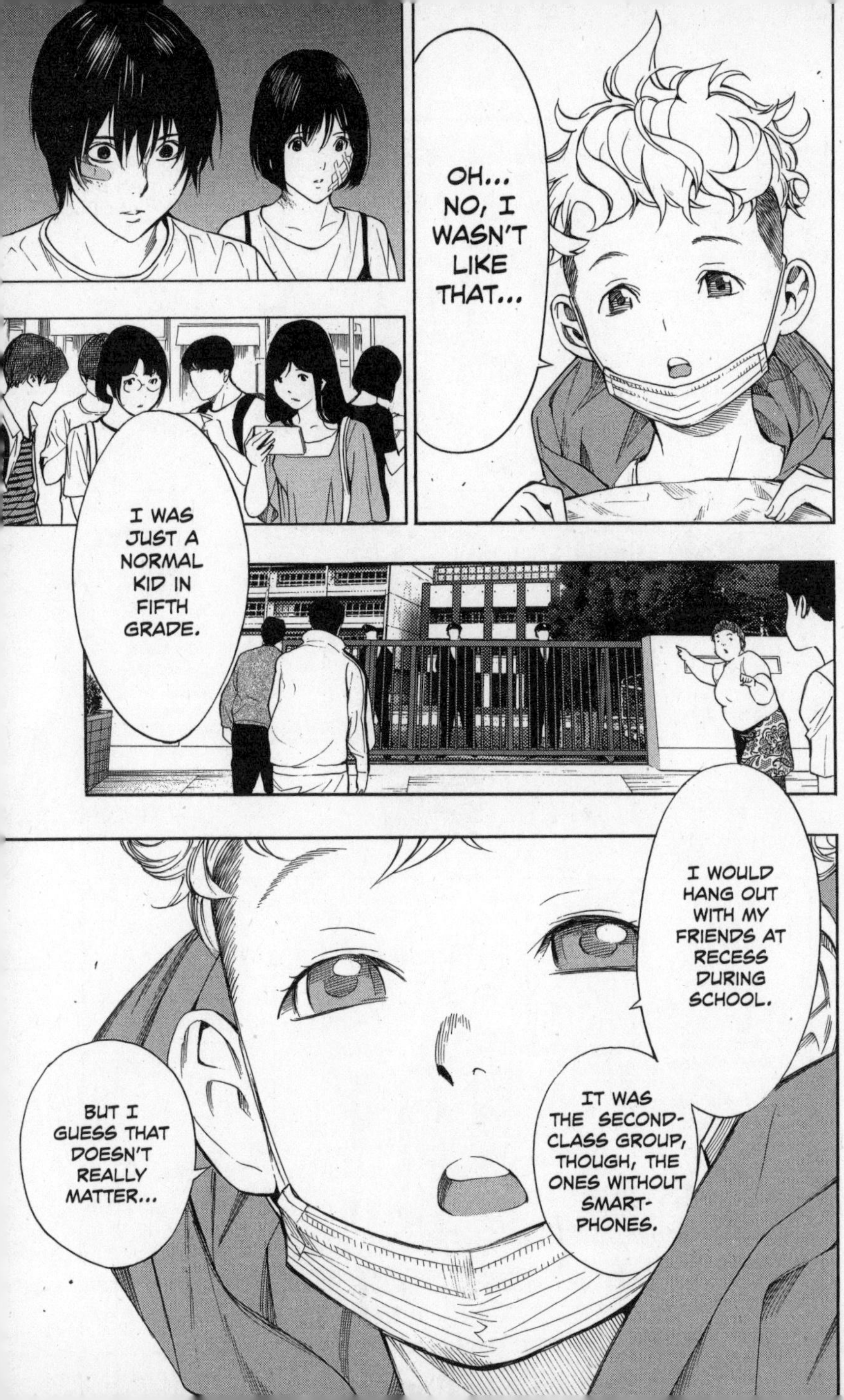
OH... NO, I WASN'T LIKE THAT...
I WAS JUST A NORMAL KID IN FIFTH GRADE.
I WOULD HANG OUT WITH MY FRIENDS AT RECESS DURING SCHOOL.
IT WAS THE SECOND-CLASS GROUP, THOUGH, THE ONES WITHOUT SMART-PHONES.
BUT I GUESS THAT DOESN'T REALLY MATTER...

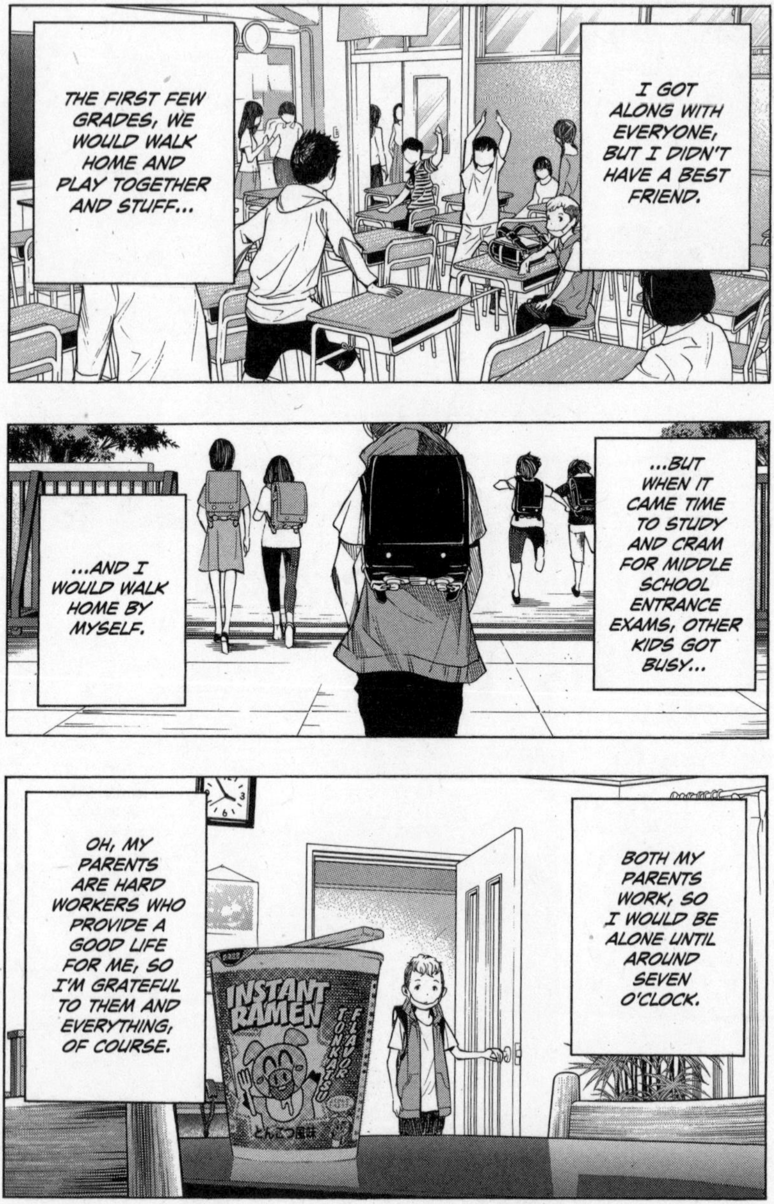
I GOT ALONG WITH EVERYONE, BUT I DIDN'T HAVE A BEST FRIEND.
THE FIRST FEW GRADES, WE WOULD WALK HOME AND PLAY TOGETHER AND STUFF...
...BUT WHEN IT CAME TIME TO STUDY AND CRAM FOR MIDDLE SCHOOL ENTRANCE EXAMS, OTHER KIDS GOT BUSY...
...AND I WOULD WALK HOME BY MYSELF.
BOTH MY PARENTS WORK, SO I WOULD BE ALONE UNTIL AROUND SEVEN O'CLOCK.
OH, MY PARENTS ARE HARD WORKERS WHO PROVIDE A GOOD LIFE FOR ME, SO I'M GRATEFUL TO THEM AND EVERYTHING, OF COURSE.
INSTANT RAMEN
TONKATSU FLAVOR
とんこつ風味

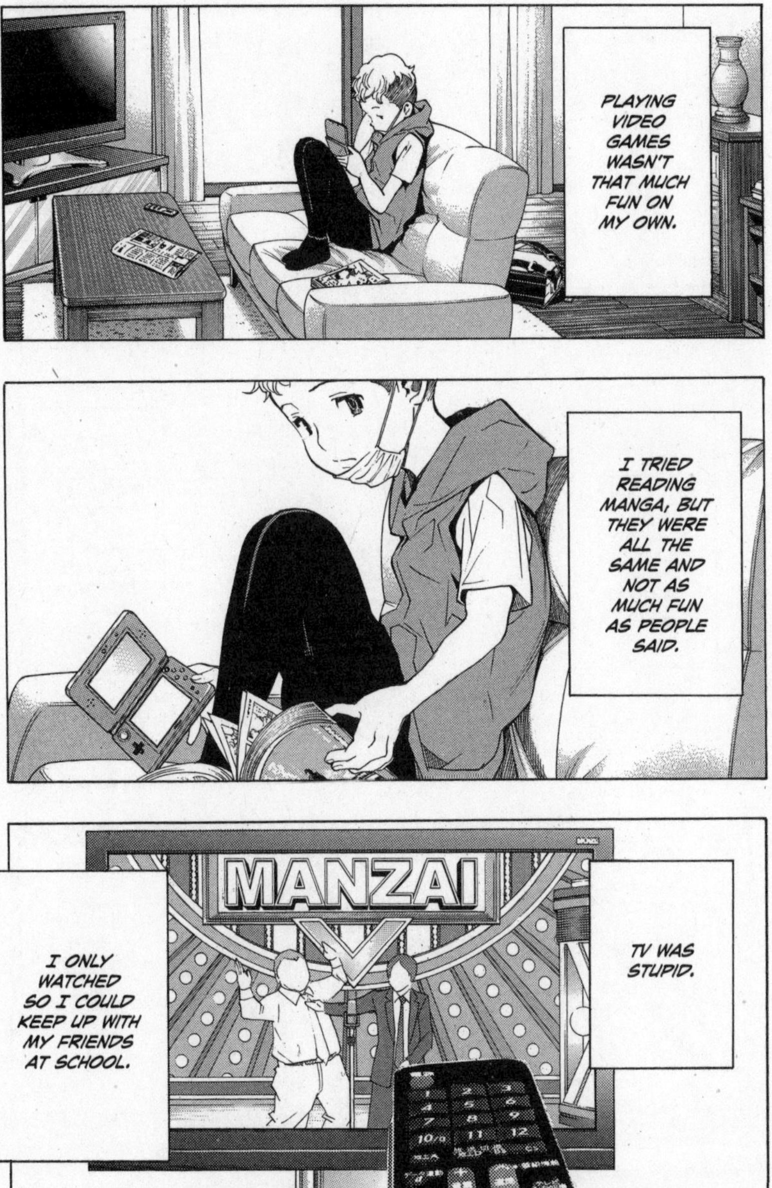
PLAYING VIDEO GAMES WASN'T THAT MUCH FUN ON MY OWN.
I TRIED READING MANGA, BUT THEY WERE ALL THE SAME AND NOT AS MUCH FUN AS PEOPLE SAID.
TV WAS STUPID.
MANZAI
I ONLY WATCHED SO I COULD KEEP UP WITH MY FRIENDS AT SCHOOL.

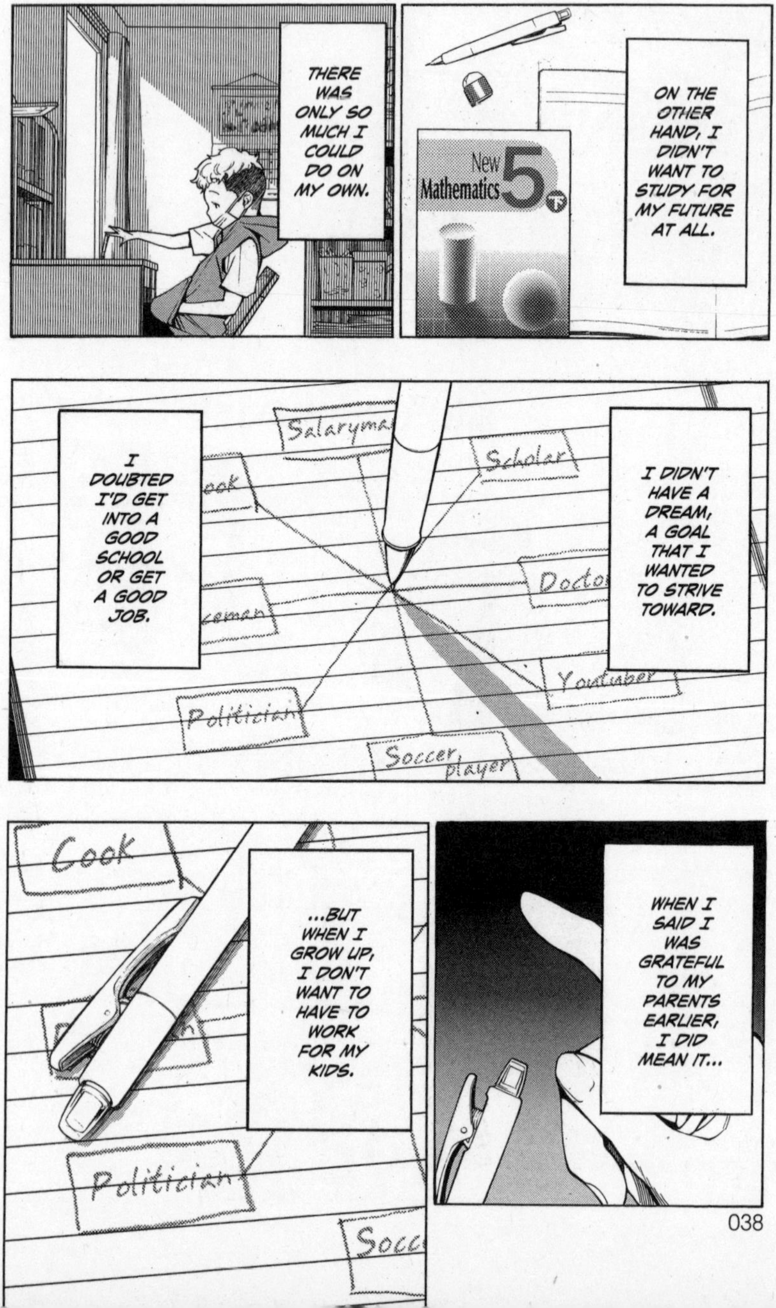
ON THE OTHER HAND, I DIDN'T WANT TO STUDY FOR MY FUTURE AT ALL.
New Mathematics 5 下
THERE WAS ONLY SO MUCH I COULD DO ON MY OWN.
I DIDN'T HAVE A DREAM, A GOAL THAT I WANTED TO STRIVE TOWARD.
Scholar
Salaryma
Doctor
Youtuber
Soccer player
Politician
I DOUBTED I'D GET INTO A GOOD SCHOOL OR GET A GOOD JOB.
WHEN I SAID I WAS GRATEFUL TO MY PARENTS EARLIER, I DID MEAN IT...
...BUT WHEN I GROW UP, I DON'T WANT TO HAVE TO WORK FOR MY KIDS.
Cook
Politician
Socce

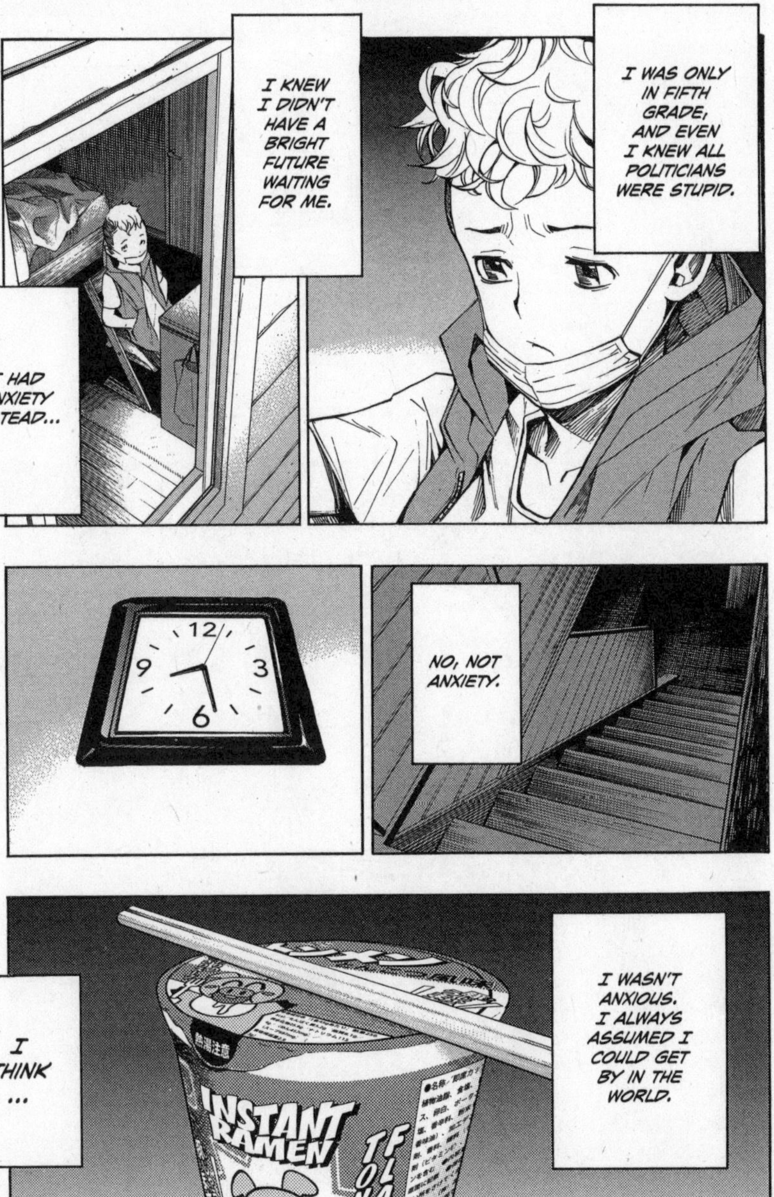
I WAS ONLY IN FIFTH GRADE, AND EVEN I KNEW ALL POLITICIANS WERE STUPID.
I KNEW I DIDN'T HAVE A BRIGHT FUTURE WAITING FOR ME.
I HAD ANXIETY INSTEAD...
NO, NOT ANXIETY.
I WASN'T ANXIOUS. I ALWAYS ASSUMED I COULD GET BY IN THE WORLD.
INSTANT RAMEN
I THINK ...

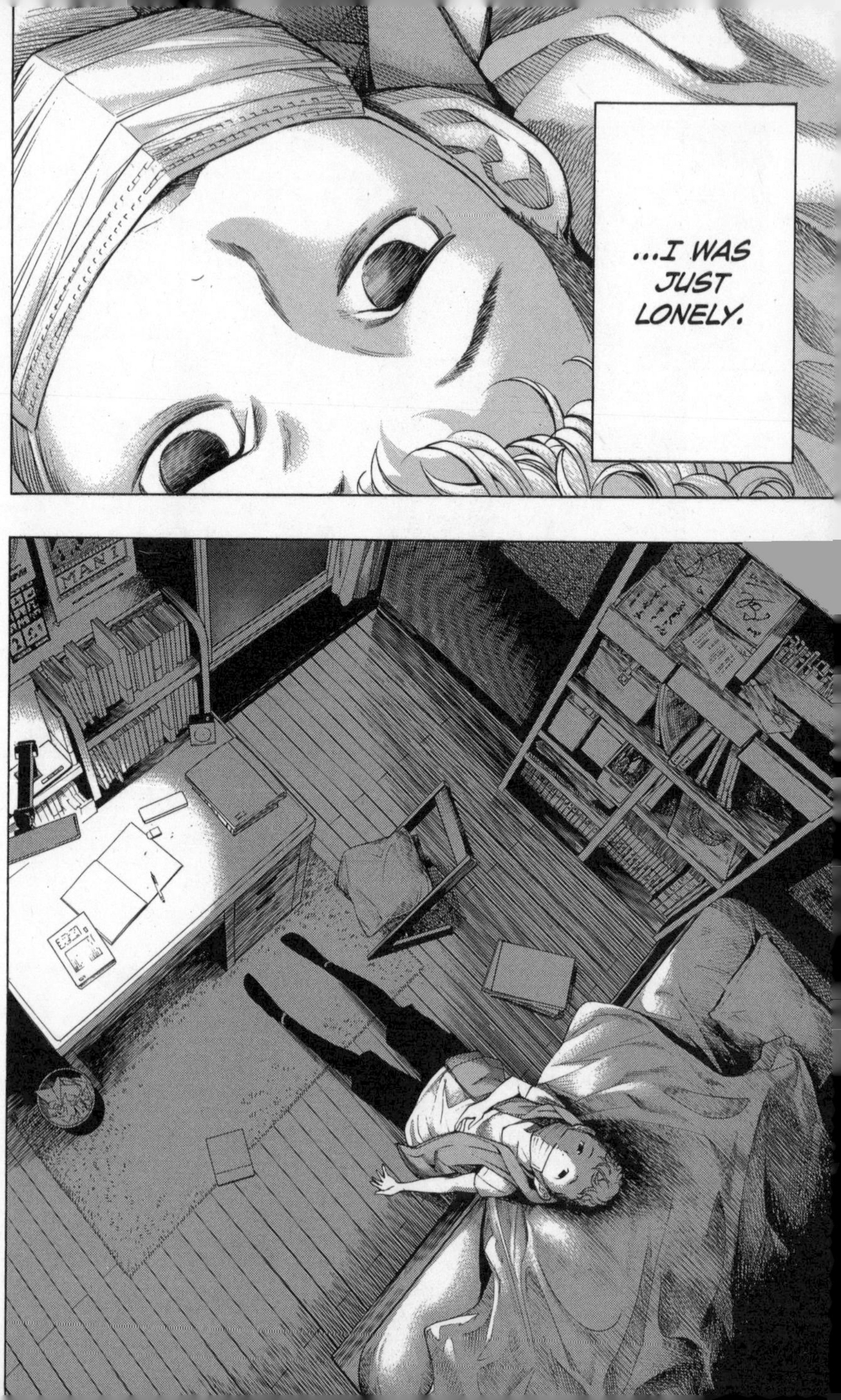
...I WAS JUST LONELY.
MANI

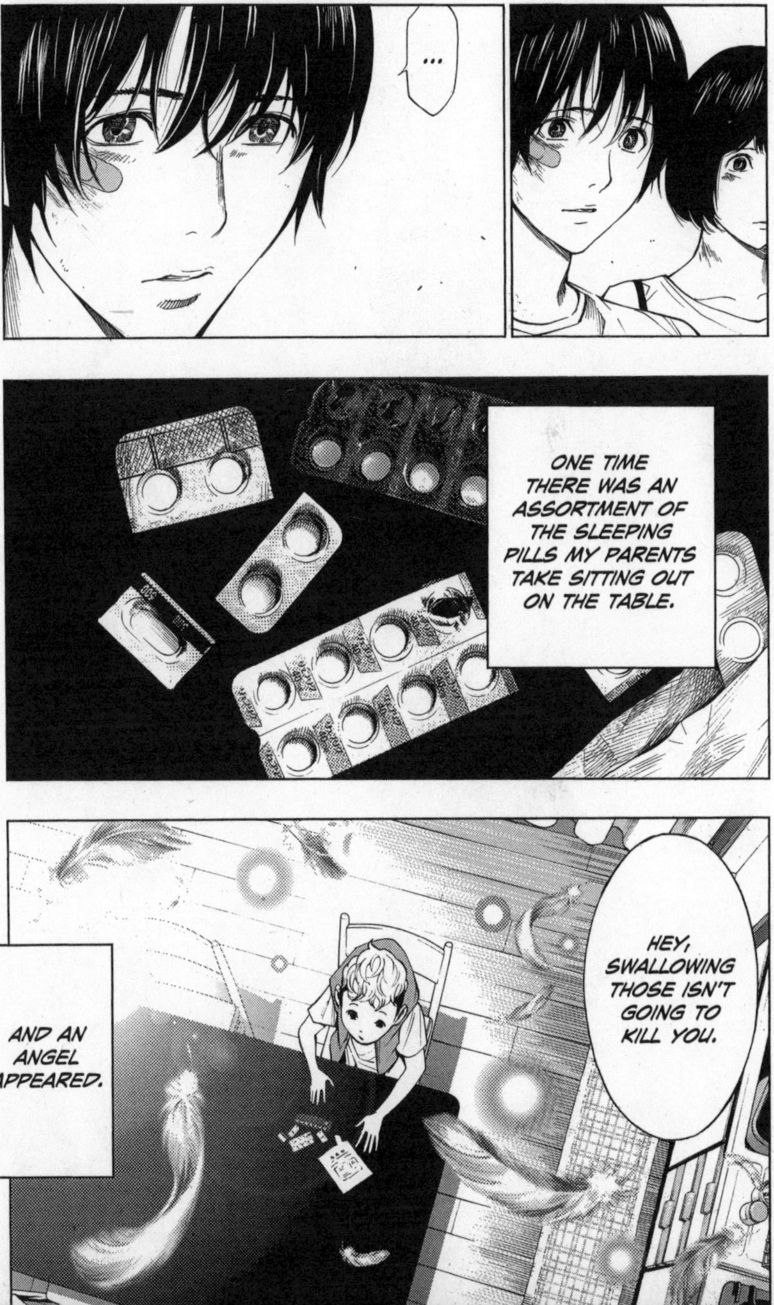
...
ONE TIME THERE WAS AN ASSORTMENT OF THE SLEEPING PILLS MY PARENTS TAKE SITTING OUT ON THE TABLE.
HEY, SWALLOWING THOSE ISN'T GOING TO KILL YOU.
AND AN ANGEL APPEARED.

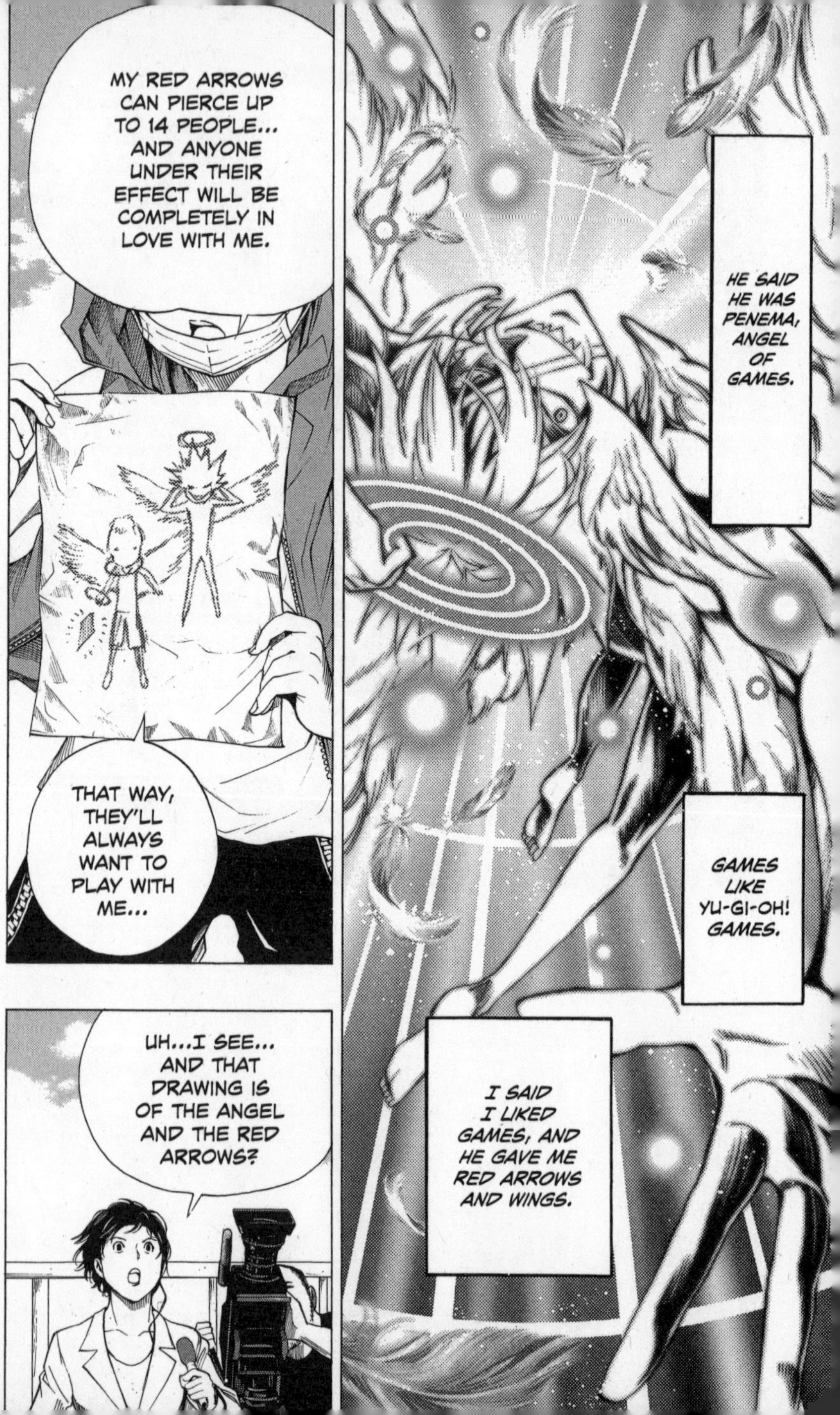
HE SAID HE WAS PENEMA, ANGEL OF GAMES.
GAMES LIKE YU-GI-OH! GAMES.
I SAID I LIKED GAMES, AND HE GAVE ME RED ARROWS AND WINGS.
MY RED ARROWS CAN PIERCE UP TO 14 PEOPLE... AND ANYONE UNDER THEIR EFFECT WILL BE COMPLETELY IN LOVE WITH ME.
THAT WAY, THEY'LL ALWAYS WANT TO PLAY WITH ME...
UH...I SEE... AND THAT DRAWING IS OF THE ANGEL AND THE RED ARROWS?

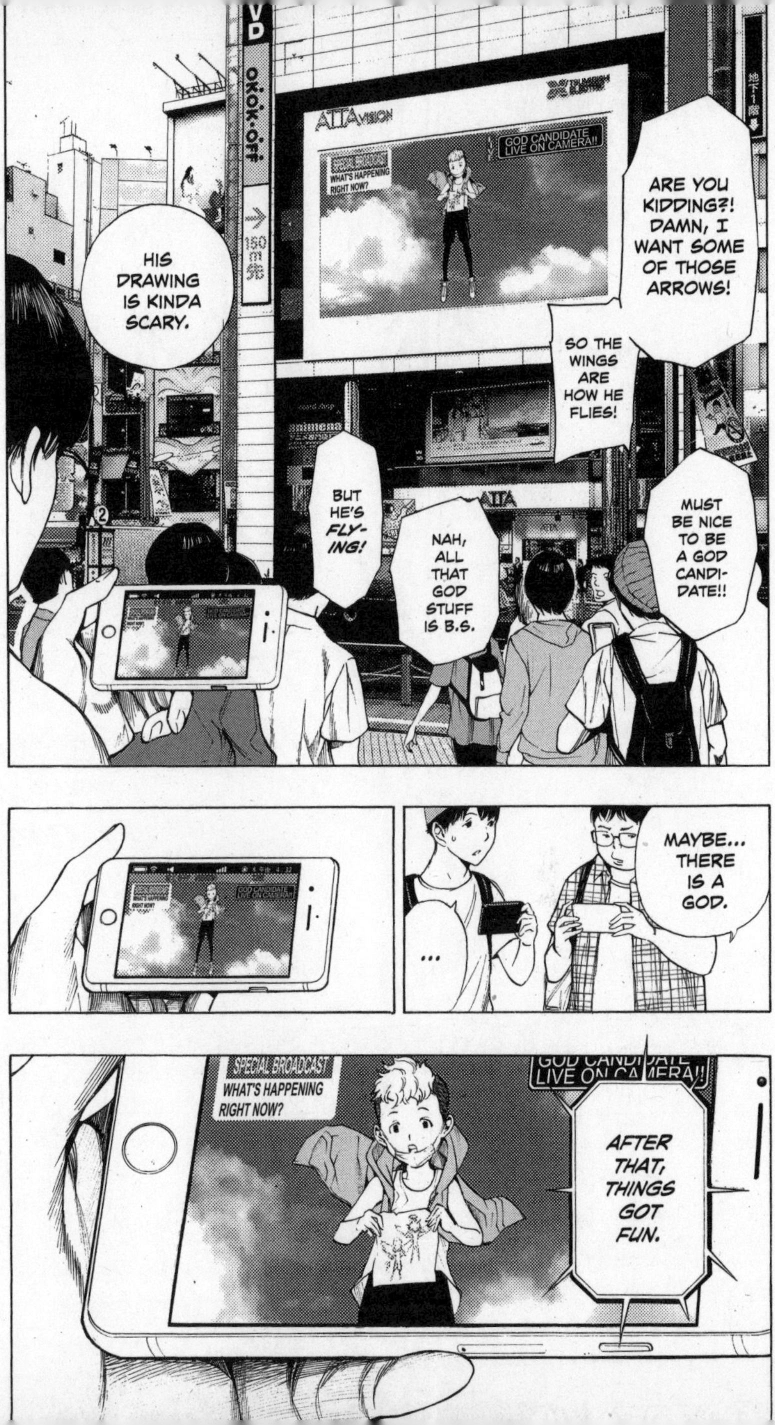
ATTA VISION
GOD CANDIDATE LIVE ON CAMERA!!
WHAT'S HAPPENING RIGHT NOW?
ARE YOU KIDDING?! DAMN, I WANT SOME OF THOSE ARROWS!
SO THE WINGS ARE HOW HE FLIES!
HIS DRAWING IS KINDA SCARY.
MUST BE NICE TO BE A GOD CANDIDATE!!
NAH, ALL THAT GOD STUFF IS B.S.
BUT HE'S *FLYING!*
MAYBE... THERE IS A GOD.
...
SPECIAL BROADCAST
WHAT'S HAPPENING RIGHT NOW?
GOD CANDIDATE LIVE ON CAMERA!!
AFTER THAT, THINGS GOT FUN.

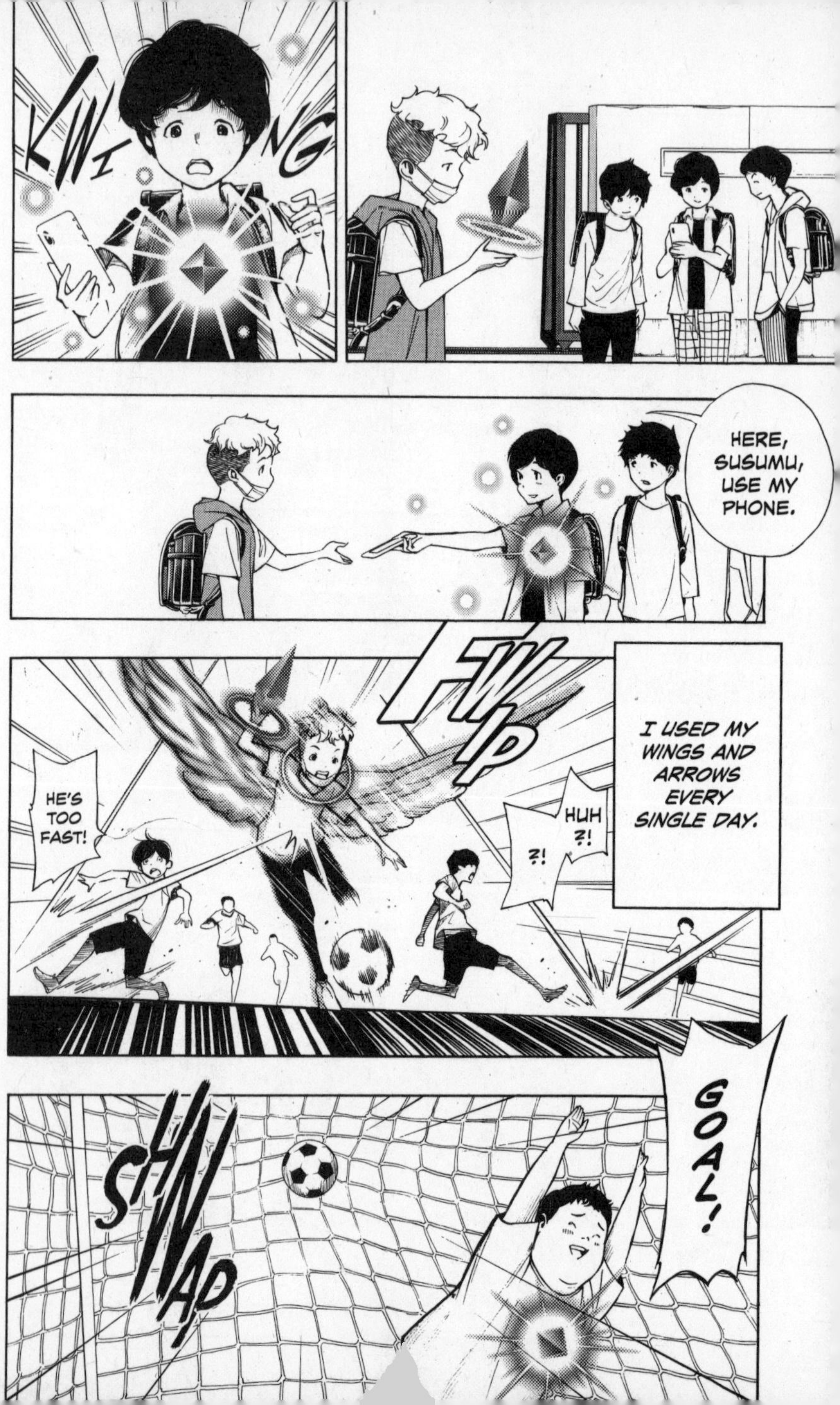
KWING
HERE, SUSUMU, USE MY PHONE.
I USED MY WINGS AND ARROWS EVERY SINGLE DAY.
FWIP
HUH ?!
?!
HE'S TOO FAST!
GOAL!
SHWAP

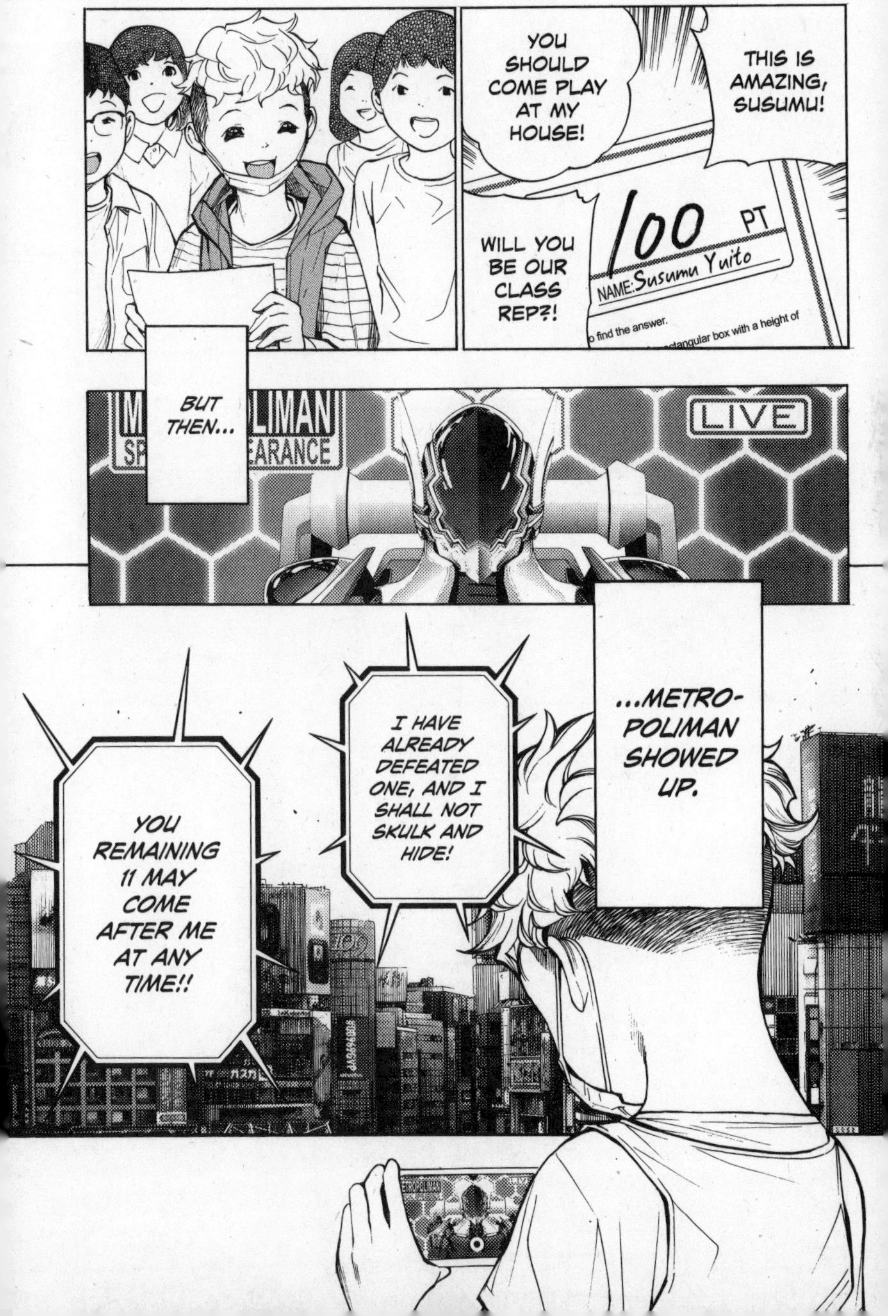
THIS IS AMAZING, SUSUMU!
YOU SHOULD COME PLAY AT MY HOUSE!
100 PT
NAME: Susumu Yuito
o find the answer.
ctangular box with a height of
WILL YOU BE OUR CLASS REP?!
LIVE
BUT THEN...
...METRO-POLIMAN SHOWED UP.
I HAVE ALREADY DEFEATED ONE, AND I SHALL NOT SKULK AND HIDE!
YOU REMAINING 11 MAY COME AFTER ME AT ANY TIME!!

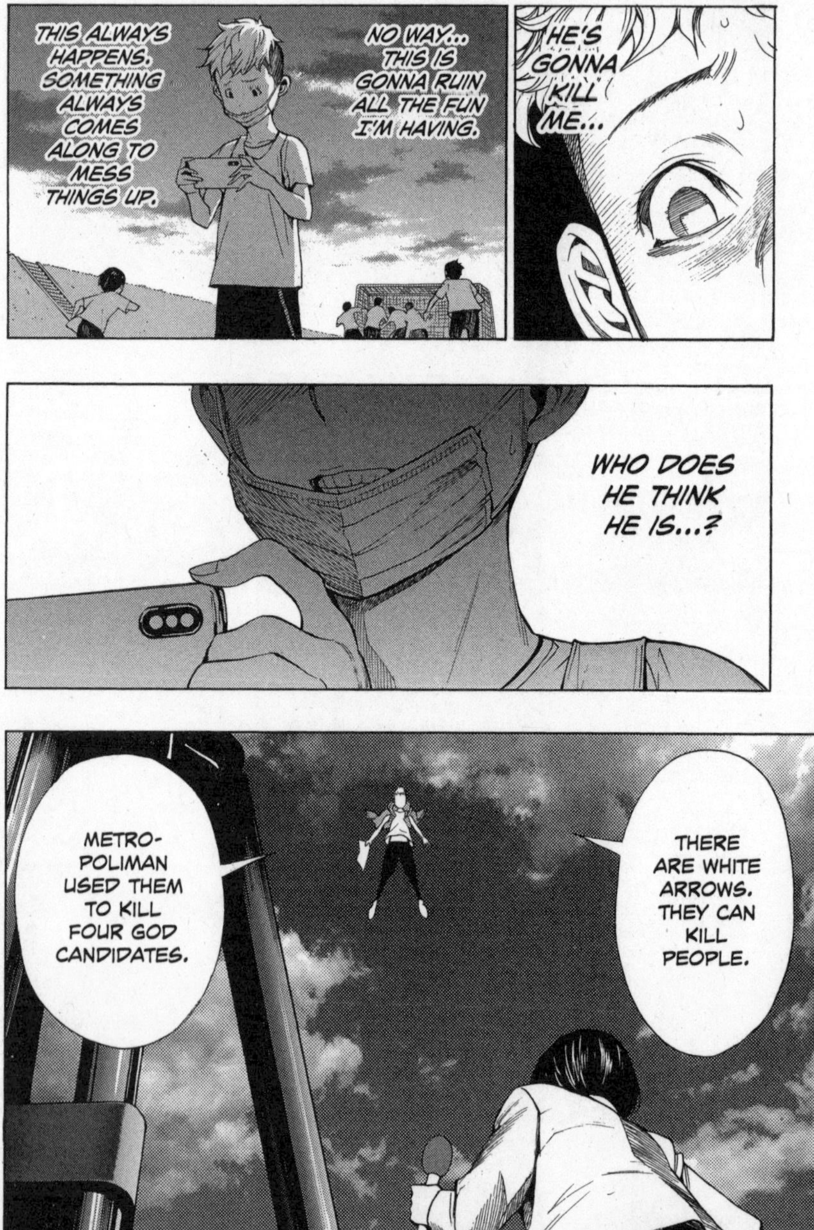
HE'S GONNA KILL ME...
NO WAY... THIS IS GONNA RUIN ALL THE FUN I'M HAVING.
THIS ALWAYS HAPPENS. SOMETHING ALWAYS COMES ALONG TO MESS THINGS UP.
WHO DOES HE THINK HE IS...?
THERE ARE WHITE ARROWS. THEY CAN KILL PEOPLE.
METRO-POLIMAN USED THEM TO KILL FOUR GOD CANDIDATES.

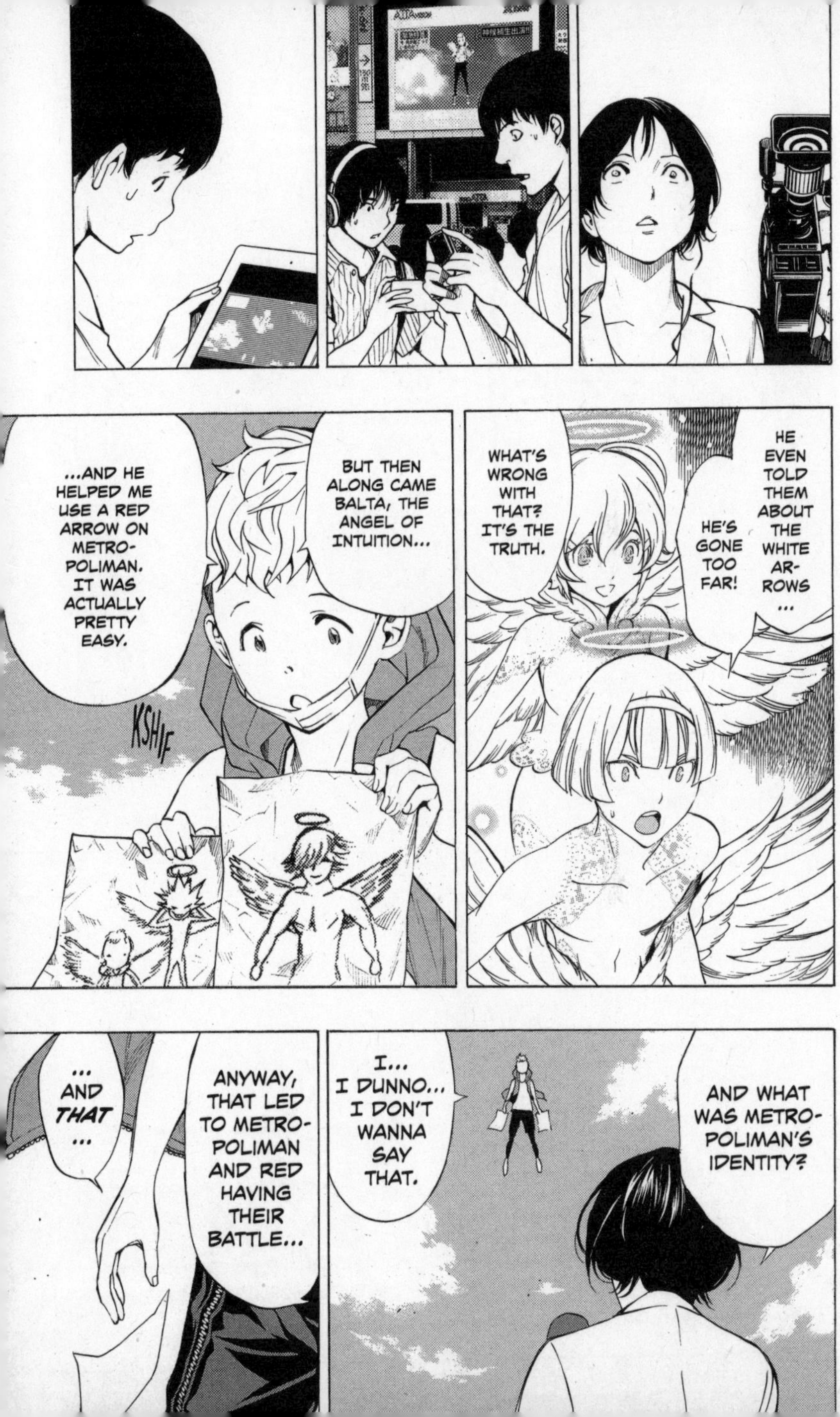
HE EVEN TOLD THEM ABOUT THE WHITE ARROWS...
HE'S GONE TOO FAR!
WHAT'S WRONG WITH THAT? IT'S THE TRUTH.
BUT THEN ALONG CAME BALTA, THE ANGEL OF INTUITION...
...AND HE HELPED ME USE A RED ARROW ON METROPOLIMAN. IT WAS ACTUALLY PRETTY EASY.
KSHIF
AND WHAT WAS METROPOLIMAN'S IDENTITY?
I... I DUNNO... I DON'T WANNA SAY THAT.
ANYWAY, THAT LED TO METROPOLIMAN AND RED HAVING THEIR BATTLE...
...AND *THAT*...

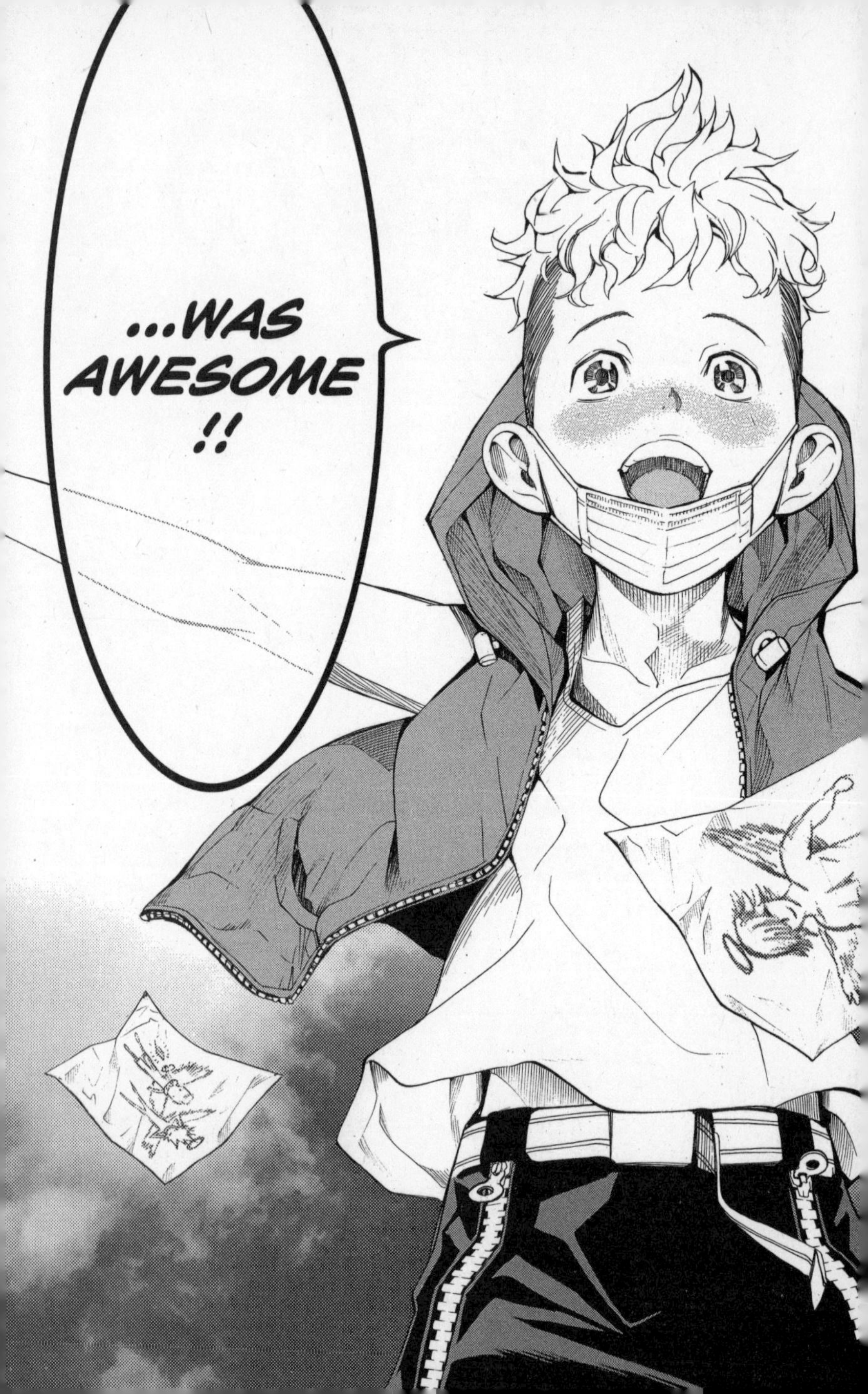
...WAS AWESOME !!

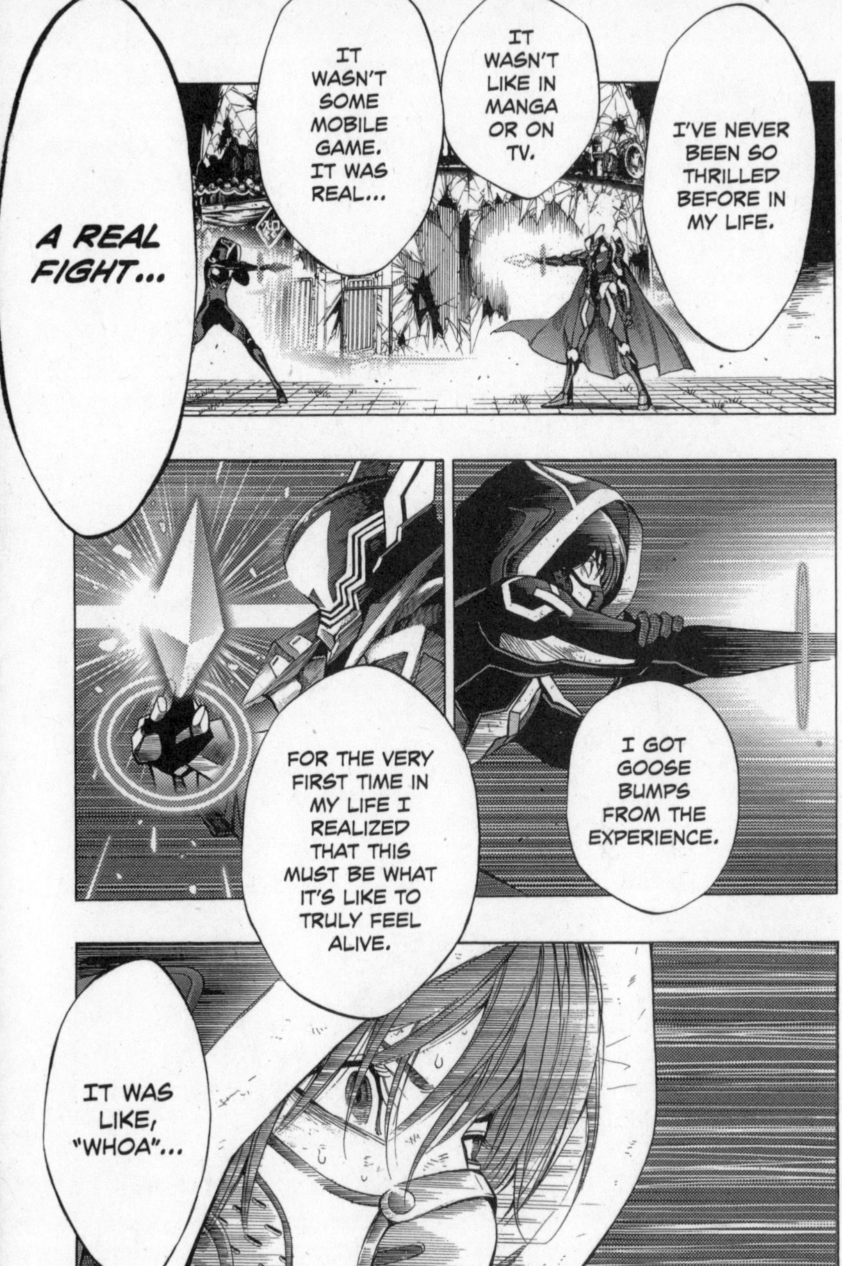
I'VE NEVER BEEN SO THRILLED BEFORE IN MY LIFE.
IT WASN'T LIKE IN MANGA OR ON TV.
IT WASN'T SOME MOBILE GAME. IT WAS REAL...
A REAL FIGHT...
I GOT GOOSE BUMPS FROM THE EXPERIENCE.
FOR THE VERY FIRST TIME IN MY LIFE I REALIZED THAT THIS MUST BE WHAT IT'S LIKE TO TRULY FEEL ALIVE.
IT WAS LIKE, "WHOA"...

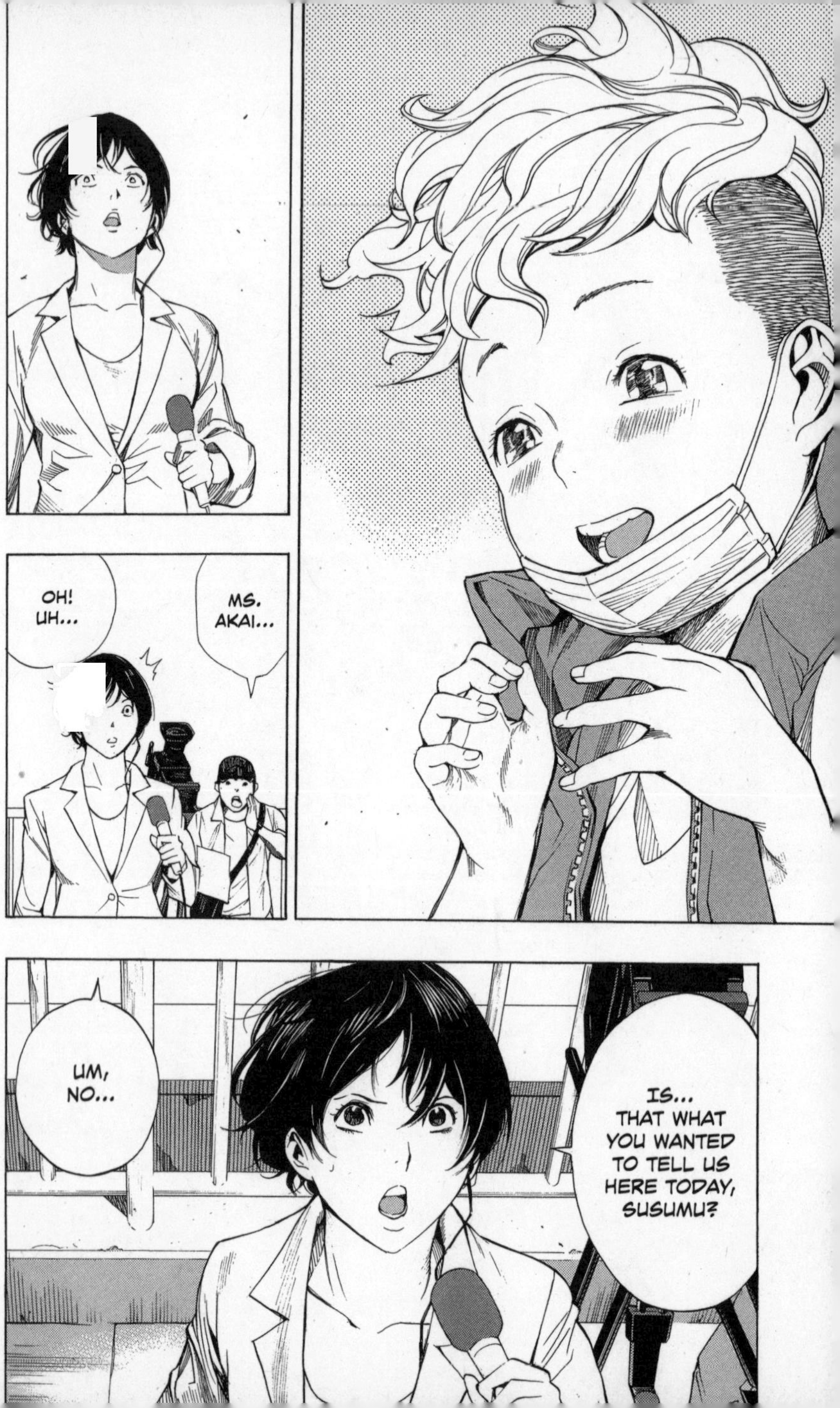
MS. AKAI...
OH! UH...
IS... THAT WHAT YOU WANTED TO TELL US HERE TODAY, SUSUMU?
UM, NO...

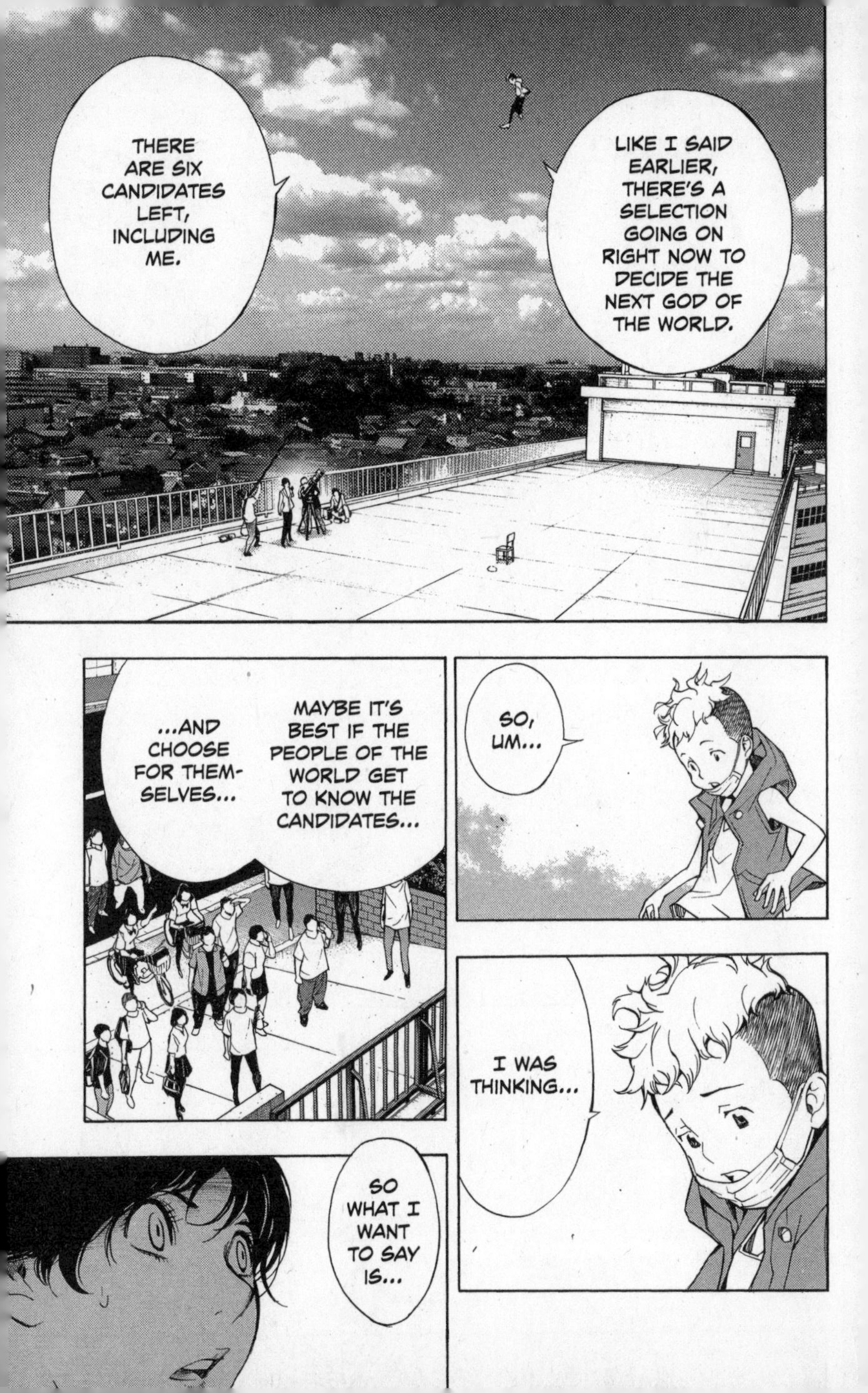
LIKE I SAID EARLIER, THERE'S A SELECTION GOING ON RIGHT NOW TO DECIDE THE NEXT GOD OF THE WORLD.
THERE ARE SIX CANDIDATES LEFT, INCLUDING ME.
SO, UM...
I WAS THINKING...
MAYBE IT'S BEST IF THE PEOPLE OF THE WORLD GET TO KNOW THE CANDIDATES...
...AND CHOOSE FOR THEMSELVES...
SO WHAT I WANT TO SAY IS...

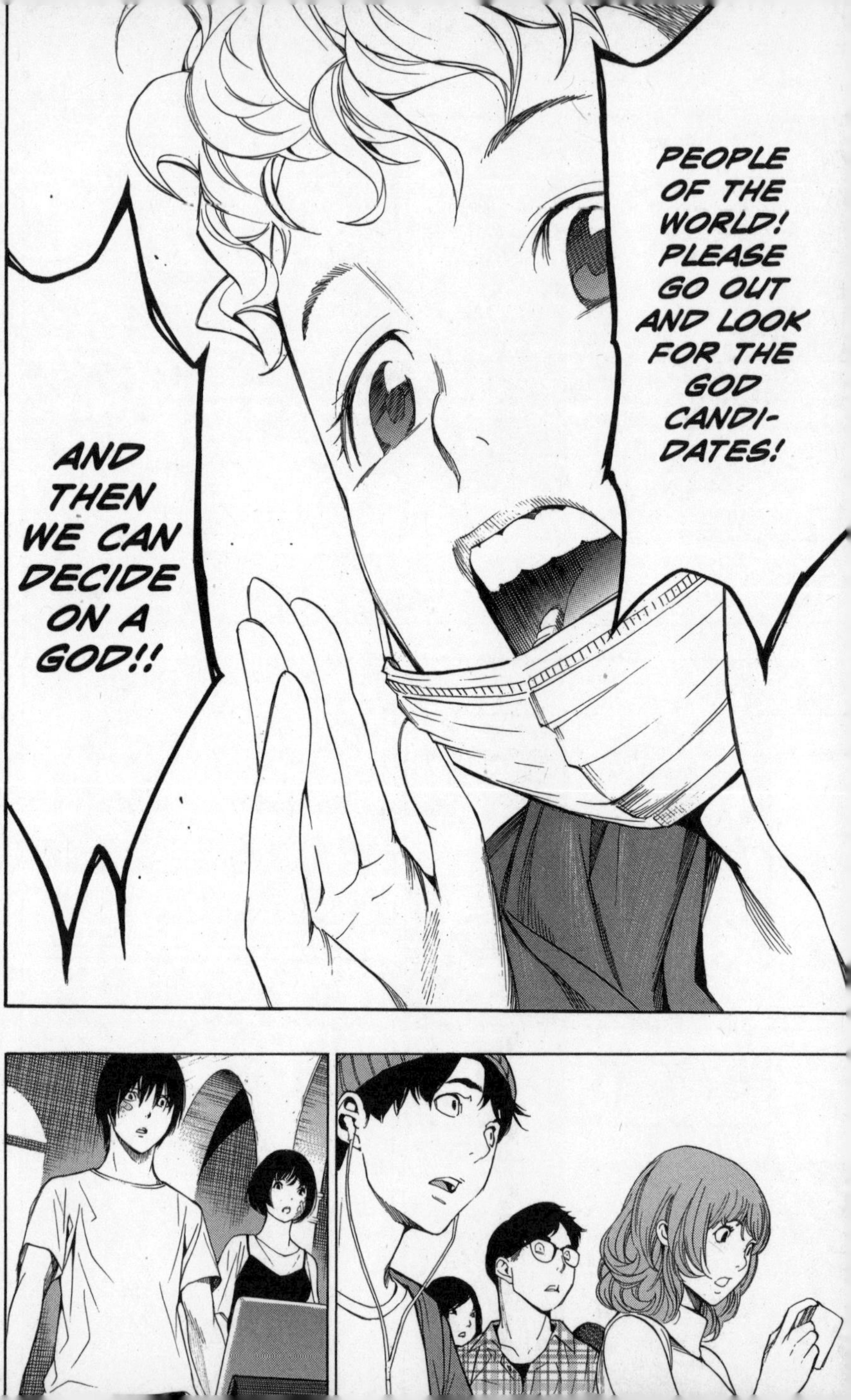
PEOPLE OF THE WORLD! PLEASE GO OUT AND LOOK FOR THE GOD CANDI-DATES!
AND THEN WE CAN DECIDE ON A GOD!!

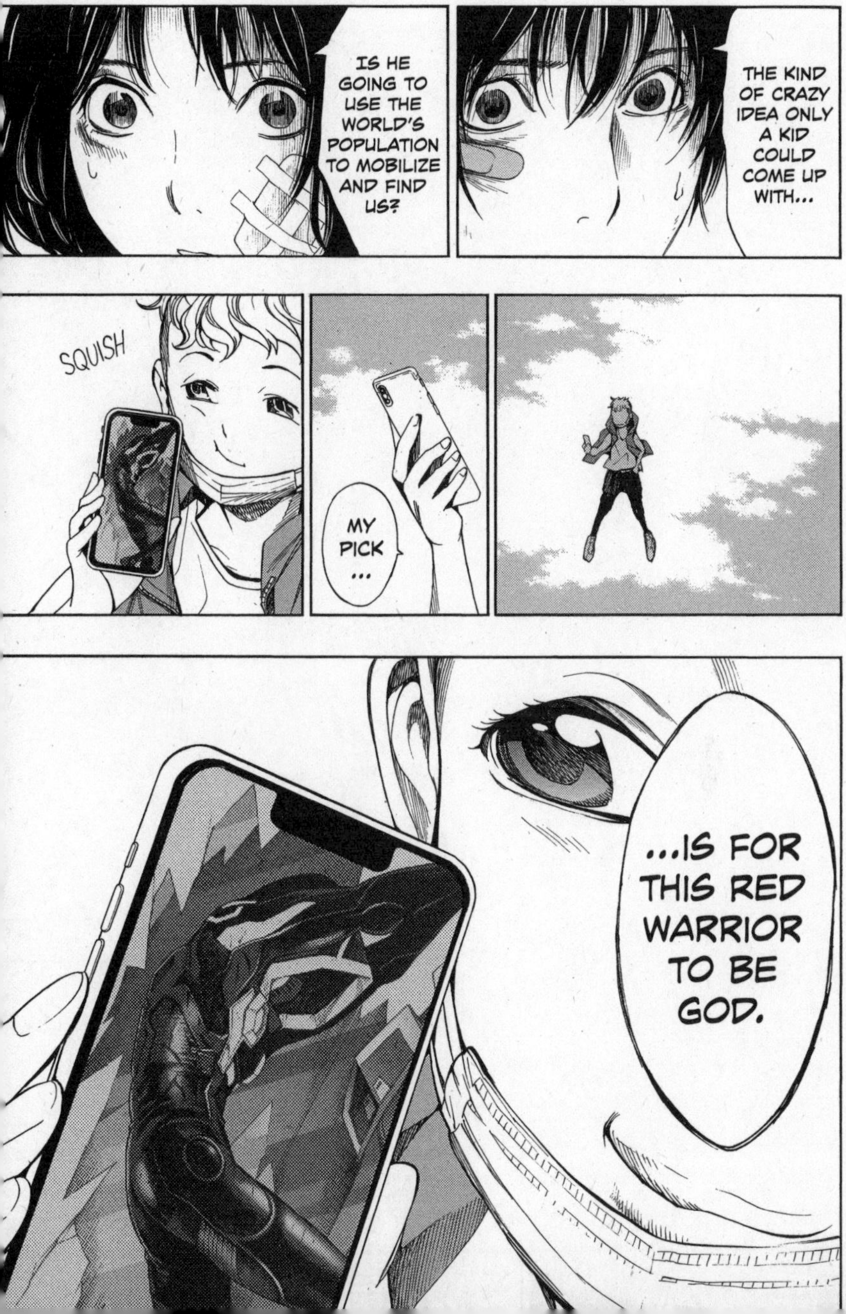
THE KIND OF CRAZY IDEA ONLY A KID COULD COME UP WITH...
IS HE GOING TO USE THE WORLD'S POPULATION TO MOBILIZE AND FIND US?
MY PICK ...
SQUISH
...IS FOR THIS RED WARRIOR TO BE GOD.

#29 Diffused Power

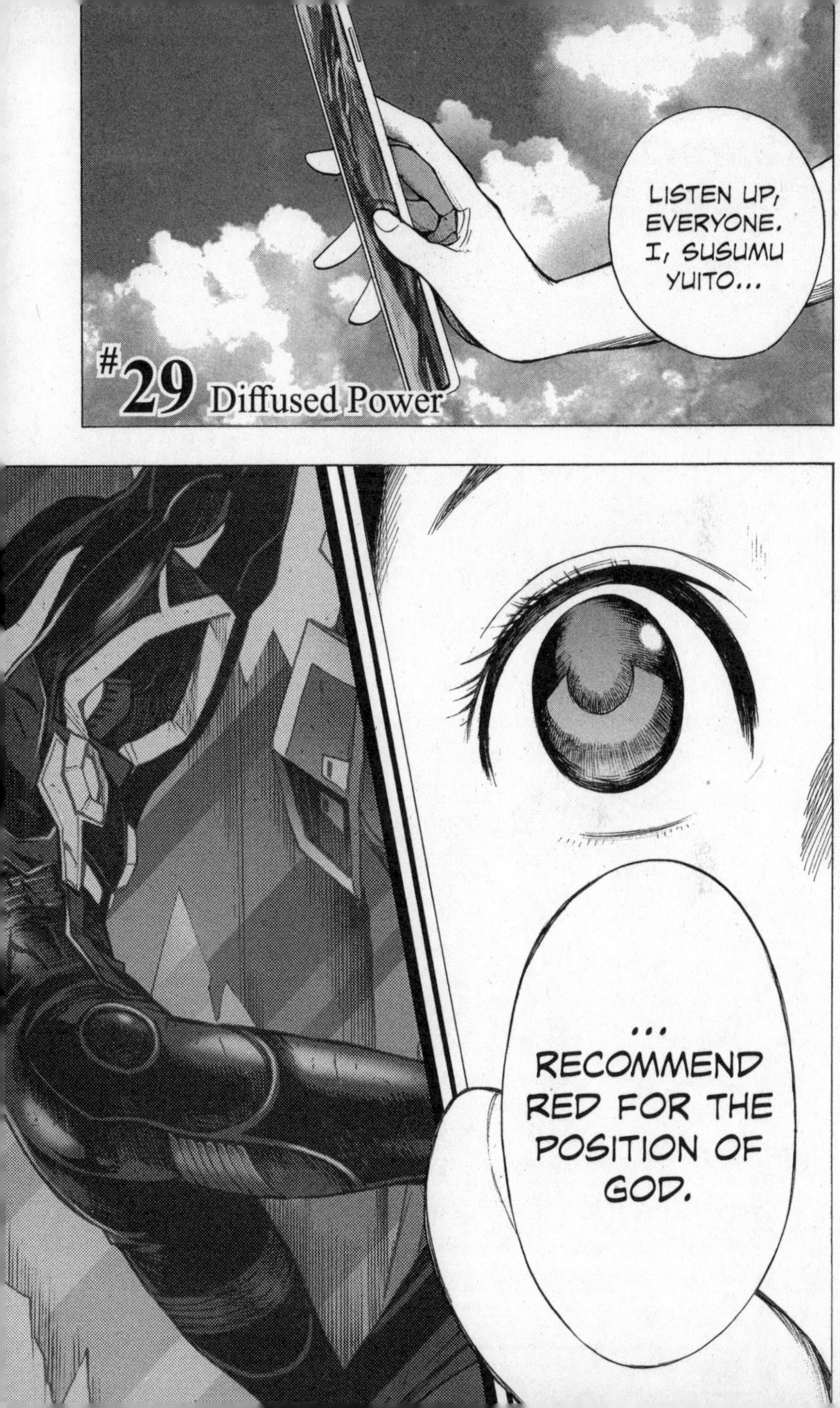
LISTEN UP, EVERYONE. I, SUSUMU YUITO...
... RECOMMEND RED FOR THE POSITION OF GOD.

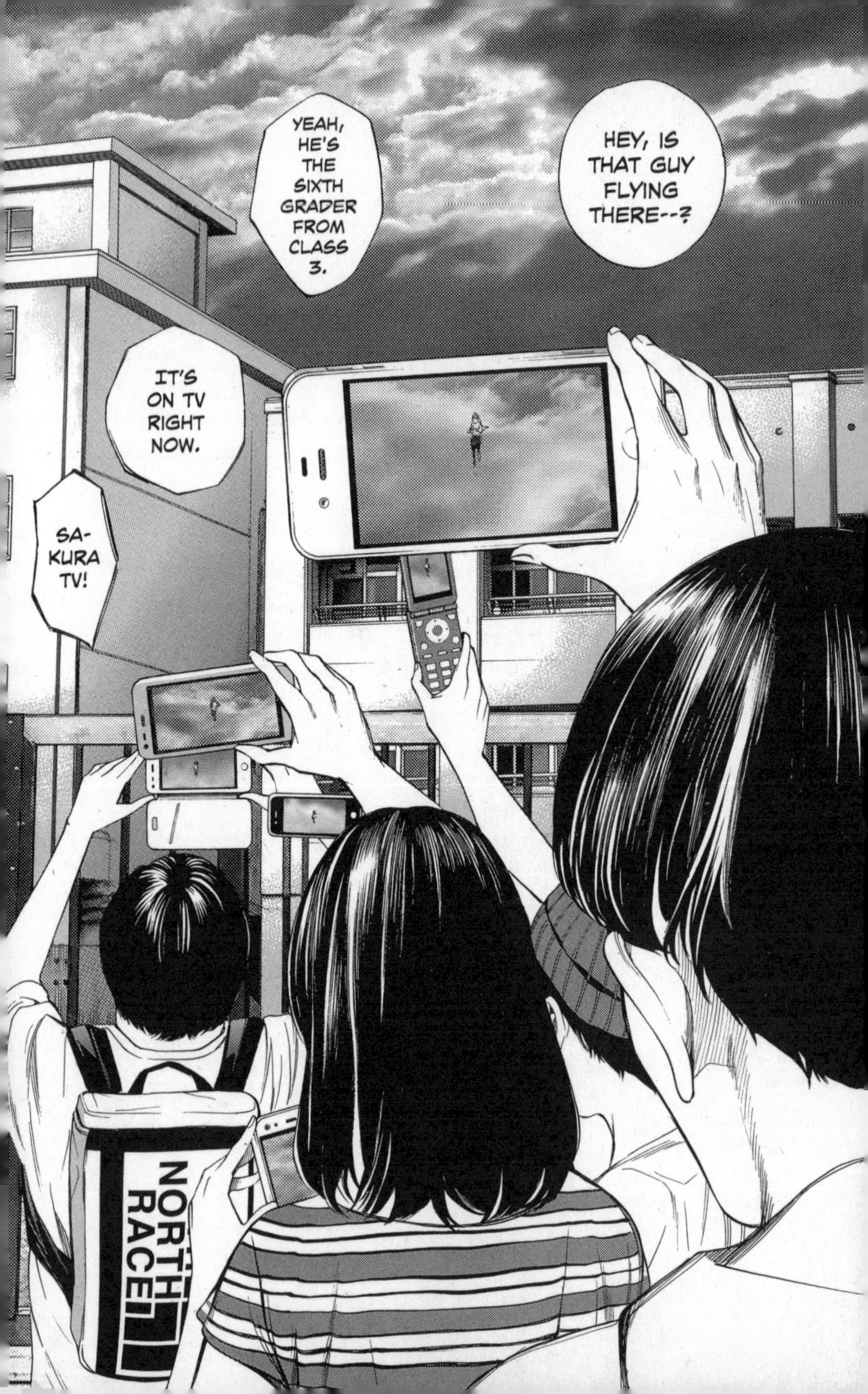
HEY, IS THAT GUY FLYING THERE--?
YEAH, HE'S THE SIXTH GRADER FROM CLASS 3.
IT'S ON TV RIGHT NOW.
SA-KURA TV!
NORTH RACE

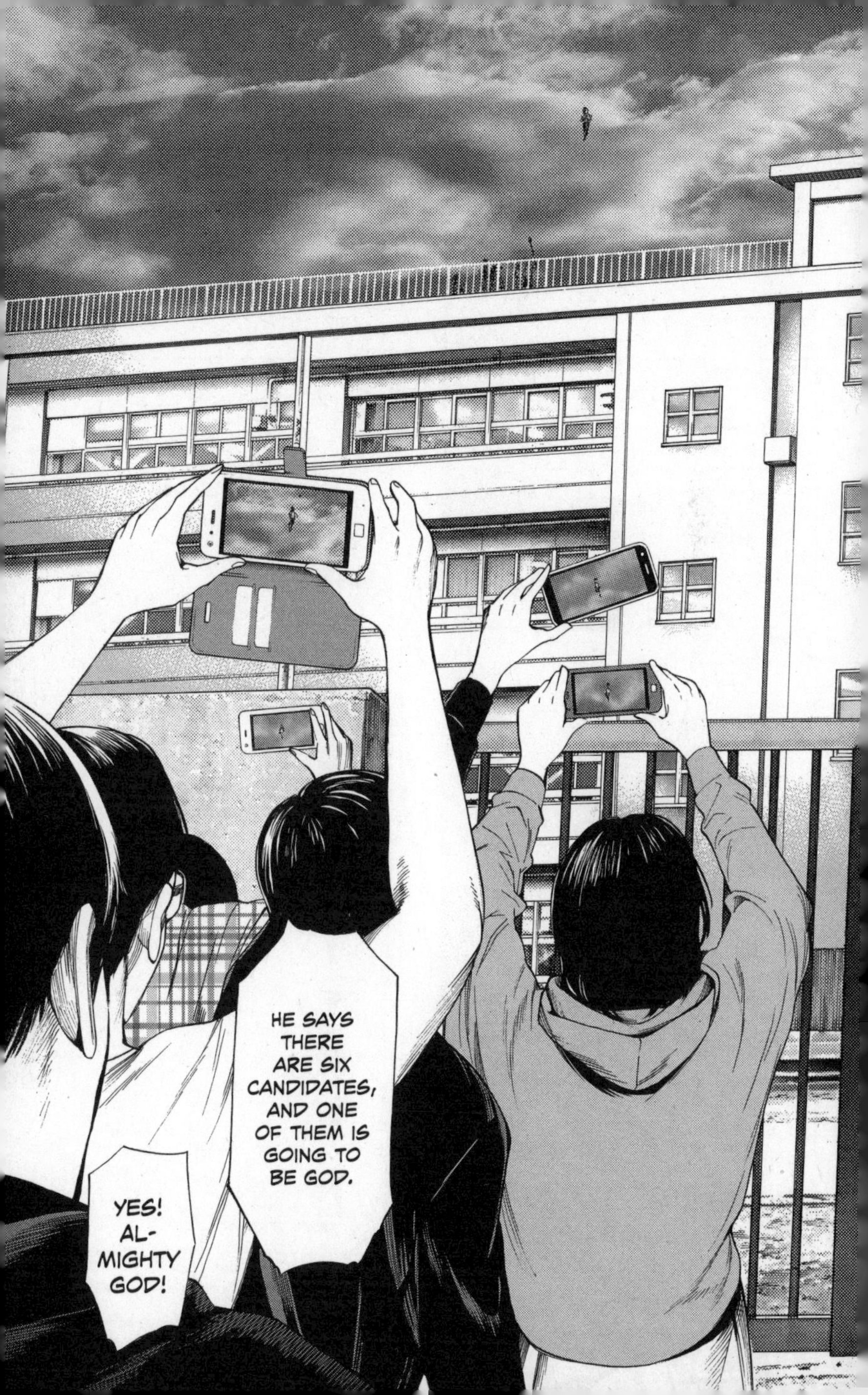
HE SAYS THERE ARE SIX CANDIDATES, AND ONE OF THEM IS GOING TO BE GOD.
YES! AL-MIGHTY GOD!

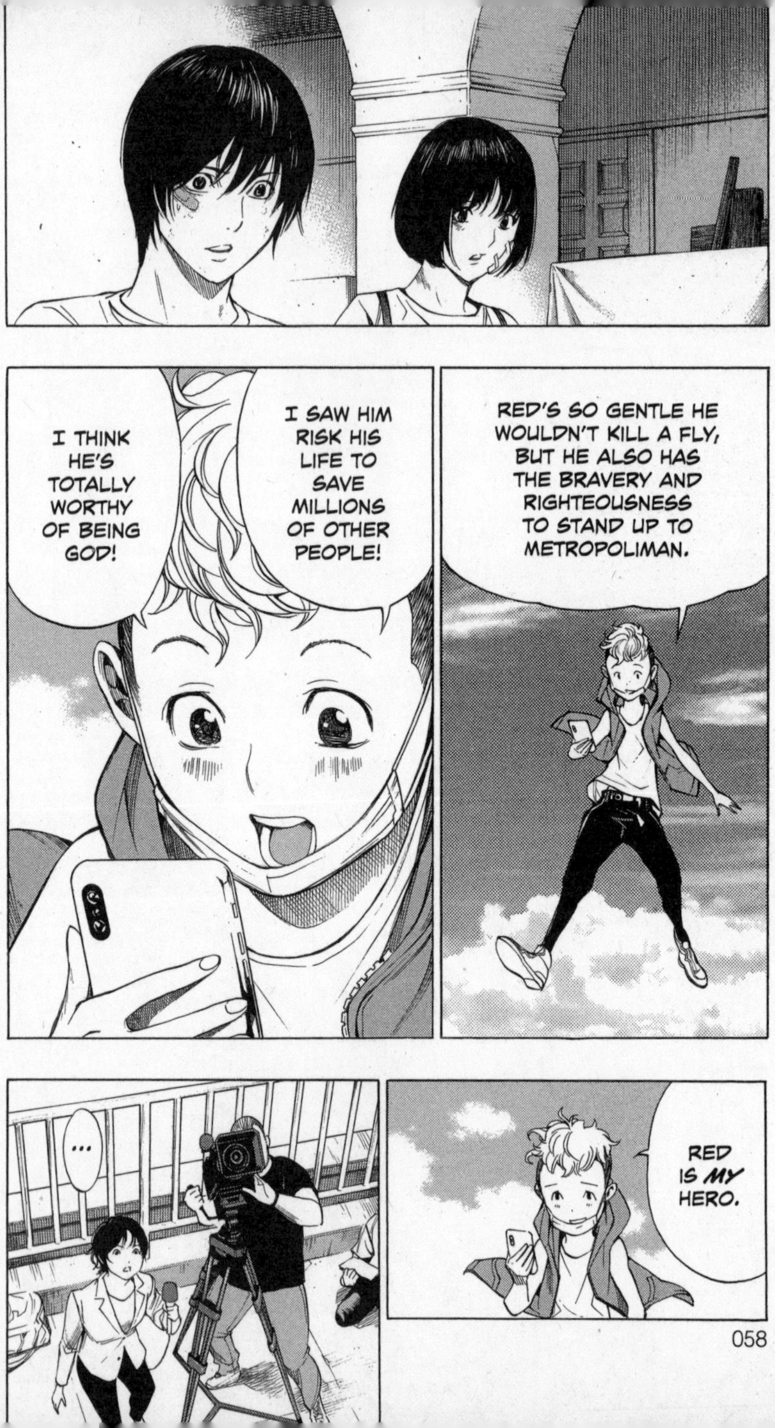
RED'S SO GENTLE HE WOULDN'T KILL A FLY, BUT HE ALSO HAS THE BRAVERY AND RIGHTEOUSNESS TO STAND UP TO METROPOLIMAN.
I SAW HIM RISK HIS LIFE TO SAVE MILLIONS OF OTHER PEOPLE!
I THINK HE'S TOTALLY WORTHY OF BEING GOD!
RED IS *MY* HERO.
...

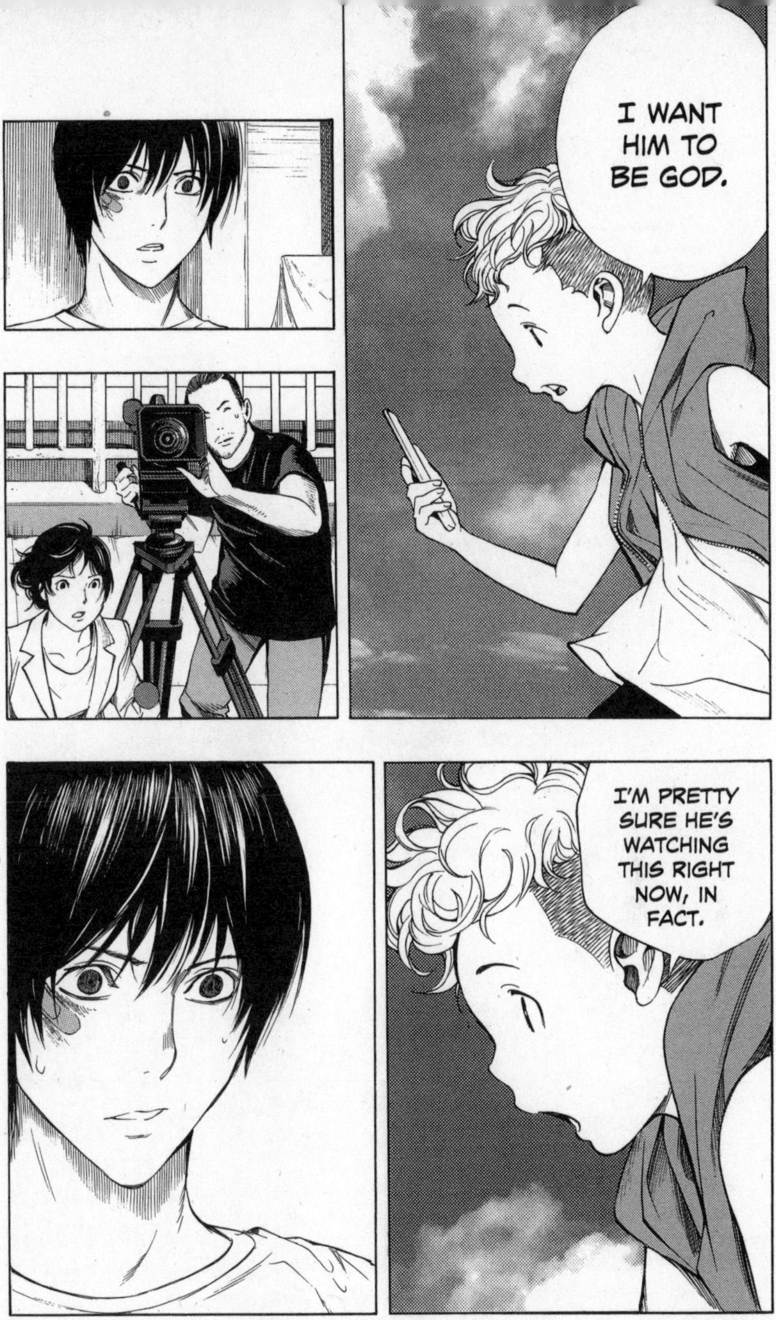
I WANT HIM TO BE GOD.
I'M PRETTY SURE HE'S WATCHING THIS RIGHT NOW, IN FACT.

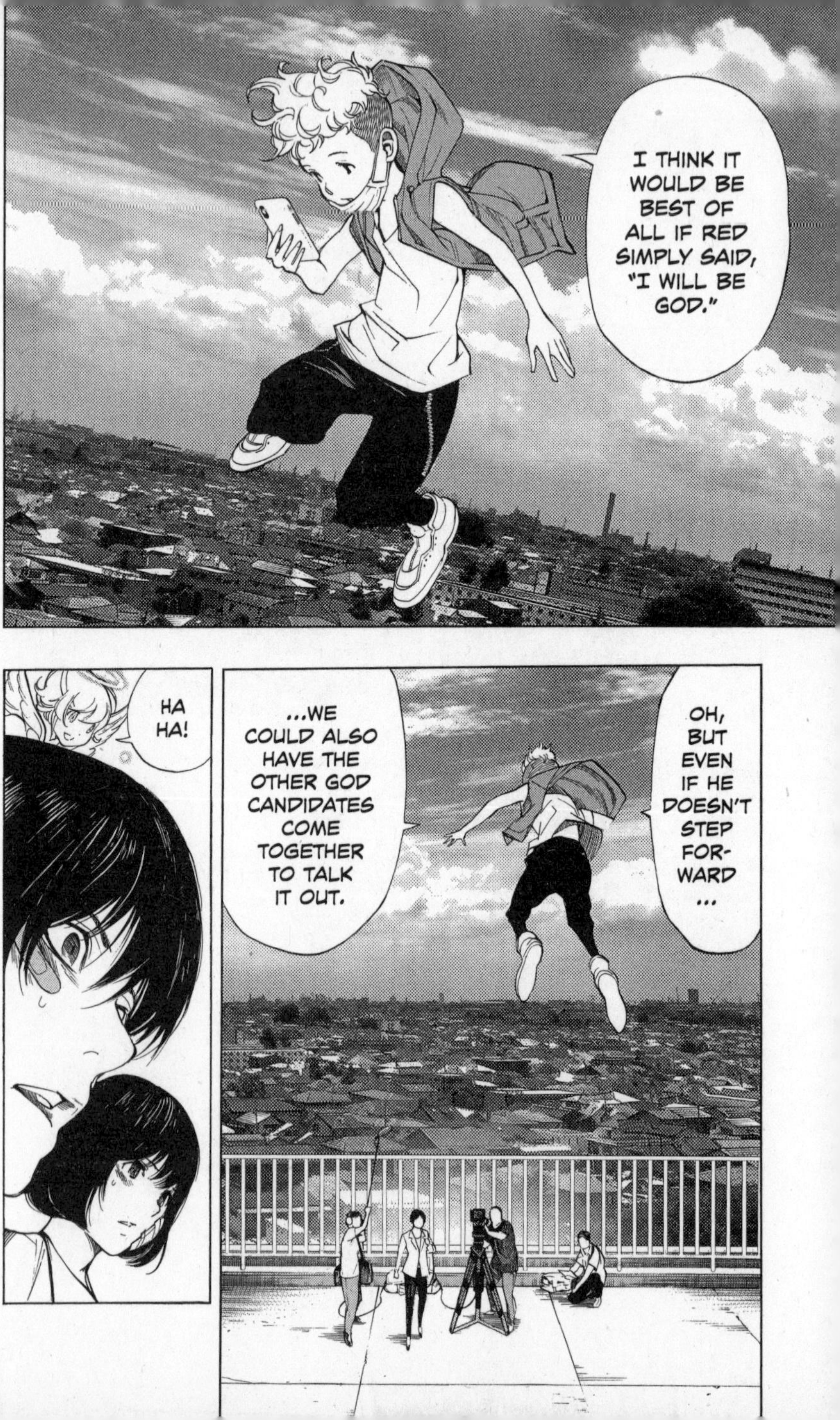
I THINK IT WOULD BE BEST OF ALL IF RED SIMPLY SAID, "I WILL BE GOD."
OH, BUT EVEN IF HE DOESN'T STEP FOR-WARD...
...WE COULD ALSO HAVE THE OTHER GOD CANDIDATES COME TOGETHER TO TALK IT OUT.
HA HA!

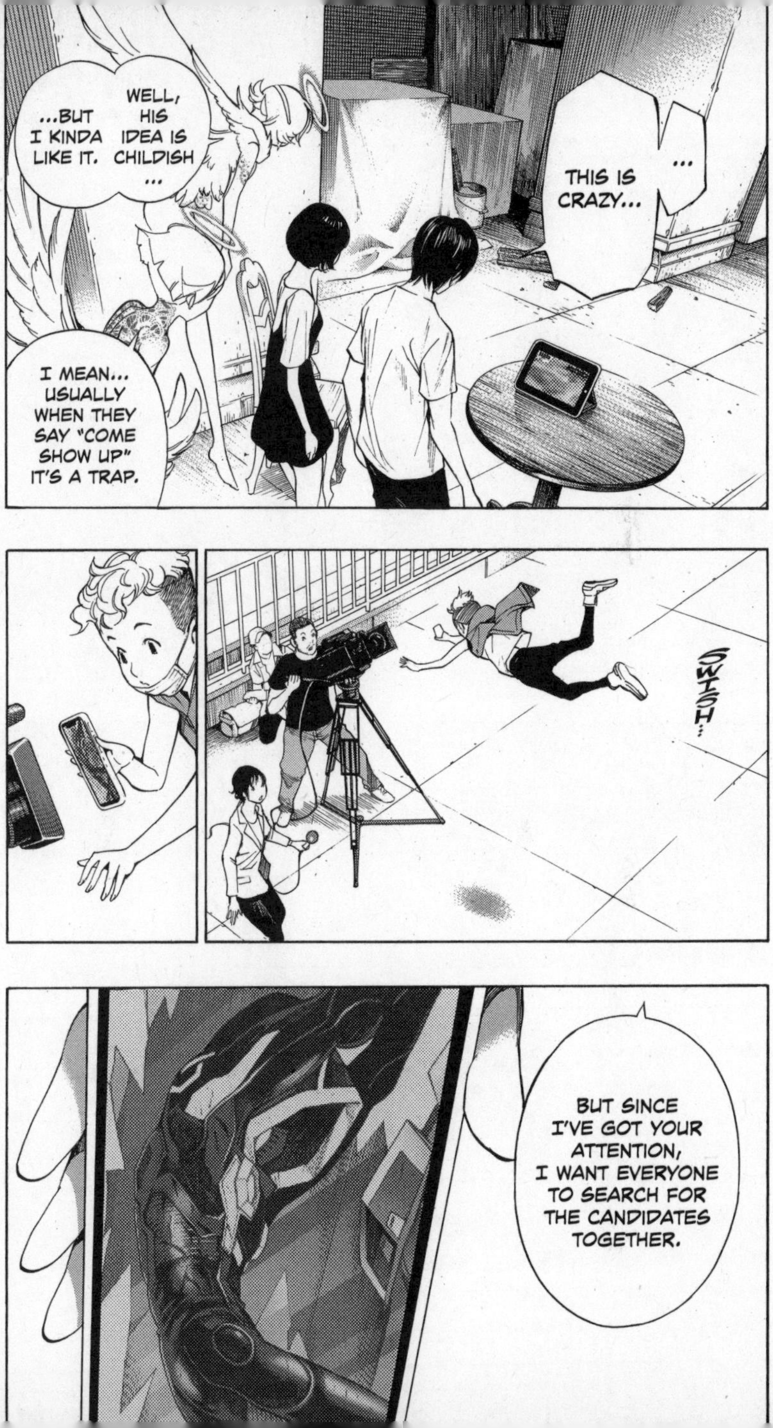
...
THIS IS CRAZY...
WELL, HIS IDEA IS CHILDISH ...
...BUT I KINDA LIKE IT.
I MEAN... USUALLY WHEN THEY SAY "COME SHOW UP" IT'S A TRAP.
SWISH...
BUT SINCE I'VE GOT YOUR ATTENTION, I WANT EVERYONE TO SEARCH FOR THE CANDIDATES TOGETHER.

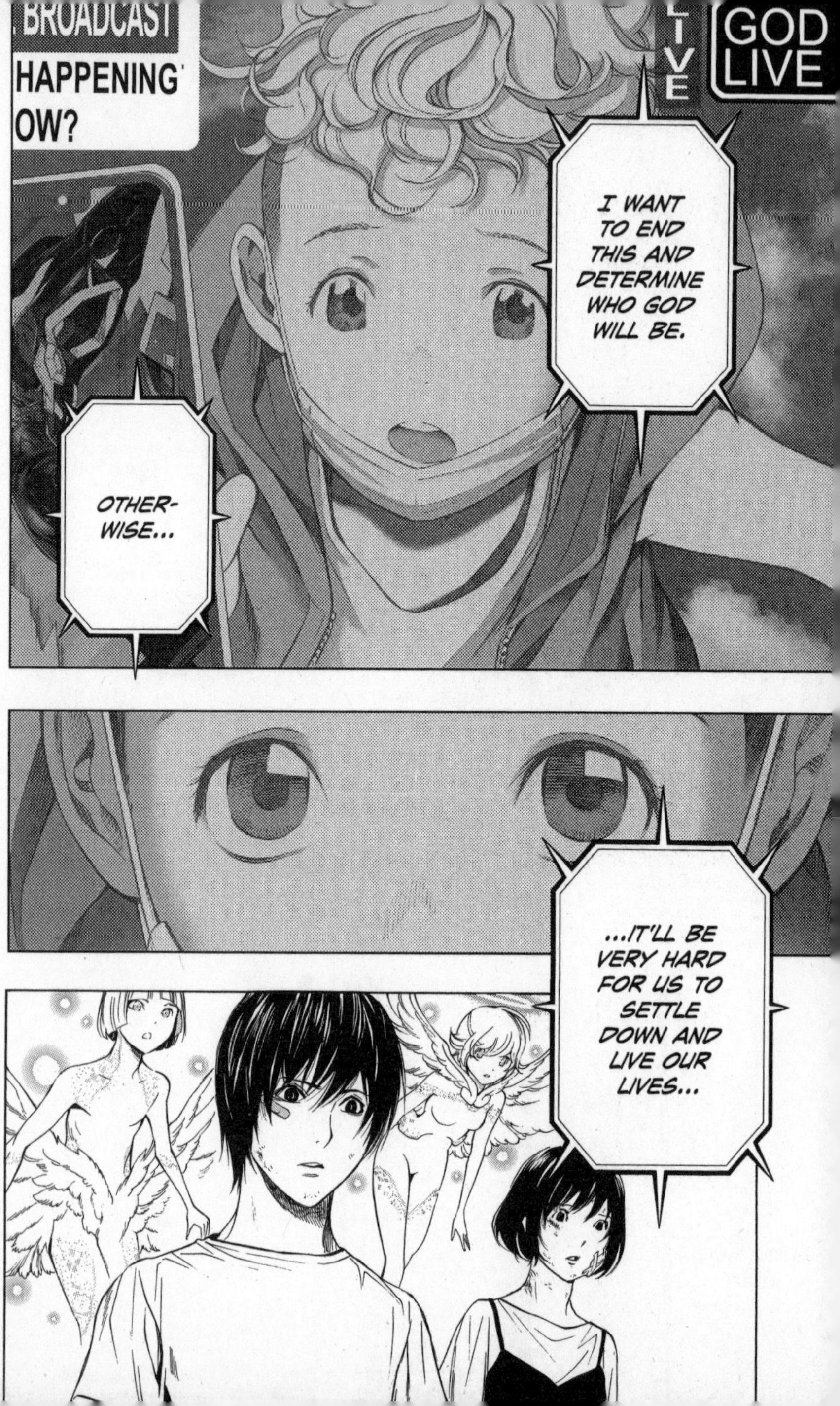
BROADCAST
HAPPENING
OW?
LIVE
GOD LIVE
I WANT TO END THIS AND DETERMINE WHO GOD WILL BE.
OTHER-WISE...
...IT'LL BE VERY HARD FOR US TO SETTLE DOWN AND LIVE OUR LIVES...

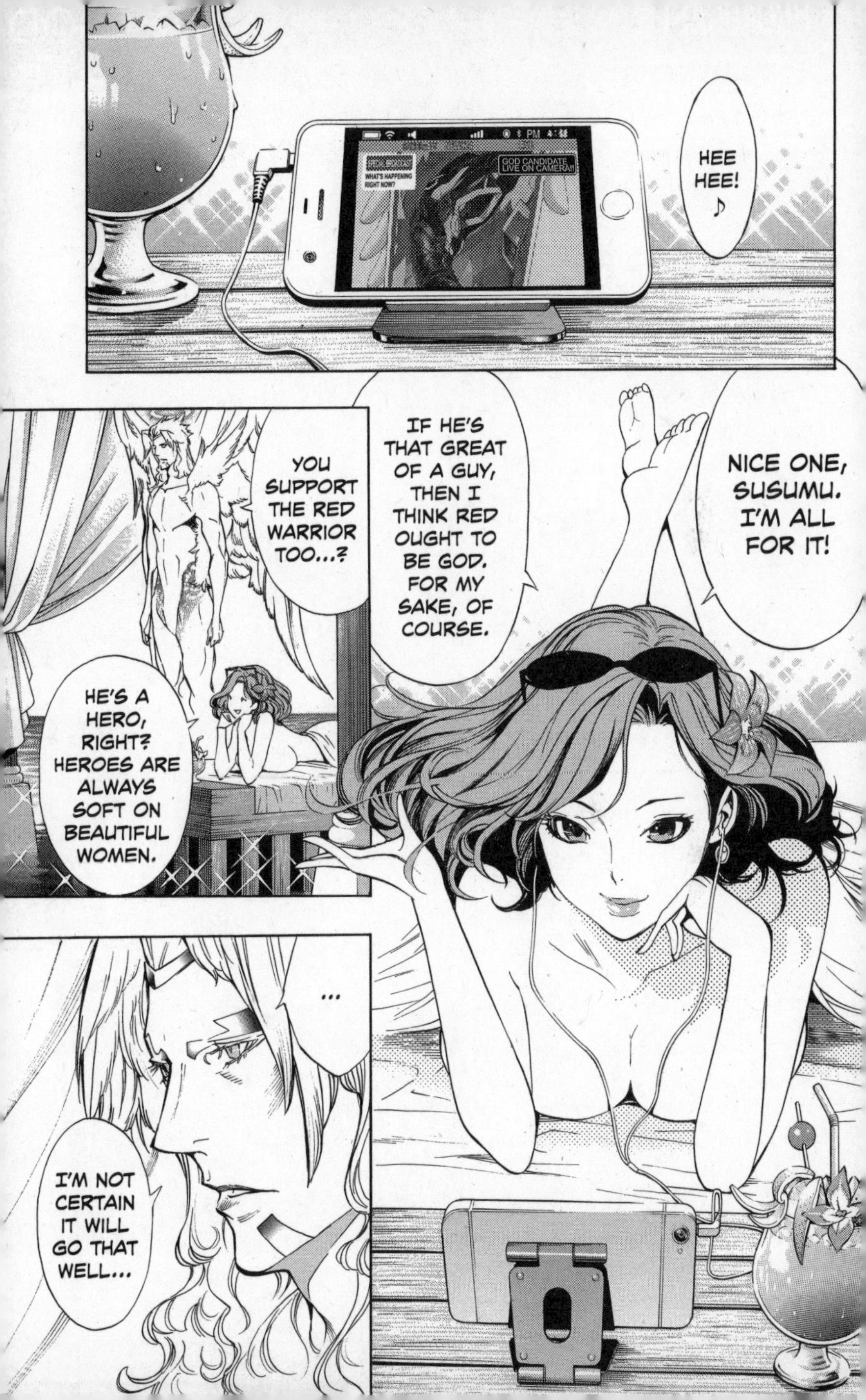
HEE HEE! ♪
GOD CANDIDATE LIVE ON CAMERA!!
WHAT'S HAPPENING RIGHT NOW?
NICE ONE, SUSUMU. I'M ALL FOR IT!
IF HE'S THAT GREAT OF A GUY, THEN I THINK RED OUGHT TO BE GOD. FOR MY SAKE, OF COURSE.
YOU SUPPORT THE RED WARRIOR TOO...?
HE'S A HERO, RIGHT? HEROES ARE ALWAYS SOFT ON BEAUTIFUL WOMEN.
...
I'M NOT CERTAIN IT WILL GO THAT WELL...

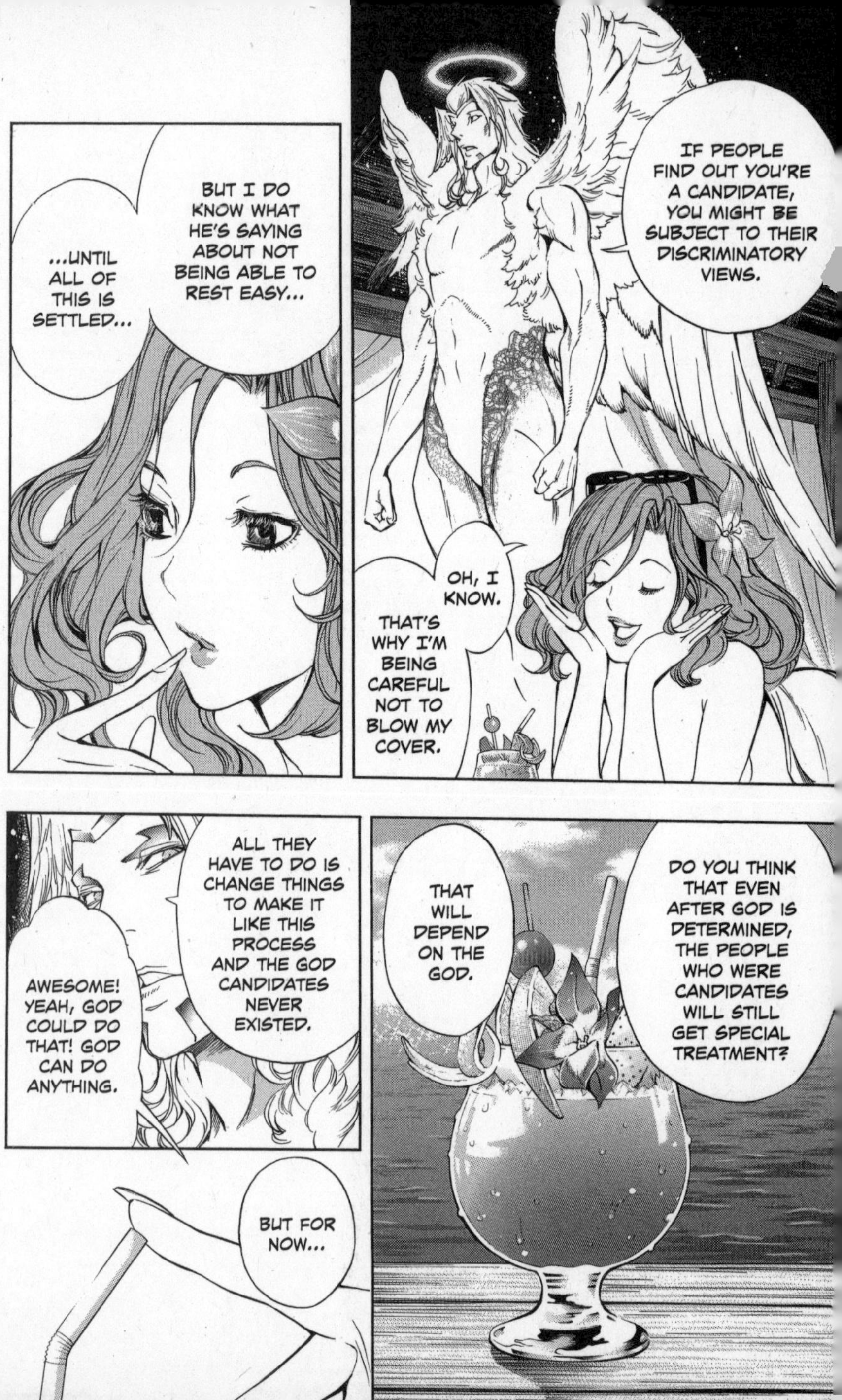
IF PEOPLE FIND OUT YOU'RE A CANDIDATE, YOU MIGHT BE SUBJECT TO THEIR DISCRIMINATORY VIEWS.
OH, I KNOW.
THAT'S WHY I'M BEING CAREFUL NOT TO BLOW MY COVER.
BUT I DO KNOW WHAT HE'S SAYING ABOUT NOT BEING ABLE TO REST EASY...
...UNTIL ALL OF THIS IS SETTLED...
DO YOU THINK THAT EVEN AFTER GOD IS DETERMINED, THE PEOPLE WHO WERE CANDIDATES WILL STILL GET SPECIAL TREATMENT?
THAT WILL DEPEND ON THE GOD.
ALL THEY HAVE TO DO IS CHANGE THINGS TO MAKE IT LIKE THIS PROCESS AND THE GOD CANDIDATES NEVER EXISTED.
AWESOME! YEAH, GOD COULD DO THAT! GOD CAN DO ANYTHING.
BUT FOR NOW...

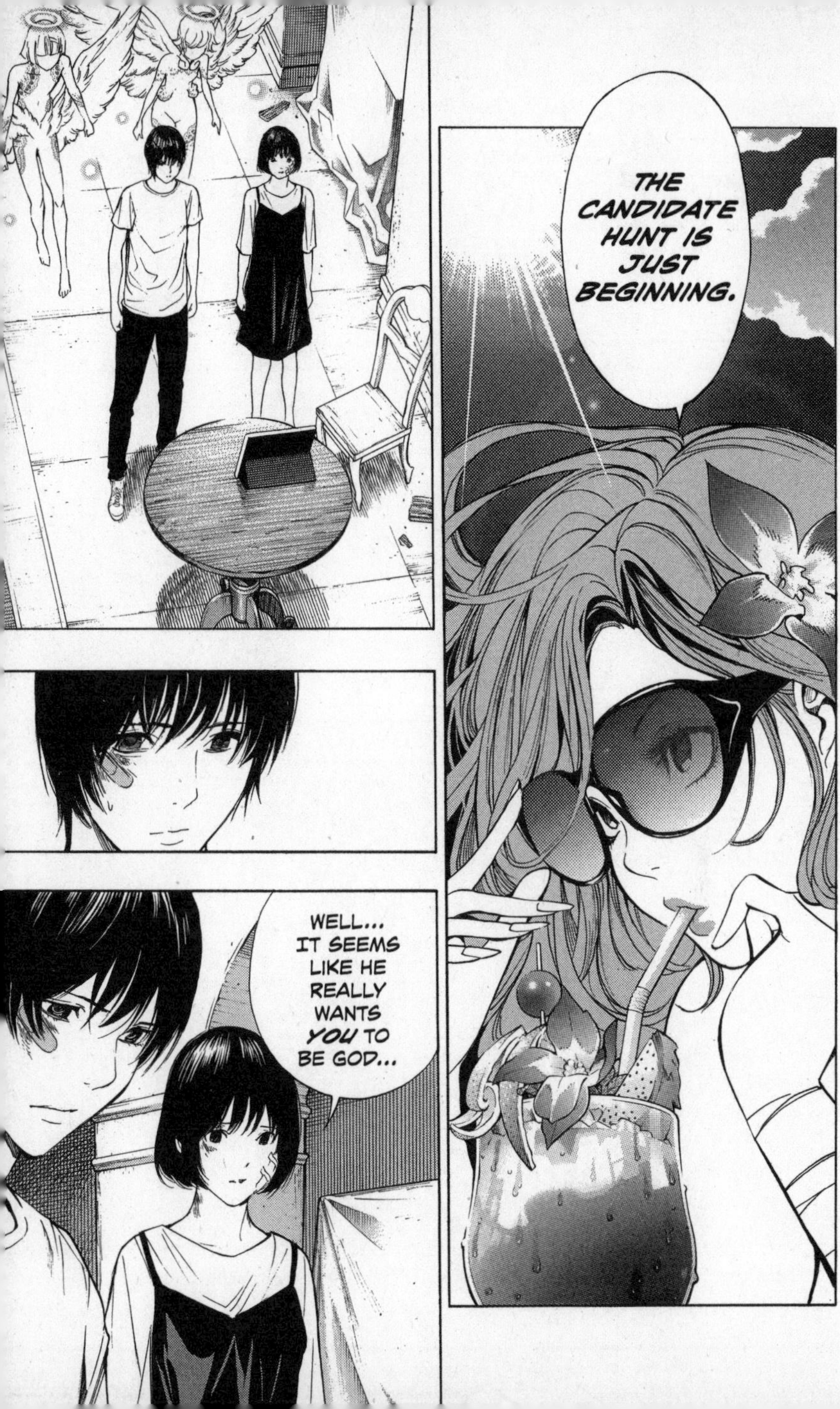
THE CANDIDATE HUNT IS JUST BEGINNING.
WELL... IT SEEMS LIKE HE REALLY WANTS *YOU* TO BE GOD...

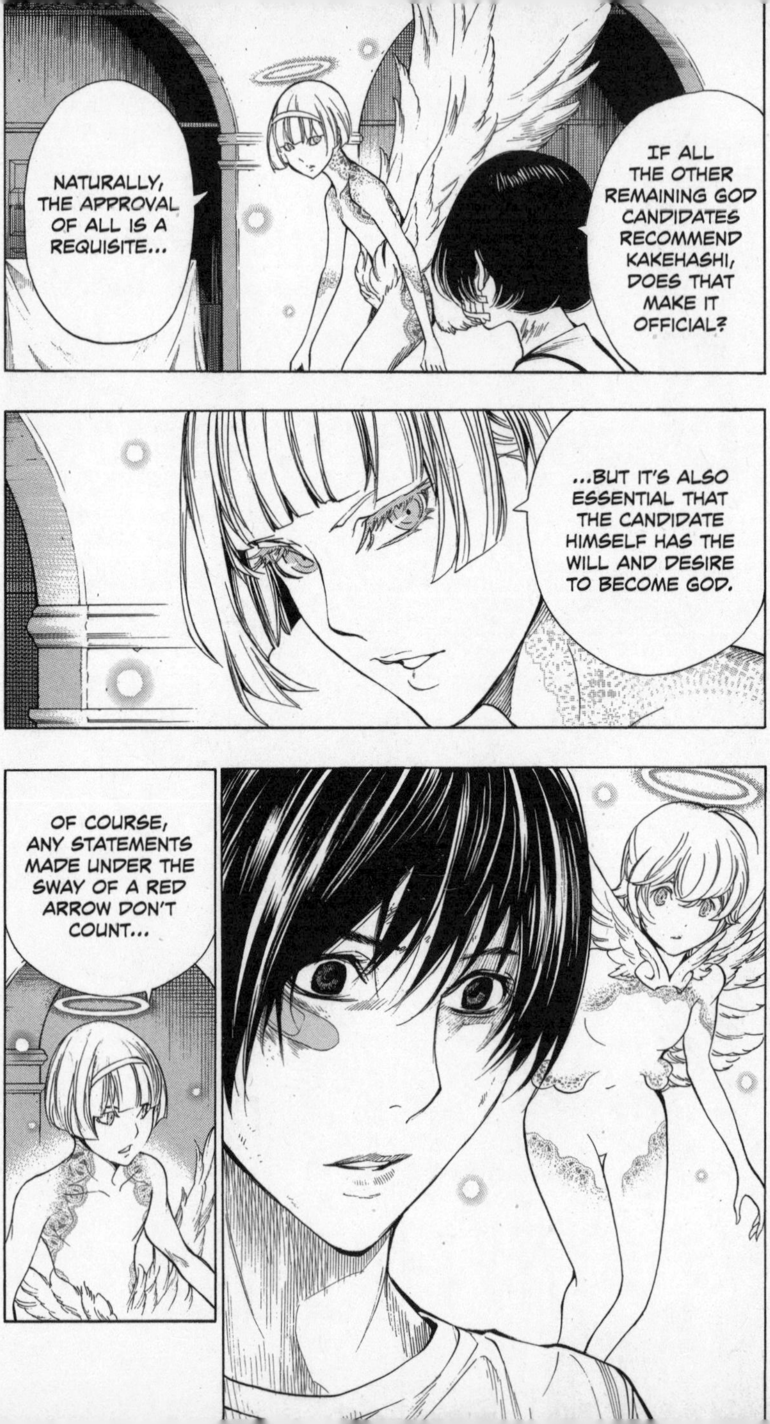
IF ALL THE OTHER REMAINING GOD CANDIDATES RECOMMEND KAKEHASHI, DOES THAT MAKE IT OFFICIAL?
NATURALLY, THE APPROVAL OF ALL IS A REQUISITE...
...BUT IT'S ALSO ESSENTIAL THAT THE CANDIDATE HIMSELF HAS THE WILL AND DESIRE TO BECOME GOD.
OF COURSE, ANY STATEMENTS MADE UNDER THE SWAY OF A RED ARROW DON'T COUNT...

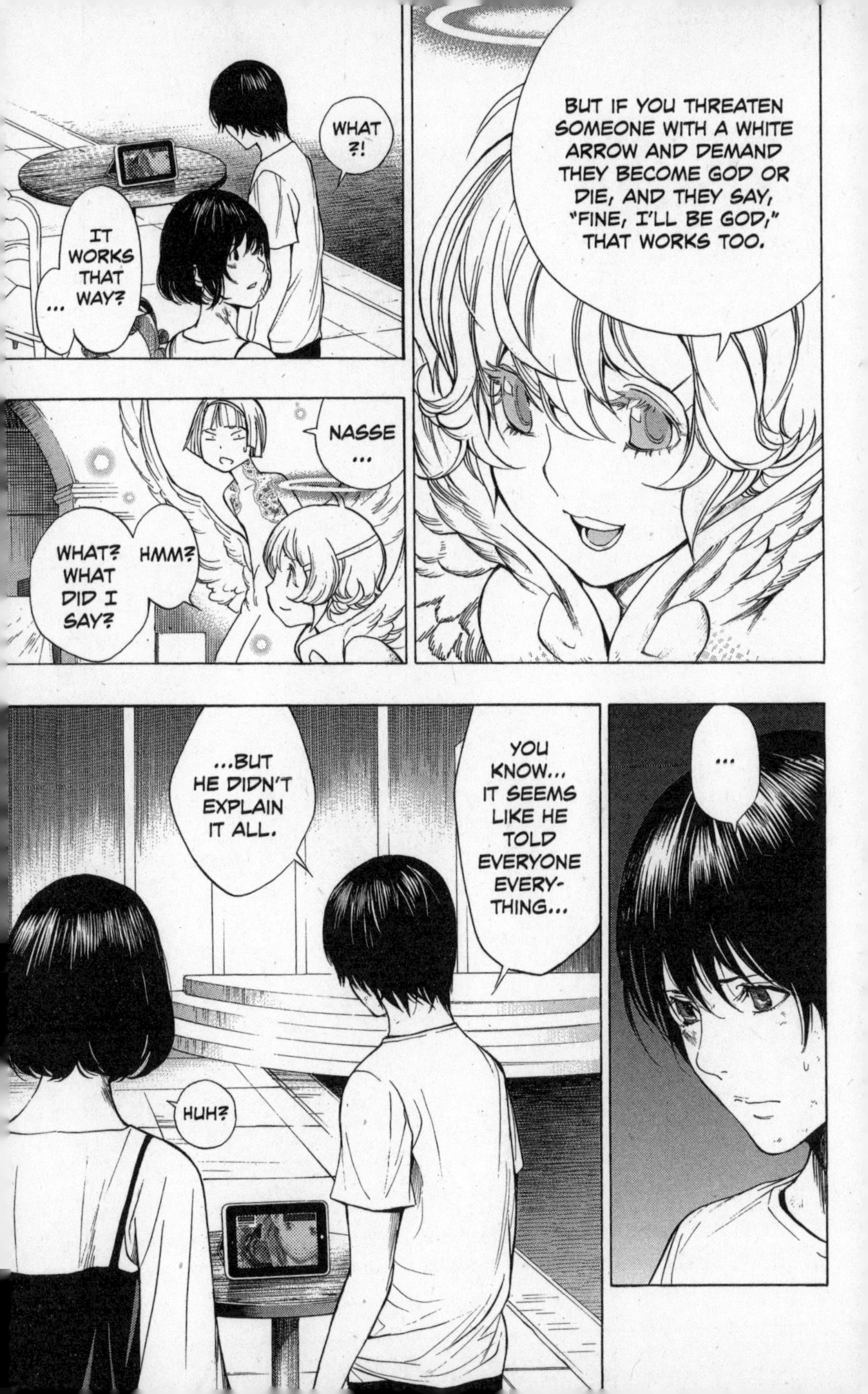
BUT IF YOU THREATEN SOMEONE WITH A WHITE ARROW AND DEMAND THEY BECOME GOD OR DIE, AND THEY SAY, "FINE, I'LL BE GOD," THAT WORKS TOO.
WHAT ?!
IT WORKS THAT WAY?
...
NASSE ...
HMM?
WHAT? WHAT DID I SAY?
...
YOU KNOW... IT SEEMS LIKE HE TOLD EVERYONE EVERY-THING...
...BUT HE DIDN'T EXPLAIN IT ALL.
HUH?

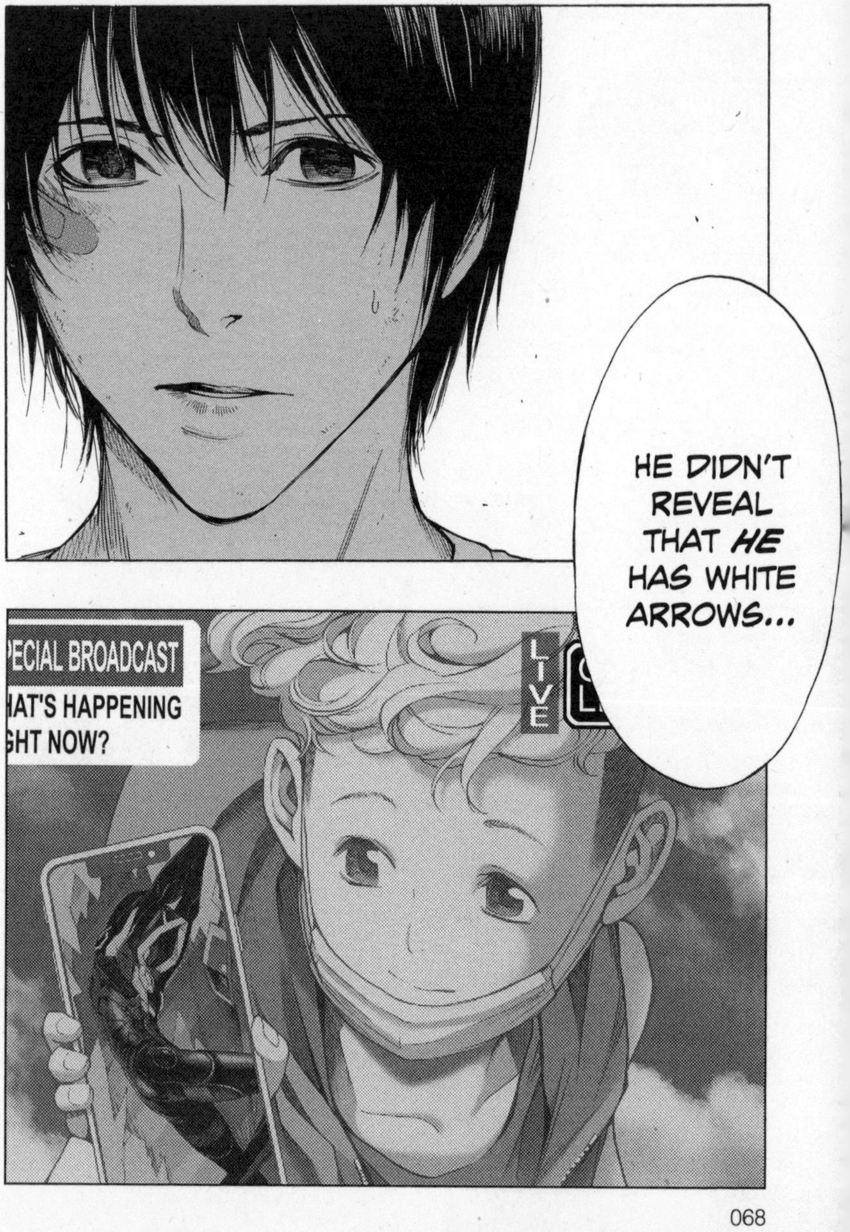
HE DIDN'T REVEAL THAT *HE* HAS WHITE ARROWS...
PECIAL BROADCAST
HAT'S HAPPENING
GHT NOW?
LIVE

KRRK

CLASS 1-3

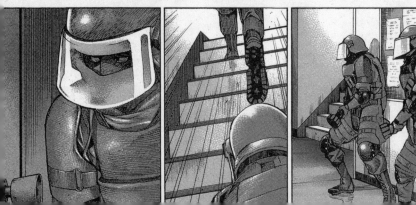

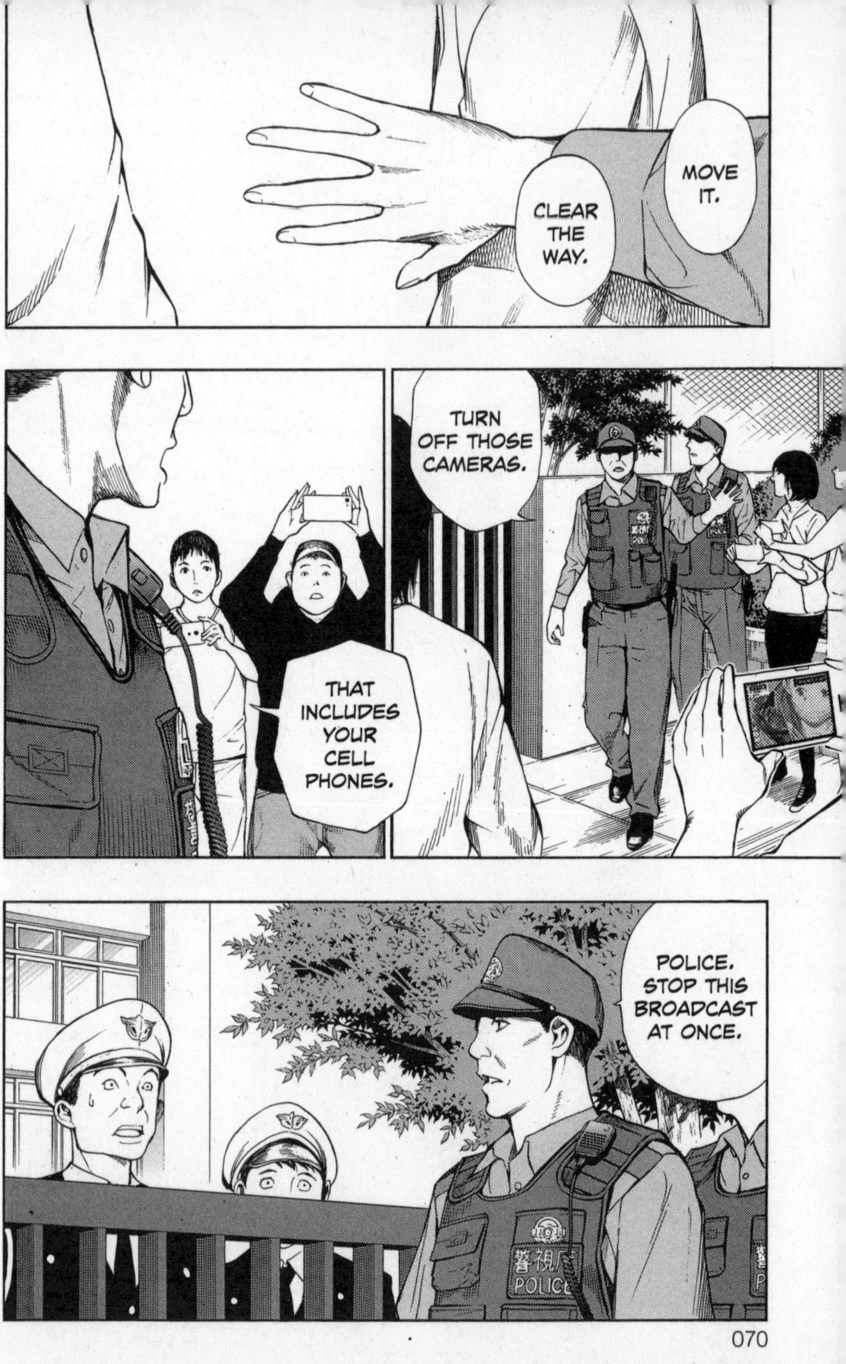
MOVE IT.
CLEAR THE WAY.
TURN OFF THOSE CAMERAS.
THAT INCLUDES YOUR CELL PHONES.
POLICE. STOP THIS BROADCAST AT ONCE.

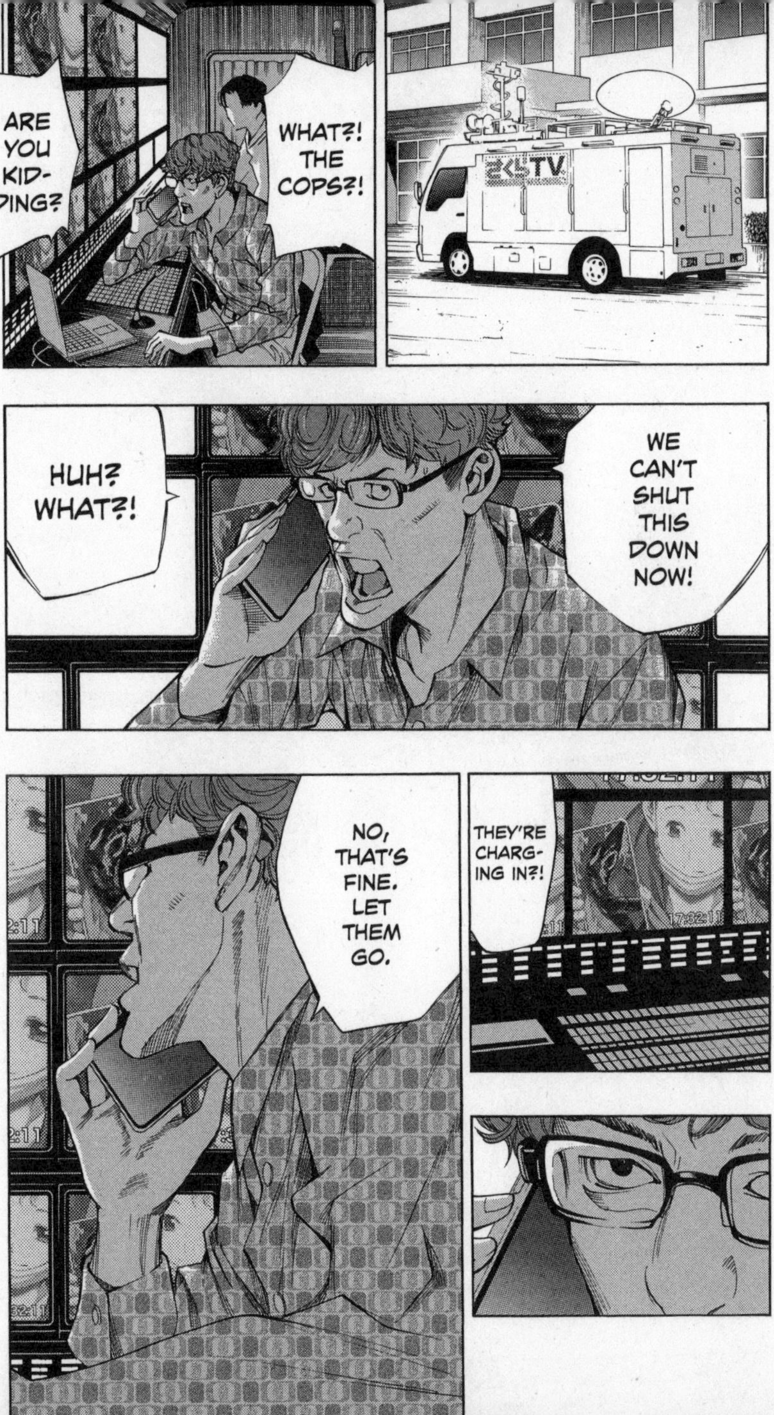
WHAT?! THE COPS?!
ARE YOU KID-DING?
WE CAN'T SHUT THIS DOWN NOW!
HUH? WHAT?!
THEY'RE CHARG-ING IN?!
NO, THAT'S FINE. LET THEM GO.

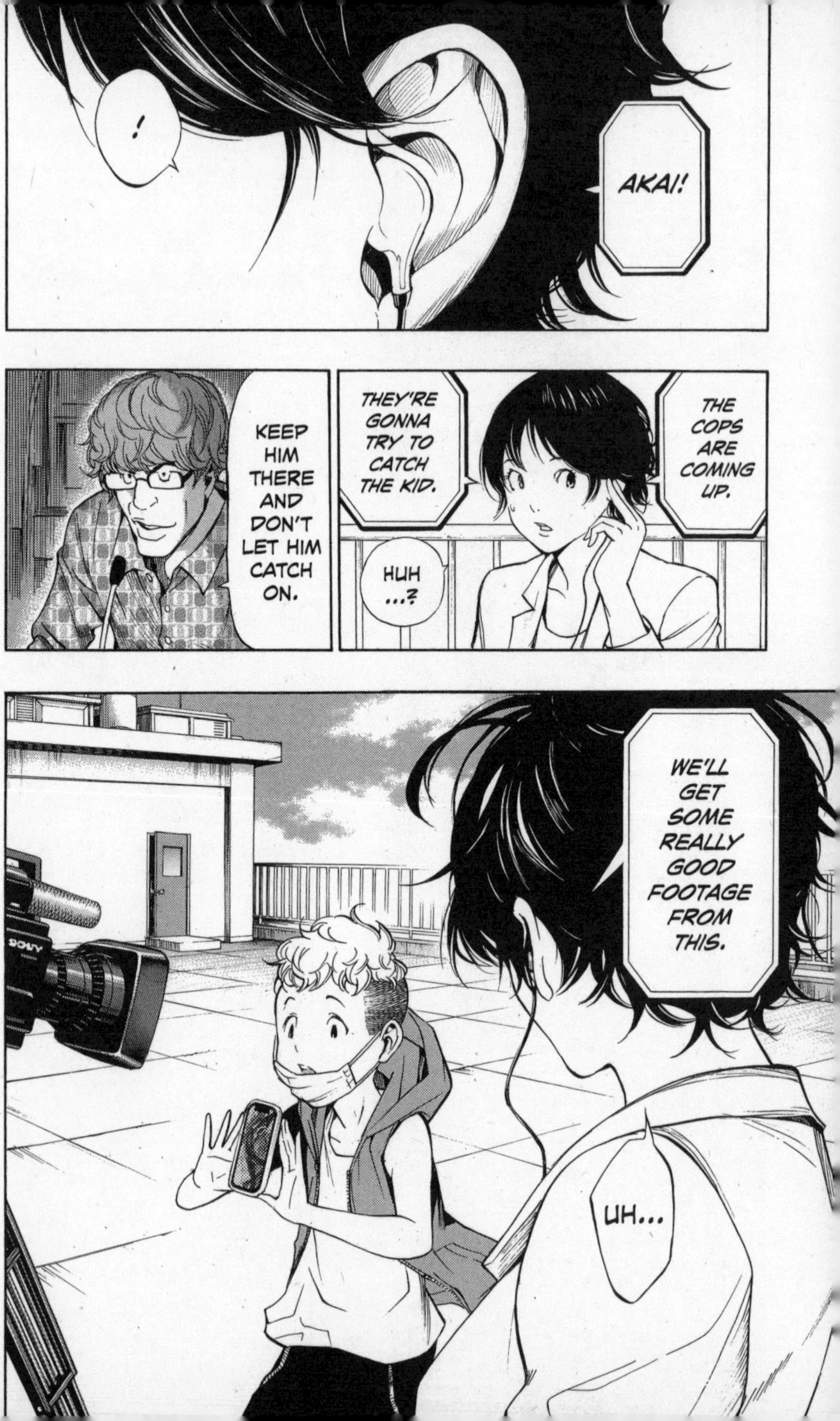
AKAI!
!
THE COPS ARE COMING UP.
THEY'RE GONNA TRY TO CATCH THE KID.
HUH ...?
KEEP HIM THERE AND DON'T LET HIM CATCH ON.
WE'LL GET SOME REALLY GOOD FOOTAGE FROM THIS.
UH...

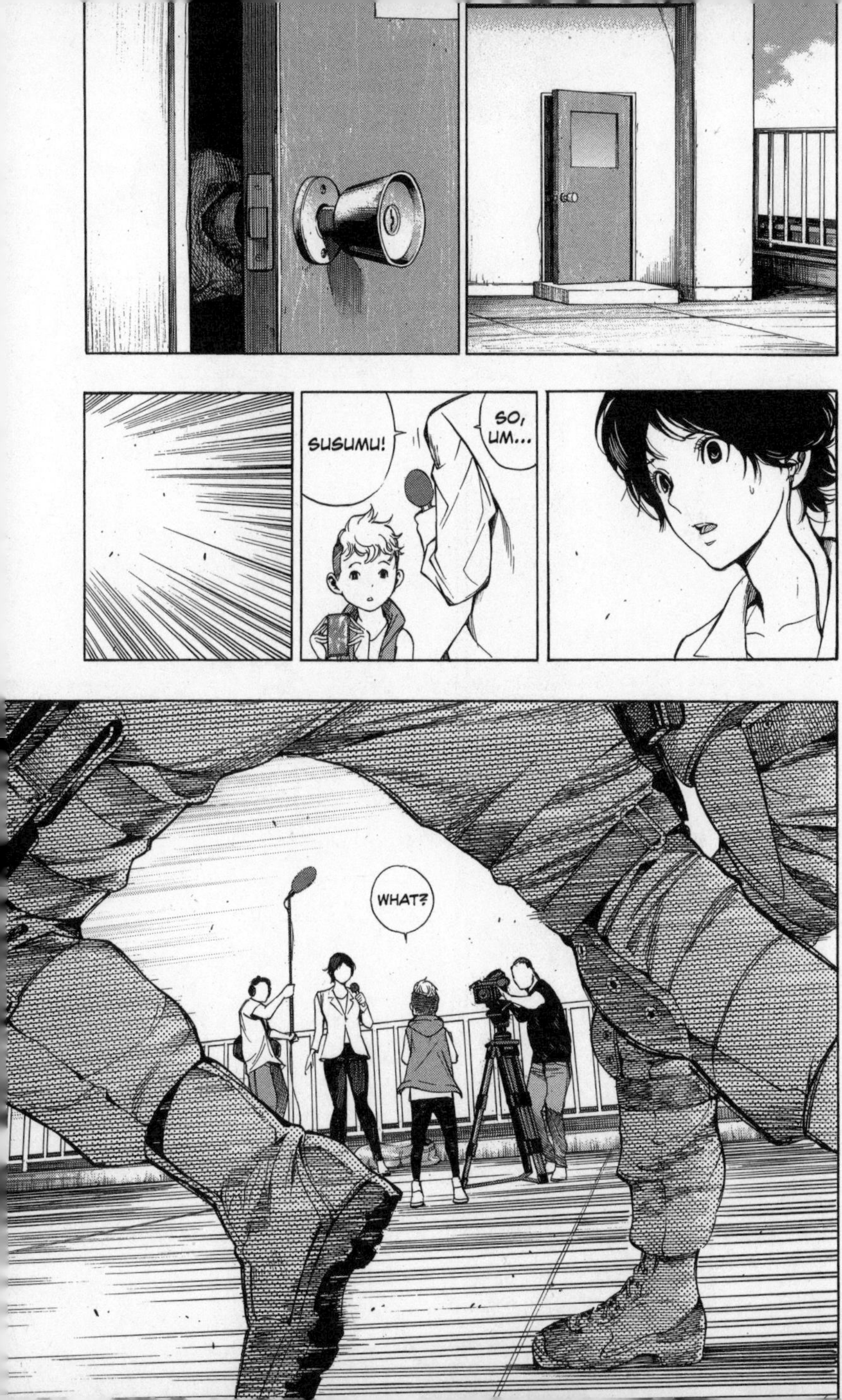
SO, UM...
SUSUMU!
WHAT?

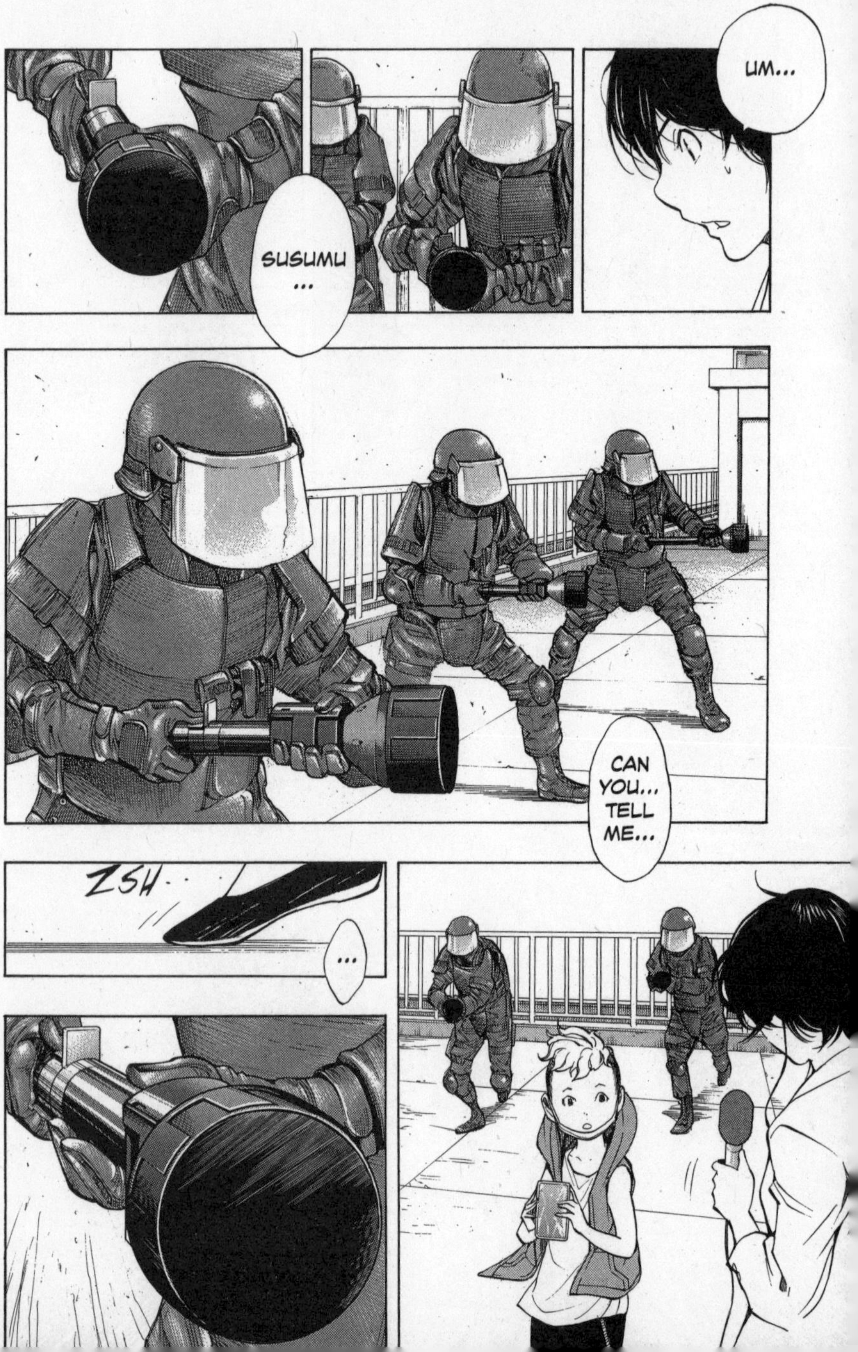
UM...
SUSUMU...
CAN YOU... TELL ME...
ZSH
...

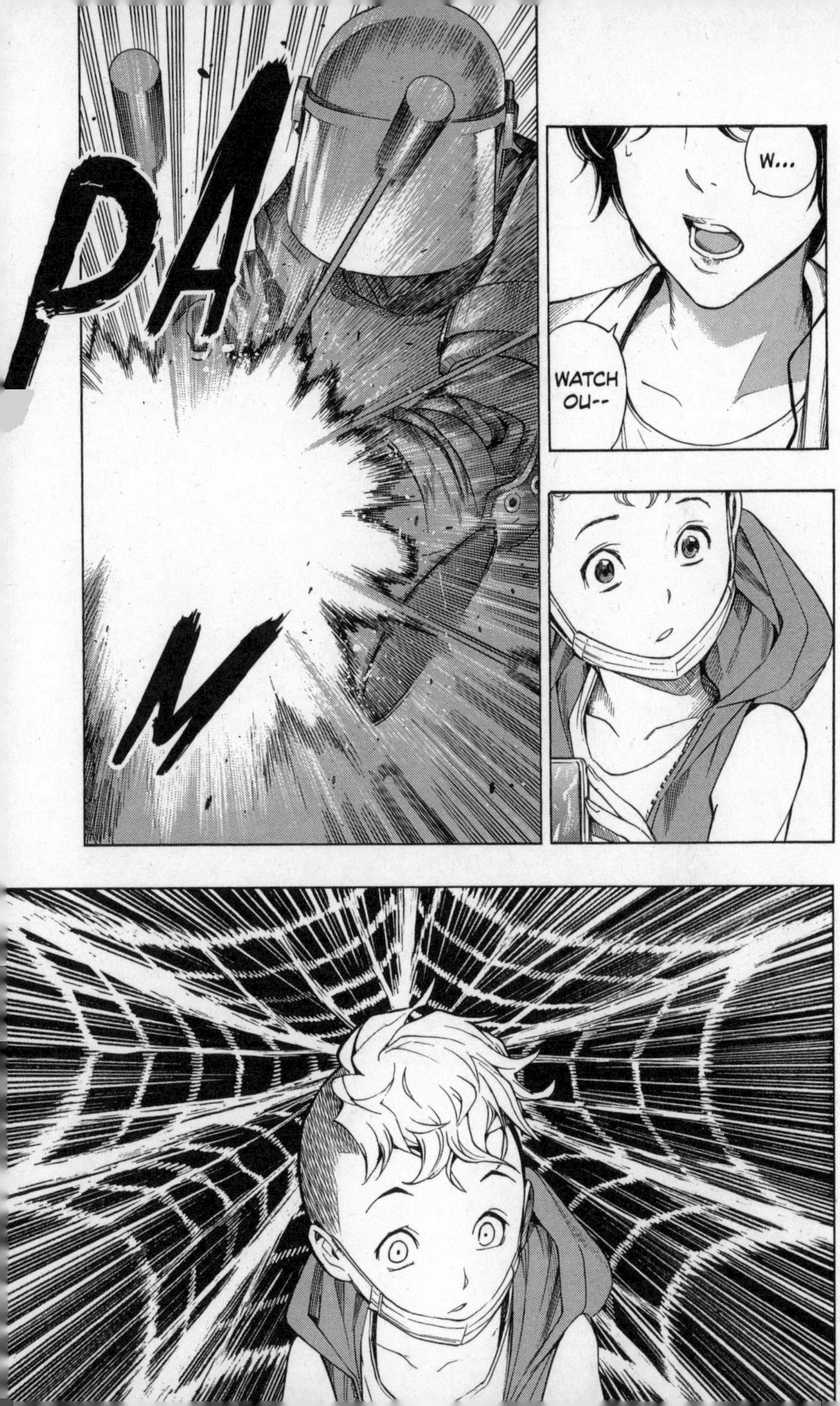
W...
WATCH OU--
PAM

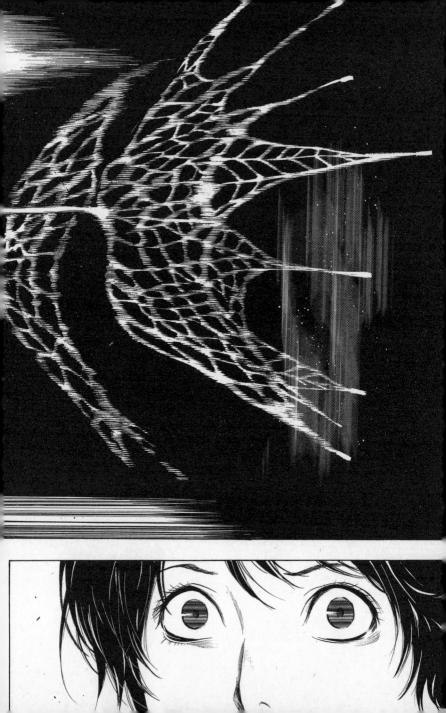

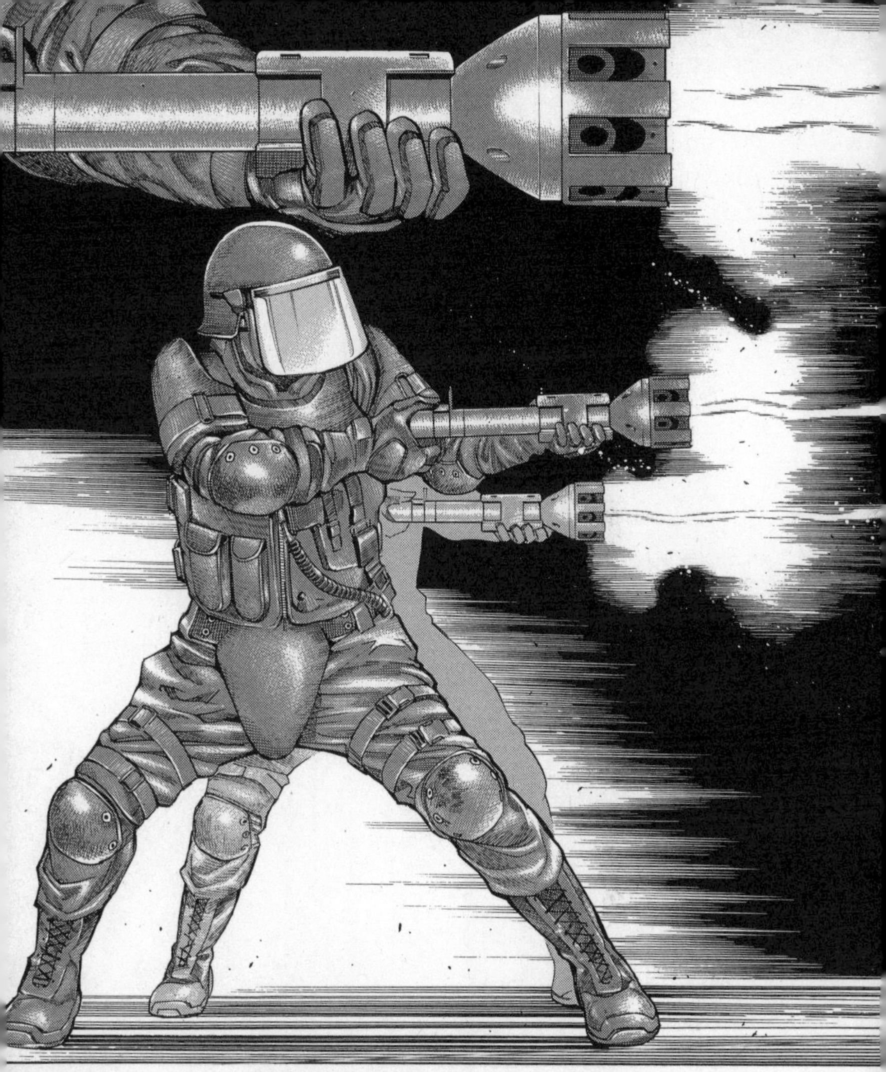
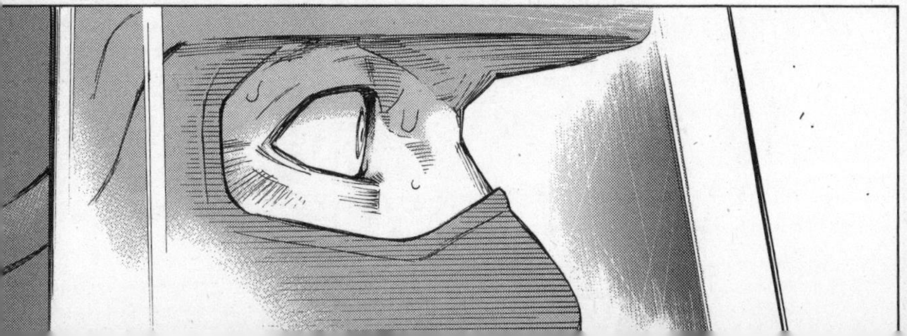

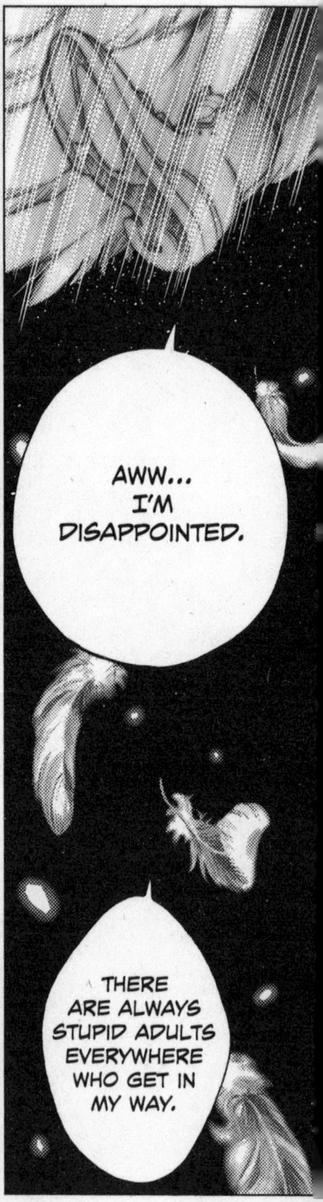
AWW... I'M DISAPPOINTED.
THERE ARE ALWAYS STUPID ADULTS EVERYWHERE WHO GET IN MY WAY.

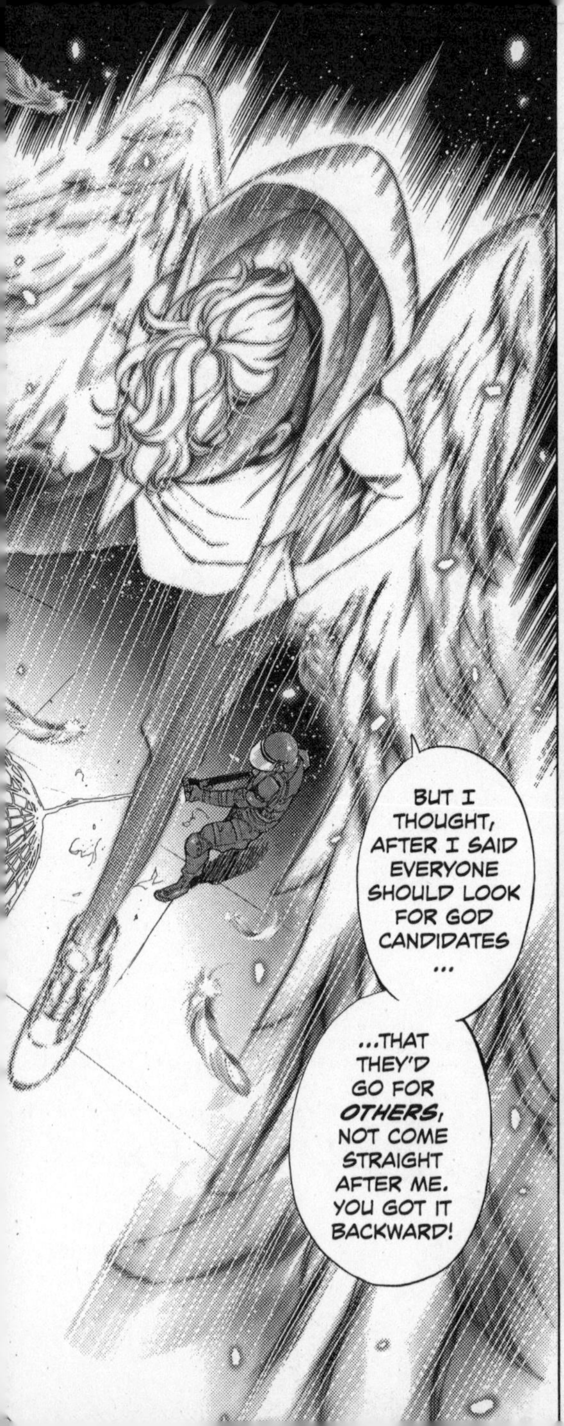
BUT I THOUGHT, AFTER I SAID EVERYONE SHOULD LOOK FOR GOD CANDIDATES ...
...THAT THEY'D GO FOR *OTHERS*, NOT COME STRAIGHT AFTER ME. YOU GOT IT BACKWARD!

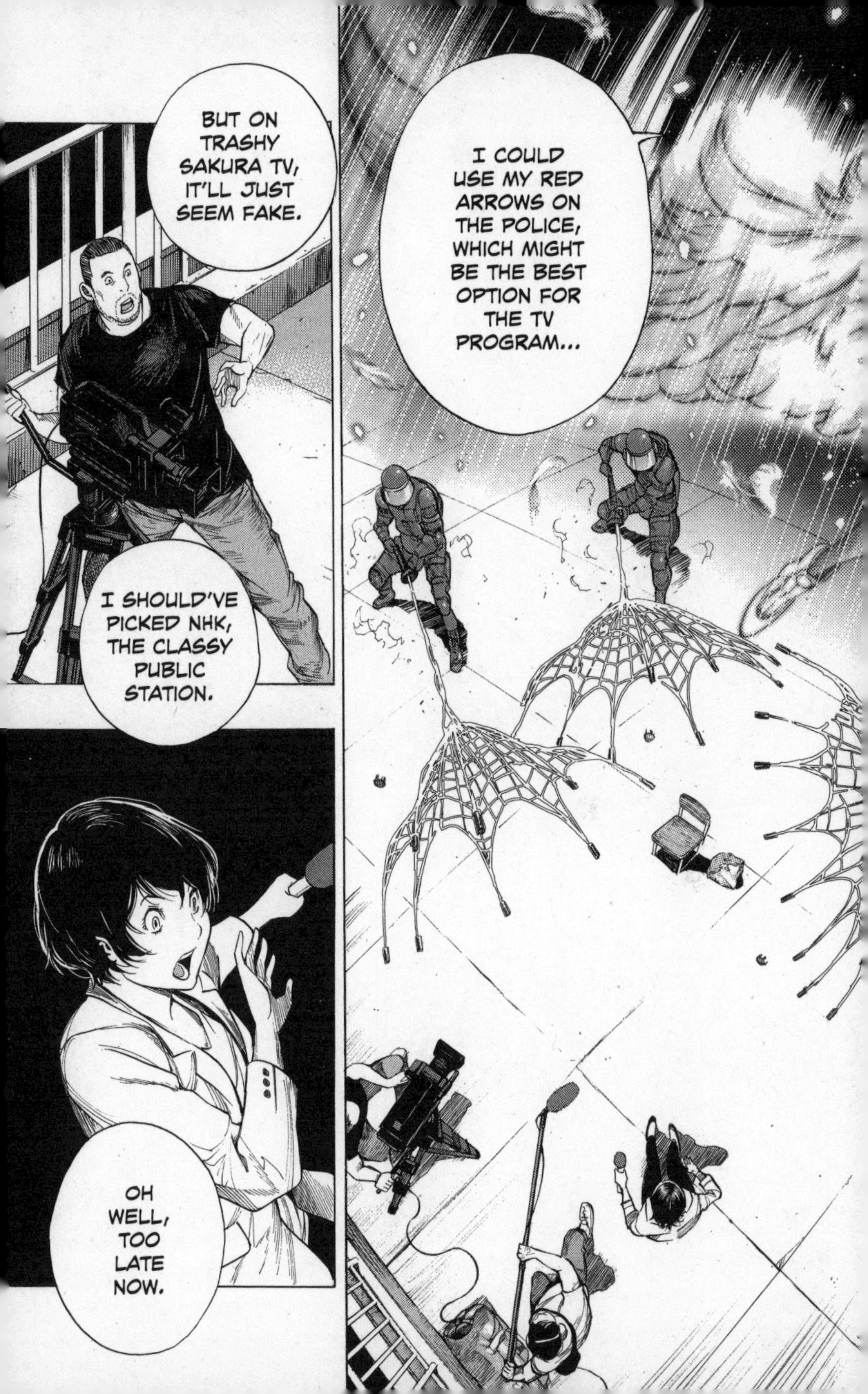
I COULD USE MY RED ARROWS ON THE POLICE, WHICH MIGHT BE THE BEST OPTION FOR THE TV PROGRAM...
BUT ON TRASHY SAKURA TV, IT'LL JUST SEEM FAKE.
I SHOULD'VE PICKED NHK, THE CLASSY PUBLIC STATION.
OH WELL, TOO LATE NOW.

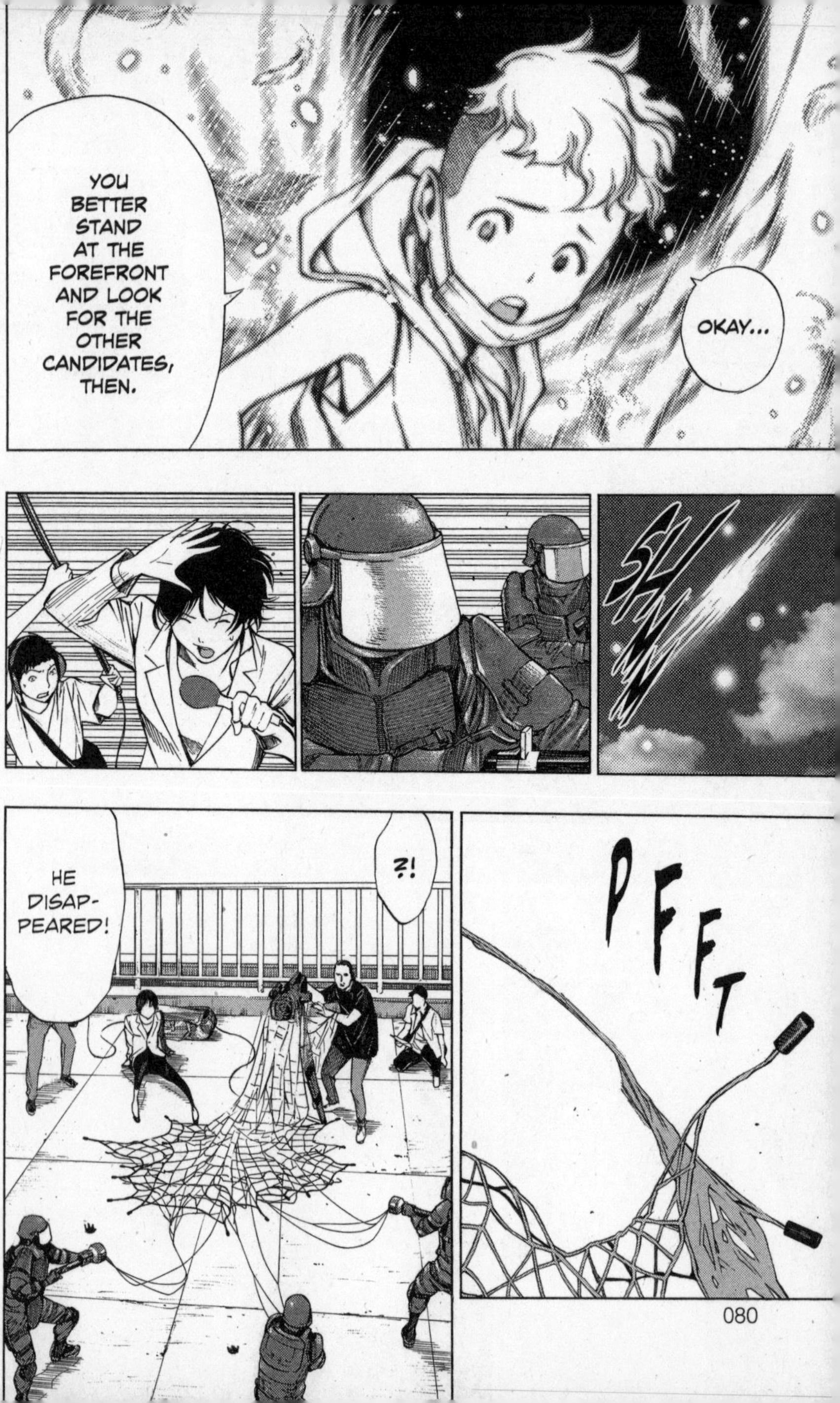
YOU BETTER STAND AT THE FOREFRONT AND LOOK FOR THE OTHER CANDIDATES, THEN.
OKAY...
SHWM
PFFT
?!
HE DISAP-PEARED!

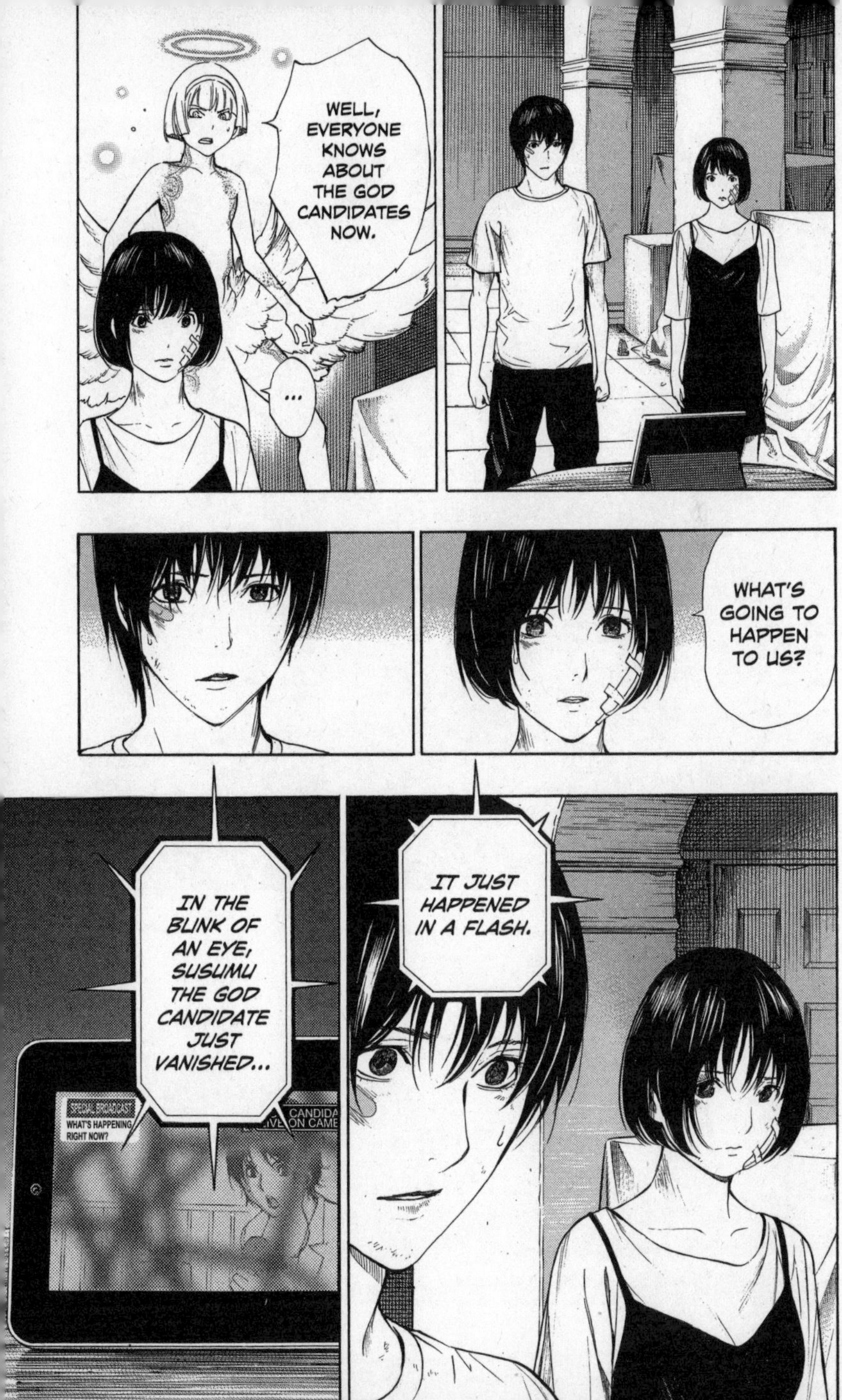
WELL, EVERYONE KNOWS ABOUT THE GOD CANDIDATES NOW.
...
WHAT'S GOING TO HAPPEN TO US?
IT JUST HAPPENED IN A FLASH.
IN THE BLINK OF AN EYE, SUSUMU THE GOD CANDIDATE JUST VANISHED...
SPECIAL BROADCAST
WHAT'S HAPPENING RIGHT NOW?

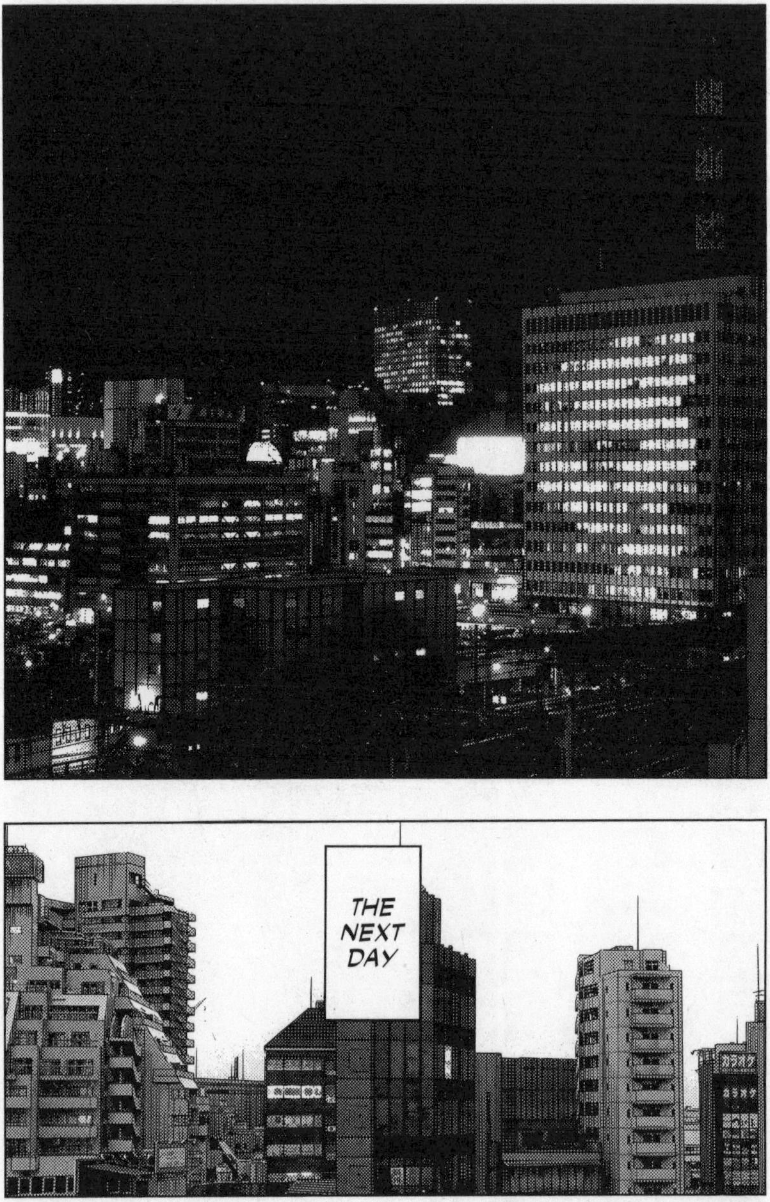
THE NEXT DAY

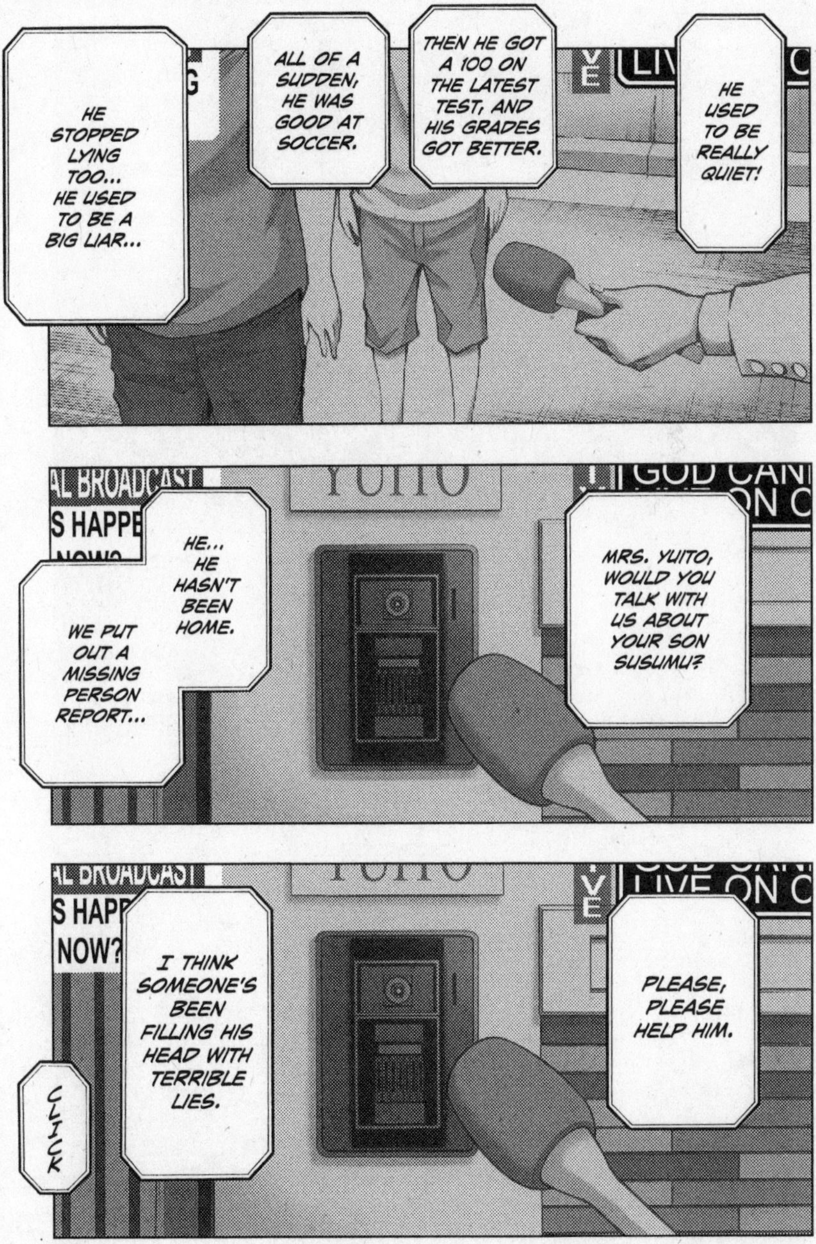
HE USED TO BE REALLY QUIET!
THEN HE GOT A 100 ON THE LATEST TEST, AND HIS GRADES GOT BETTER.
ALL OF A SUDDEN, HE WAS GOOD AT SOCCER.
HE STOPPED LYING TOO... HE USED TO BE A BIG LIAR...
MRS. YUITO, WOULD YOU TALK WITH US ABOUT YOUR SON SUSUMU?
HE... HE HASN'T BEEN HOME.
WE PUT OUT A MISSING PERSON REPORT...
PLEASE, PLEASE HELP HIM.
I THINK SOMEONE'S BEEN FILLING HIS HEAD WITH TERRIBLE LIES.
CLICK

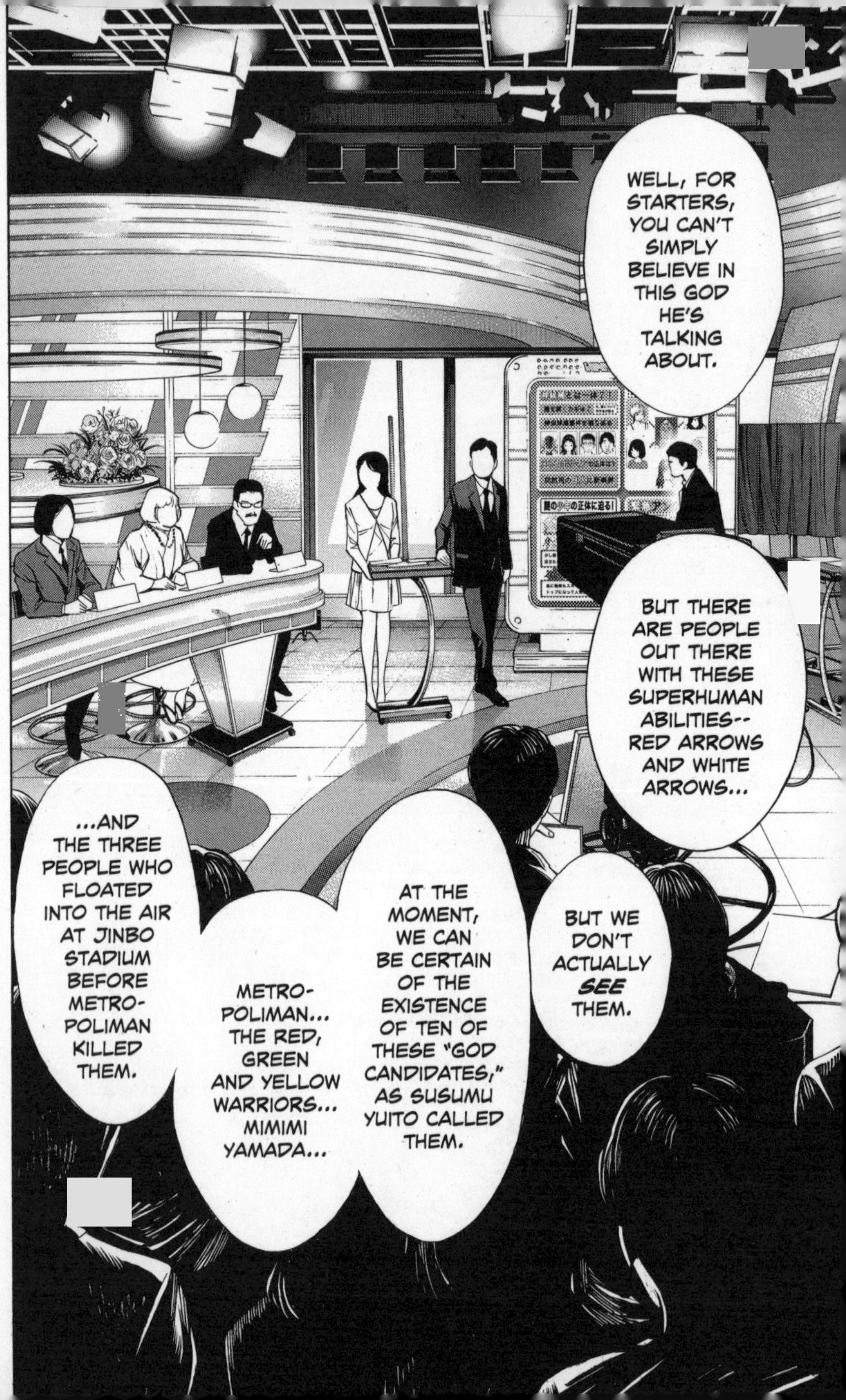
WELL, FOR STARTERS, YOU CAN'T SIMPLY BELIEVE IN THIS GOD HE'S TALKING ABOUT.
BUT THERE ARE PEOPLE OUT THERE WITH THESE SUPERHUMAN ABILITIES-- RED ARROWS AND WHITE ARROWS...
BUT WE DON'T ACTUALLY *SEE* THEM.
AT THE MOMENT, WE CAN BE CERTAIN OF THE EXISTENCE OF TEN OF THESE "GOD CANDIDATES," AS SUSUMU YUITO CALLED THEM.
METRO-POLIMAN... THE RED, GREEN AND YELLOW WARRIORS... MIMIMI YAMADA...
...AND THE THREE PEOPLE WHO FLOATED INTO THE AIR AT JINBO STADIUM BEFORE METRO-POLIMAN KILLED THEM.

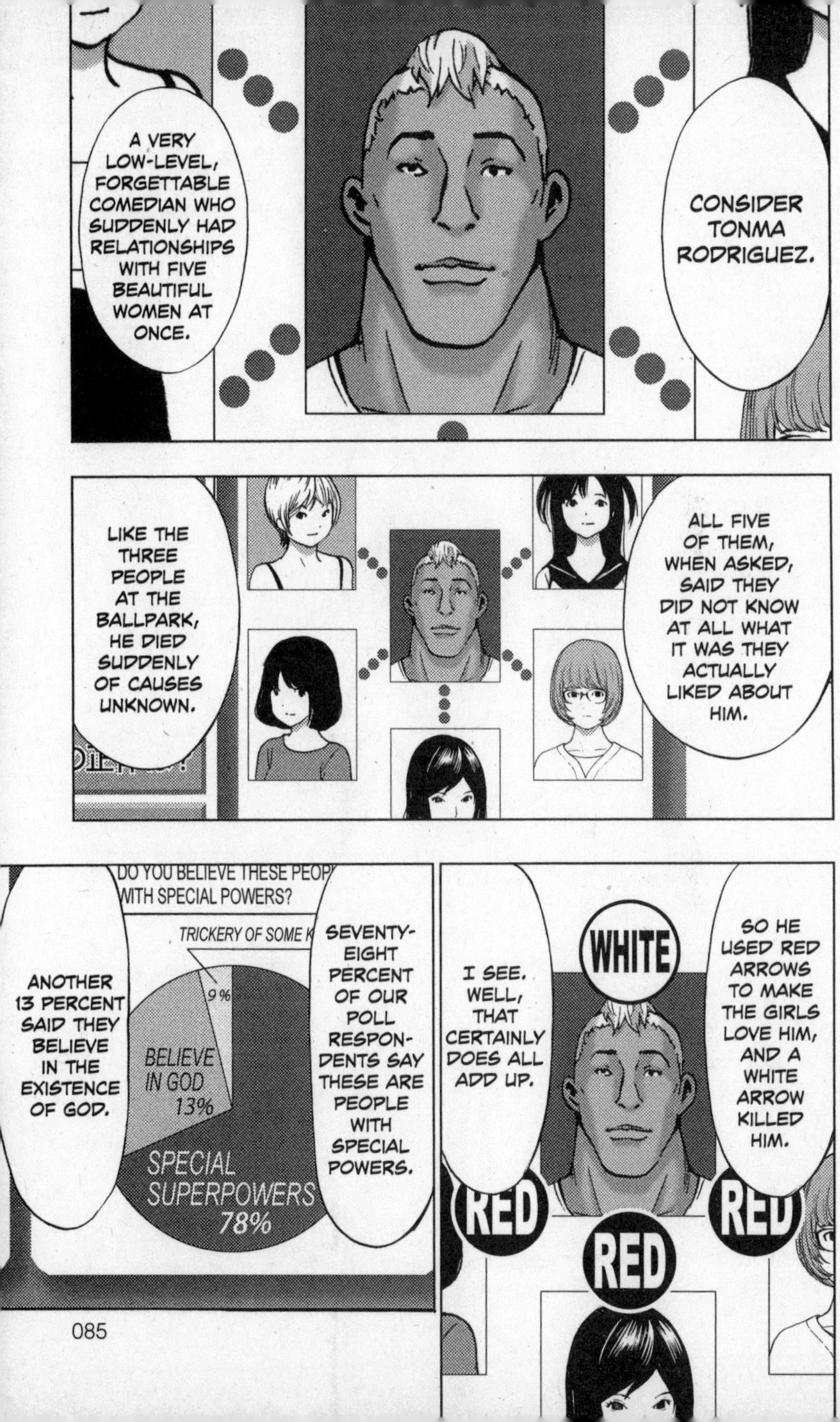
CONSIDER TONMA RODRIGUEZ.
A VERY LOW-LEVEL, FORGETTABLE COMEDIAN WHO SUDDENLY HAD RELATIONSHIPS WITH FIVE BEAUTIFUL WOMEN AT ONCE.
ALL FIVE OF THEM, WHEN ASKED, SAID THEY DID NOT KNOW AT ALL WHAT IT WAS THEY ACTUALLY LIKED ABOUT HIM.
LIKE THE THREE PEOPLE AT THE BALLPARK, HE DIED SUDDENLY OF CAUSES UNKNOWN.
SO HE USED RED ARROWS TO MAKE THE GIRLS LOVE HIM, AND A WHITE ARROW KILLED HIM.
WHITE
RED
RED
RED
I SEE. WELL, THAT CERTAINLY DOES ALL ADD UP.
DO YOU BELIEVE THESE PEOP
WITH SPECIAL POWERS?
TRICKERY OF SOME K
9%
BELIEVE IN GOD 13%
SPECIAL SUPERPOWERS 78%
SEVENTY-EIGHT PERCENT OF OUR POLL RESPON-DENTS SAY THESE ARE PEOPLE WITH SPECIAL POWERS.
ANOTHER 13 PERCENT SAID THEY BELIEVE IN THE EXISTENCE OF GOD.

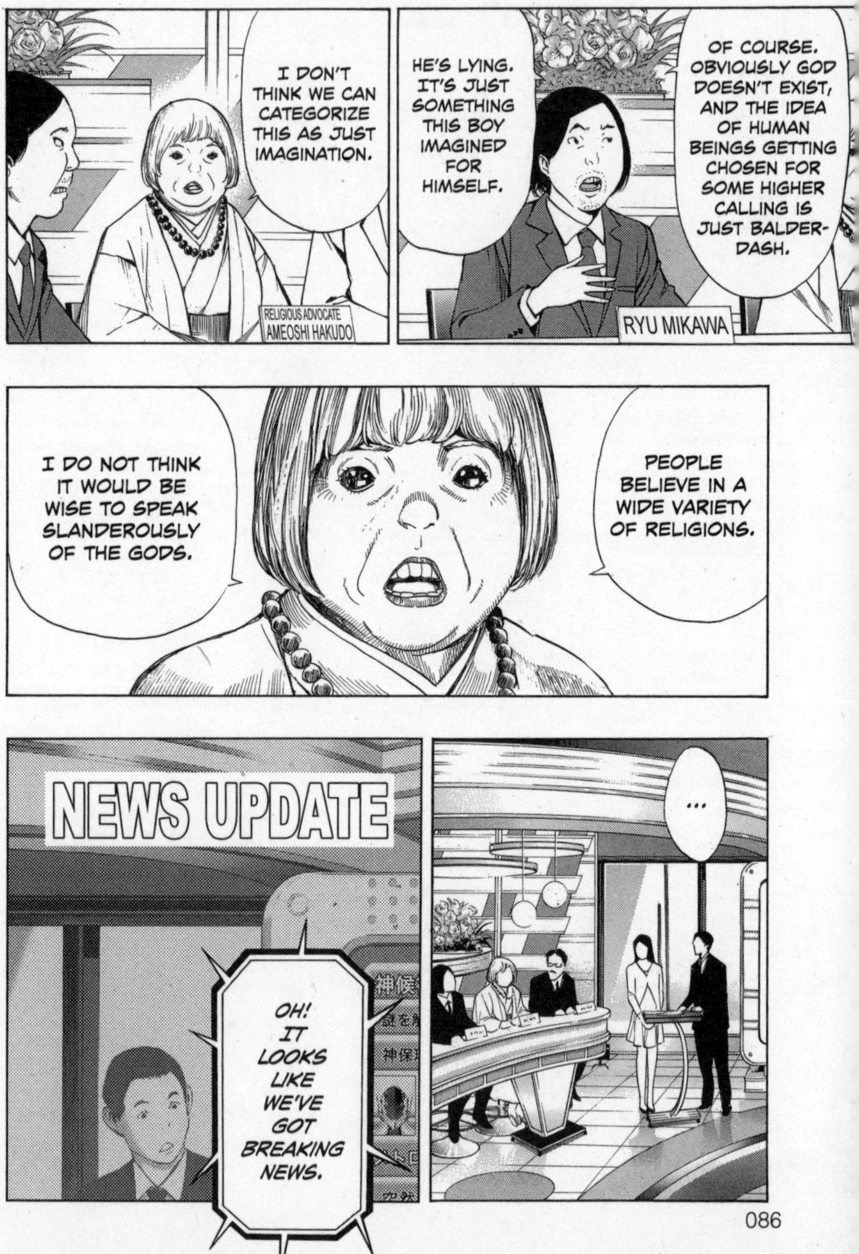
RYU MIKAWA
OF COURSE. OBVIOUSLY GOD DOESN'T EXIST, AND THE IDEA OF HUMAN BEINGS GETTING CHOSEN FOR SOME HIGHER CALLING IS JUST BALDER-DASH.
HE'S LYING. IT'S JUST SOMETHING THIS BOY IMAGINED FOR HIMSELF.
I DON'T THINK WE CAN CATEGORIZE THIS AS JUST IMAGINATION.
RELIGIOUS ADVOCATE
AMEOSHI HAKUDO
PEOPLE BELIEVE IN A WIDE VARIETY OF RELIGIONS.
I DO NOT THINK IT WOULD BE WISE TO SPEAK SLANDEROUSLY OF THE GODS.
...
NEWS UPDATE
OH! IT LOOKS LIKE WE'VE GOT BREAKING NEWS.

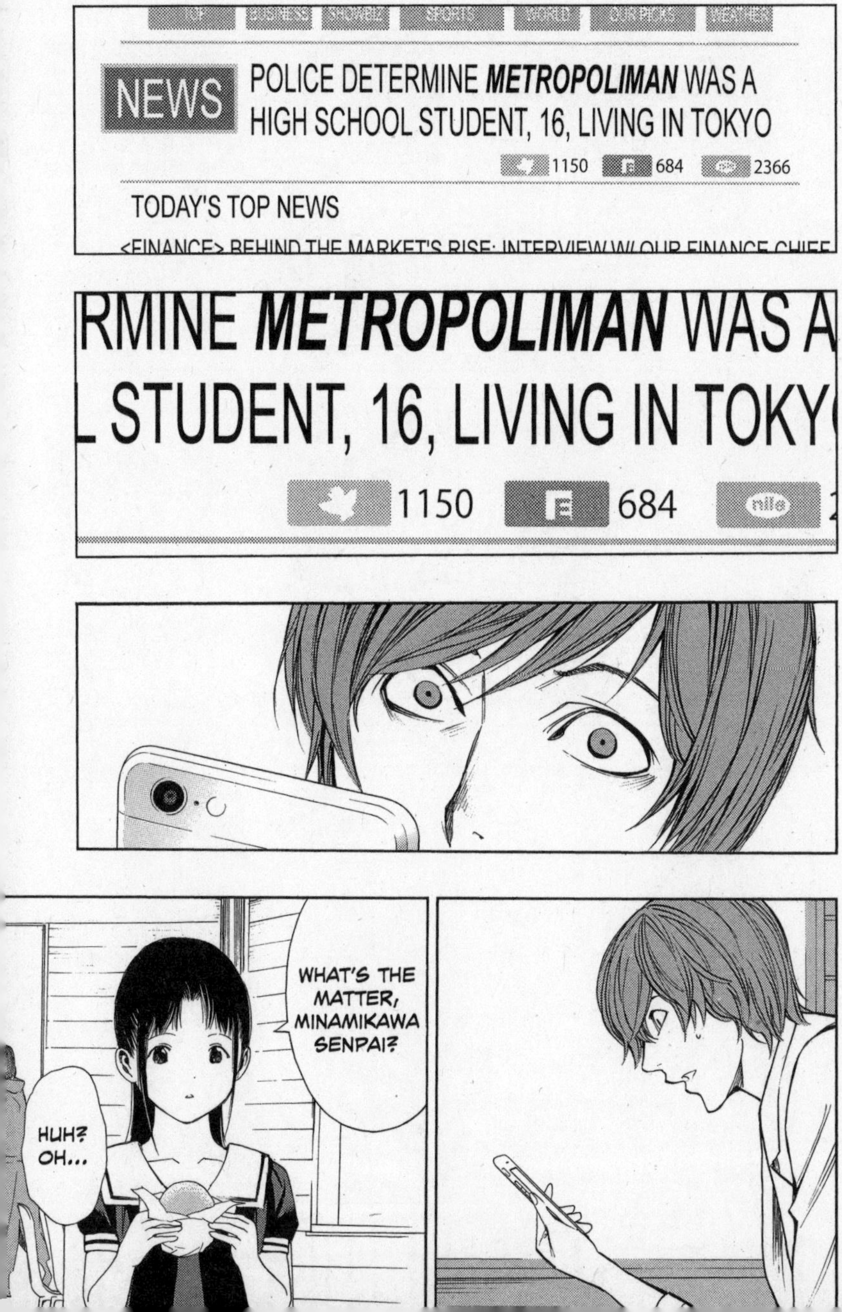

TOP BUSINESS SHOWBIZ SPORTS WORLD OUR PICKS WEATHER
NEWS
POLICE DETERMINE METROPOLIMAN WAS A HIGH SCHOOL STUDENT, 16, LIVING IN TOKYO
1150 684 2366
TODAY'S TOP NEWS
<FINANCE> BEHIND THE MARKET'S RISE: INTERVIEW W/ OUR FINANCE CHIEF
RMINE METROPOLIMAN WAS A
L STUDENT, 16, LIVING IN TOKY
1150 684
WHAT'S THE MATTER, MINAMIKAWA SENPAI?
HUH? OH...

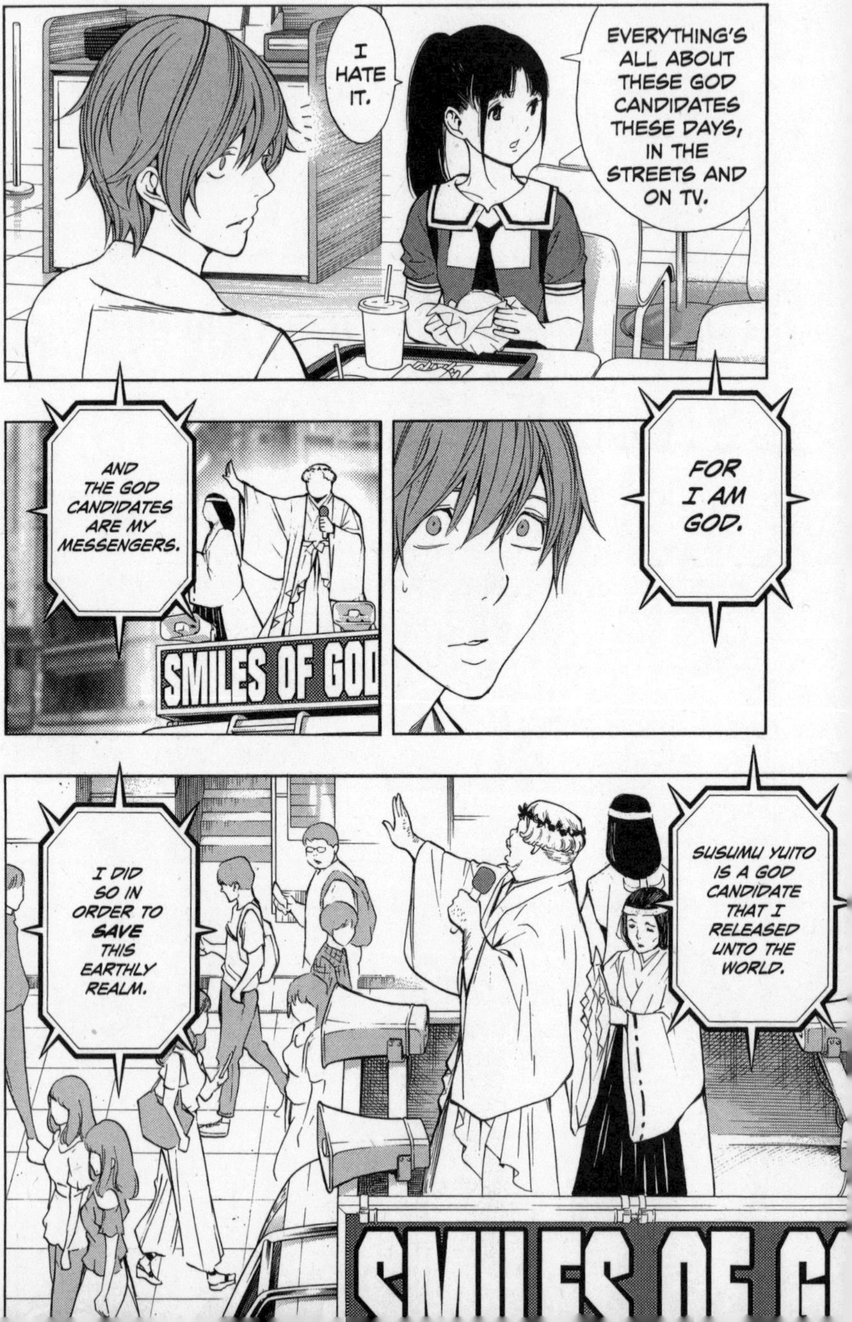
EVERYTHING'S ALL ABOUT THESE GOD CANDIDATES THESE DAYS, IN THE STREETS AND ON TV.
I HATE IT.
FOR I AM GOD.
AND THE GOD CANDIDATES ARE MY MESSENGERS.
SMILES OF GOD
SUSUMU YUITO IS A GOD CANDIDATE THAT I RELEASED UNTO THE WORLD.
I DID SO IN ORDER TO SAVE THIS EARTHLY REALM.

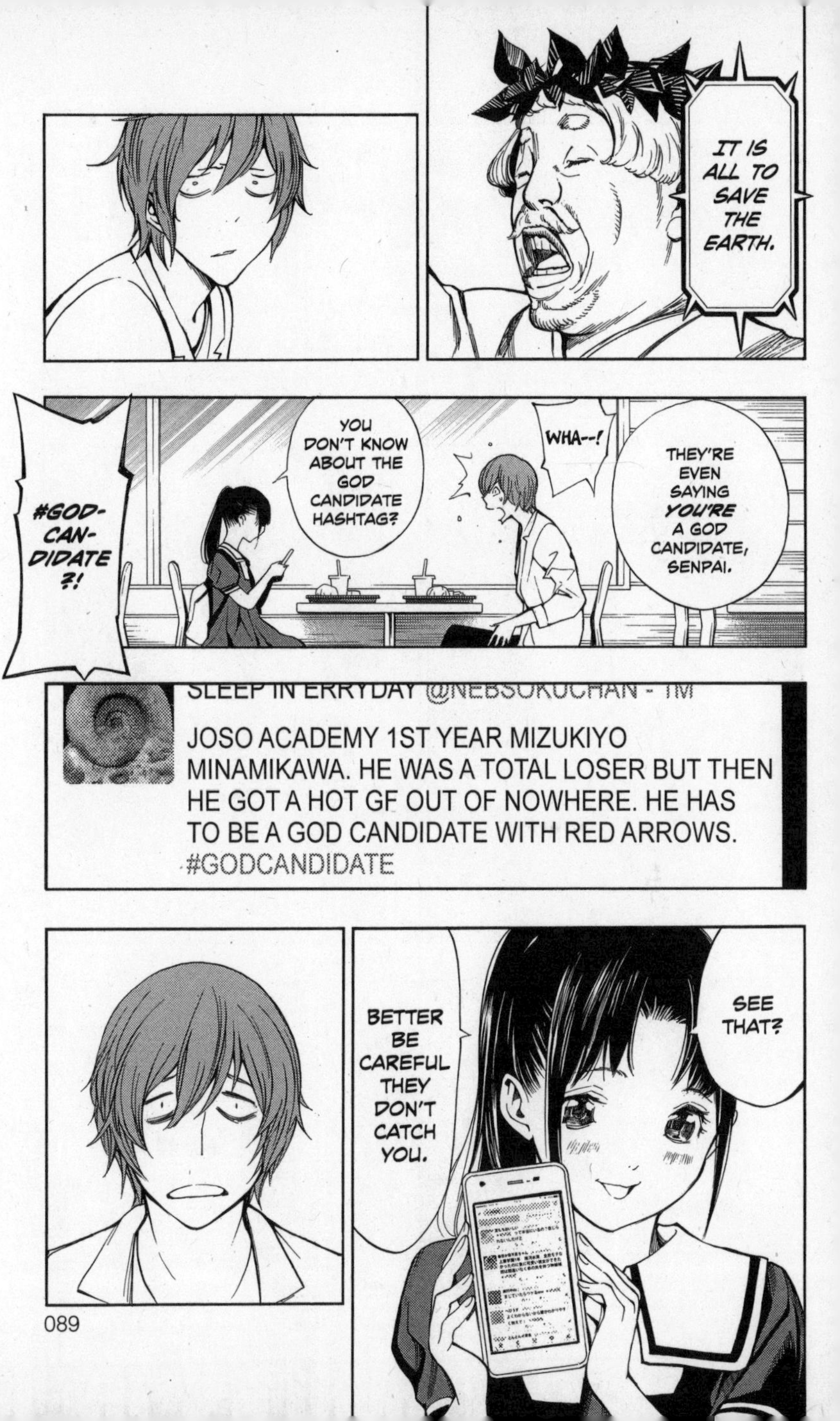
IT IS ALL TO SAVE THE EARTH.
THEY'RE EVEN SAYING YOU'RE A GOD CANDIDATE, SENPAI.
WHA--!
YOU DON'T KNOW ABOUT THE GOD CANDIDATE HASHTAG?
#GOD-CAN-DIDATE?!
SLEEP IN ERRYDAY @NEBSOKUCHAN - 1M
JOSO ACADEMY 1ST YEAR MIZUKIYO MINAMIKAWA. HE WAS A TOTAL LOSER BUT THEN HE GOT A HOT GF OUT OF NOWHERE. HE HAS TO BE A GOD CANDIDATE WITH RED ARROWS. #GODCANDIDATE
SEE THAT?
BETTER BE CAREFUL THEY DON'T CATCH YOU.

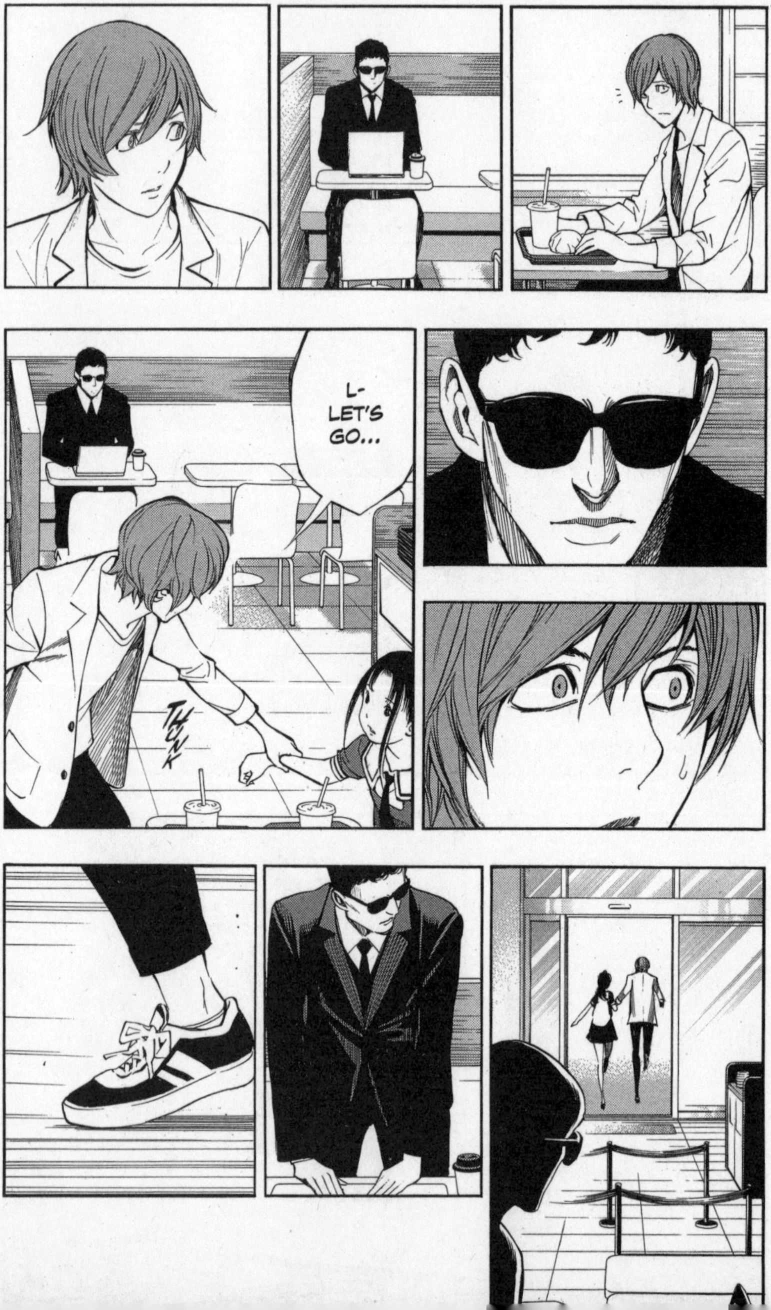

L- LET'S GO...
THUNK

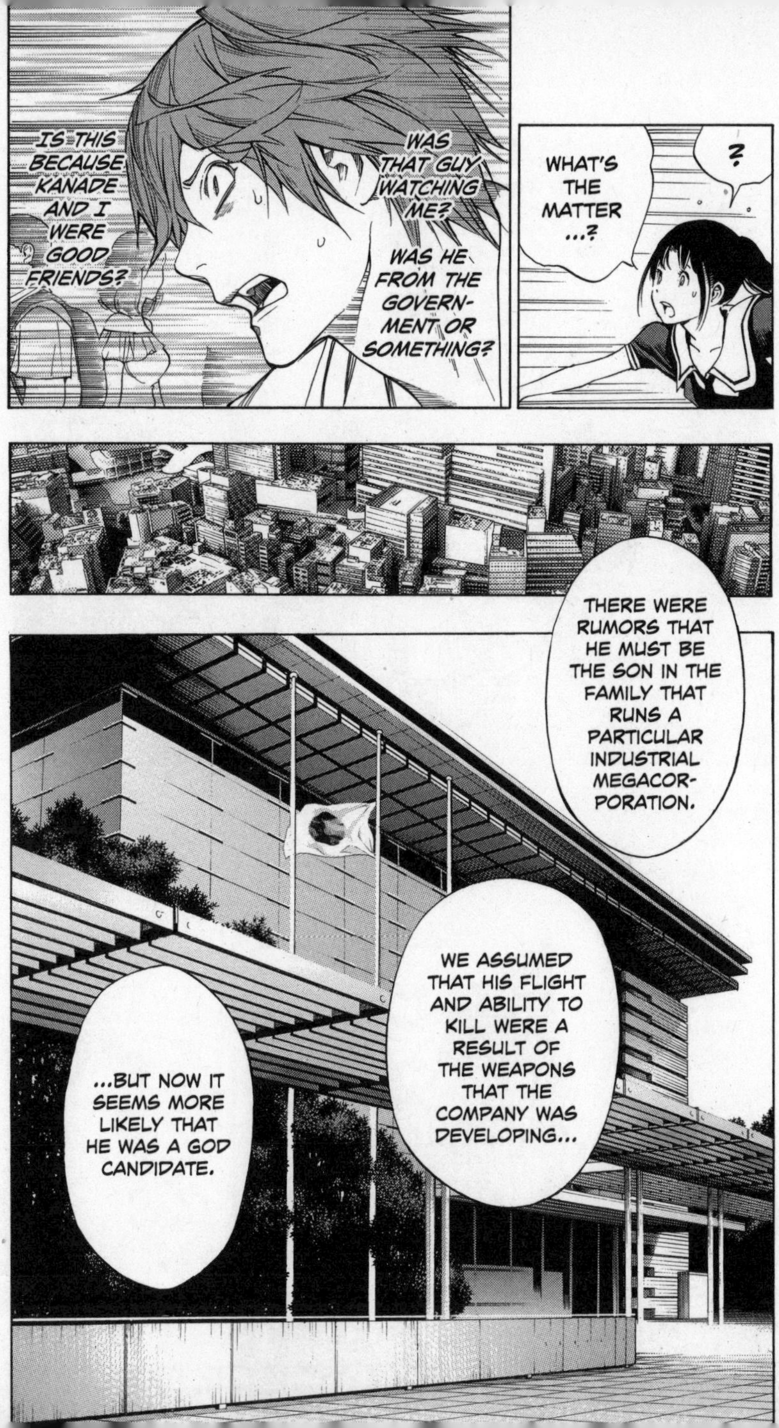
?
WHAT'S THE MATTER ...?
WAS THAT GUY WATCHING ME?
WAS HE FROM THE GOVERNMENT OR SOMETHING?
IS THIS BECAUSE KANADE AND I WERE GOOD FRIENDS?
THERE WERE RUMORS THAT HE MUST BE THE SON IN THE FAMILY THAT RUNS A PARTICULAR INDUSTRIAL MEGACORPORATION.
WE ASSUMED THAT HIS FLIGHT AND ABILITY TO KILL WERE A RESULT OF THE WEAPONS THAT THE COMPANY WAS DEVELOPING...
...BUT NOW IT SEEMS MORE LIKELY THAT HE WAS A GOD CANDIDATE.

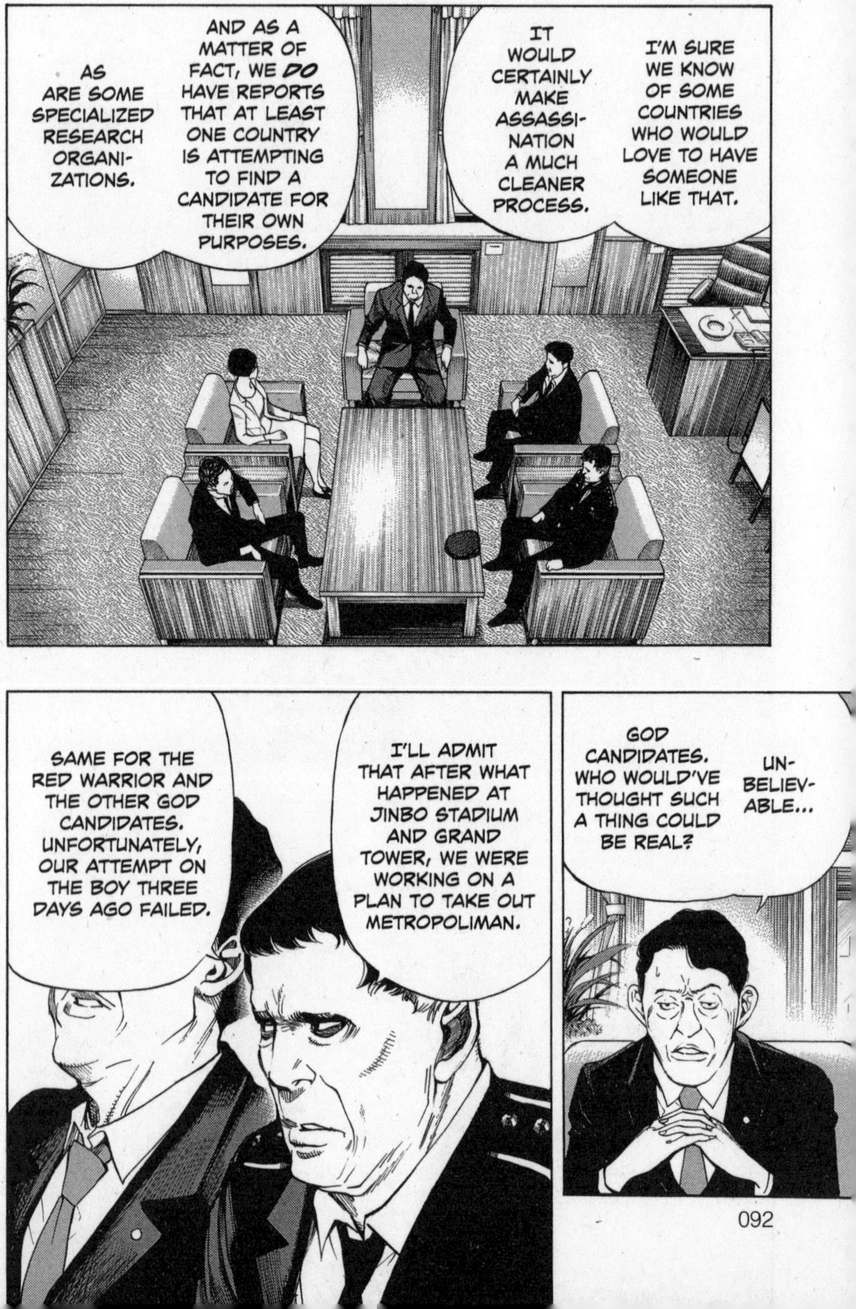
I'M SURE WE KNOW OF SOME COUNTRIES WHO WOULD LOVE TO HAVE SOMEONE LIKE THAT.
IT WOULD CERTAINLY MAKE ASSASSINATION A MUCH CLEANER PROCESS.
AND AS A MATTER OF FACT, WE *DO* HAVE REPORTS THAT AT LEAST ONE COUNTRY IS ATTEMPTING TO FIND A CANDIDATE FOR THEIR OWN PURPOSES.
AS ARE SOME SPECIALIZED RESEARCH ORGANIZATIONS.
UNBELIEVABLE...
GOD CANDIDATES. WHO WOULD'VE THOUGHT SUCH A THING COULD BE REAL?
I'LL ADMIT THAT AFTER WHAT HAPPENED AT JINBO STADIUM AND GRAND TOWER, WE WERE WORKING ON A PLAN TO TAKE OUT METROPOLIMAN.
SAME FOR THE RED WARRIOR AND THE OTHER GOD CANDIDATES. UNFORTUNATELY, OUR ATTEMPT ON THE BOY THREE DAYS AGO FAILED.

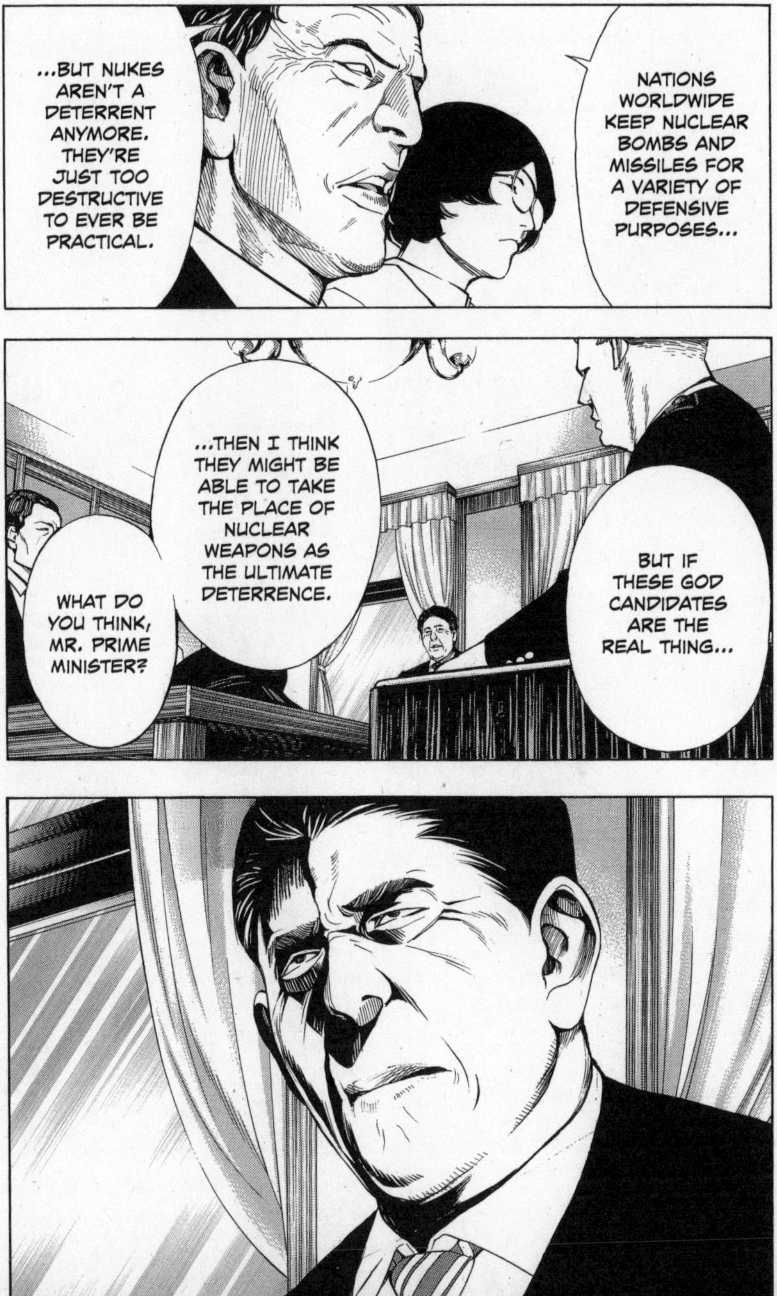
NATIONS WORLDWIDE KEEP NUCLEAR BOMBS AND MISSILES FOR A VARIETY OF DEFENSIVE PURPOSES...
...BUT NUKES AREN'T A DETERRENT ANYMORE. THEY'RE JUST TOO DESTRUCTIVE TO EVER BE PRACTICAL.
BUT IF THESE GOD CANDIDATES ARE THE REAL THING...
...THEN I THINK THEY MIGHT BE ABLE TO TAKE THE PLACE OF NUCLEAR WEAPONS AS THE ULTIMATE DETERRENCE.
WHAT DO YOU THINK, MR. PRIME MINISTER?

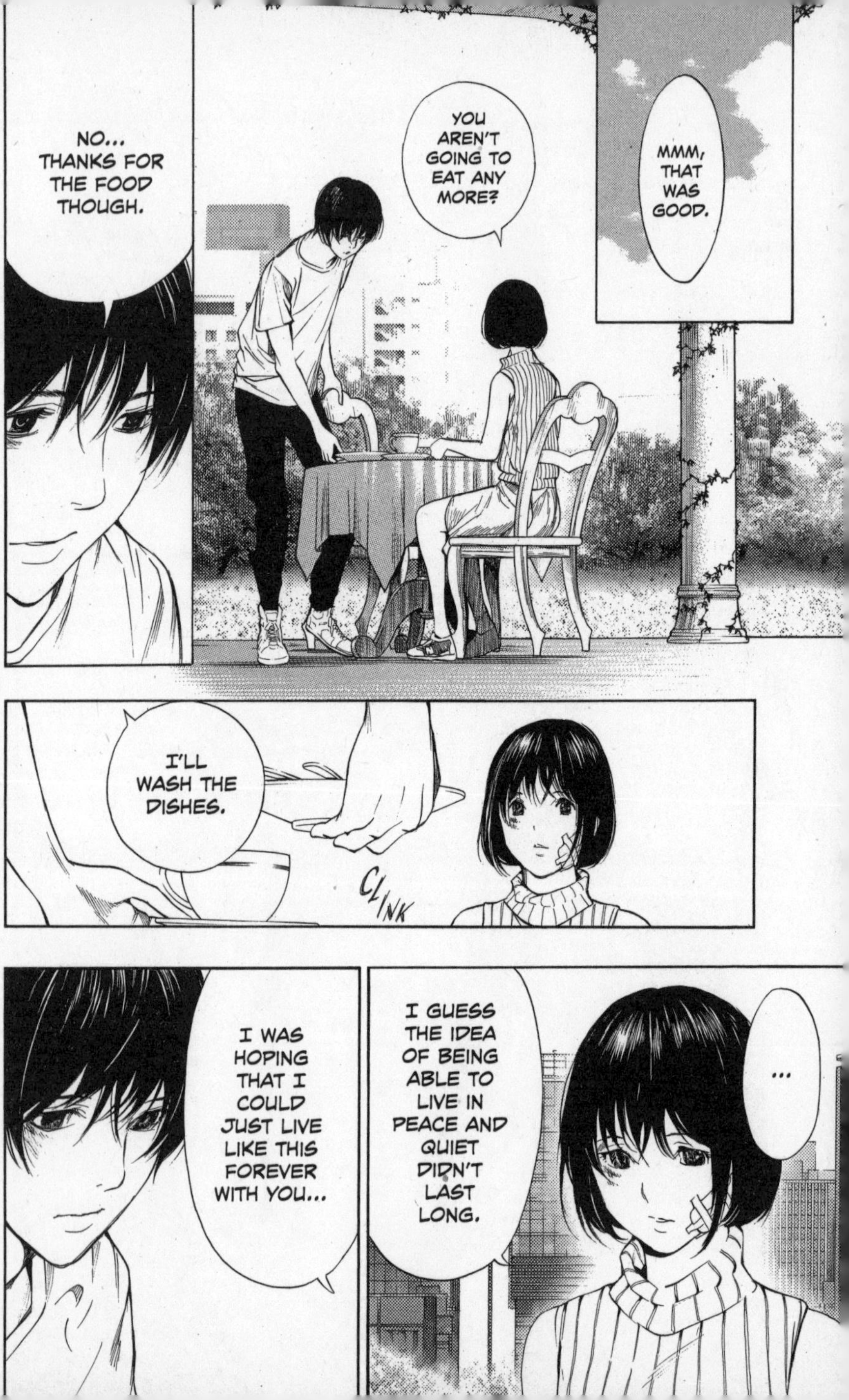
MMM, THAT WAS GOOD.
YOU AREN'T GOING TO EAT ANY MORE?
NO... THANKS FOR THE FOOD THOUGH.
I'LL WASH THE DISHES.
CLINK
...
I GUESS THE IDEA OF BEING ABLE TO LIVE IN PEACE AND QUIET DIDN'T LAST LONG.
I WAS HOPING THAT I COULD JUST LIVE LIKE THIS FOREVER WITH YOU...

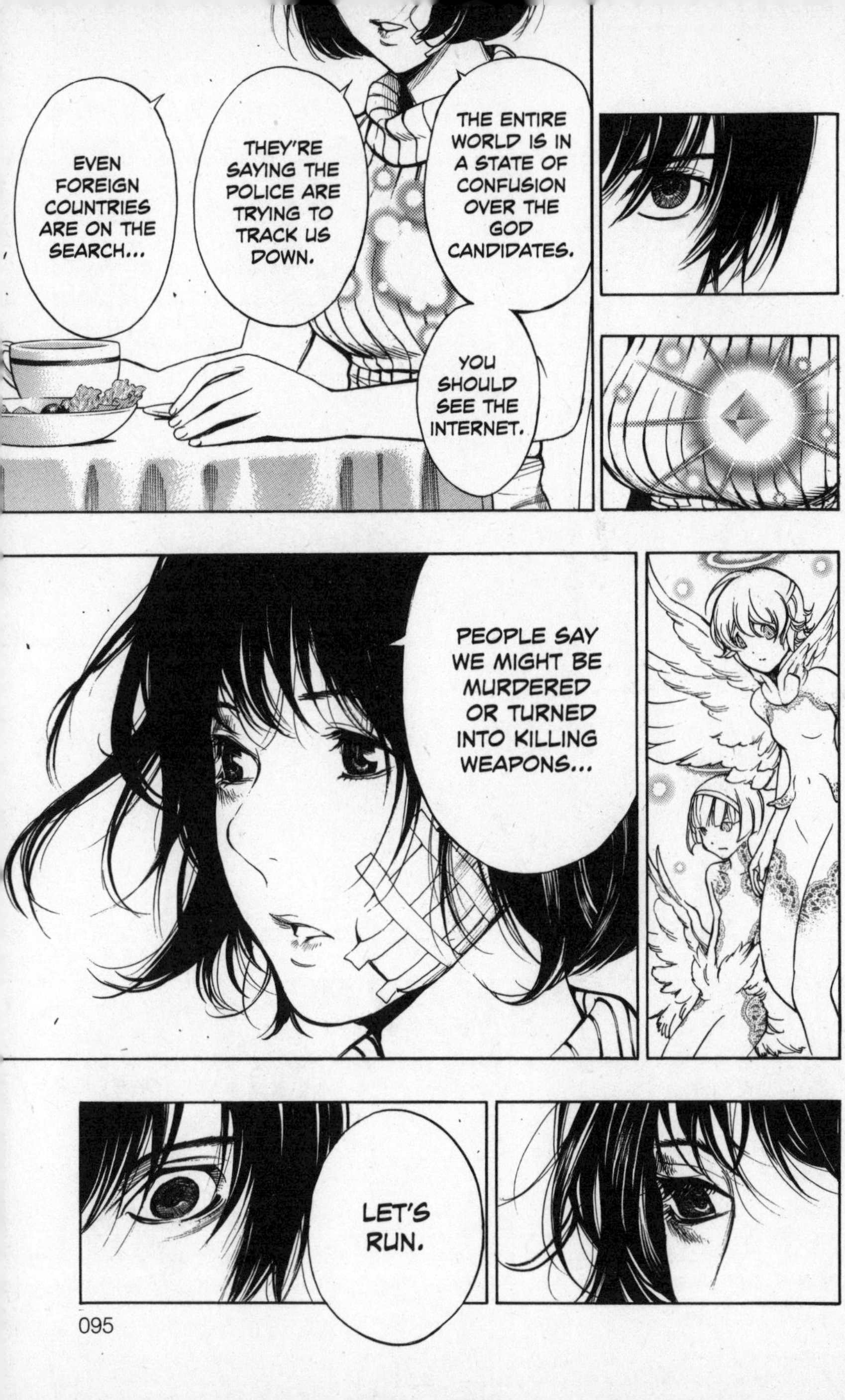
THE ENTIRE WORLD IS IN A STATE OF CONFUSION OVER THE GOD CANDIDATES.
YOU SHOULD SEE THE INTERNET.
THEY'RE SAYING THE POLICE ARE TRYING TO TRACK US DOWN.
EVEN FOREIGN COUNTRIES ARE ON THE SEARCH...
PEOPLE SAY WE MIGHT BE MURDERED OR TURNED INTO KILLING WEAPONS...
LET'S RUN.

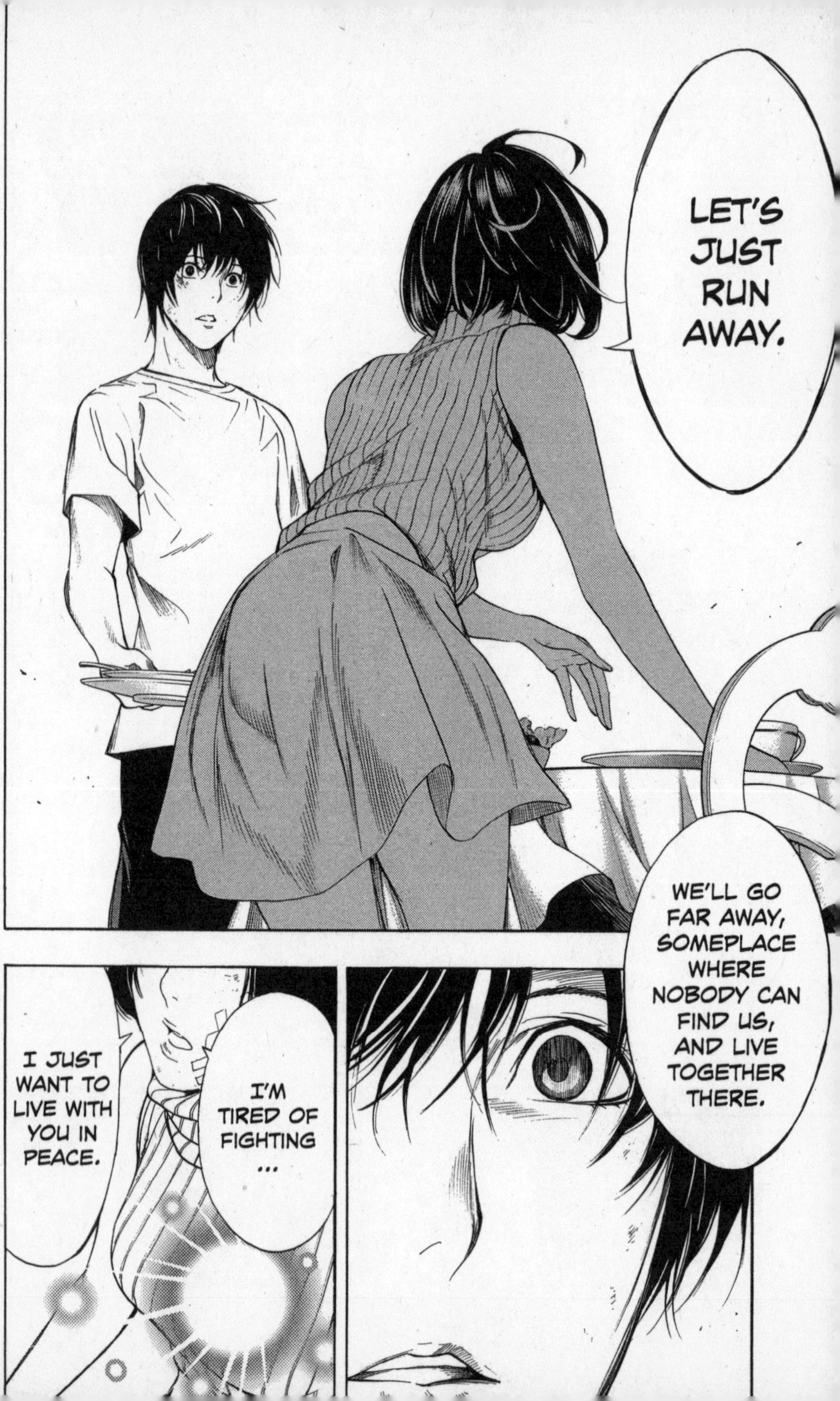
LET'S JUST RUN AWAY.
WE'LL GO FAR AWAY, SOMEPLACE WHERE NOBODY CAN FIND US, AND LIVE TOGETHER THERE.
I'M TIRED OF FIGHTING...
I JUST WANT TO LIVE WITH YOU IN PEACE.

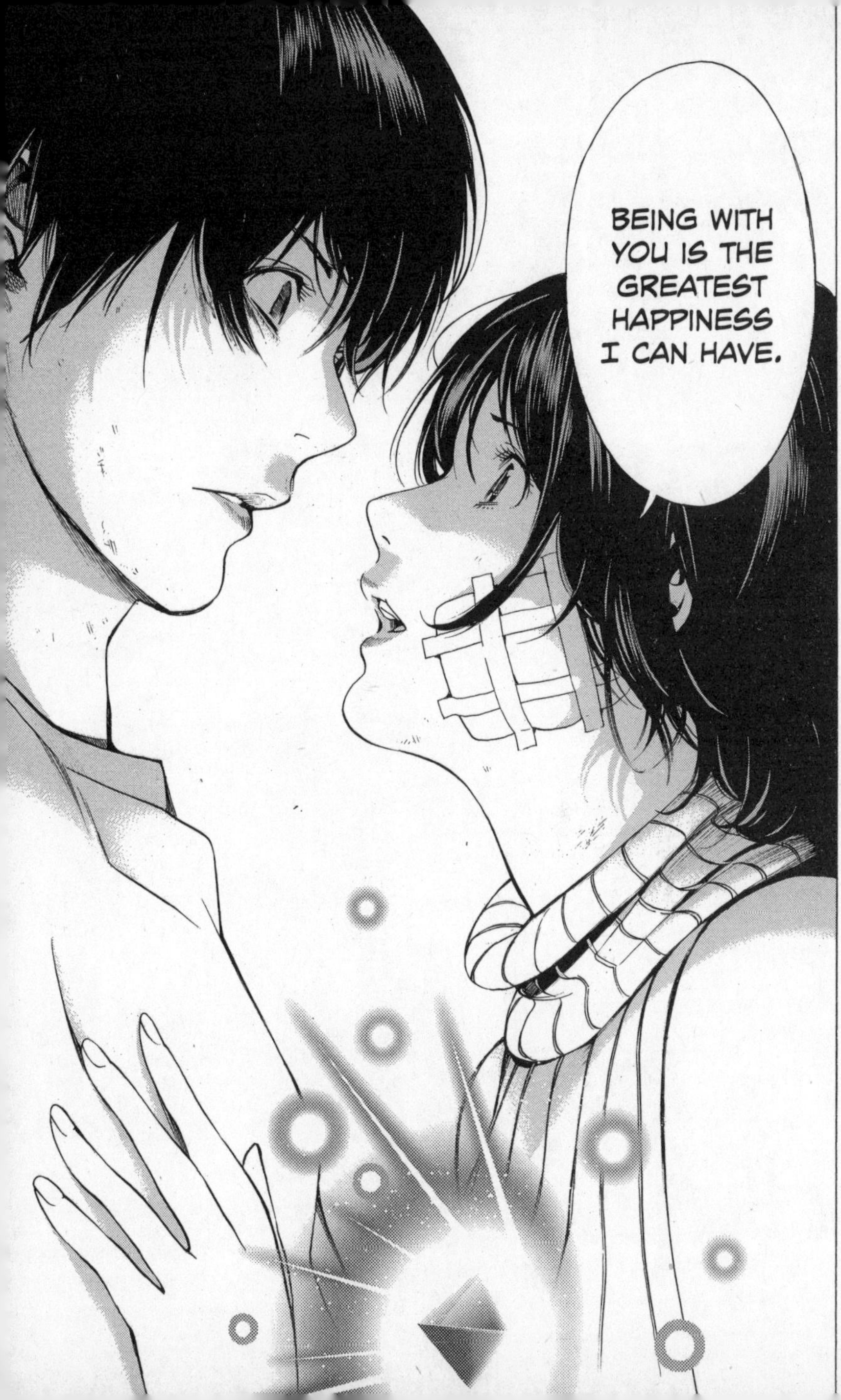
BEING WITH YOU IS THE GREATEST HAPPINESS I CAN HAVE.

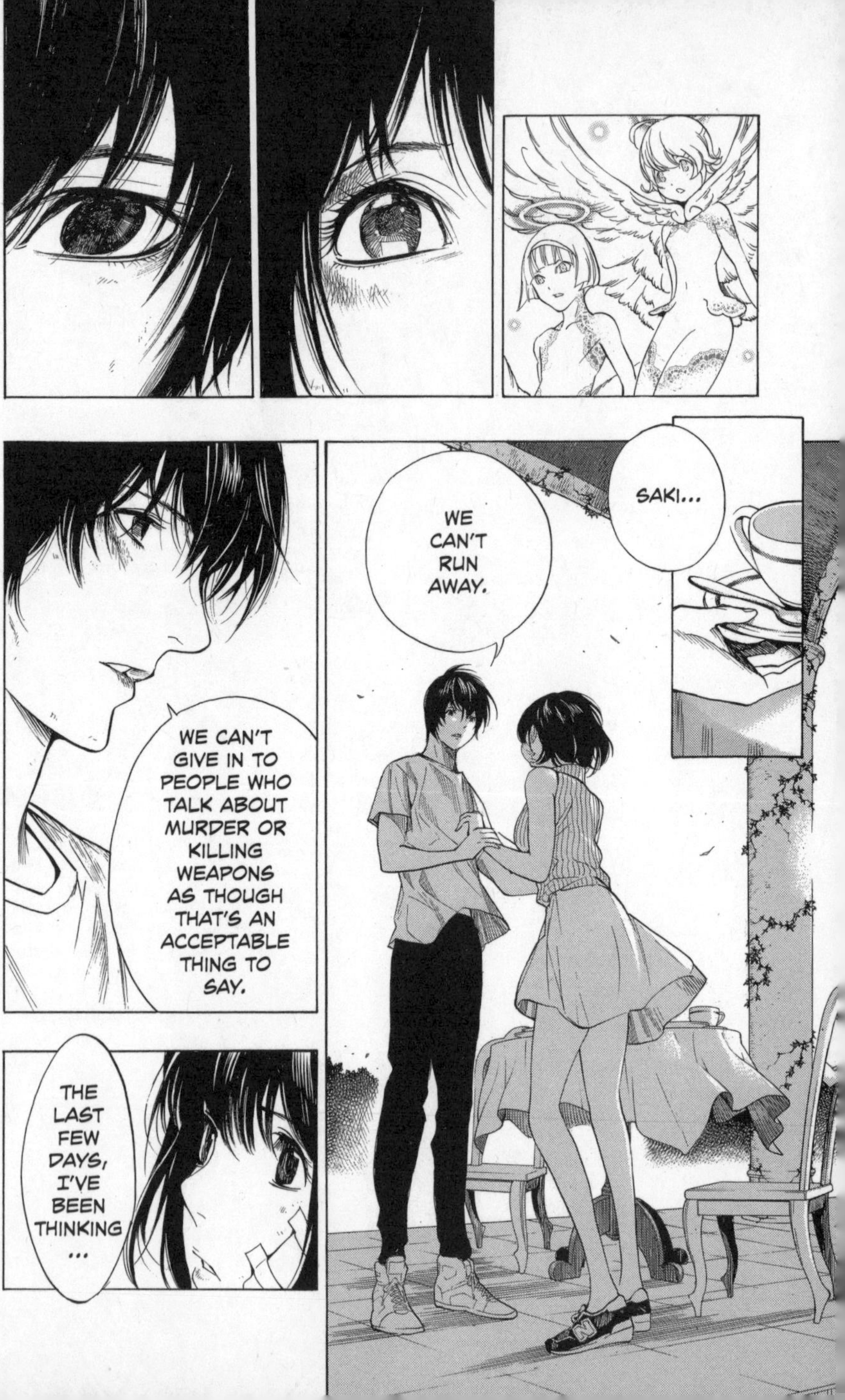
SAKI...
WE CAN'T RUN AWAY.
WE CAN'T GIVE IN TO PEOPLE WHO TALK ABOUT MURDER OR KILLING WEAPONS AS THOUGH THAT'S AN ACCEPTABLE THING TO SAY.
THE LAST FEW DAYS, I'VE BEEN THINKING...

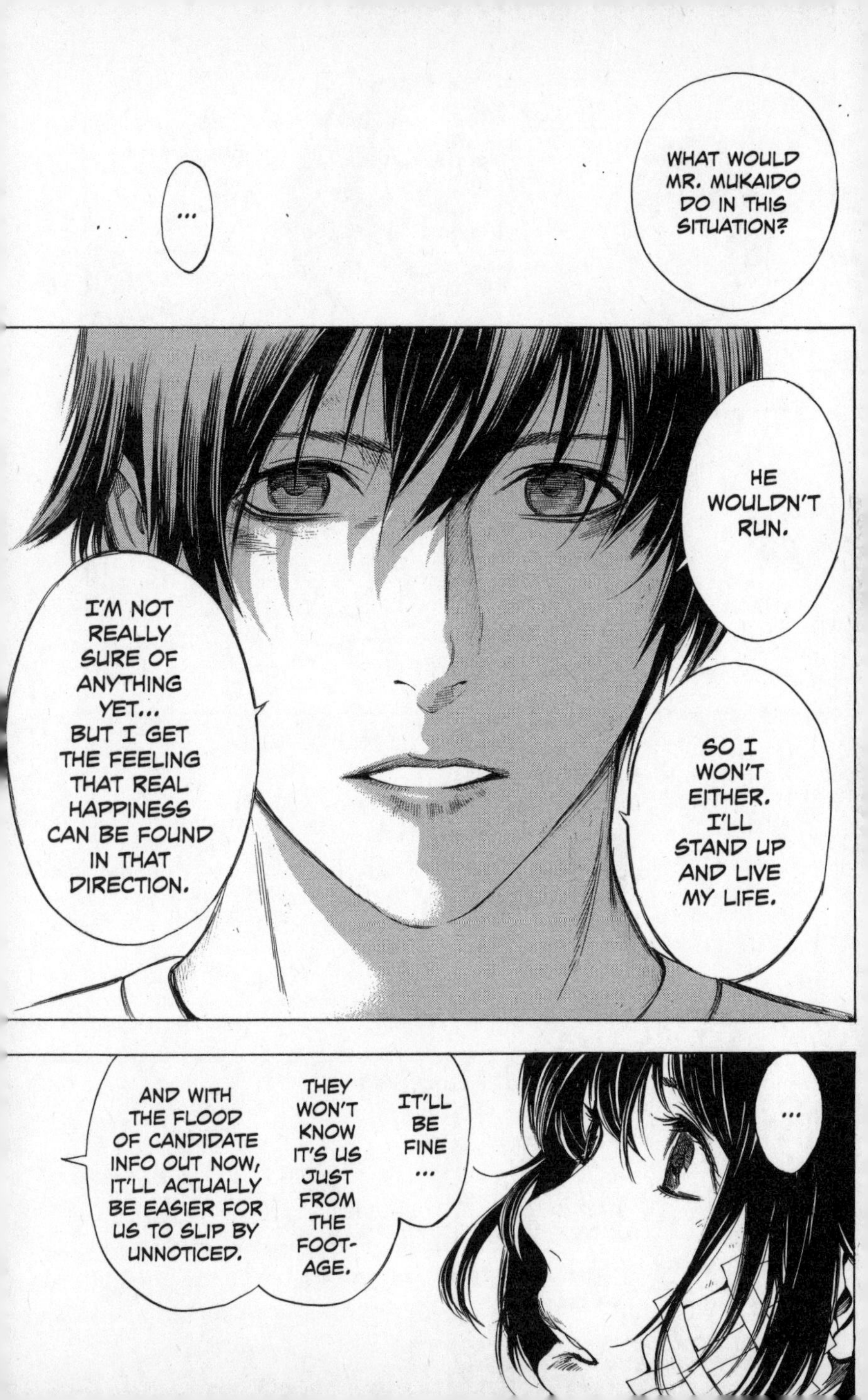
WHAT WOULD MR. MUKAIDO DO IN THIS SITUATION?
...
HE WOULDN'T RUN.
SO I WON'T EITHER. I'LL STAND UP AND LIVE MY LIFE.
I'M NOT REALLY SURE OF ANYTHING YET... BUT I GET THE FEELING THAT REAL HAPPINESS CAN BE FOUND IN THAT DIRECTION.
...
IT'LL BE FINE ...
THEY WON'T KNOW IT'S US JUST FROM THE FOOT-AGE.
AND WITH THE FLOOD OF CANDIDATE INFO OUT NOW, IT'LL ACTUALLY BE EASIER FOR US TO SLIP BY UNNOTICED.

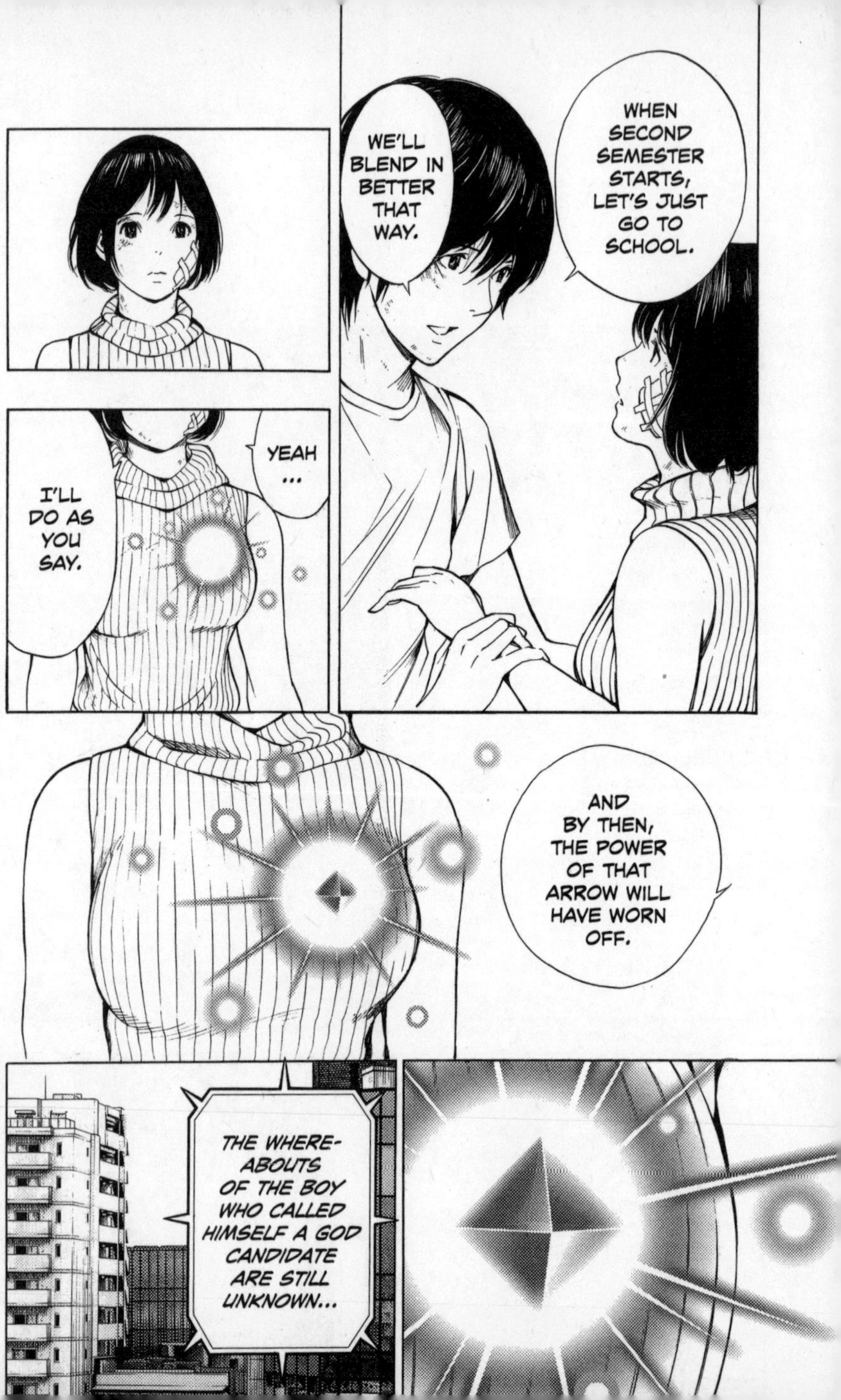
WHEN SECOND SEMESTER STARTS, LET'S JUST GO TO SCHOOL.
WE'LL BLEND IN BETTER THAT WAY.
YEAH...
I'LL DO AS YOU SAY.
AND BY THEN, THE POWER OF THAT ARROW WILL HAVE WORN OFF.
THE WHERE-ABOUTS OF THE BOY WHO CALLED HIMSELF A GOD CANDIDATE ARE STILL UNKNOWN...

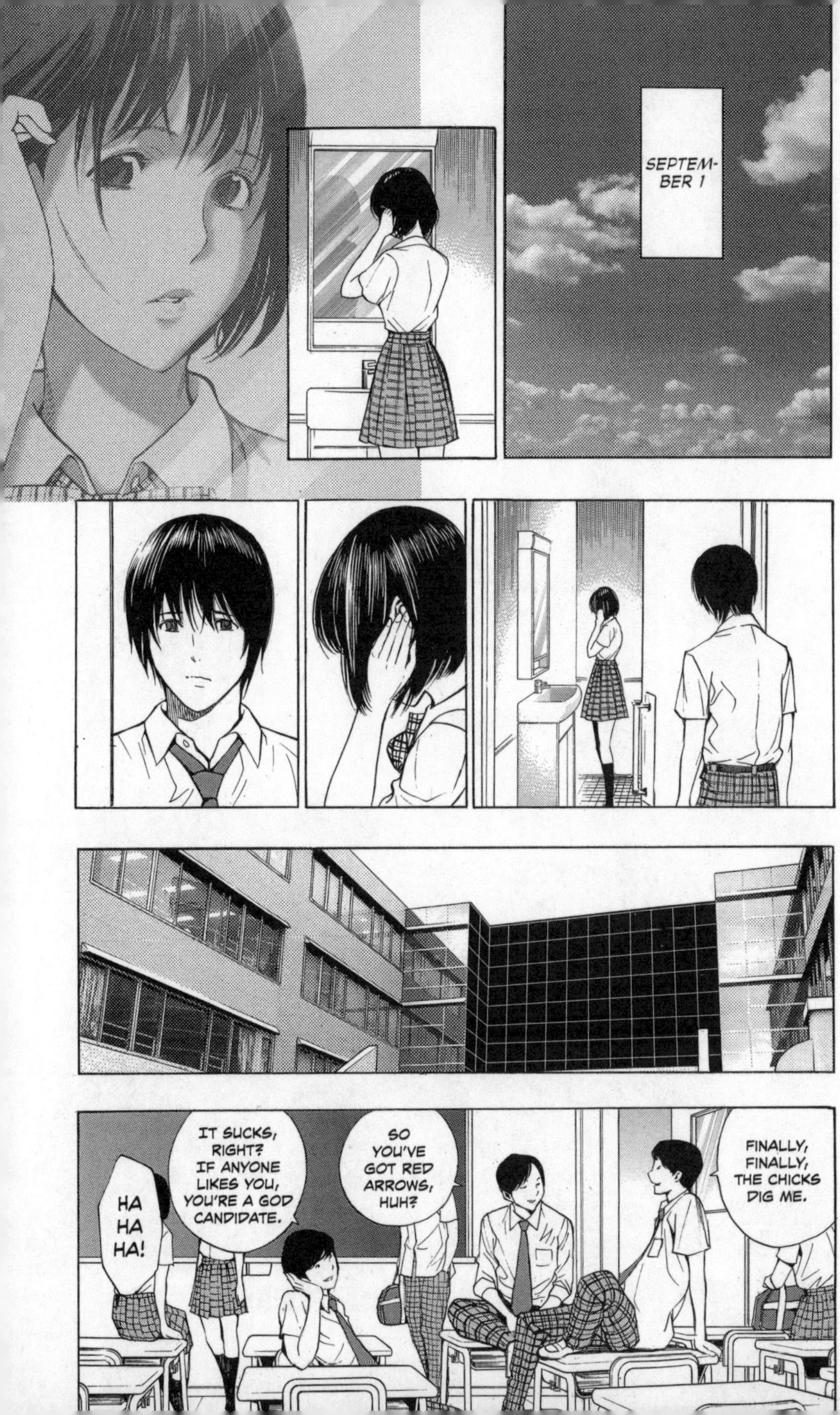
SEPTEMBER 1
FINALLY, FINALLY, THE CHICKS DIG ME.
SO YOU'VE GOT RED ARROWS, HUH?
IT SUCKS, RIGHT? IF ANYONE LIKES YOU, YOU'RE A GOD CANDIDATE.
HA HA HA!

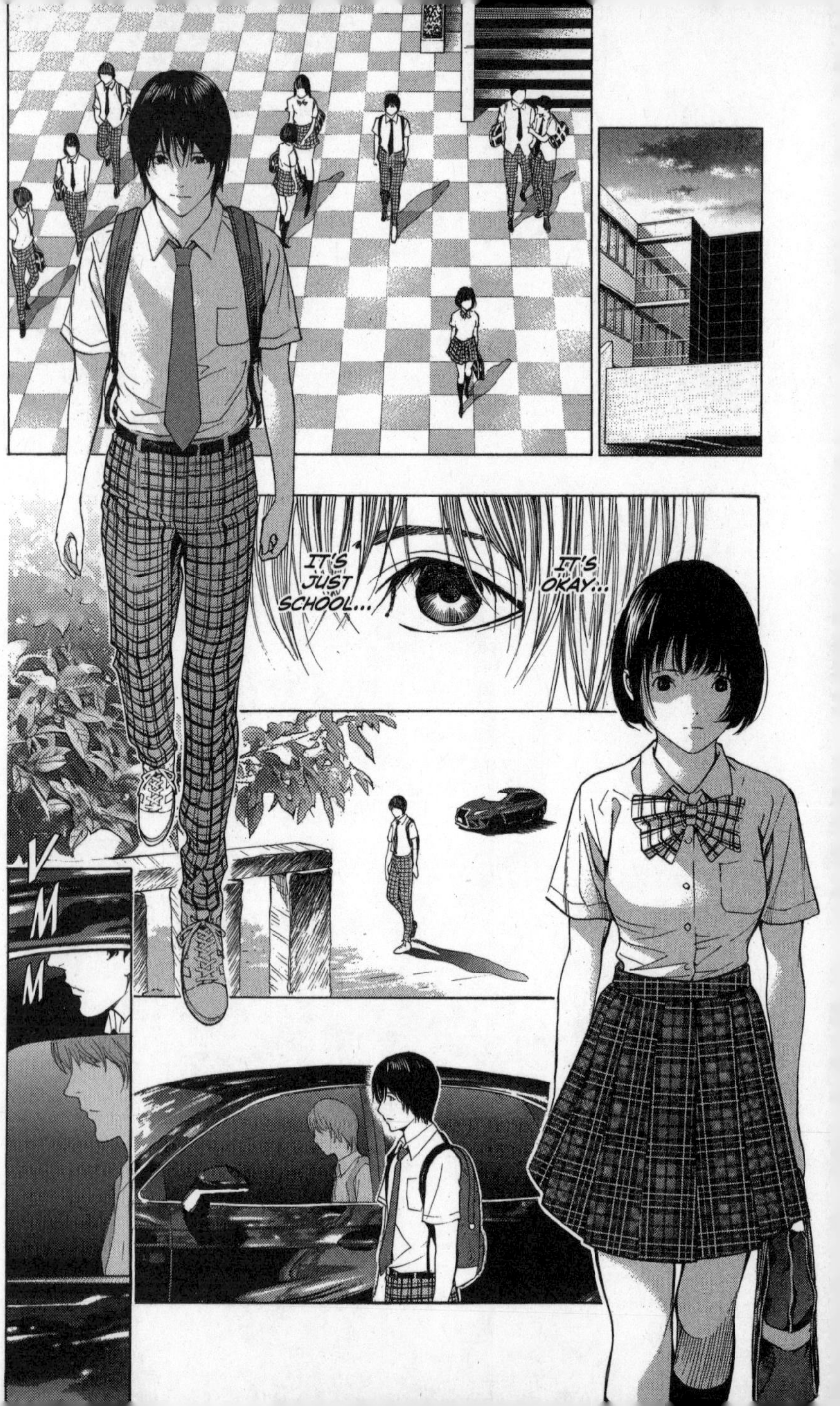
IT'S OKAY...
IT'S JUST SCHOOL...
VMM

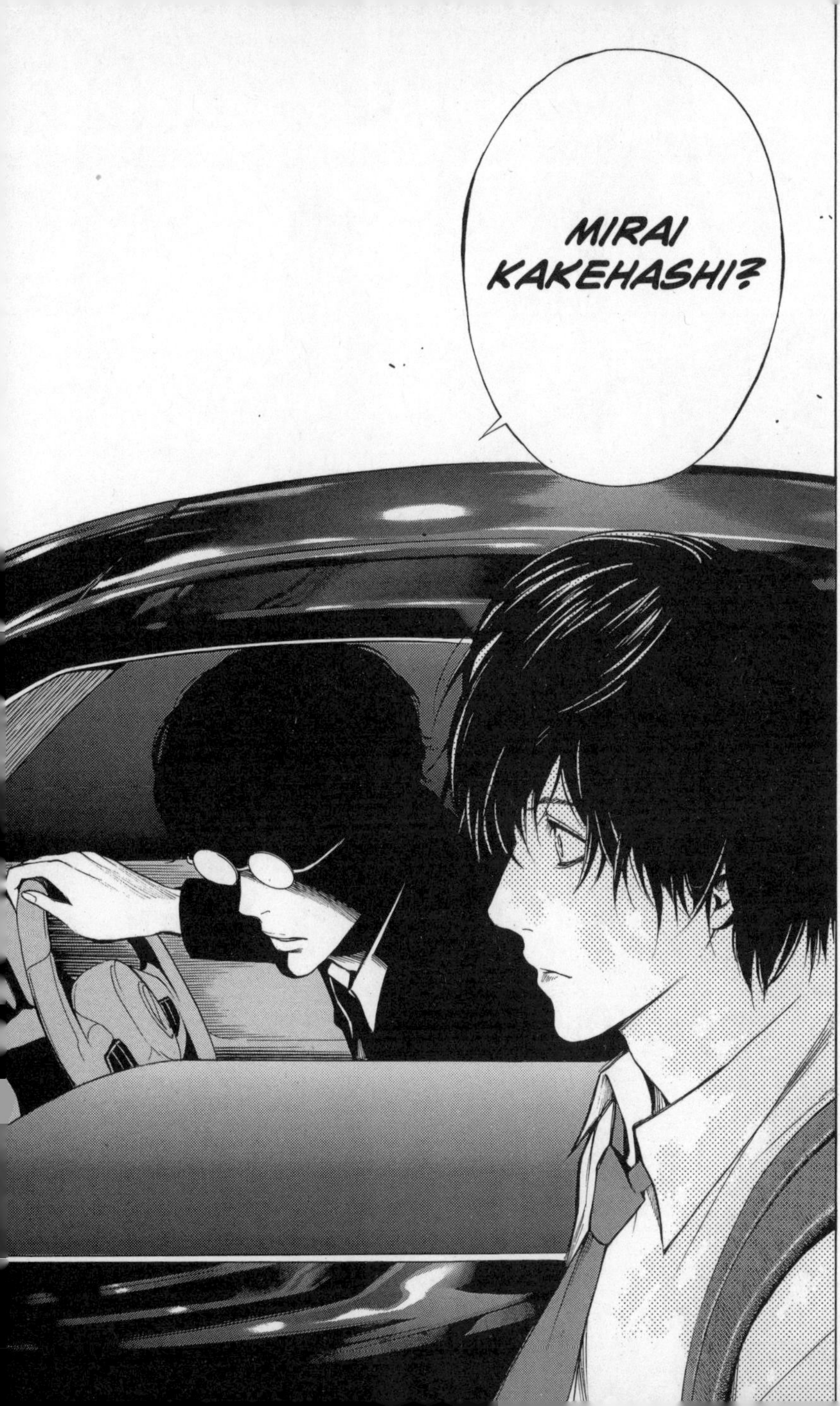
MIRAI KAKEHASHI?

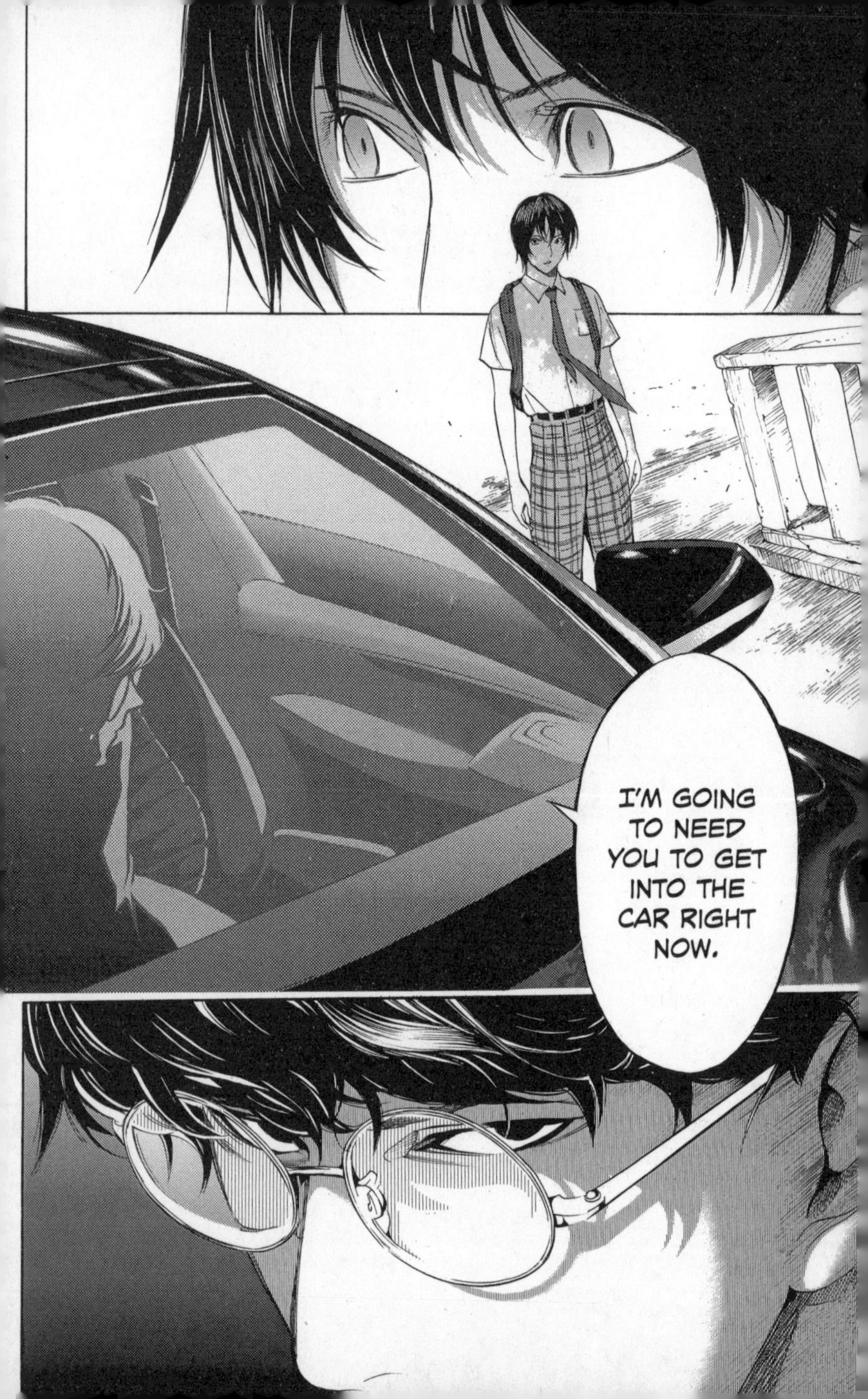
I'M GOING TO NEED YOU TO GET INTO THE CAR RIGHT NOW.

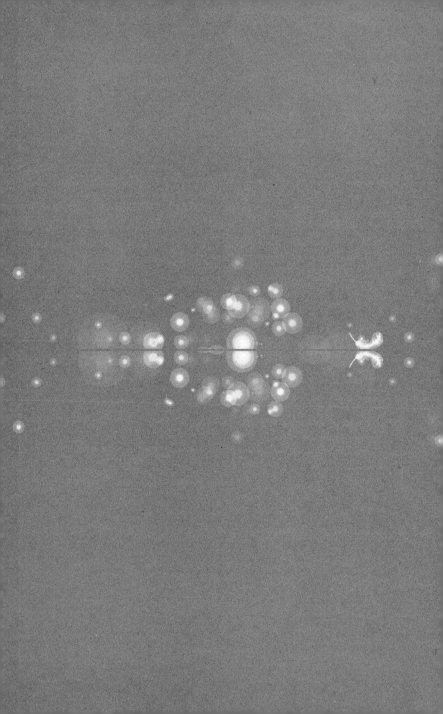

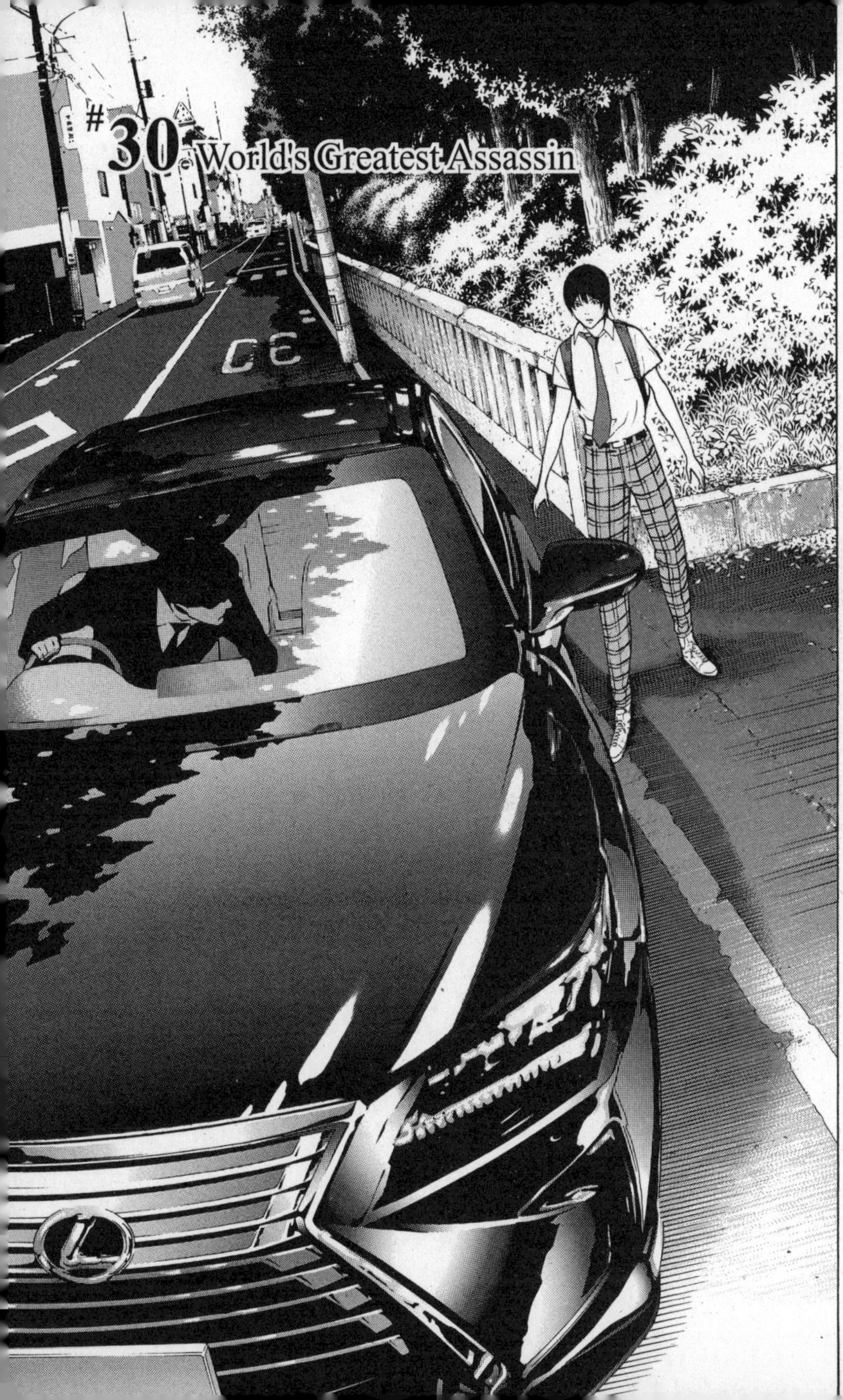

#30 World's Greatest Assassin

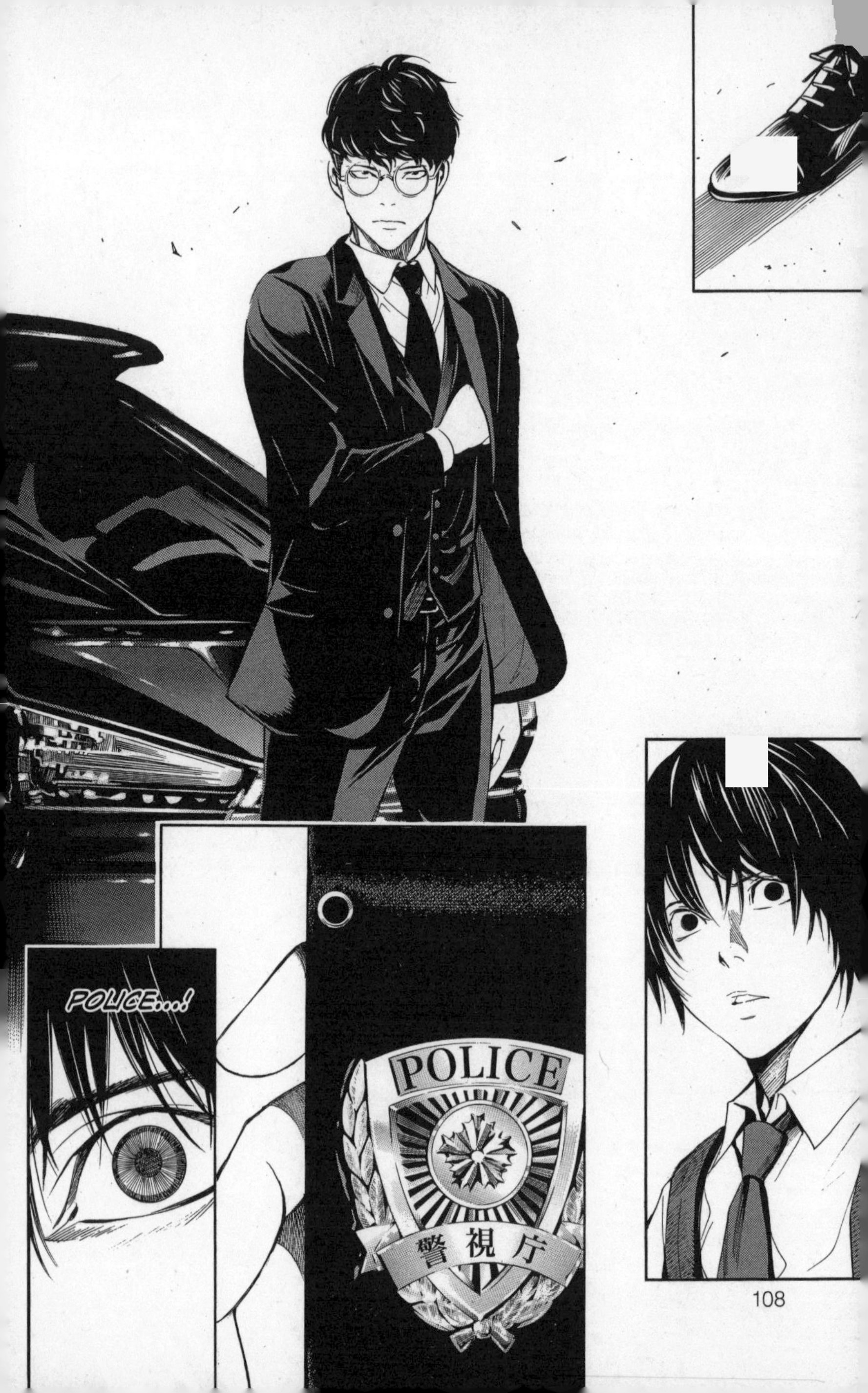
POLICE...!
POLICE
警視庁

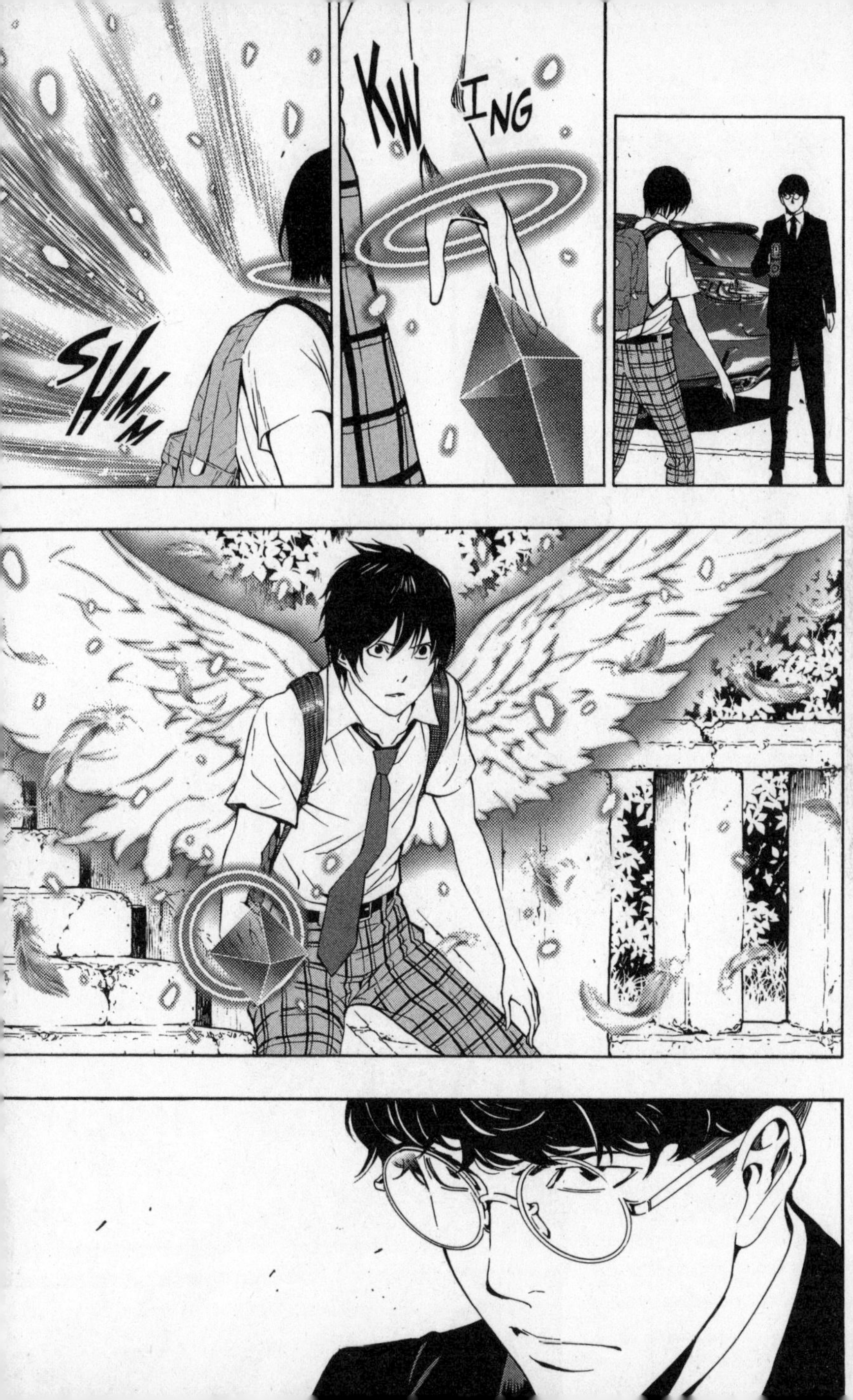
KWING
SHMM

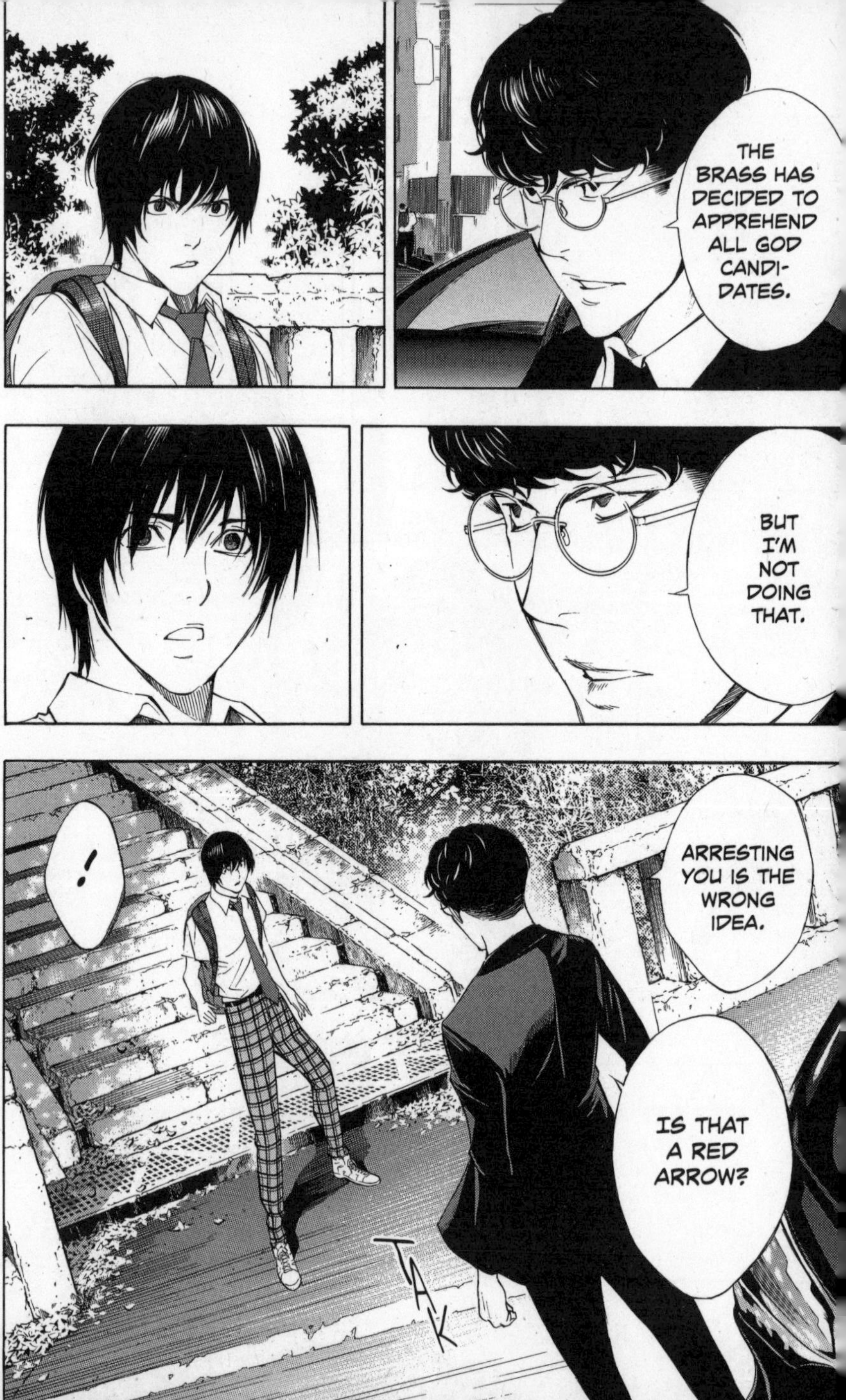
THE BRASS HAS DECIDED TO APPREHEND ALL GOD CANDIDATES.
BUT I'M NOT DOING THAT.
ARRESTING YOU IS THE WRONG IDEA.
IS THAT A RED ARROW?
!
TAK

IS IT RED? OR WHITE?

...

THE KIND THAT MAKES YOU FALL IN LOVE? OR THE KIND THAT MAKES YOU DIE?

TAK

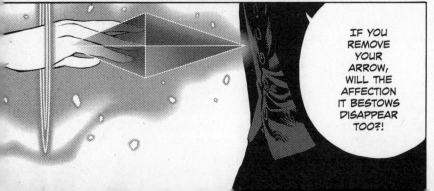

IF YOU REMOVE YOUR ARROW, WILL THE AFFECTION IT BESTOWS DISAPPEAR TOO?!

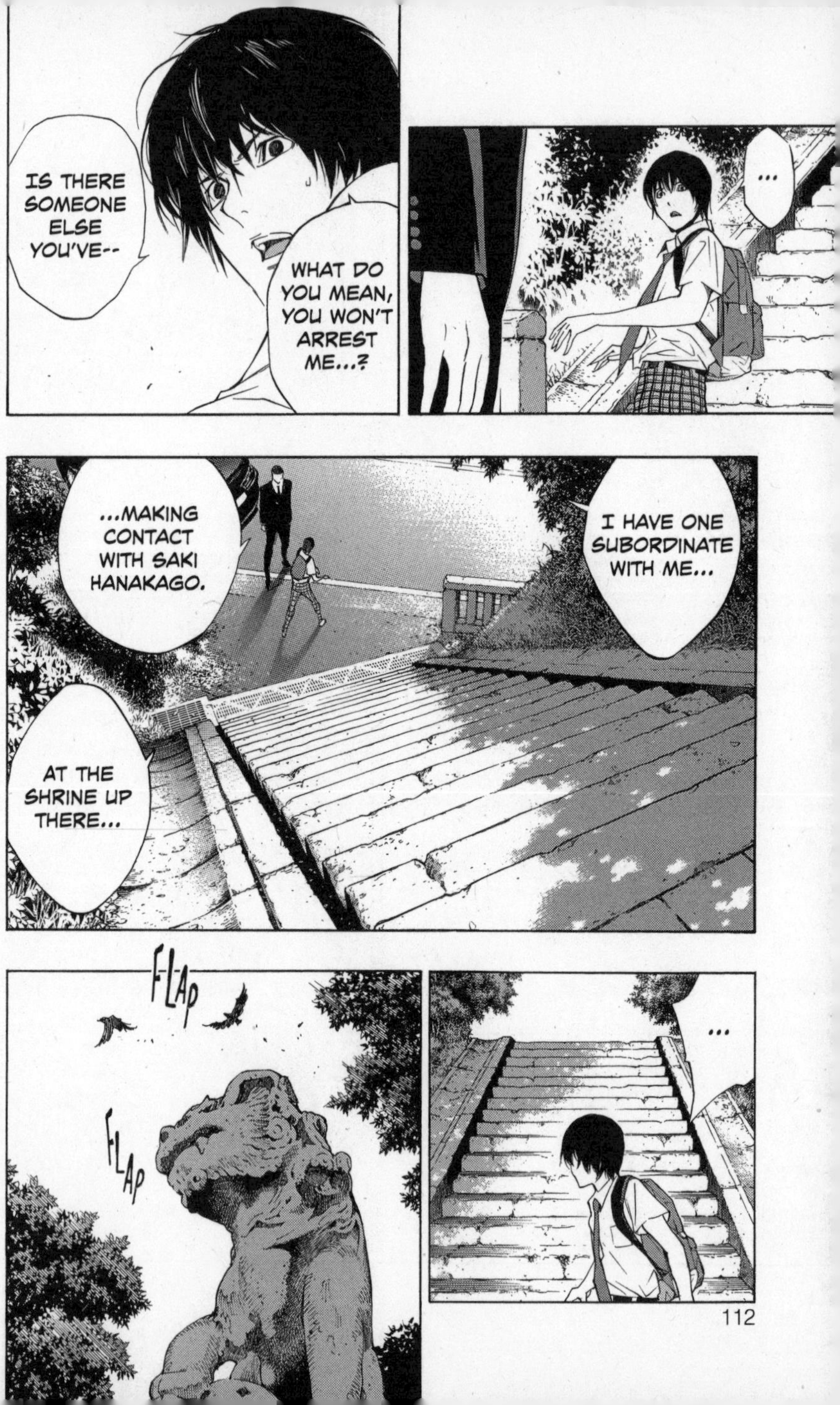
...
WHAT DO YOU MEAN, YOU WON'T ARREST ME...?
IS THERE SOMEONE ELSE YOU'VE--
I HAVE ONE SUBORDINATE WITH ME...
...MAKING CONTACT WITH SAKI HANAKAGO.
AT THE SHRINE UP THERE...
...
F-LAP
FLAP

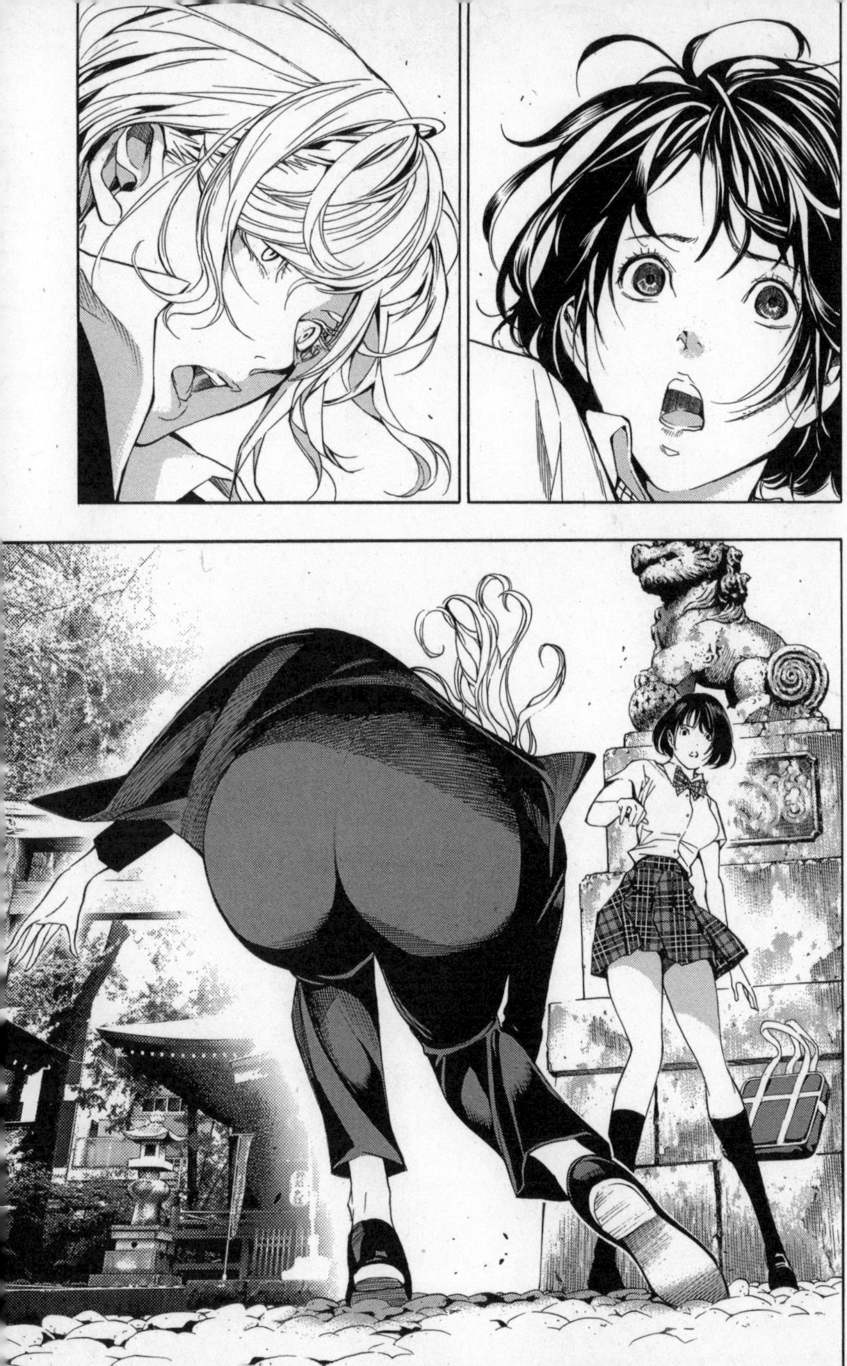

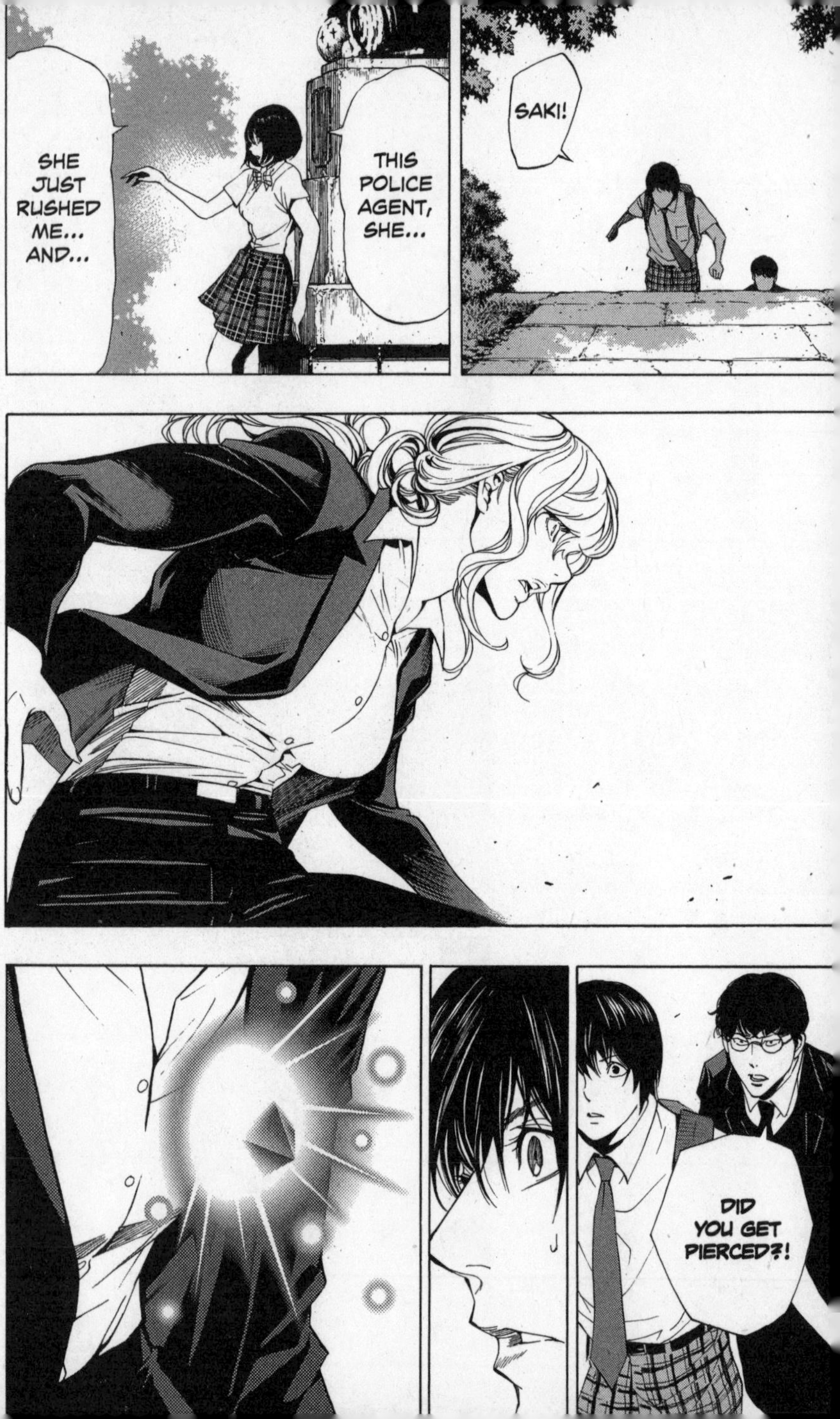
SAKI!
THIS POLICE AGENT, SHE...
SHE JUST RUSHED ME... AND...
DID YOU GET PIERCED?!

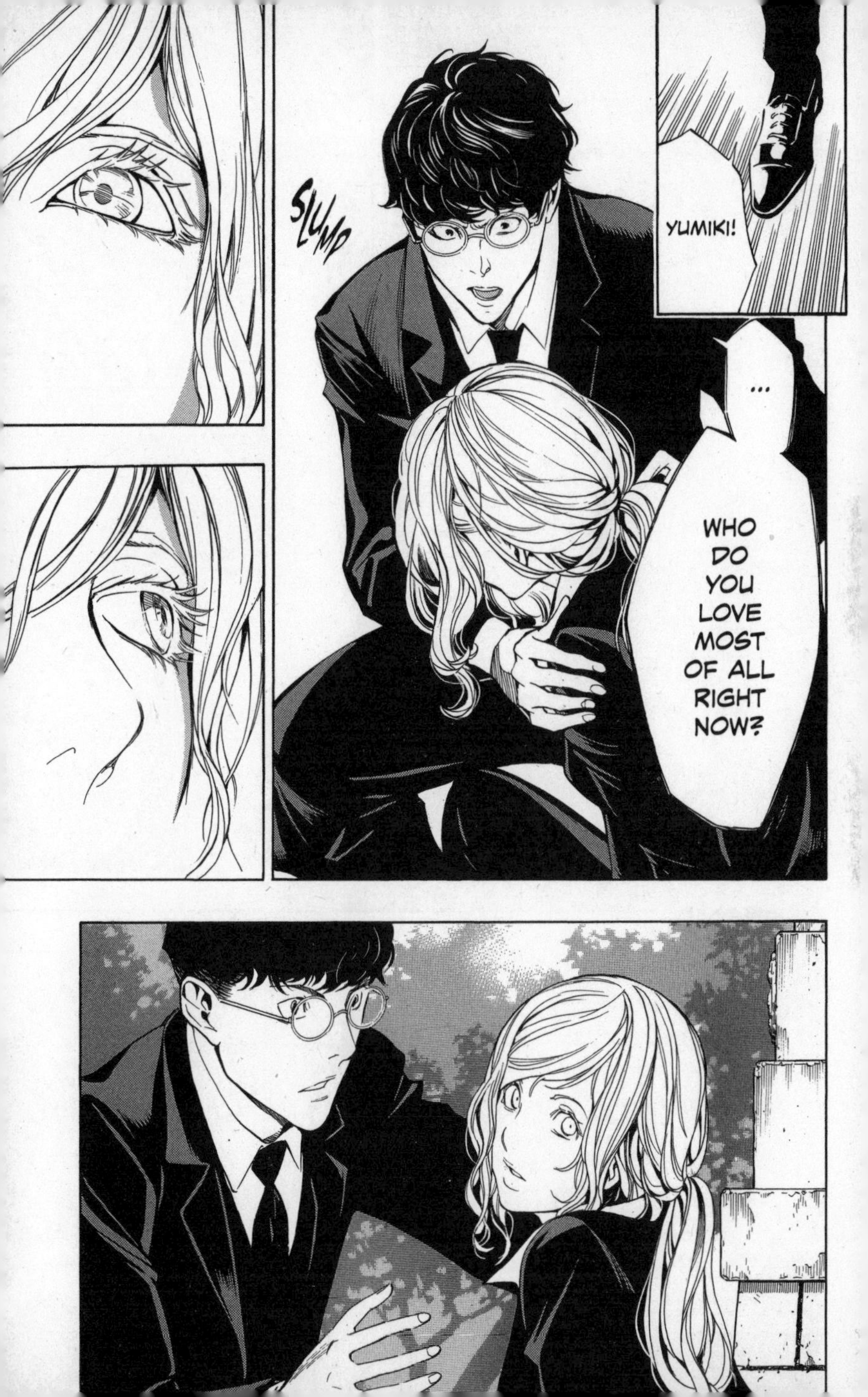
YUMIKI!
SLUMP
...
WHO DO YOU LOVE MOST OF ALL RIGHT NOW?

IN PUBLIC AND IN PRIVATE, WE HAVE ABSOLUTE RESPECT AND TRUST FOR ONE ANOTHER.

YUMIKI IS BOTH A VERY FAITHFUL SUBORDINATE OF MINE... AND THE WOMAN WHO PROMISED HER FUTURE TO ME.

INCRED-IBLE...

I'M SORRY.

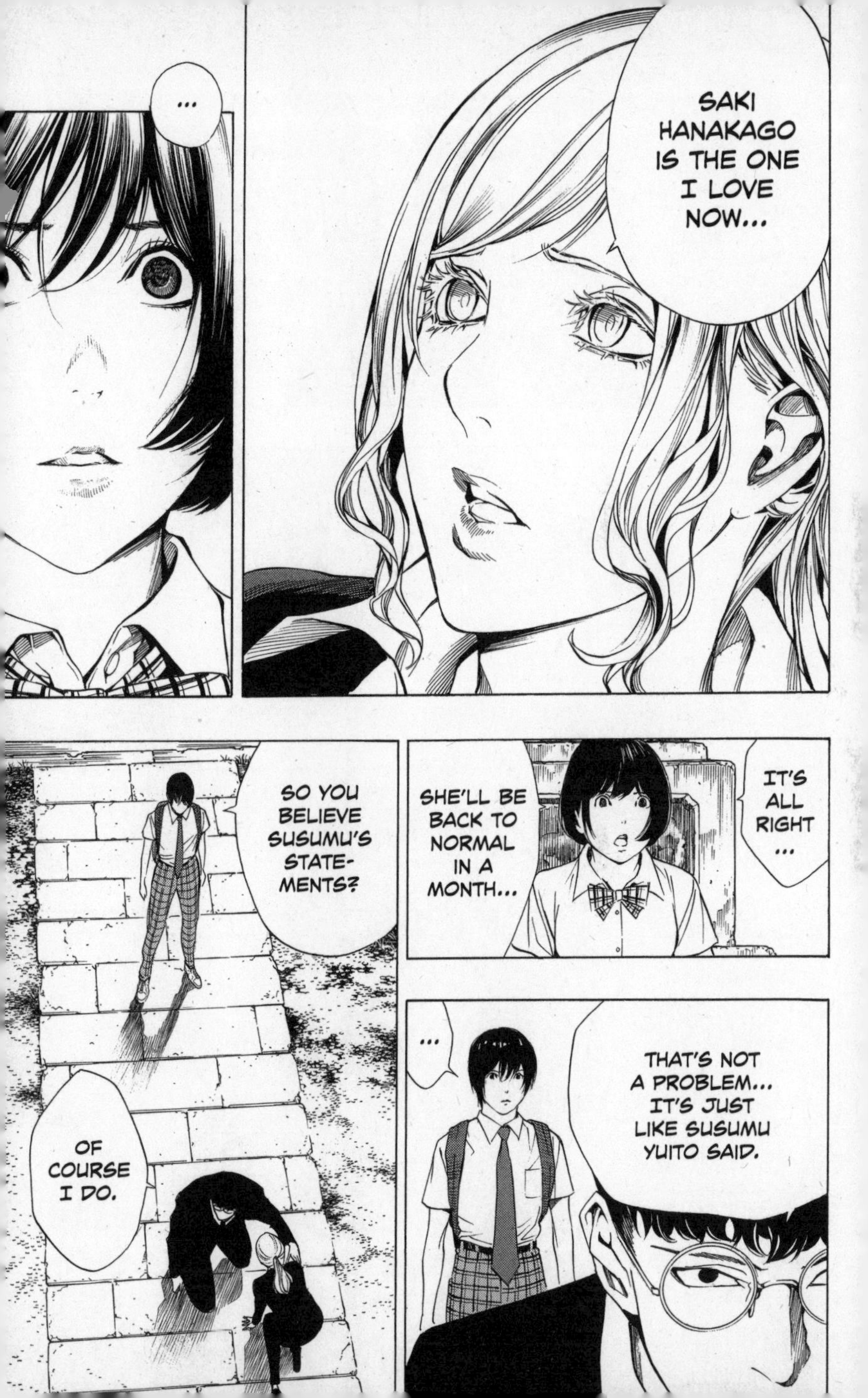
SAKI HANAKAGO IS THE ONE I LOVE NOW...
...
IT'S ALL RIGHT ...
SHE'LL BE BACK TO NORMAL IN A MONTH...
THAT'S NOT A PROBLEM... IT'S JUST LIKE SUSUMU YUITO SAID.
...
SO YOU BELIEVE SUSUMU'S STATE-MENTS?
OF COURSE I DO.

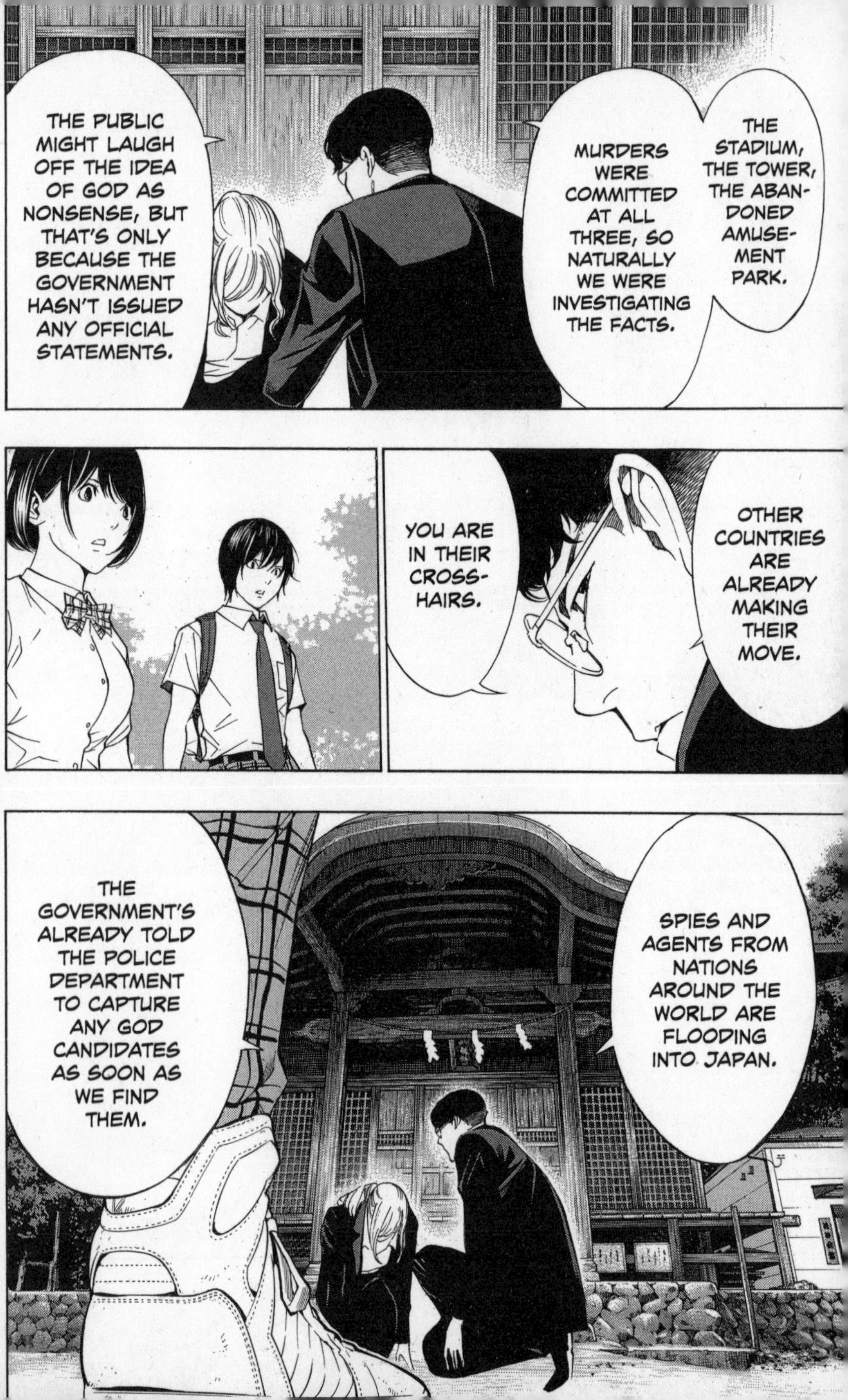
THE STADIUM, THE TOWER, THE ABAN-DONED AMUSE-MENT PARK.
MURDERS WERE COMMITTED AT ALL THREE, SO NATURALLY WE WERE INVESTIGATING THE FACTS.
THE PUBLIC MIGHT LAUGH OFF THE IDEA OF GOD AS NONSENSE, BUT THAT'S ONLY BECAUSE THE GOVERNMENT HASN'T ISSUED ANY OFFICIAL STATEMENTS.
OTHER COUNTRIES ARE ALREADY MAKING THEIR MOVE.
YOU ARE IN THEIR CROSS-HAIRS.
SPIES AND AGENTS FROM NATIONS AROUND THE WORLD ARE FLOODING INTO JAPAN.
THE GOVERNMENT'S ALREADY TOLD THE POLICE DEPARTMENT TO CAPTURE ANY GOD CANDIDATES AS SOON AS WE FIND THEM.

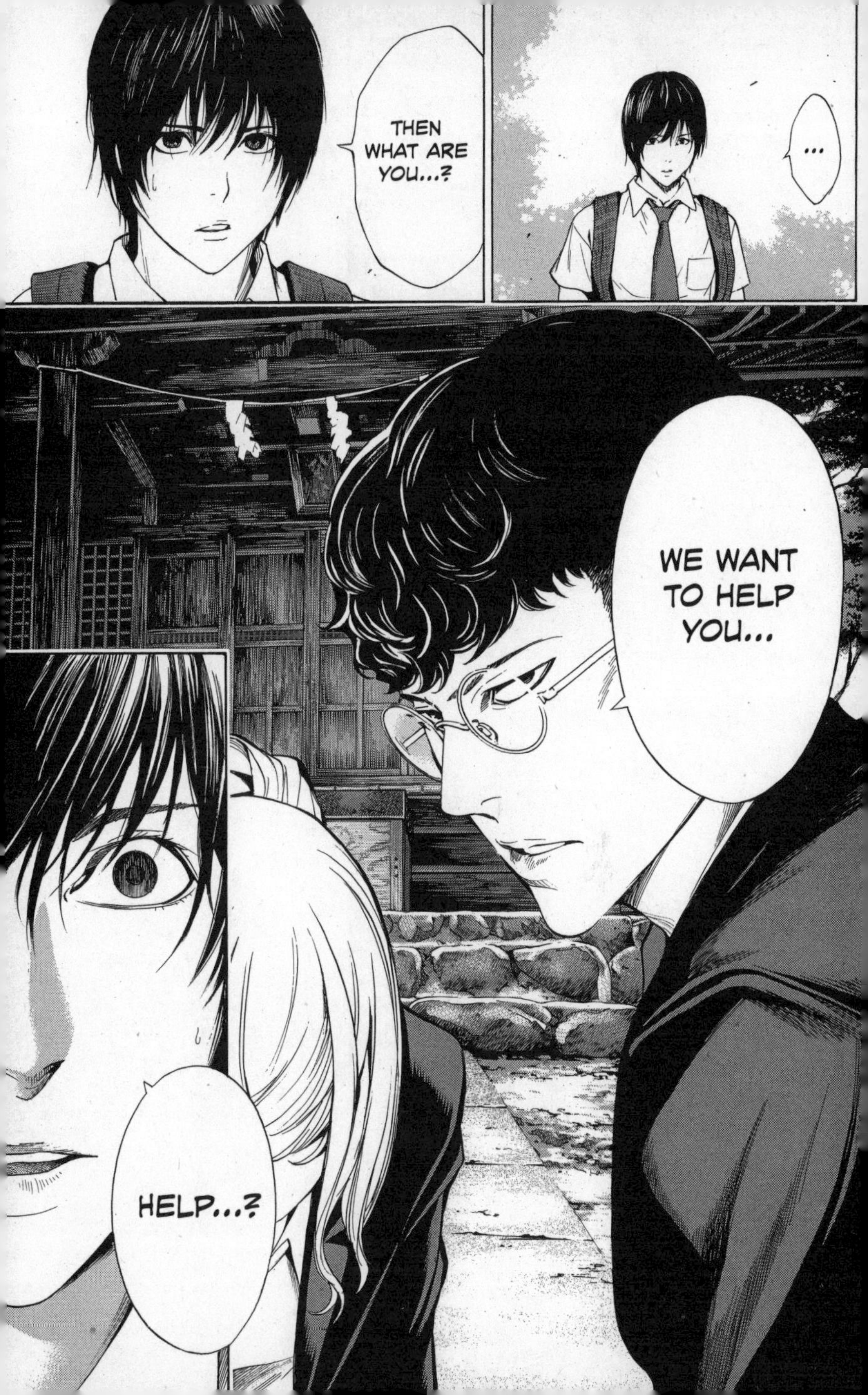
...
THEN WHAT ARE YOU...?
WE WANT TO HELP YOU...
HELP...?

IF WE WERE GOING TO CAPTURE YOU, WE'D DO IT WITH A TEAM WHILE YOU'RE SLEEPING.

FSSHH...

THAT'S RIGHT...

BUT IT'S ONLY A MATTER OF TIME UNTIL YOU'RE DISCOVERED.

THEY DON'T REALIZE THAT YOU'RE GOD CANDIDATES YET.

ZSH

THIS PLACE IS TOO VISIBLE.

WILL YOU COME WITH US?

WE ARE ORDINARY HUMAN BEINGS. BESIDES...

I UNDERSTAND YOUR SENSE OF CAUTION, BUT THERE'S NO REASON TO BE AFRAID OF US.

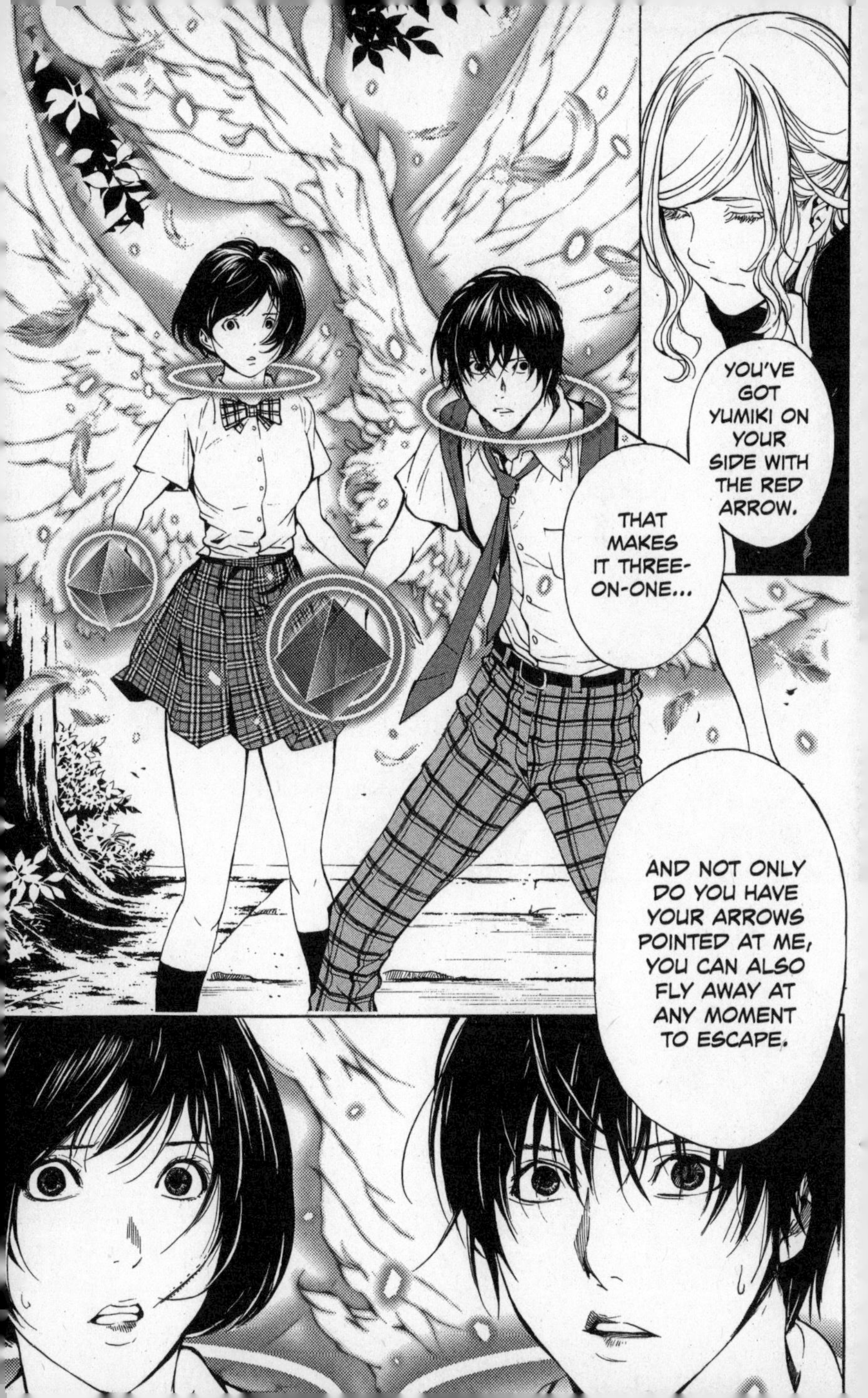
YOU'VE GOT YUMIKI ON YOUR SIDE WITH THE RED ARROW.
THAT MAKES IT THREE-ON-ONE...
AND NOT ONLY DO YOU HAVE YOUR ARROWS POINTED AT ME, YOU CAN ALSO FLY AWAY AT ANY MOMENT TO ESCAPE.

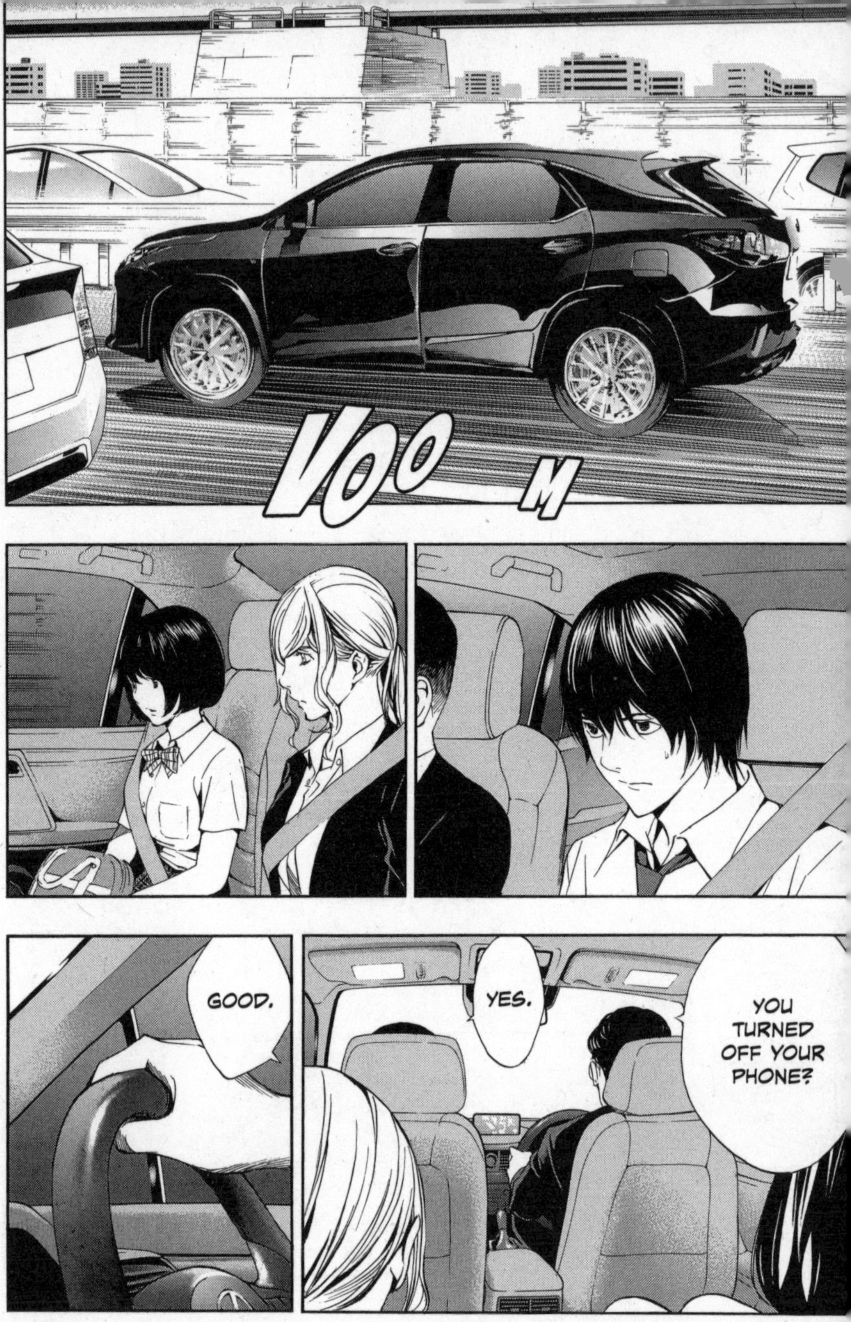
VOOOM
YOU TURNED OFF YOUR PHONE?
YES.
GOOD.

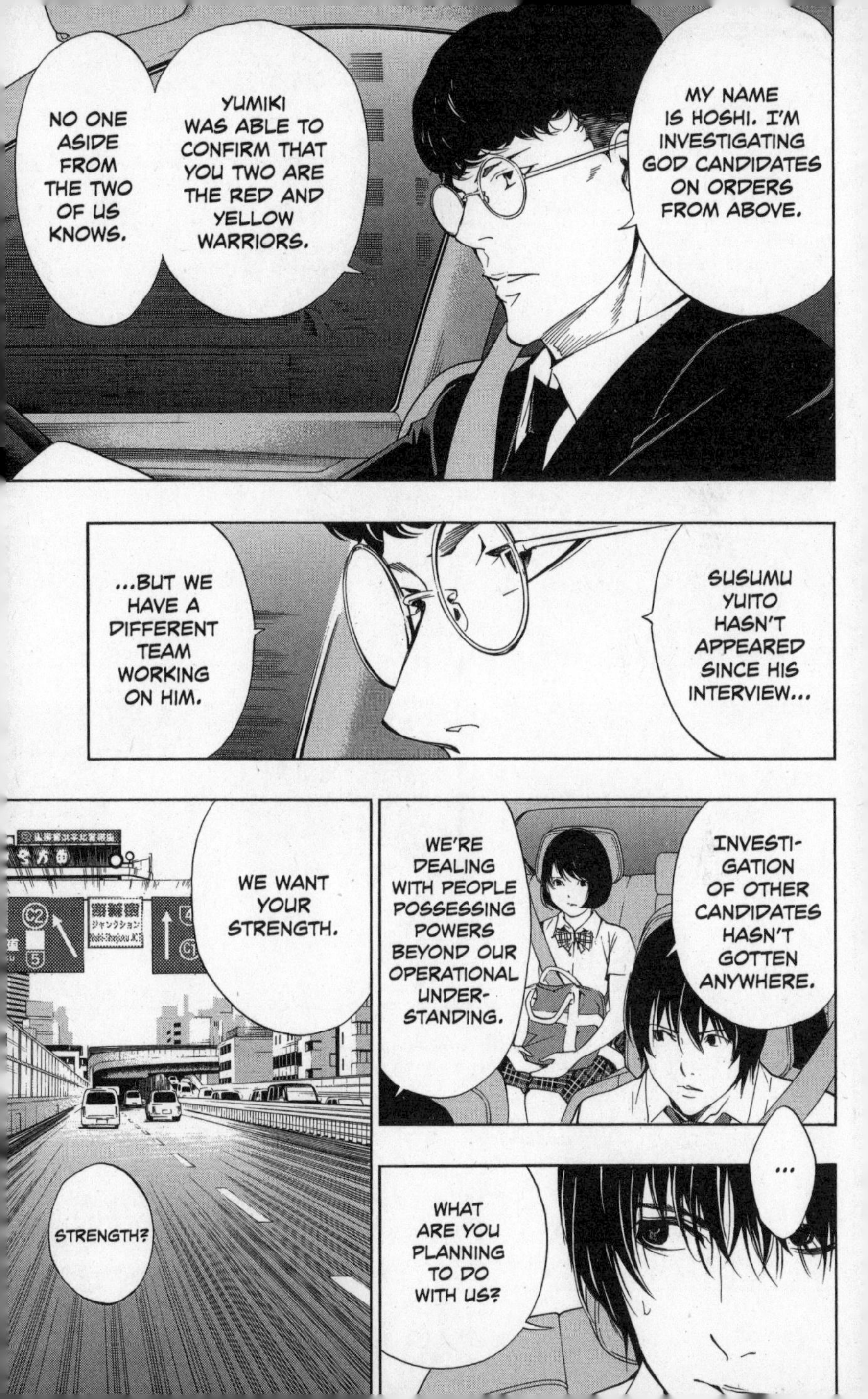
MY NAME IS HOSHI. I'M INVESTIGATING GOD CANDIDATES ON ORDERS FROM ABOVE.
YUMIKI WAS ABLE TO CONFIRM THAT YOU TWO ARE THE RED AND YELLOW WARRIORS.
NO ONE ASIDE FROM THE TWO OF US KNOWS.
SUSUMU YUITO HASN'T APPEARED SINCE HIS INTERVIEW...
...BUT WE HAVE A DIFFERENT TEAM WORKING ON HIM.
INVESTI-GATION OF OTHER CANDIDATES HASN'T GOTTEN ANYWHERE.
WE'RE DEALING WITH PEOPLE POSSESSING POWERS BEYOND OUR OPERATIONAL UNDER-STANDING.
...
WHAT ARE YOU PLANNING TO DO WITH US?
WE WANT YOUR STRENGTH.
STRENGTH?

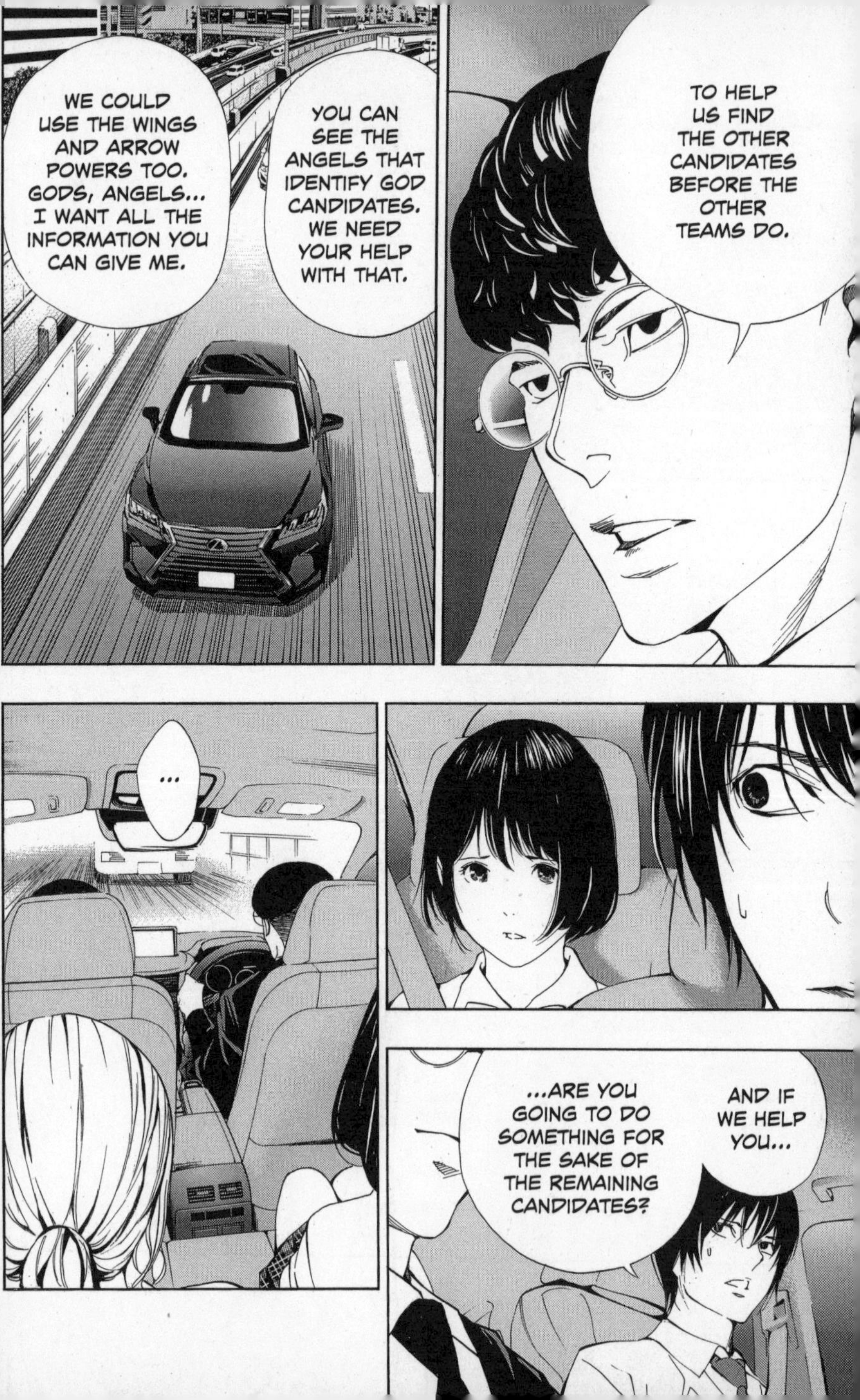
TO HELP US FIND THE OTHER CANDIDATES BEFORE THE OTHER TEAMS DO.
YOU CAN SEE THE ANGELS THAT IDENTIFY GOD CANDIDATES. WE NEED YOUR HELP WITH THAT.
WE COULD USE THE WINGS AND ARROW POWERS TOO. GODS, ANGELS... I WANT ALL THE INFORMATION YOU CAN GIVE ME.
AND IF WE HELP YOU...
...ARE YOU GOING TO DO SOMETHING FOR THE SAKE OF THE REMAINING CANDIDATES?
...

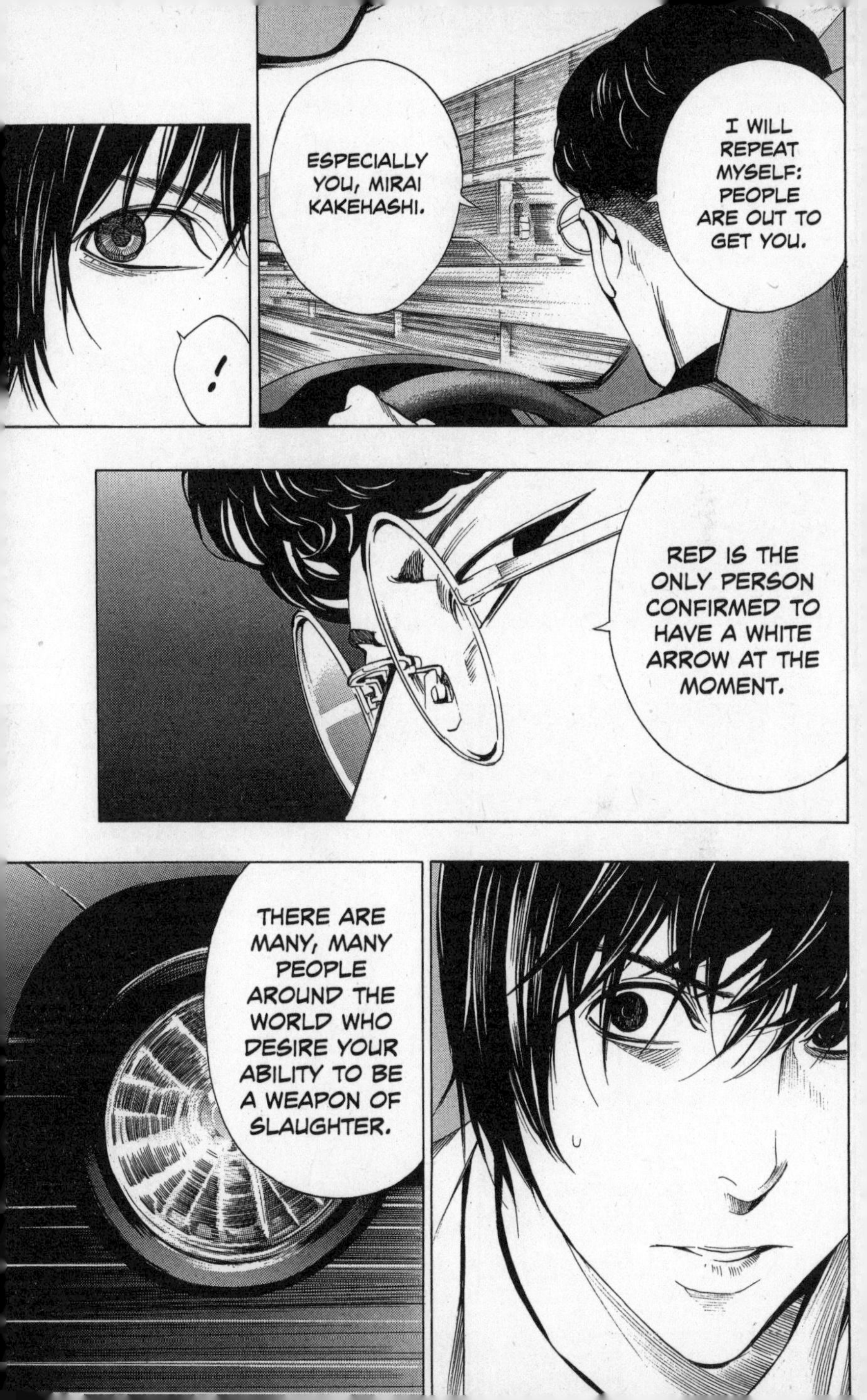
I WILL REPEAT MYSELF: PEOPLE ARE OUT TO GET YOU.
ESPECIALLY YOU, MIRAI KAKEHASHI.
!
RED IS THE ONLY PERSON CONFIRMED TO HAVE A WHITE ARROW AT THE MOMENT.
THERE ARE MANY, MANY PEOPLE AROUND THE WORLD WHO DESIRE YOUR ABILITY TO BE A WEAPON OF SLAUGHTER.

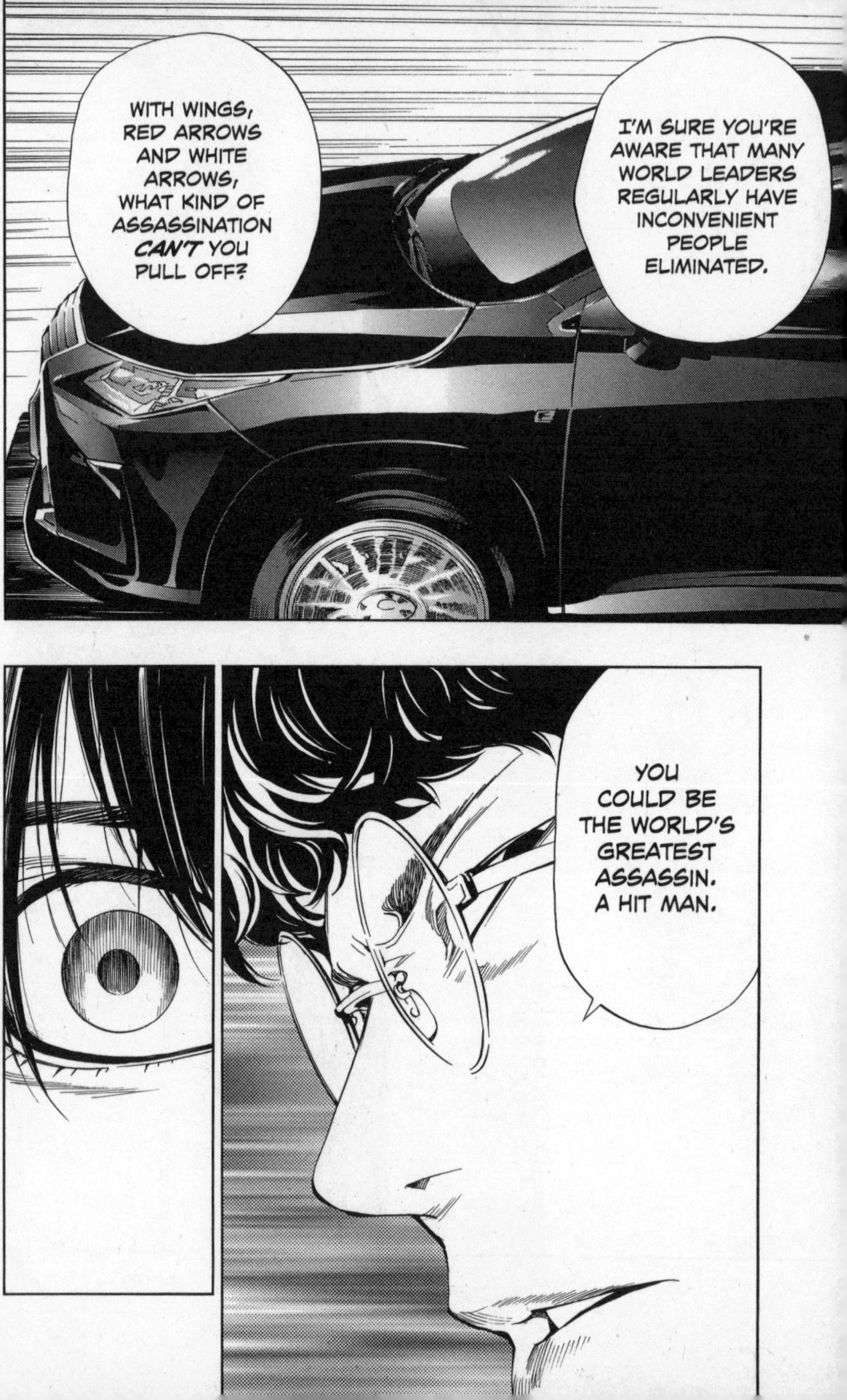
I'M SURE YOU'RE AWARE THAT MANY WORLD LEADERS REGULARLY HAVE INCONVENIENT PEOPLE ELIMINATED.
WITH WINGS, RED ARROWS AND WHITE ARROWS, WHAT KIND OF ASSASSINATION *CAN'T* YOU PULL OFF?
YOU COULD BE THE WORLD'S GREATEST ASSASSIN. A HIT MAN.

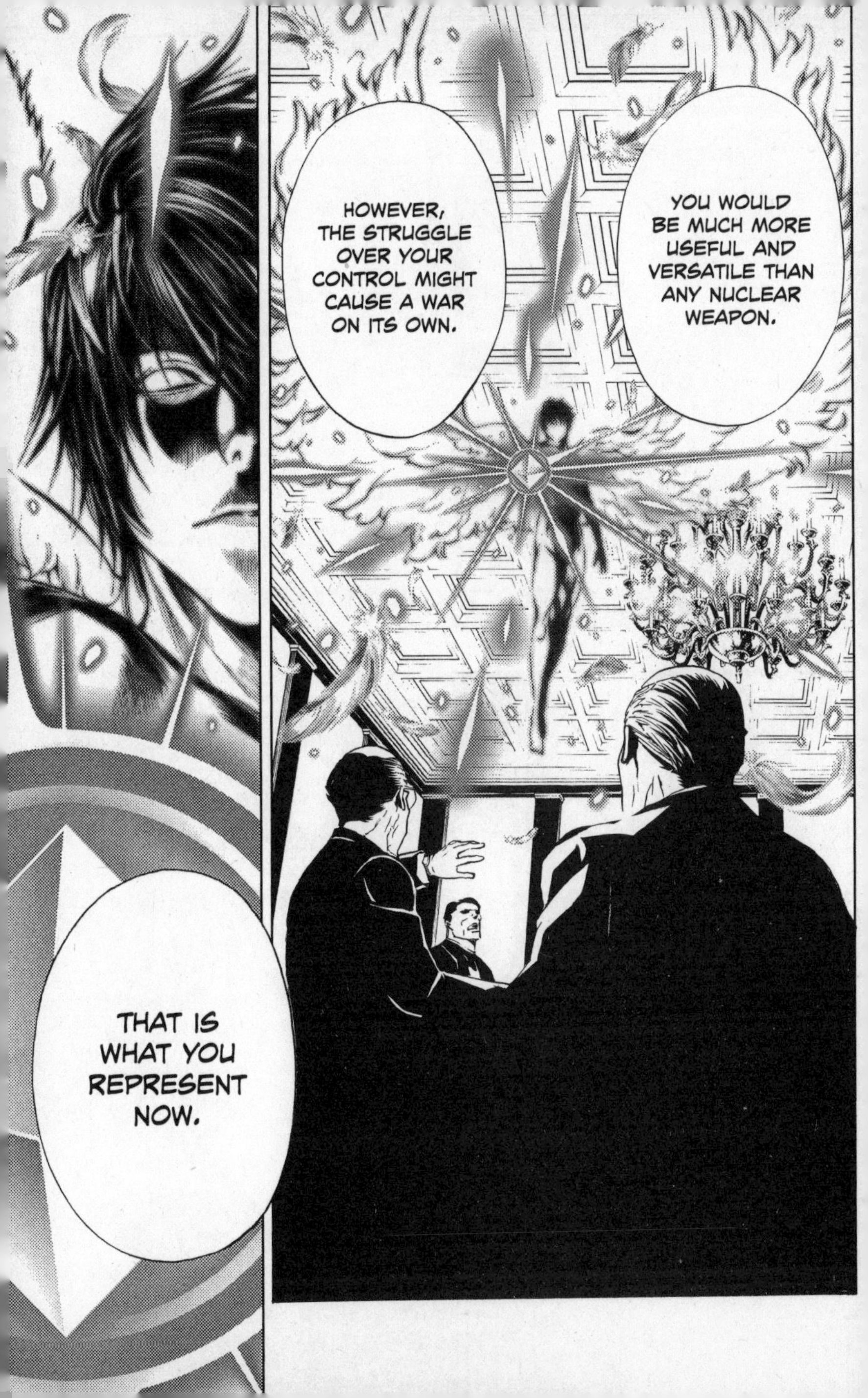
YOU WOULD BE MUCH MORE USEFUL AND VERSATILE THAN ANY NUCLEAR WEAPON.
HOWEVER, THE STRUGGLE OVER YOUR CONTROL MIGHT CAUSE A WAR ON ITS OWN.
THAT IS WHAT YOU REPRESENT NOW.

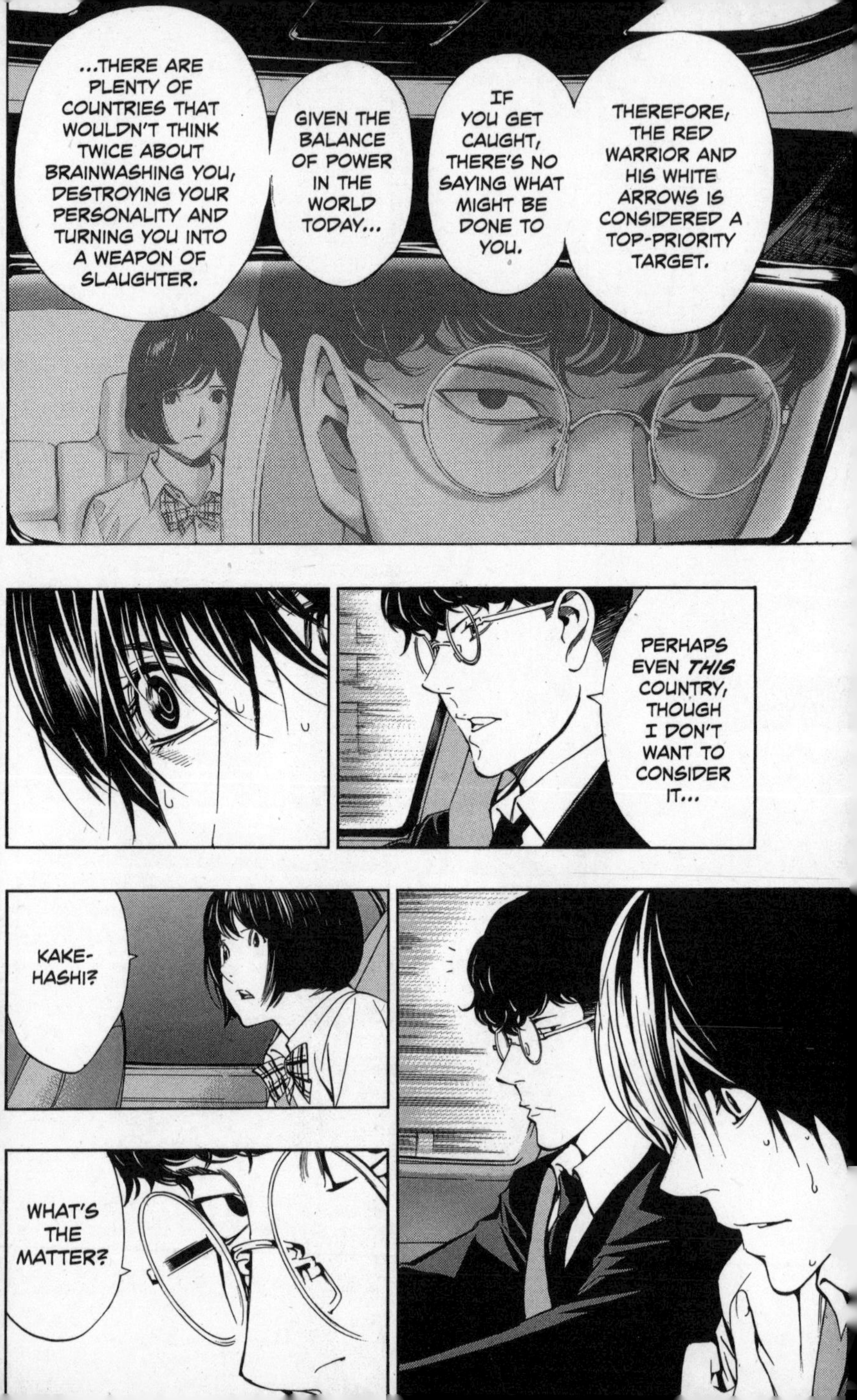
THEREFORE, THE RED WARRIOR AND HIS WHITE ARROWS IS CONSIDERED A TOP-PRIORITY TARGET.
IF YOU GET CAUGHT, THERE'S NO SAYING WHAT MIGHT BE DONE TO YOU.
GIVEN THE BALANCE OF POWER IN THE WORLD TODAY...
...THERE ARE PLENTY OF COUNTRIES THAT WOULDN'T THINK TWICE ABOUT BRAINWASHING YOU, DESTROYING YOUR PERSONALITY AND TURNING YOU INTO A WEAPON OF SLAUGHTER.
PERHAPS EVEN *THIS* COUNTRY, THOUGH I DON'T WANT TO CONSIDER IT...
KAKE-HASHI?
WHAT'S THE MATTER?

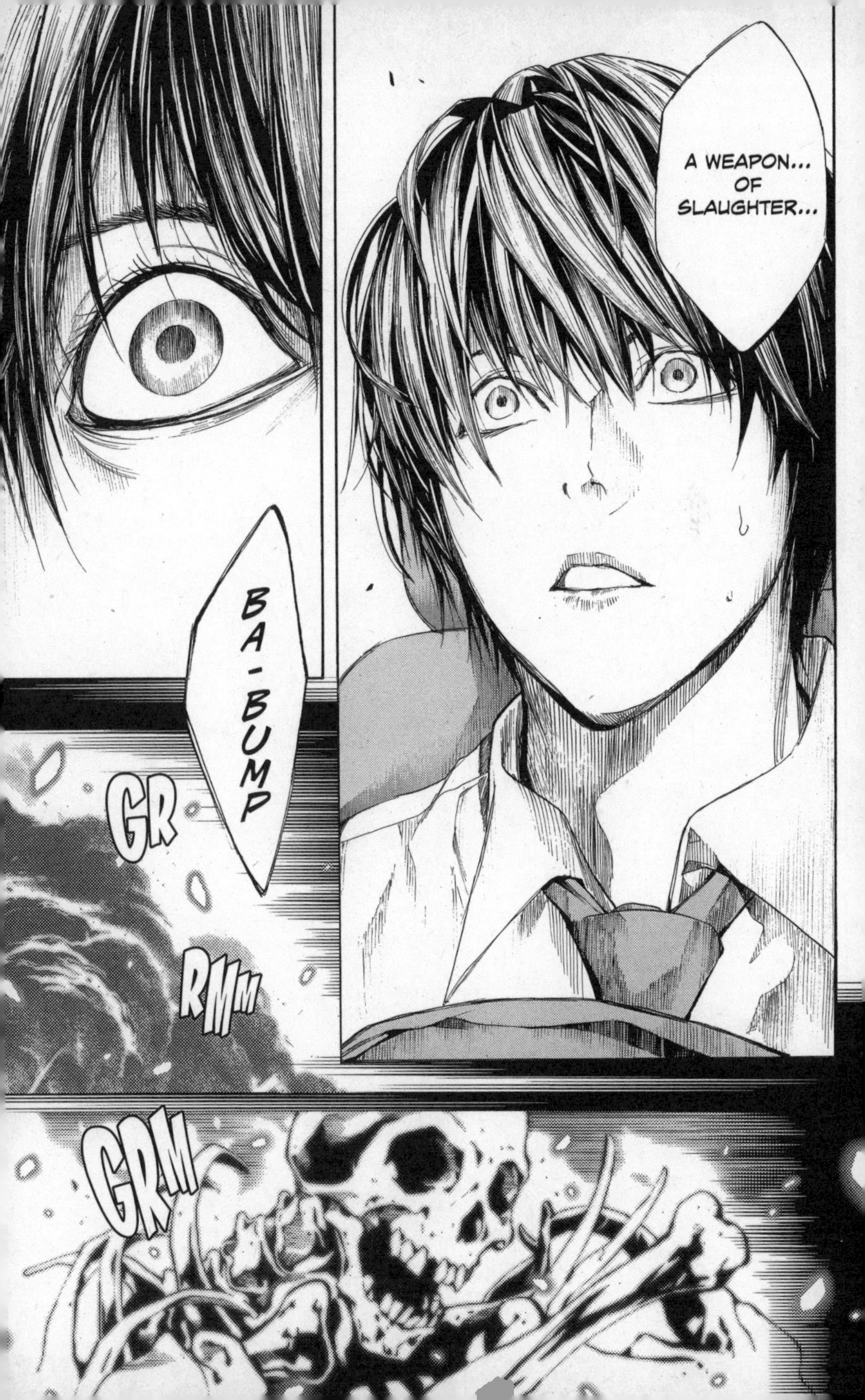
A WEAPON... OF SLAUGHTER...
BA-BUMP
GR
RMM
GRM

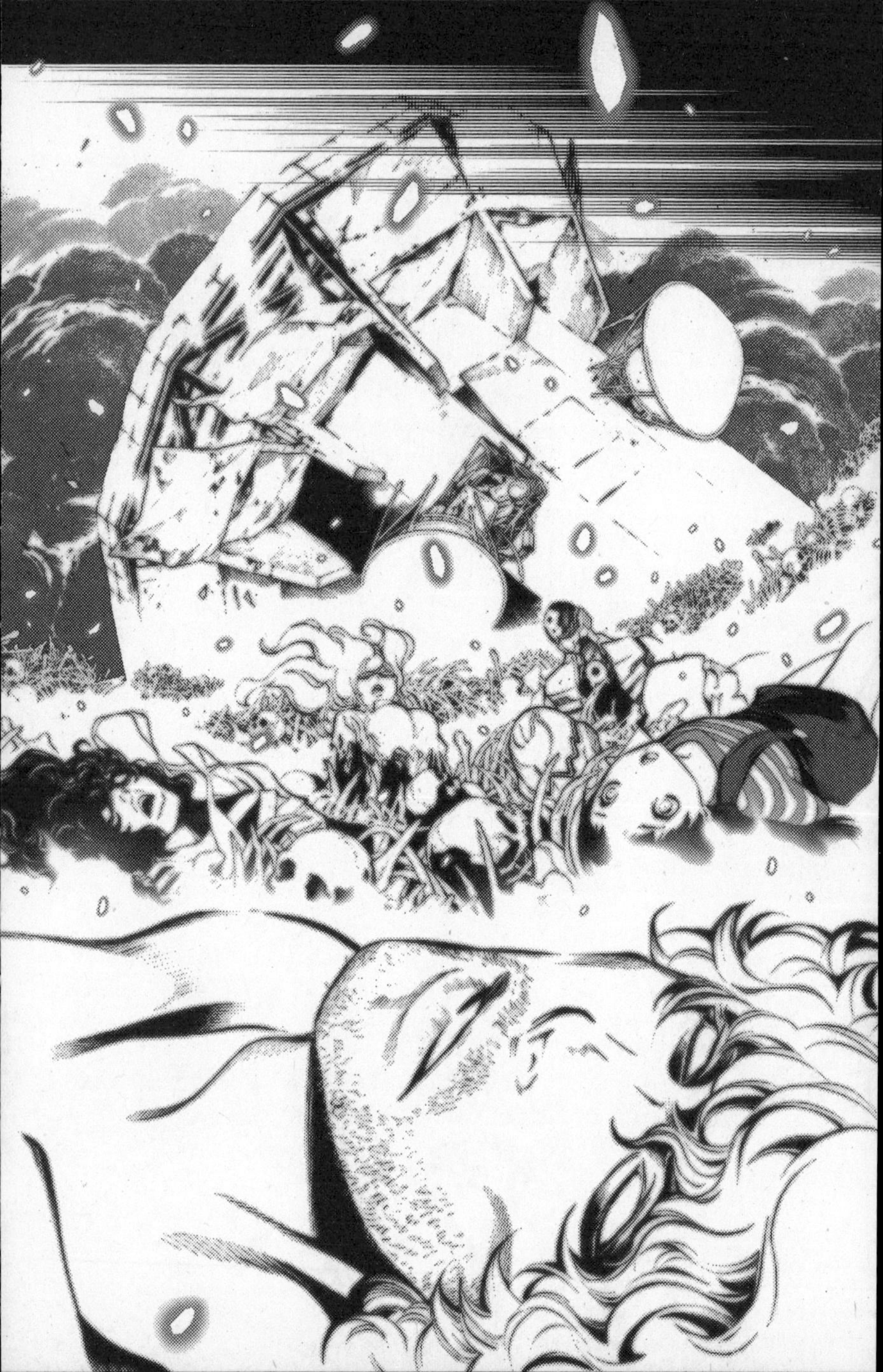

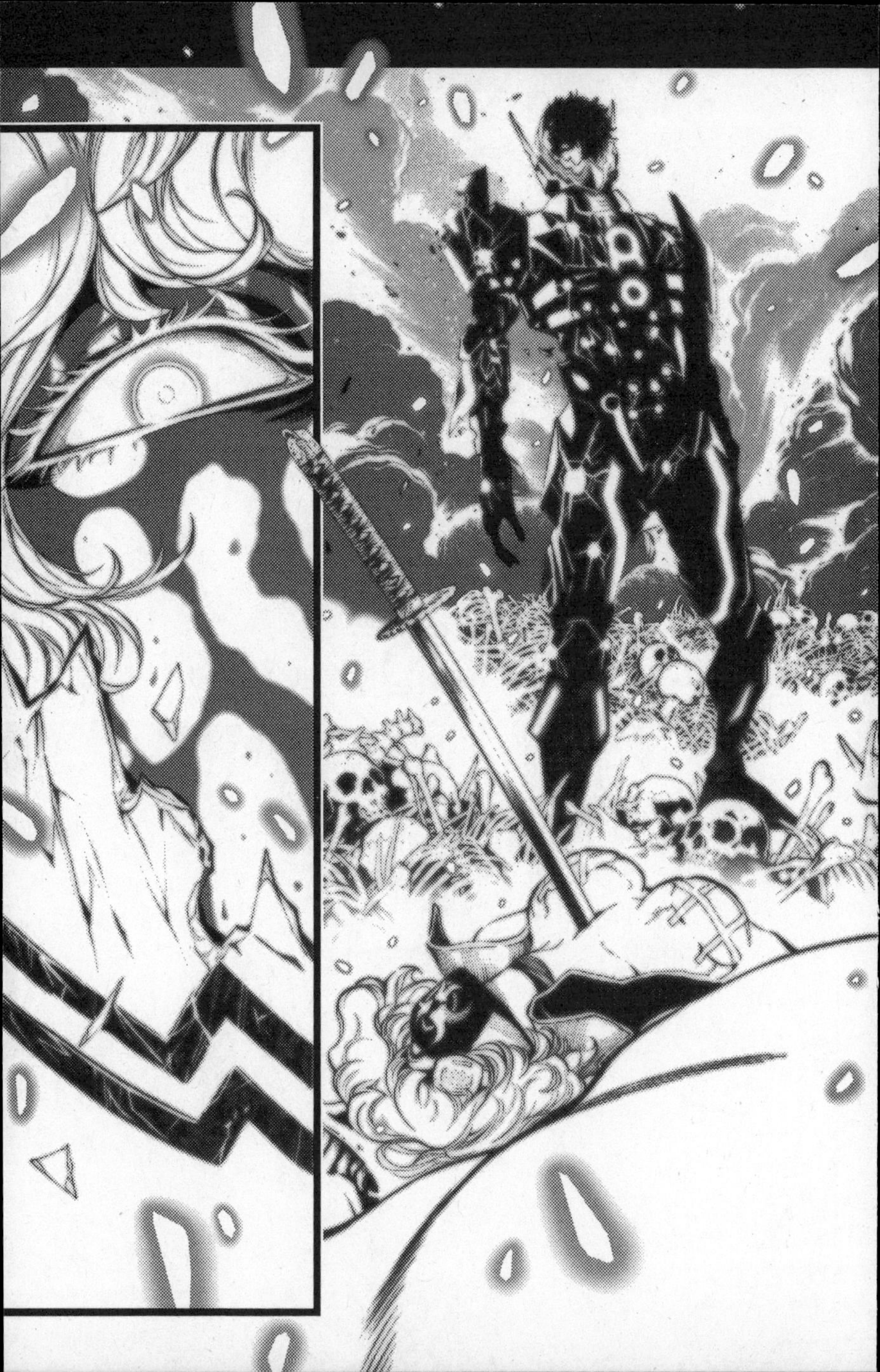

GRP...

....!

HUFF!

HUFF!

I'LL *NEVER* BE THAT...

I WON'T BE LIKE THAT...

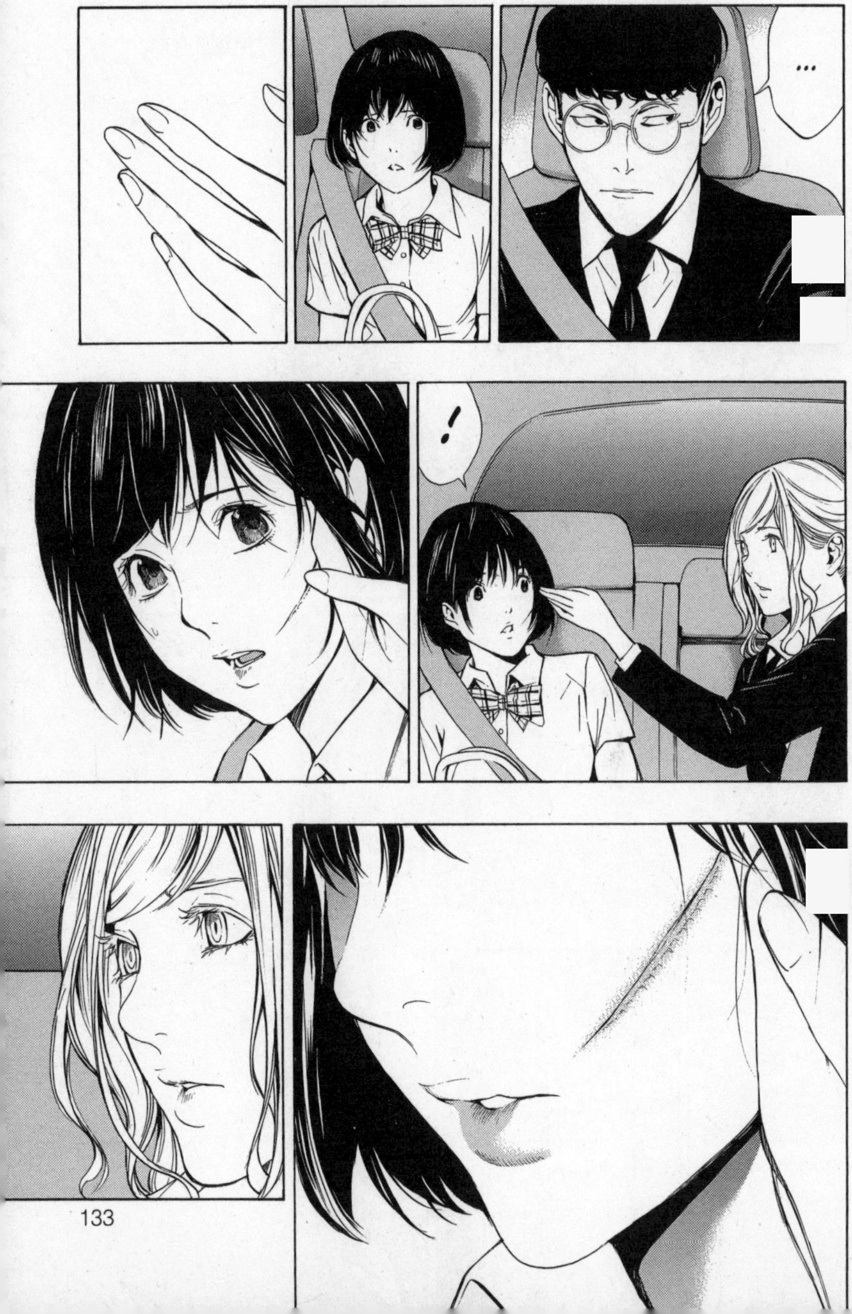
...
!

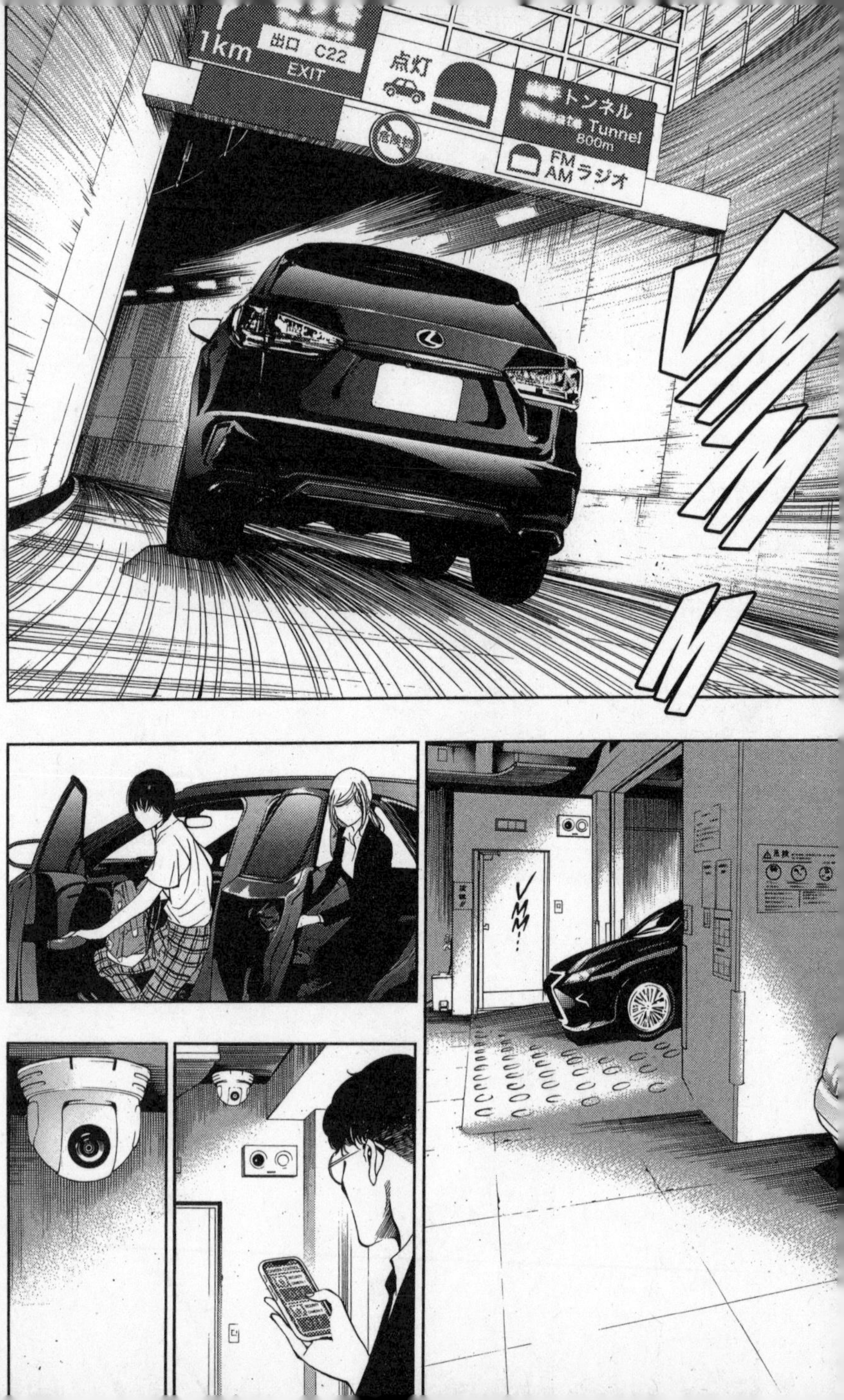
1km
出口 C22
EXIT
点灯
トンネル
Tunnel
800m
FM
AMラジオ
VMMM
VMM!!

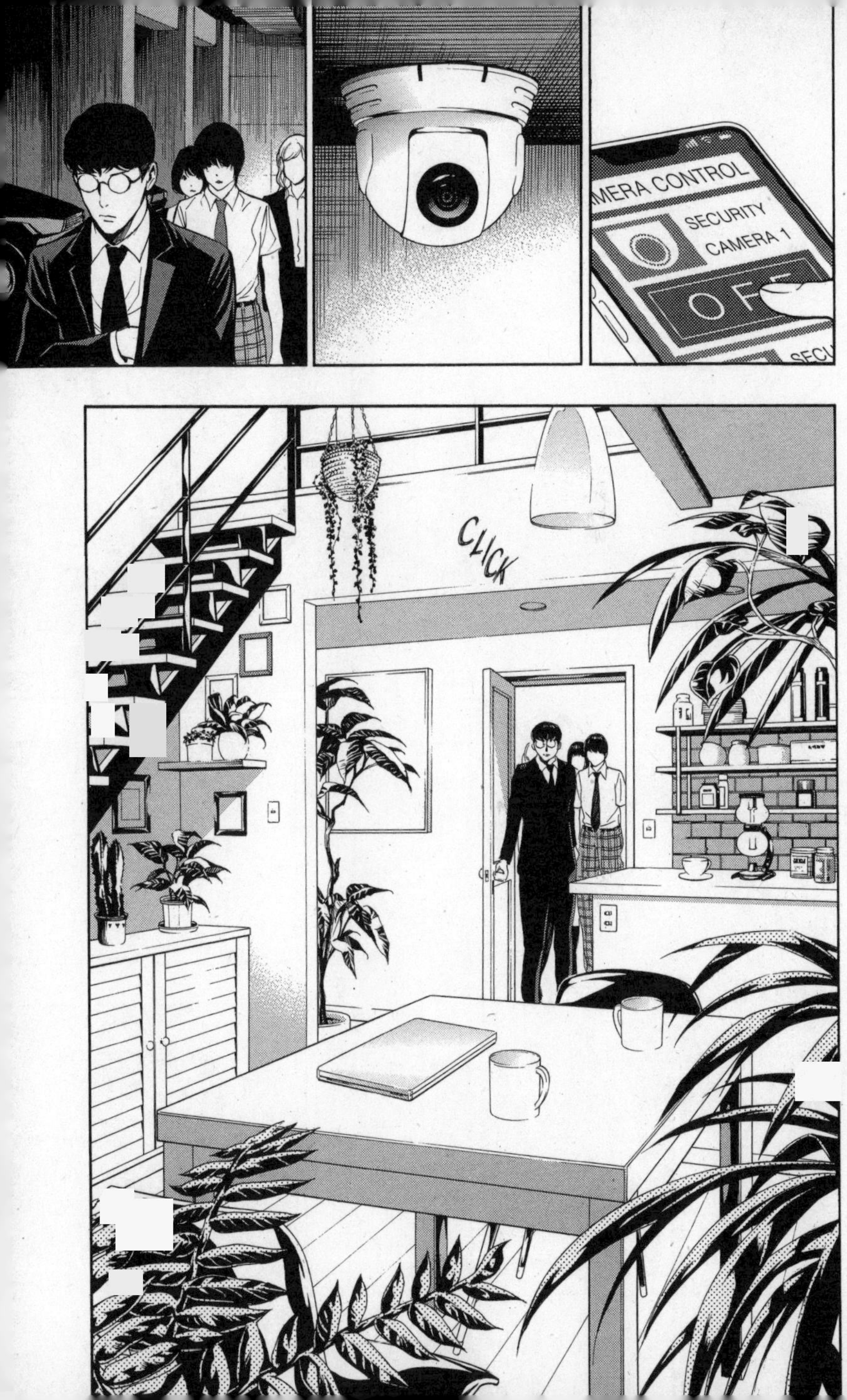
MERA CONTROL
SECURITY
CAMERA 1
CLICK

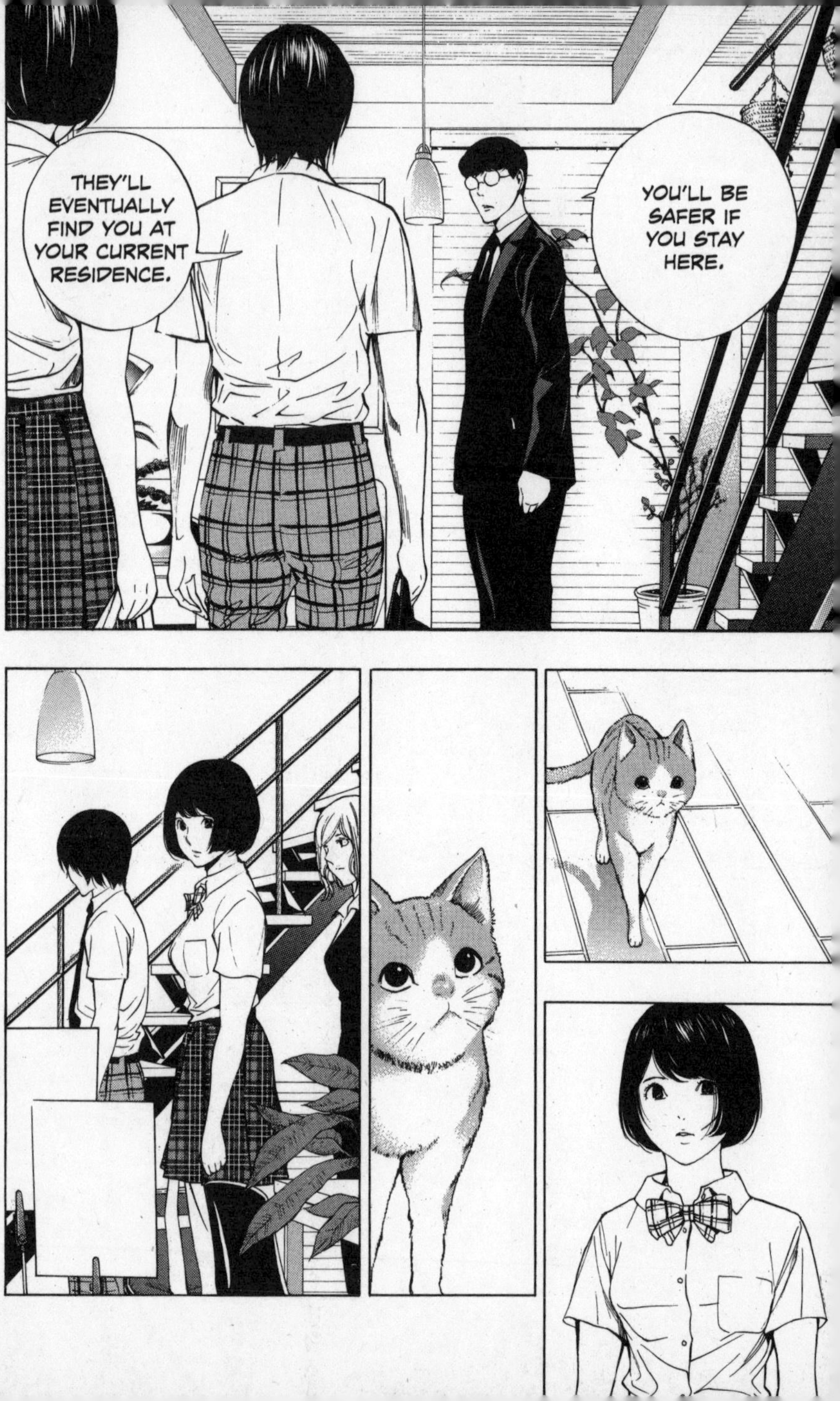
YOU'LL BE SAFER IF YOU STAY HERE.
THEY'LL EVENTUALLY FIND YOU AT YOUR CURRENT RESIDENCE.

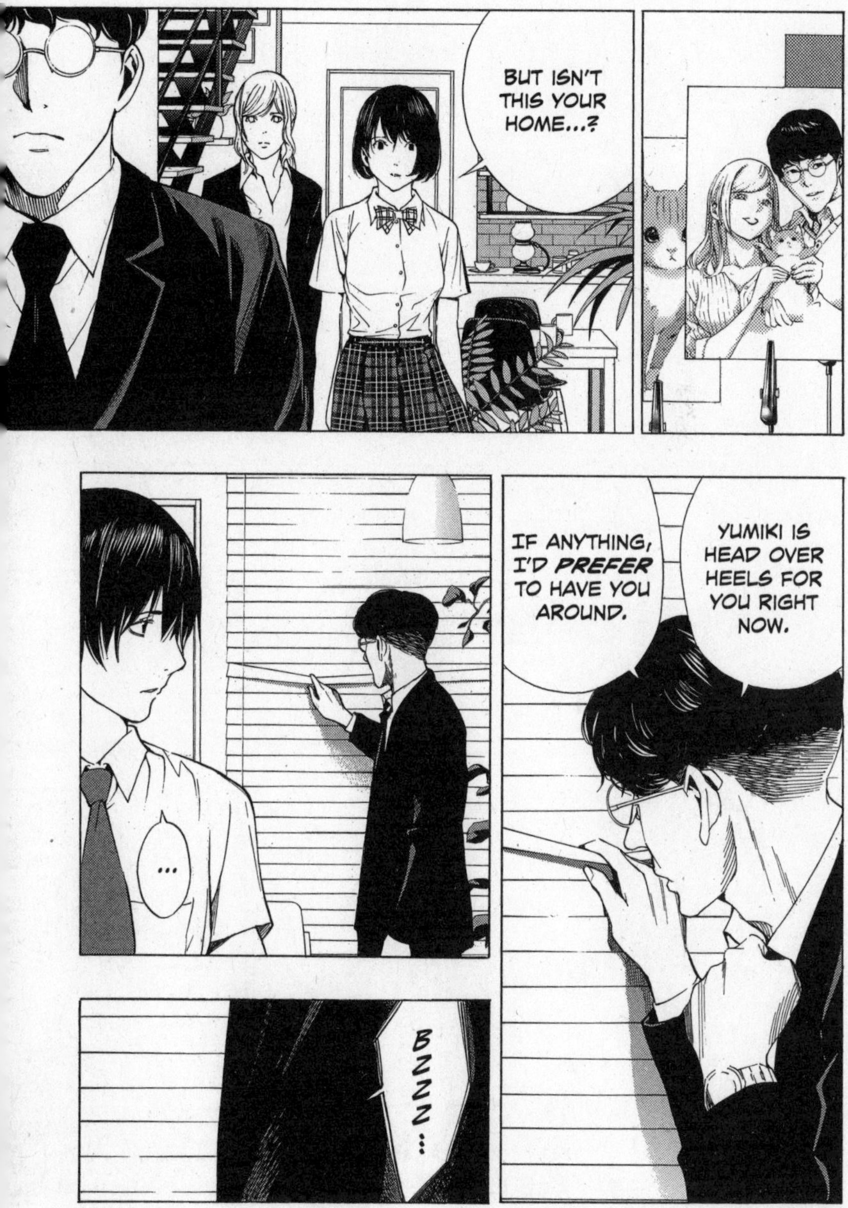
BUT ISN'T THIS YOUR HOME...?
YUMIKI IS HEAD OVER HEELS FOR YOU RIGHT NOW.
IF ANYTHING, I'D *PREFER* TO HAVE YOU AROUND.
...
BZZZ...

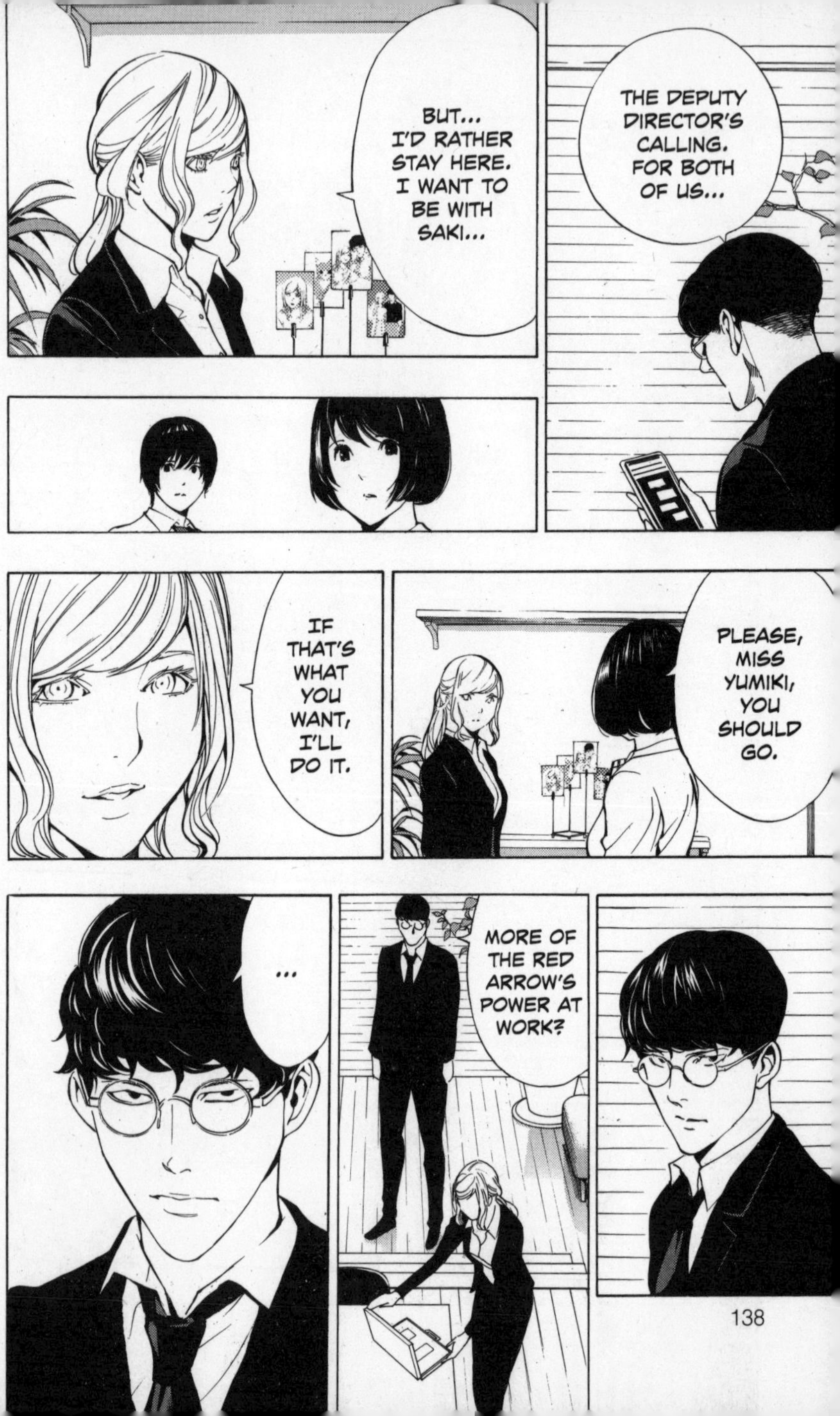
THE DEPUTY DIRECTOR'S CALLING. FOR BOTH OF US...
BUT... I'D RATHER STAY HERE. I WANT TO BE WITH SAKI...
PLEASE, MISS YUMIKI, YOU SHOULD GO.
IF THAT'S WHAT YOU WANT, I'LL DO IT.
MORE OF THE RED ARROW'S POWER AT WORK?
...

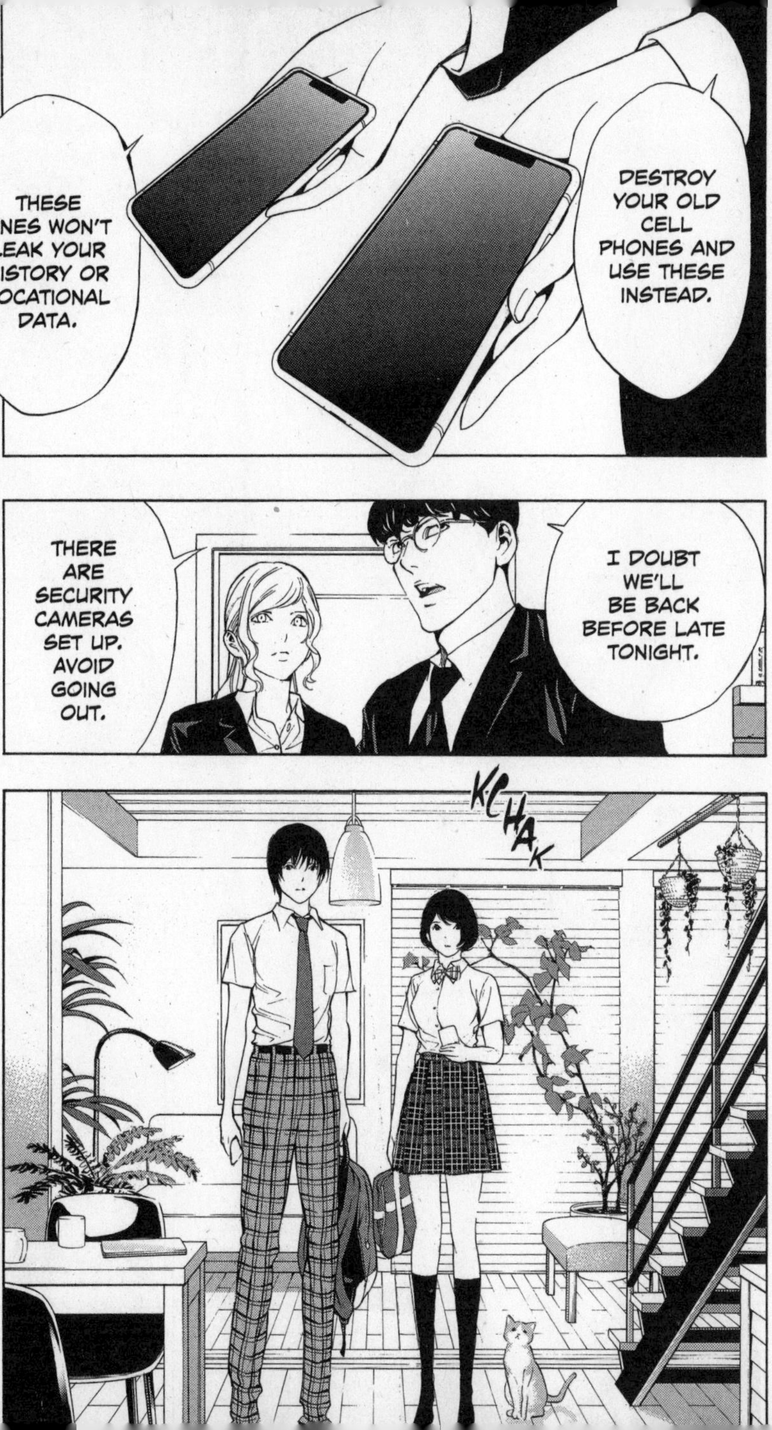
DESTROY YOUR OLD CELL PHONES AND USE THESE INSTEAD.
THESE ONES WON'T LEAK YOUR HISTORY OR LOCATIONAL DATA.
I DOUBT WE'LL BE BACK BEFORE LATE TONIGHT.
THERE ARE SECURITY CAMERAS SET UP. AVOID GOING OUT.
K-CHAK

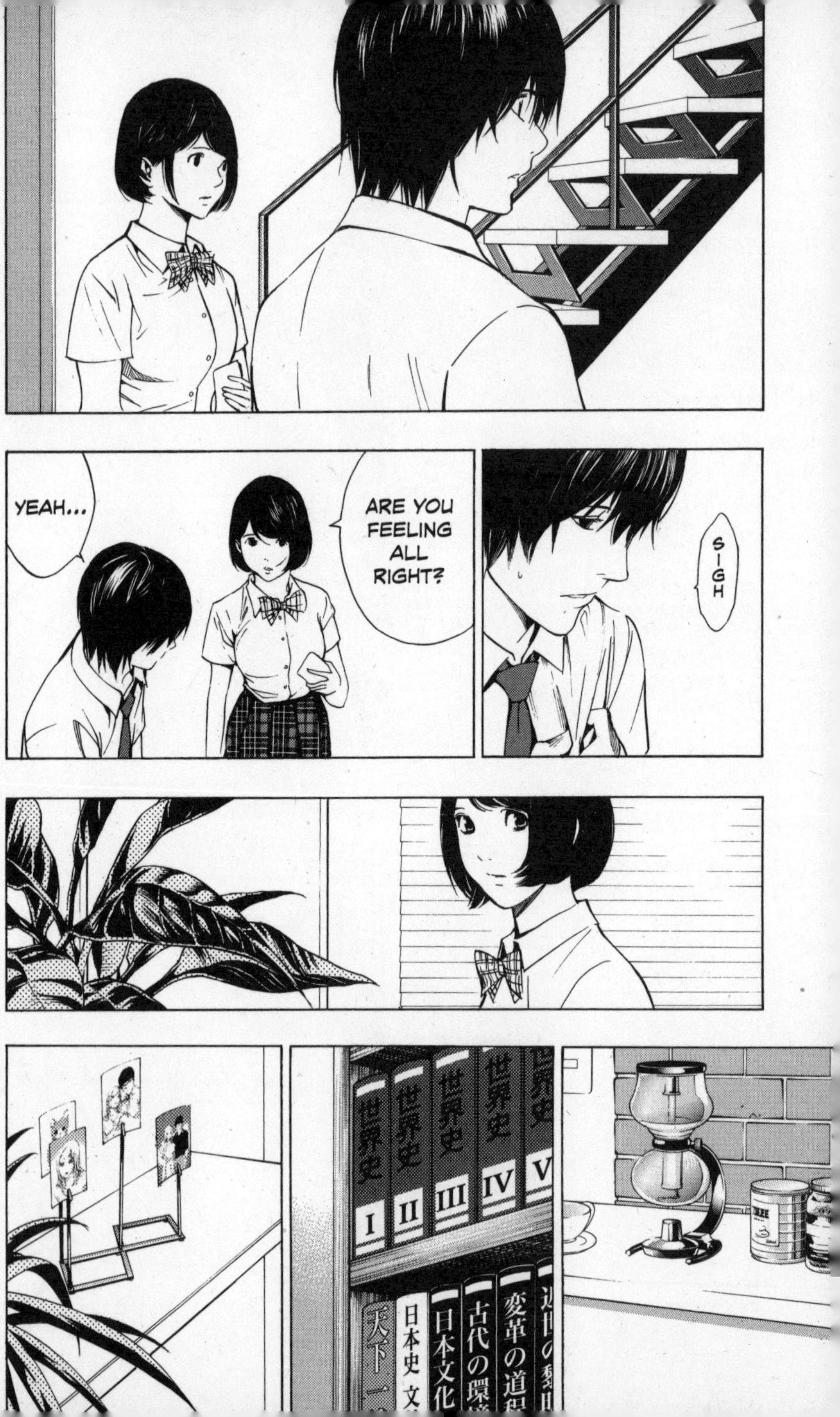

SIGH
ARE YOU FEELING ALL RIGHT?
YEAH...
世界史 I
世界史 II
世界史 III
世界史 IV
世界史 V

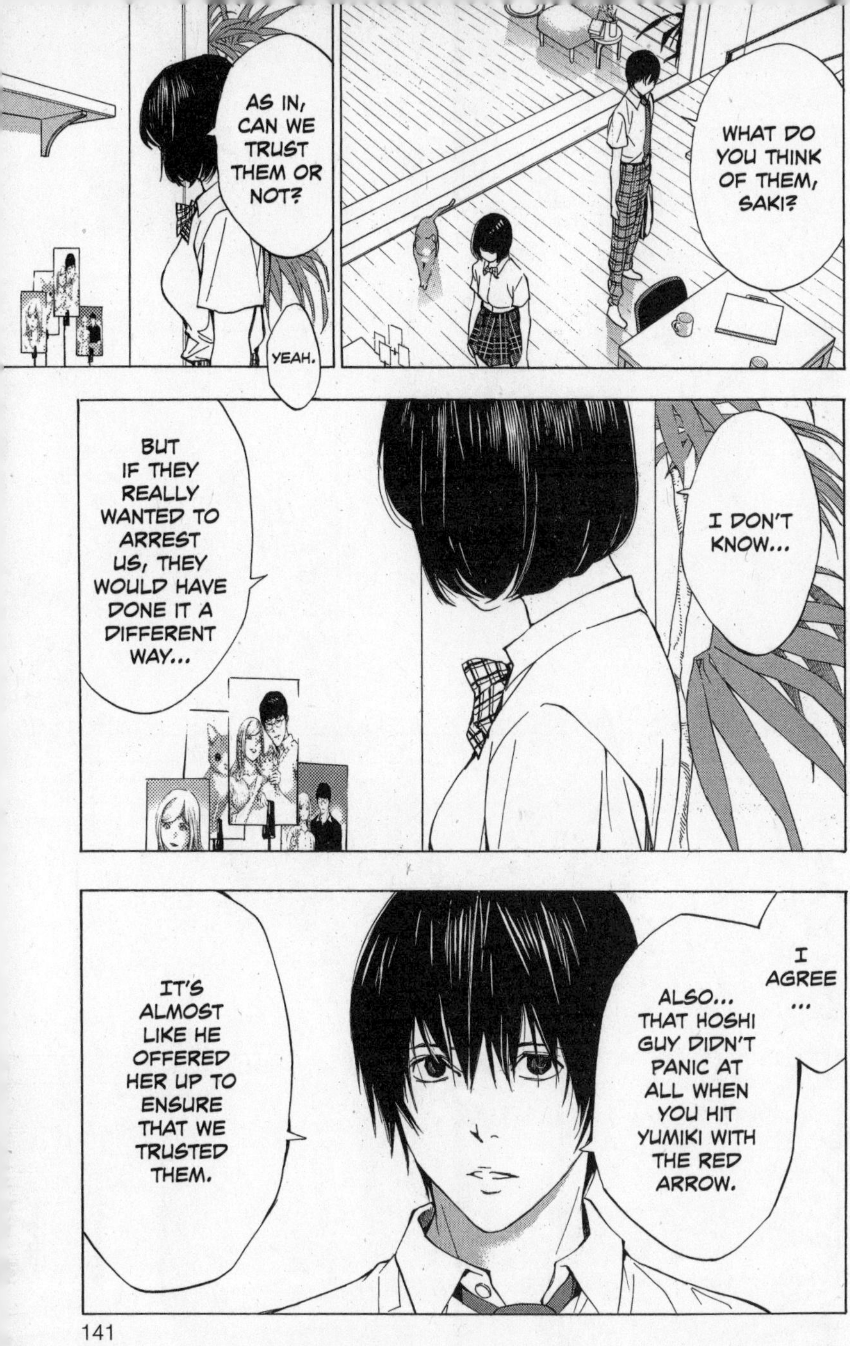
WHAT DO YOU THINK OF THEM, SAKI?
AS IN, CAN WE TRUST THEM OR NOT?
YEAH.
I DON'T KNOW...
BUT IF THEY REALLY WANTED TO ARREST US, THEY WOULD HAVE DONE IT A DIFFERENT WAY...
I AGREE...
ALSO... THAT HOSHI GUY DIDN'T PANIC AT ALL WHEN YOU HIT YUMIKI WITH THE RED ARROW.
IT'S ALMOST LIKE HE OFFERED HER UP TO ENSURE THAT WE TRUSTED THEM.

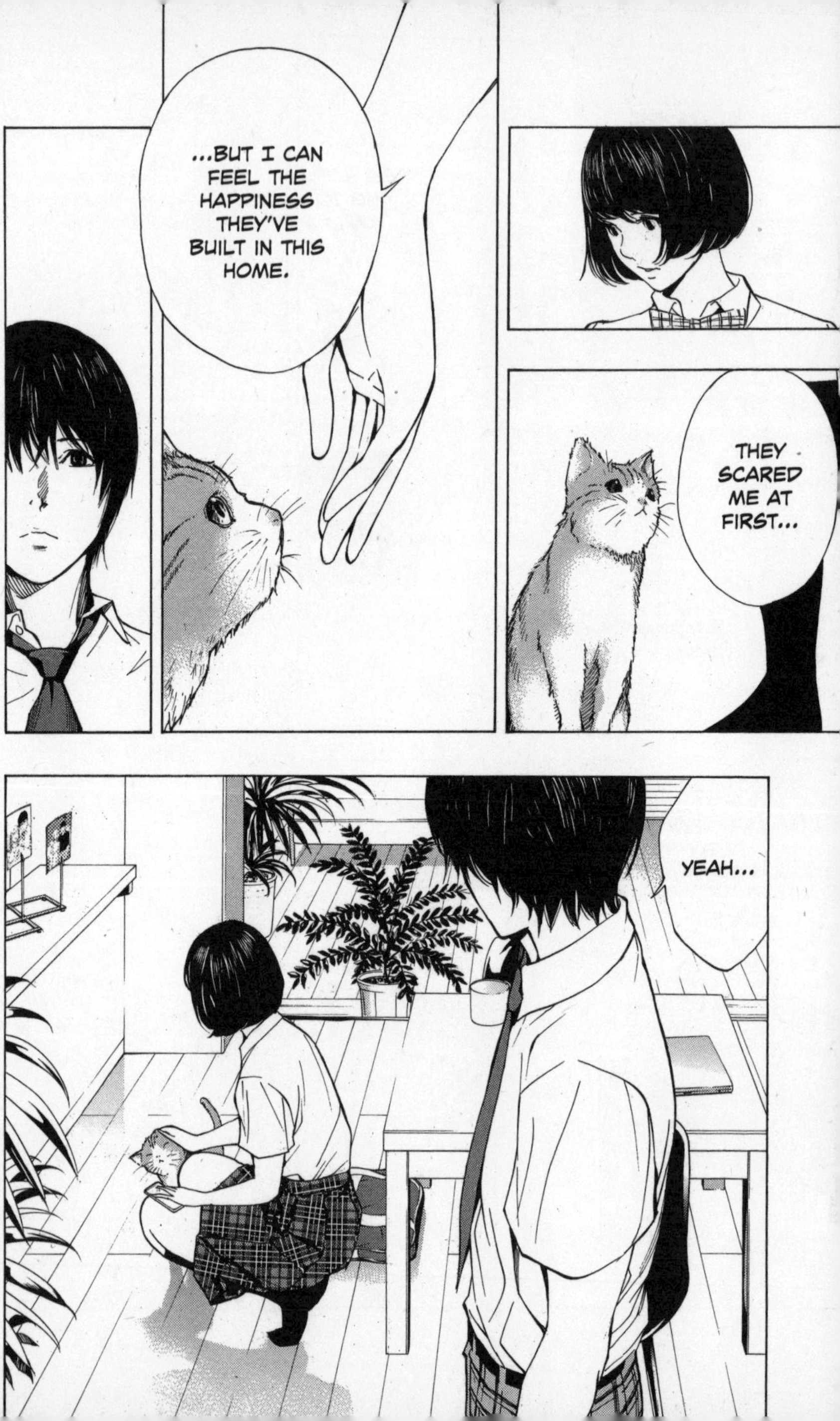
THEY SCARED ME AT FIRST...
...BUT I CAN FEEL THE HAPPINESS THEY'VE BUILT IN THIS HOME.
YEAH...

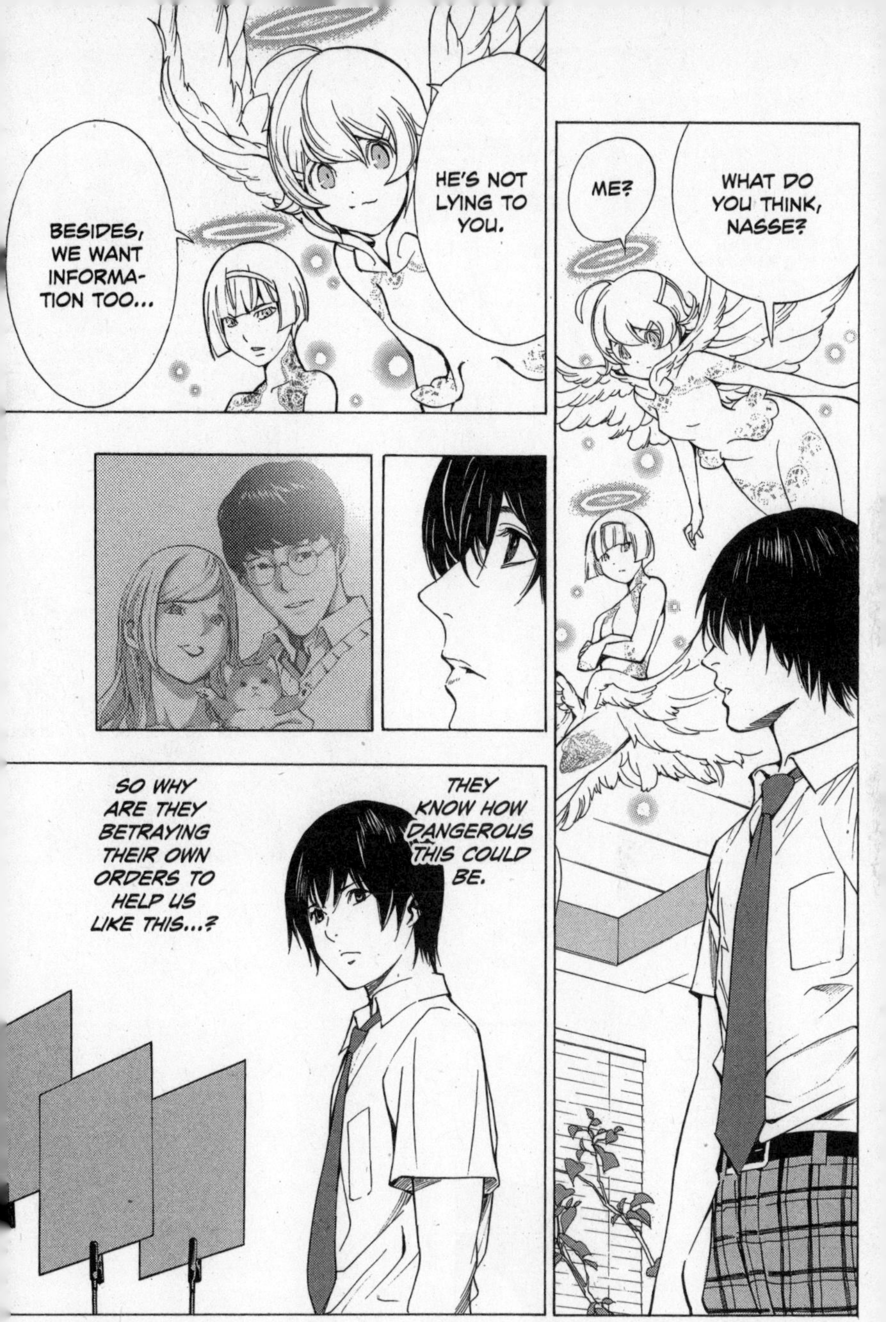
WHAT DO YOU THINK, NASSE?
ME?
HE'S NOT LYING TO YOU.
BESIDES, WE WANT INFORMATION TOO...
THEY KNOW HOW DANGEROUS THIS COULD BE.
SO WHY ARE THEY BETRAYING THEIR OWN ORDERS TO HELP US LIKE THIS...?

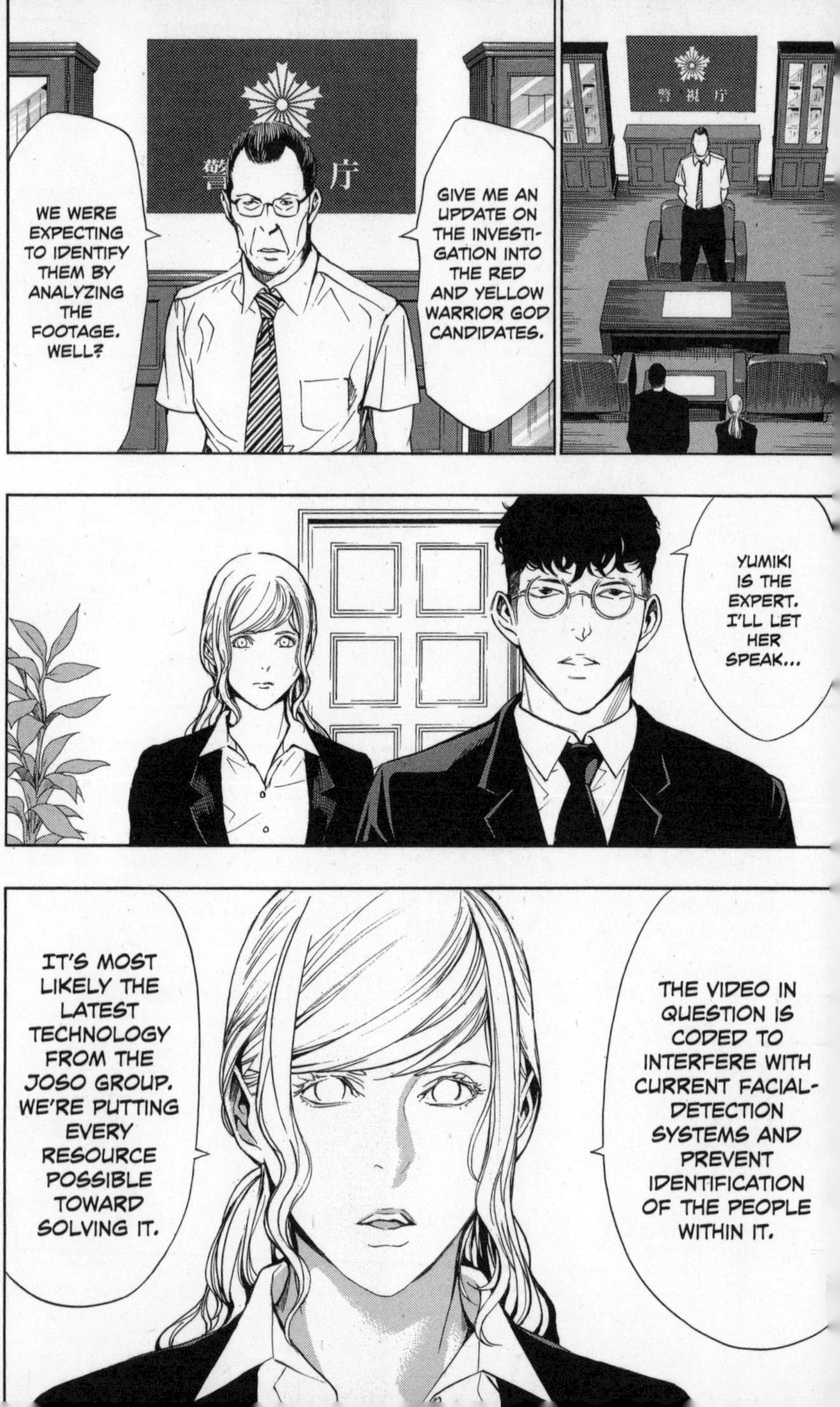
警視庁
GIVE ME AN UPDATE ON THE INVESTIGATION INTO THE RED AND YELLOW WARRIOR GOD CANDIDATES.
WE WERE EXPECTING TO IDENTIFY THEM BY ANALYZING THE FOOTAGE. WELL?
YUMIKI IS THE EXPERT. I'LL LET HER SPEAK...
THE VIDEO IN QUESTION IS CODED TO INTERFERE WITH CURRENT FACIAL-DETECTION SYSTEMS AND PREVENT IDENTIFICATION OF THE PEOPLE WITHIN IT.
IT'S MOST LIKELY THE LATEST TECHNOLOGY FROM THE JOSO GROUP. WE'RE PUTTING EVERY RESOURCE POSSIBLE TOWARD SOLVING IT.

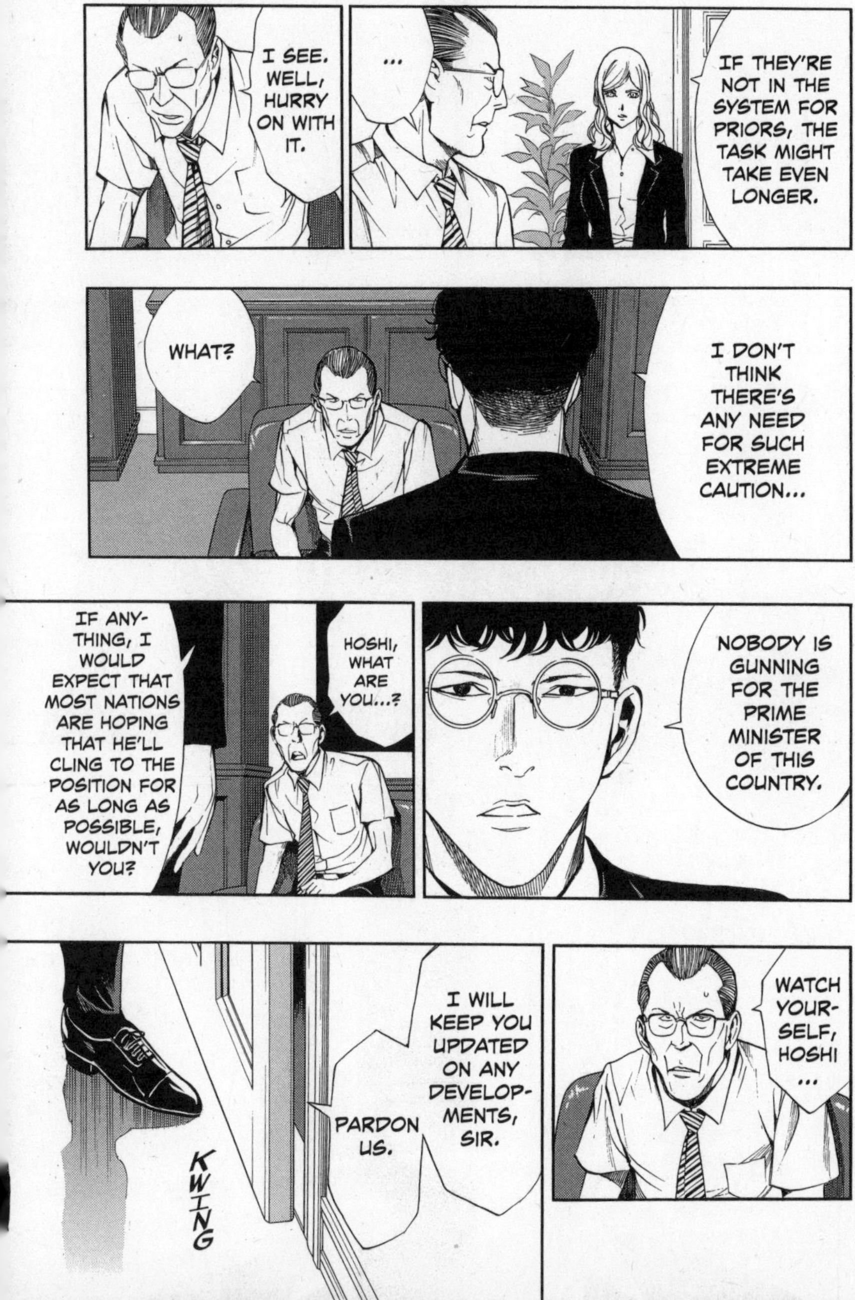

IF THEY'RE NOT IN THE SYSTEM FOR PRIORS, THE TASK MIGHT TAKE EVEN LONGER.
...
I SEE. WELL, HURRY ON WITH IT.
I DON'T THINK THERE'S ANY NEED FOR SUCH EXTREME CAUTION...
WHAT?
NOBODY IS GUNNING FOR THE PRIME MINISTER OF THIS COUNTRY.
HOSHI, WHAT ARE YOU...?
IF ANY-THING, I WOULD EXPECT THAT MOST NATIONS ARE HOPING THAT HE'LL CLING TO THE POSITION FOR AS LONG AS POSSIBLE, WOULDN'T YOU?
WATCH YOUR-SELF, HOSHI...
I WILL KEEP YOU UPDATED ON ANY DEVELOP-MENTS, SIR.
PARDON US.
KWING

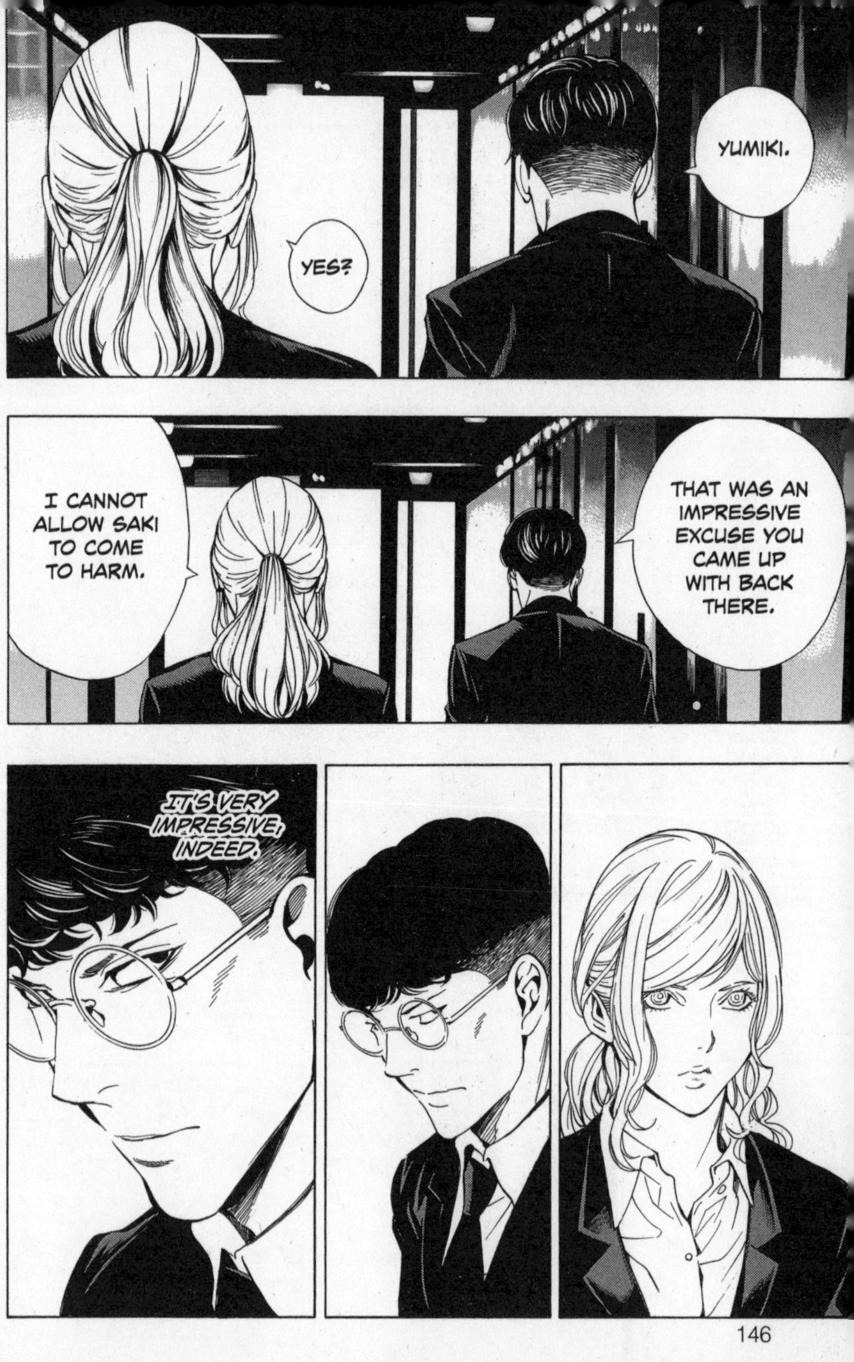
YUMIKI.
YES?
THAT WAS AN IMPRESSIVE EXCUSE YOU CAME UP WITH BACK THERE.
I CANNOT ALLOW SAKI TO COME TO HARM.
IT'S VERY IMPRESSIVE, INDEED.

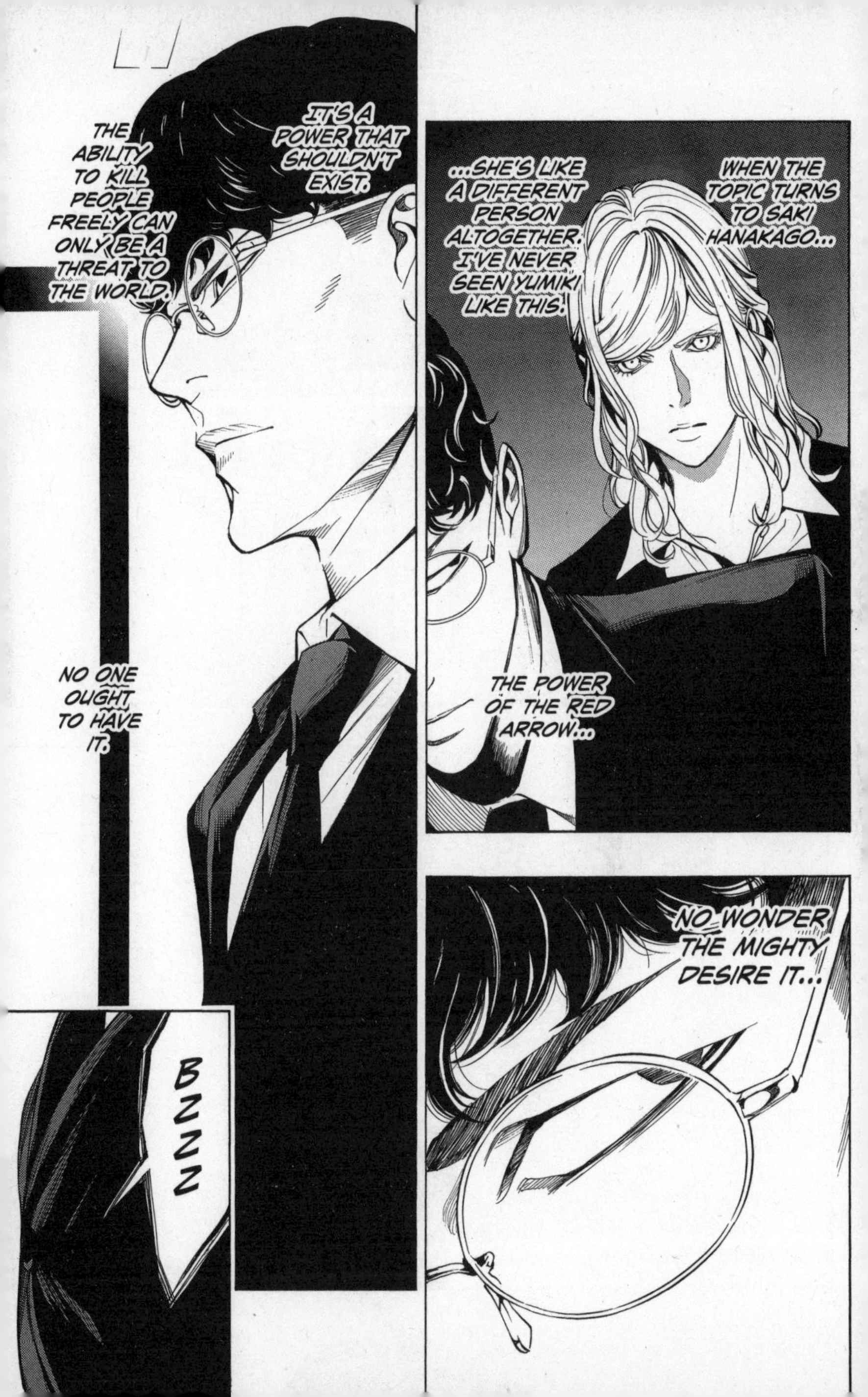
WHEN THE TOPIC TURNS TO SAKI HANAKAGO...
...SHE'S LIKE A DIFFERENT PERSON ALTOGETHER. I'VE NEVER SEEN YUMIKI LIKE THIS.
THE POWER OF THE RED ARROW...
NO WONDER THE MIGHTY DESIRE IT...
IT'S A POWER THAT SHOULDN'T EXIST.
THE ABILITY TO KILL PEOPLE FREELY CAN ONLY BE A THREAT TO THE WORLD.
NO ONE OUGHT TO HAVE IT.
BZZZ

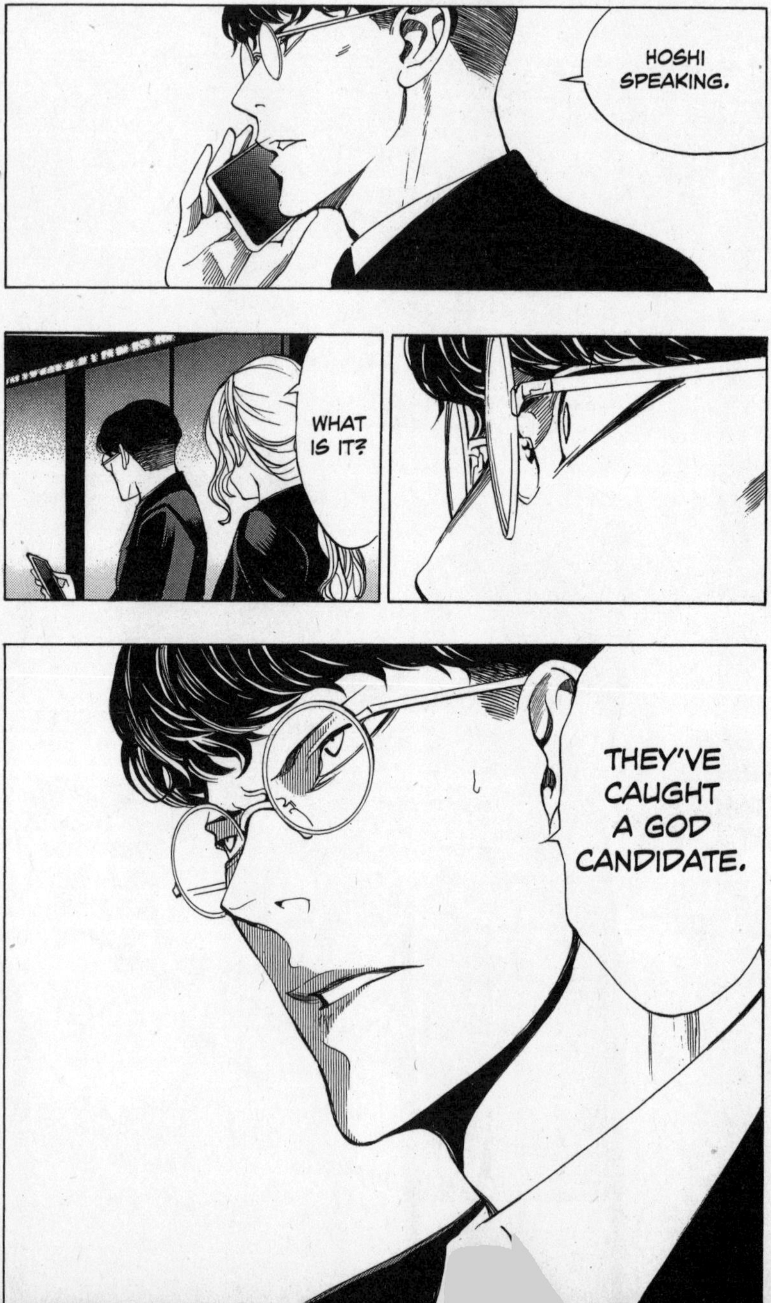
HOSHI SPEAKING.
WHAT IS IT?
THEY'VE CAUGHT A GOD CANDIDATE.

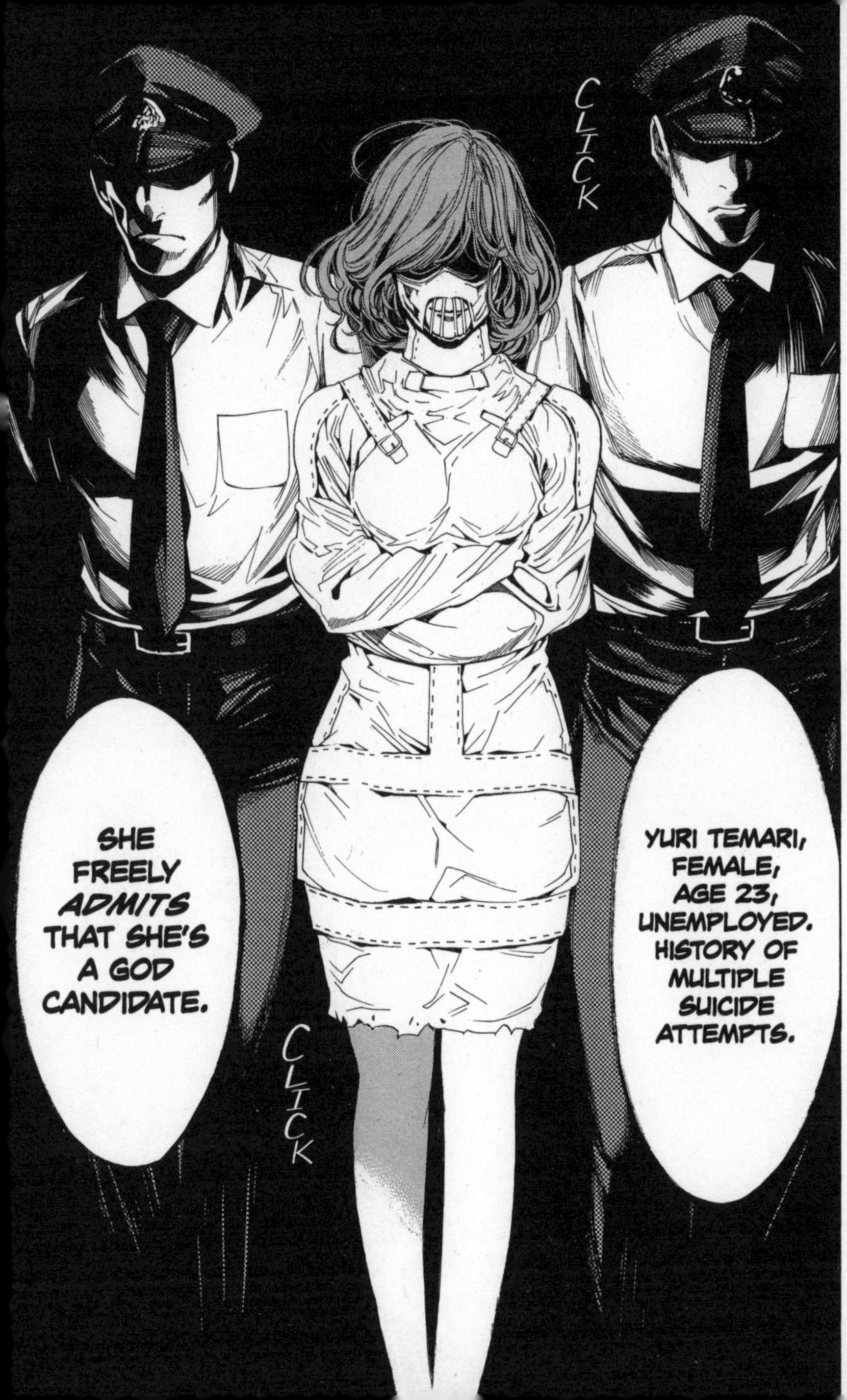
CLICK
YURI TEMARI, FEMALE, AGE 23, UNEMPLOYED. HISTORY OF MULTIPLE SUICIDE ATTEMPTS.
SHE FREELY *ADMITS* THAT SHE'S A GOD CANDIDATE.
CLICK

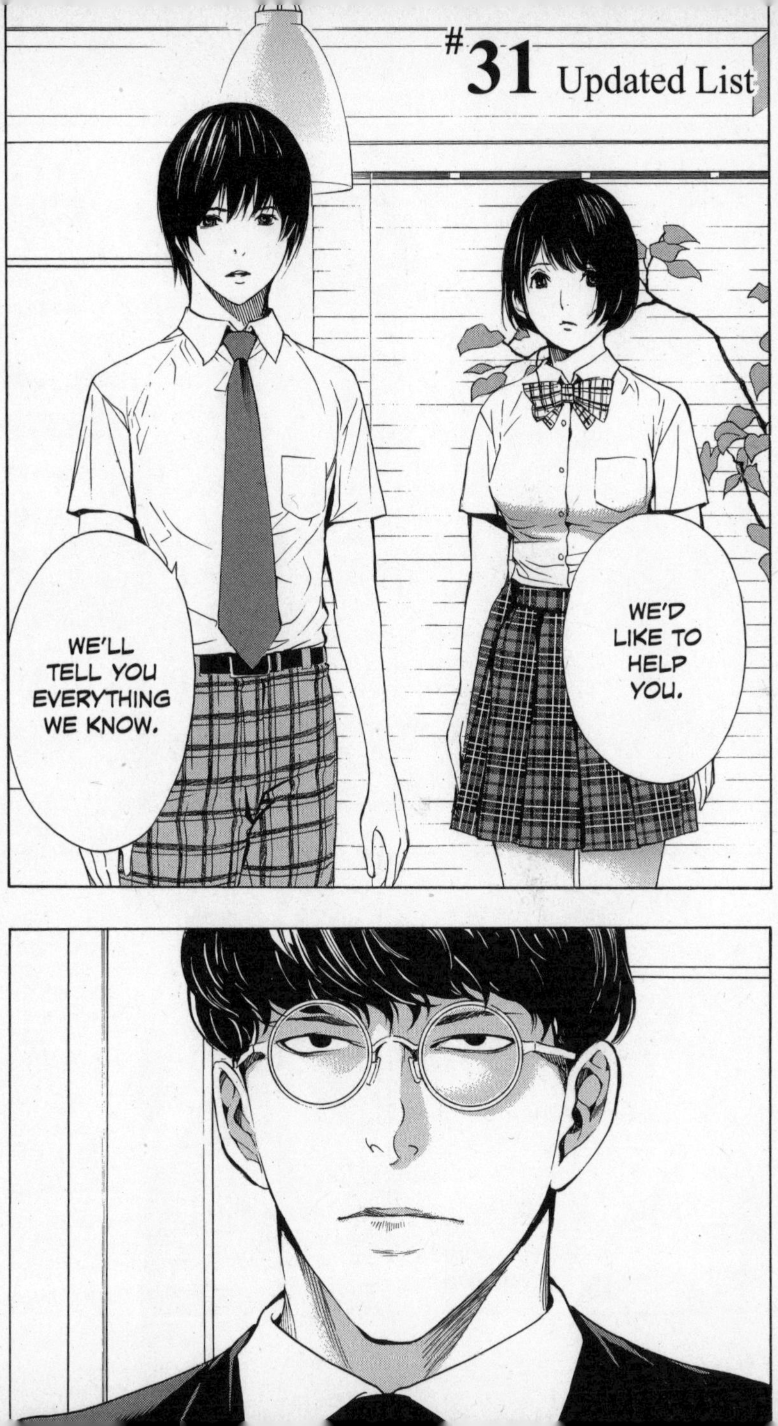
#31 Updated List
WE'D LIKE TO HELP YOU.
WE'LL TELL YOU EVERYTHING WE KNOW.

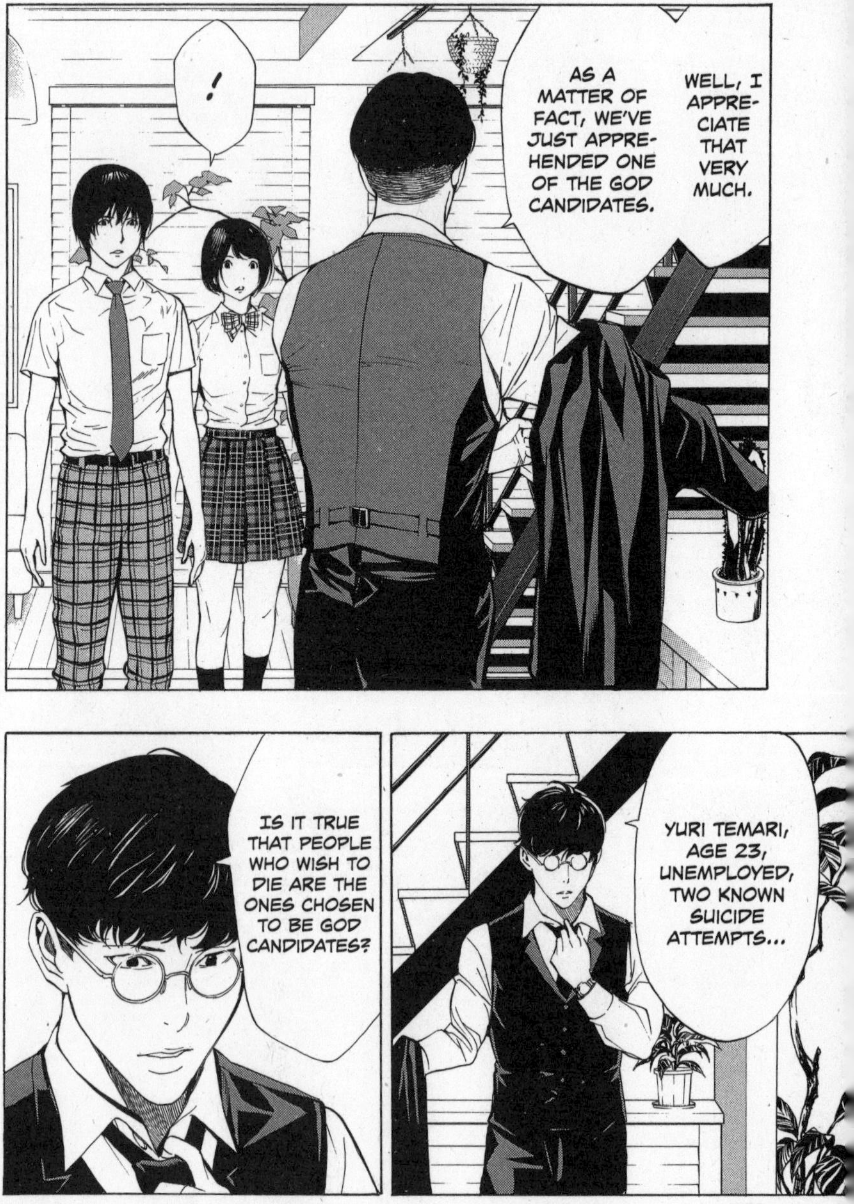
WELL, I APPRECIATE THAT VERY MUCH.
AS A MATTER OF FACT, WE'VE JUST APPREHENDED ONE OF THE GOD CANDIDATES.
!
YURI TEMARI, AGE 23, UNEMPLOYED, TWO KNOWN SUICIDE ATTEMPTS...
IS IT TRUE THAT PEOPLE WHO WISH TO DIE ARE THE ONES CHOSEN TO BE GOD CANDIDATES?

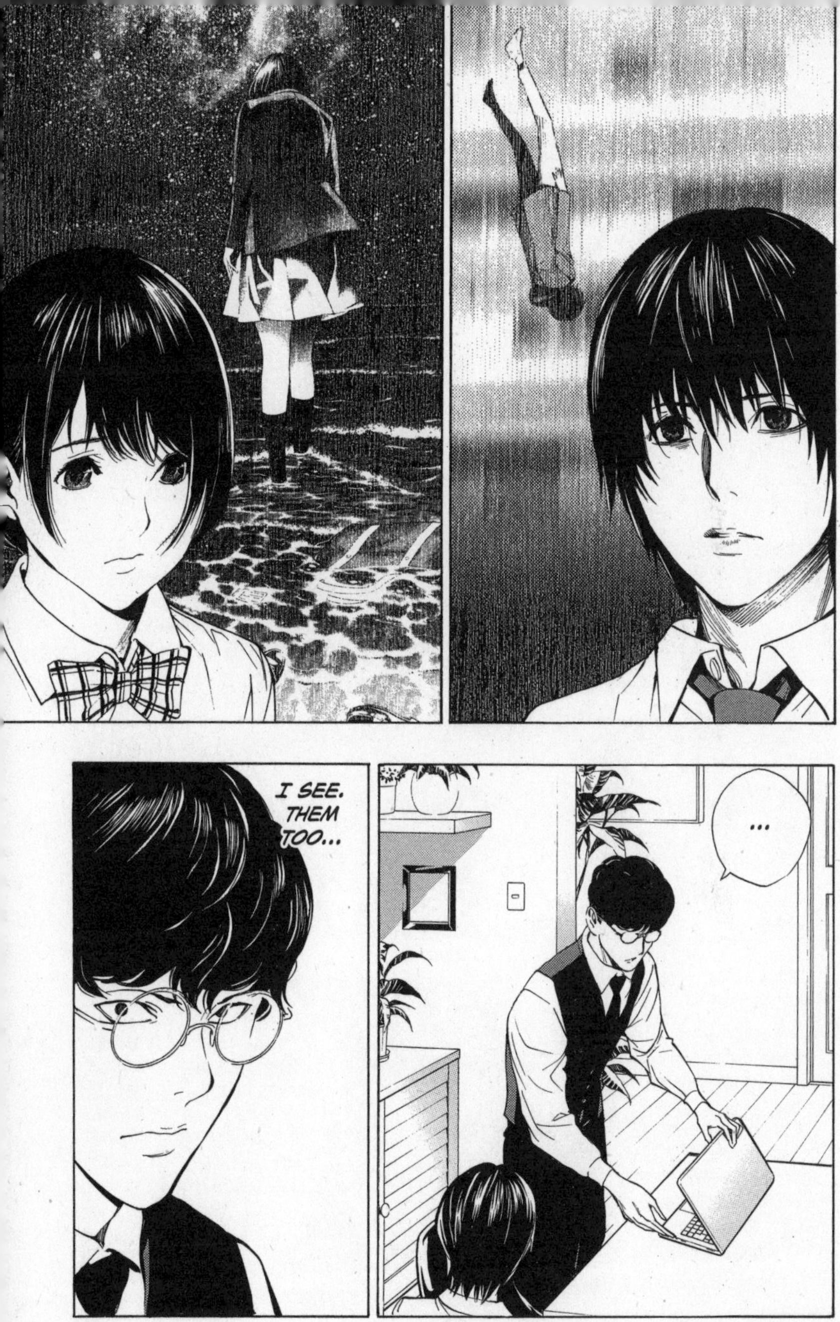
...
I SEE. THEM TOO...

SORRY FOR ASKING.

EVERYONE THINKS ABOUT DYING AT SOME POINT OR ANOTHER IN THEIR LIFE.

AND YET THE REALITY IS THAT WE HAVE MANY SUICIDES IN THIS COUNTRY. I CAN'T ACTUALLY BRING MYSELF TO BLAME PEOPLE FOR MAKING THAT DECISION.

AS A POLICEMAN, MY OFFICIAL POSITION IS TO DISAVOW THE CONCEPT OF SUICIDE.

ESPE-CIALLY WHEN WE'RE YOUNG ...

154

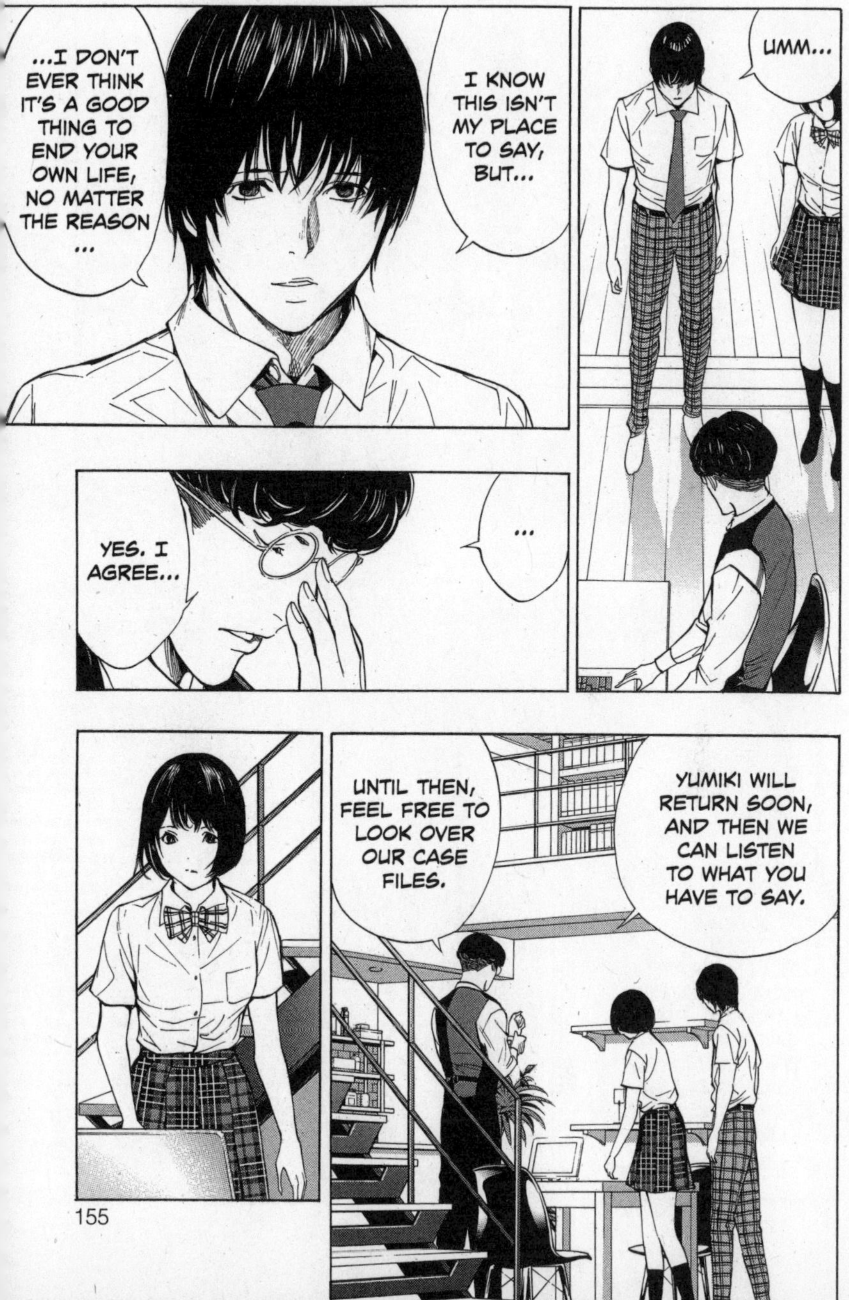
UMM...
I KNOW THIS ISN'T MY PLACE TO SAY, BUT...
...I DON'T EVER THINK IT'S A GOOD THING TO END YOUR OWN LIFE, NO MATTER THE REASON...
...
YES. I AGREE...
YUMIKI WILL RETURN SOON, AND THEN WE CAN LISTEN TO WHAT YOU HAVE TO SAY.
UNTIL THEN, FEEL FREE TO LOOK OVER OUR CASE FILES.

THIS IS OUR CURRENT LIST OF CONFIRMED CANDIDATES.

01　02　03　04　0

07　08　09　10　11　1

LOOK AT HOW MUCH INFORMATION THEY HAVE ABOUT METRO-POLIMAN...

01

CLICK

u, Ka

Birth	2
Gender	
Birthplace	Ja
Height	18
Blood type	
Occupation	Stu

Notes

Registered add
may not match
place of reside
Student of Jos
Private Acade
The person be
public figure
Metropoliman
Constructed hi
costume and d
himself Metro
before his dea

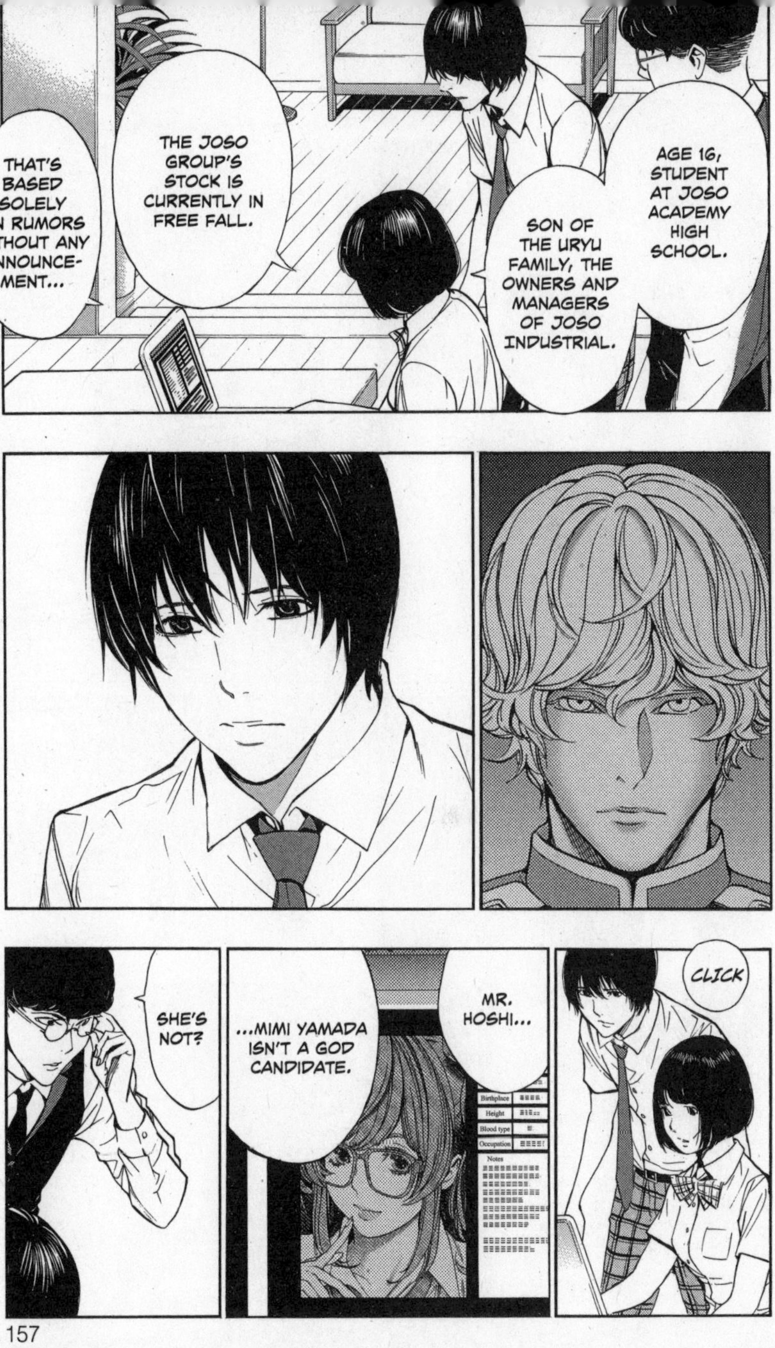
AGE 16, STUDENT AT JOSO ACADEMY HIGH SCHOOL.
SON OF THE URYU FAMILY, THE OWNERS AND MANAGERS OF JOSO INDUSTRIAL.
THE JOSO GROUP'S STOCK IS CURRENTLY IN FREE FALL.
THAT'S BASED SOLELY ON RUMORS WITHOUT ANY ANNOUNCEMENT...
CLICK
MR. HOSHI...
...MIMI YAMADA ISN'T A GOD CANDIDATE.
Birthplace
Height
Blood type
Occupation
Notes
SHE'S NOT?

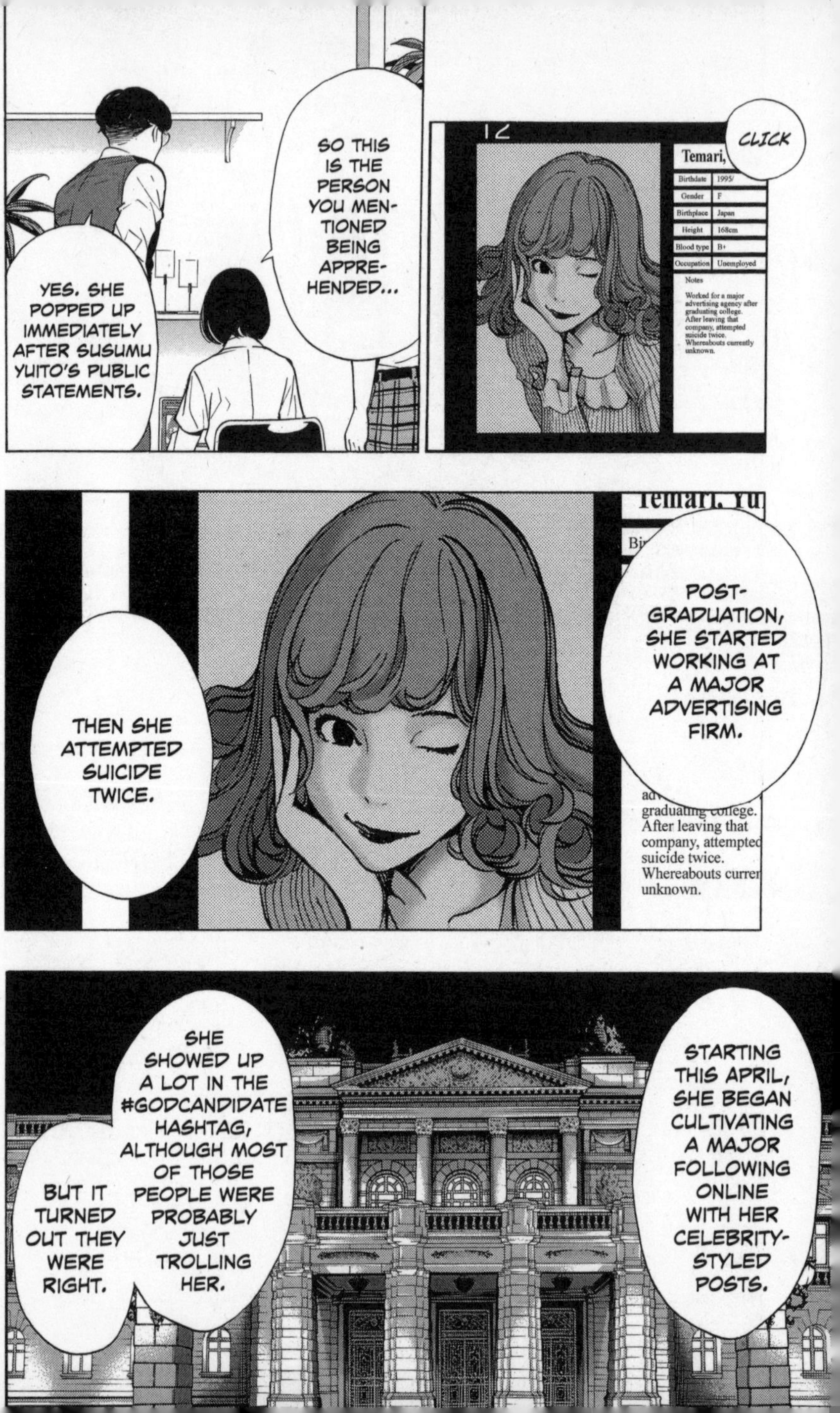
CLICK
Temari,
Birthdate 1995/
Gender F
Birthplace Japan
Height 168cm
Blood type B+
Occupation Unemployed
Notes
Worked for a major advertising agency after graduating college. After leaving that company, attempted suicide twice. Whereabouts currently unknown.
SO THIS IS THE PERSON YOU MENTIONED BEING APPREHENDED...
YES. SHE POPPED UP IMMEDIATELY AFTER SUSUMU YUITO'S PUBLIC STATEMENTS.
POST-GRADUATION, SHE STARTED WORKING AT A MAJOR ADVERTISING FIRM.
graduating college. After leaving that company, attempted suicide twice. Whereabouts curren unknown.
THEN SHE ATTEMPTED SUICIDE TWICE.
STARTING THIS APRIL, SHE BEGAN CULTIVATING A MAJOR FOLLOWING ONLINE WITH HER CELEBRITY-STYLED POSTS.
SHE SHOWED UP A LOT IN THE #GODCANDIDATE HASHTAG, ALTHOUGH MOST OF THOSE PEOPLE WERE PROBABLY JUST TROLLING HER.
BUT IT TURNED OUT THEY WERE RIGHT.

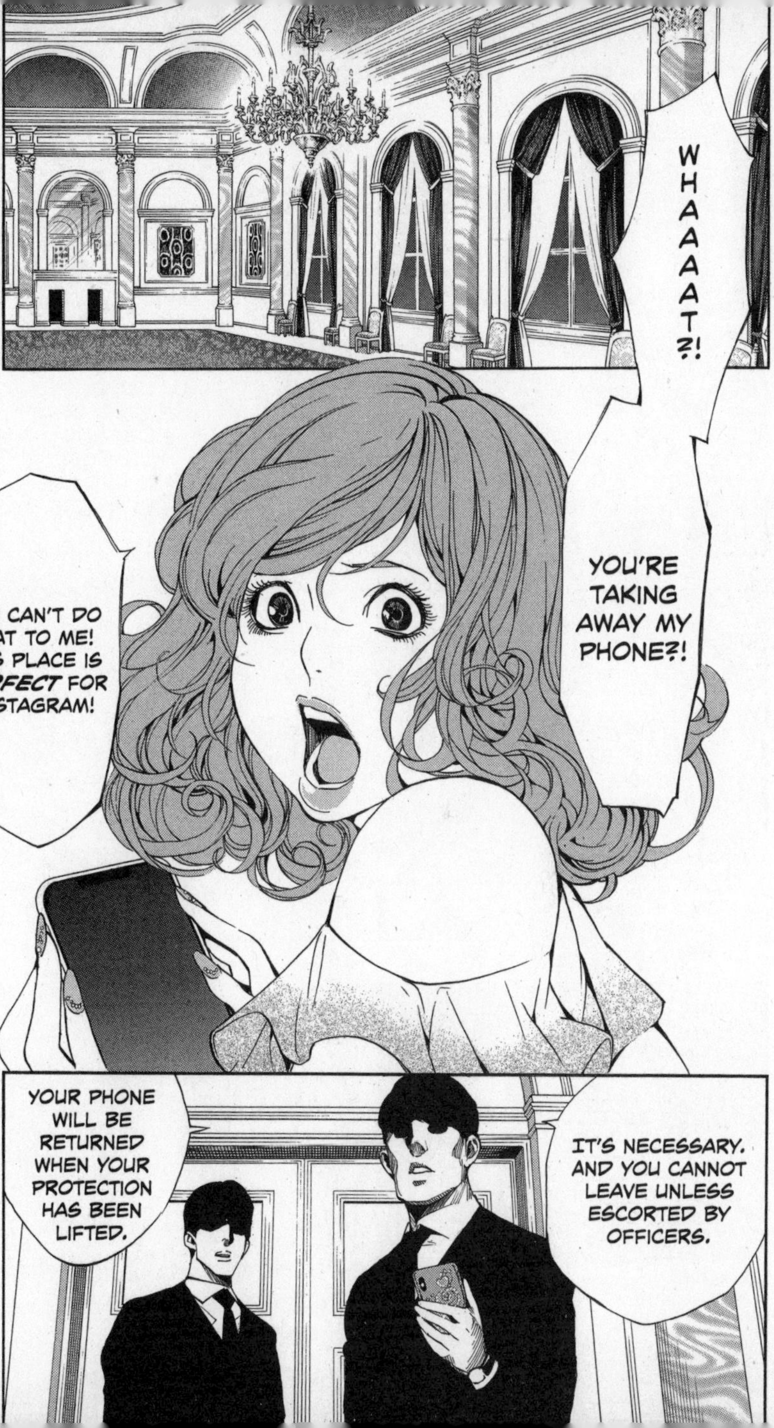
WHAAAAT?!
YOU'RE TAKING AWAY MY PHONE?!
YOU CAN'T DO THAT TO ME! THIS PLACE IS *PERFECT* FOR INSTAGRAM!
IT'S NECESSARY. AND YOU CANNOT LEAVE UNLESS ESCORTED BY OFFICERS.
YOUR PHONE WILL BE RETURNED WHEN YOUR PROTECTION HAS BEEN LIFTED.

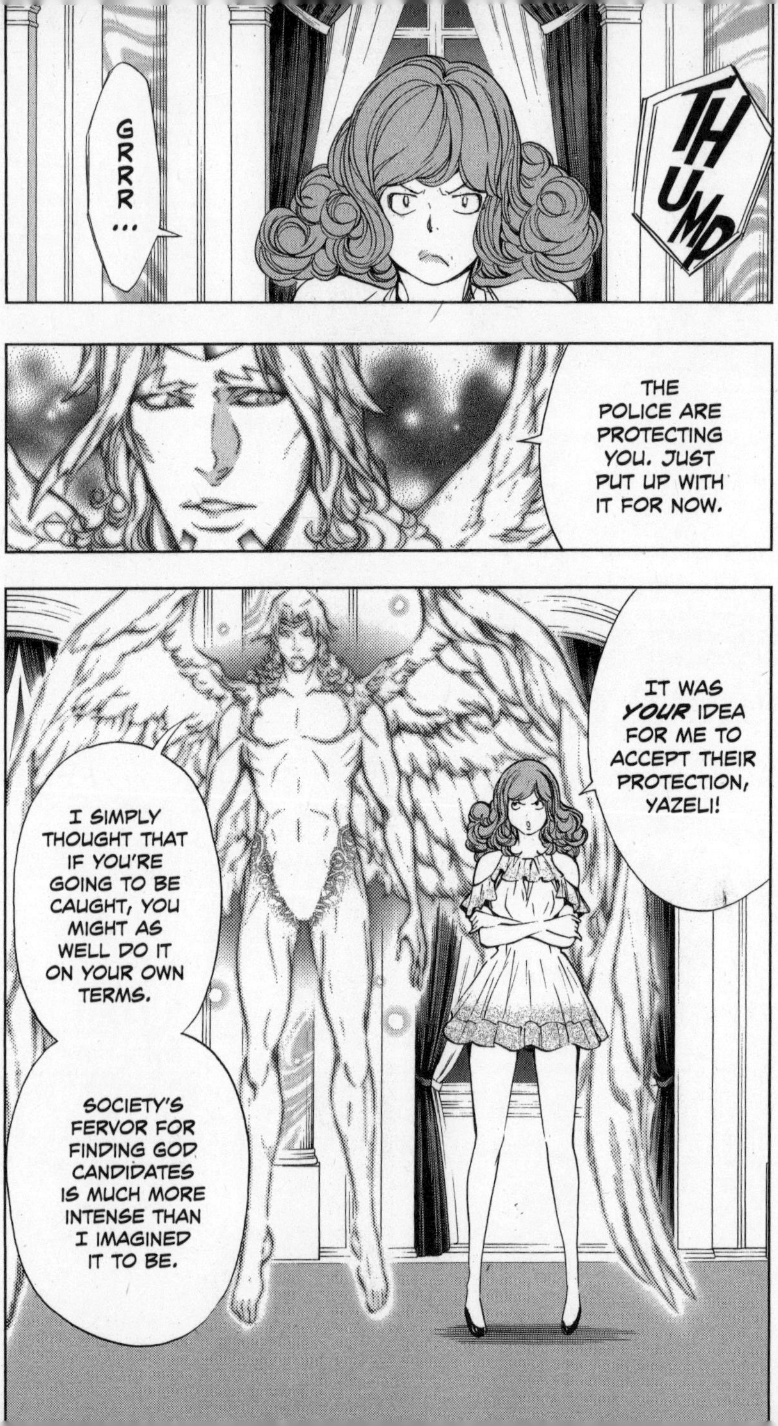
THUMP
GRRR...
THE POLICE ARE PROTECTING YOU. JUST PUT UP WITH IT FOR NOW.
IT WAS *YOUR* IDEA FOR ME TO ACCEPT THEIR PROTECTION, YAZELI!
I SIMPLY THOUGHT THAT IF YOU'RE GOING TO BE CAUGHT, YOU MIGHT AS WELL DO IT ON YOUR OWN TERMS.
SOCIETY'S FERVOR FOR FINDING GOD CANDIDATES IS MUCH MORE INTENSE THAN I IMAGINED IT TO BE.

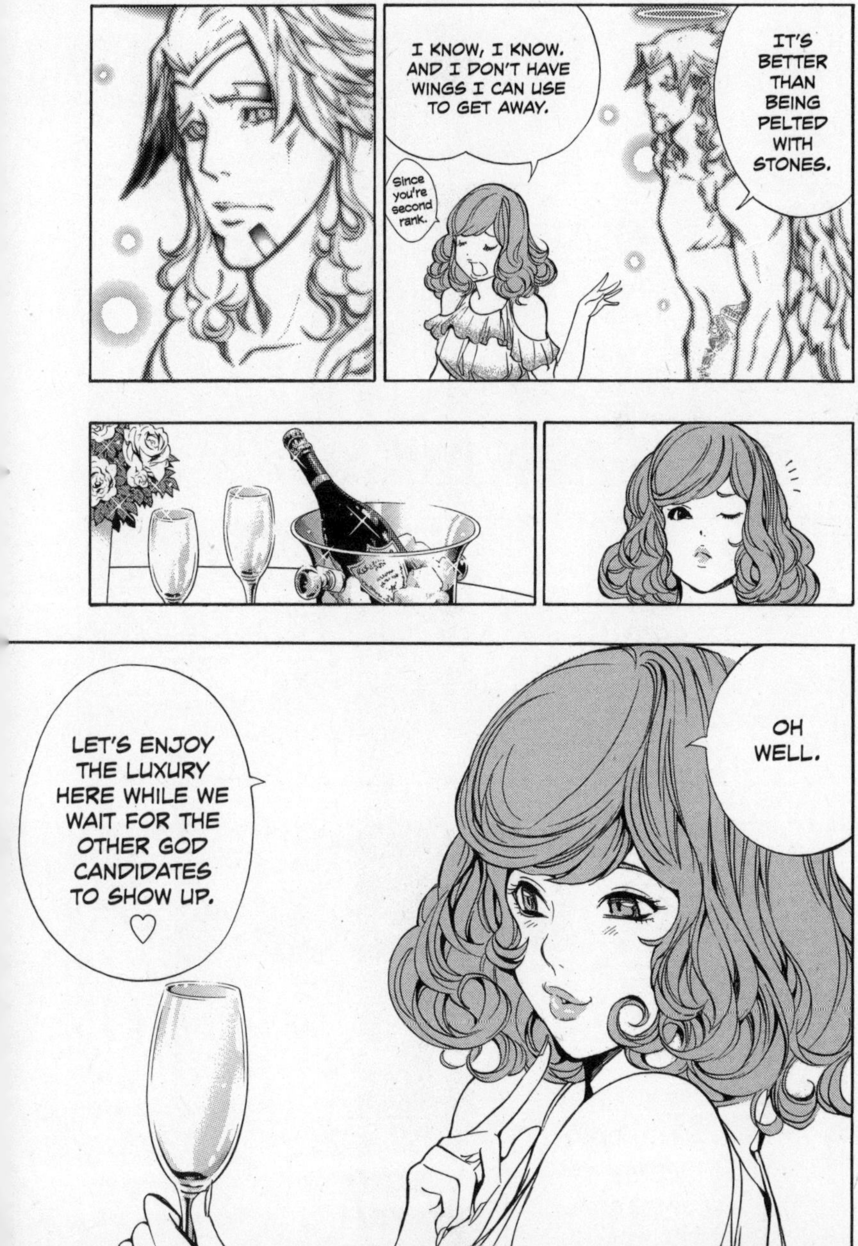
IT'S BETTER THAN BEING PELTED WITH STONES.
I KNOW, I KNOW. AND I DON'T HAVE WINGS I CAN USE TO GET AWAY.
Since you're second rank.
OH WELL.
LET'S ENJOY THE LUXURY HERE WHILE WE WAIT FOR THE OTHER GOD CANDIDATES TO SHOW UP. ♡

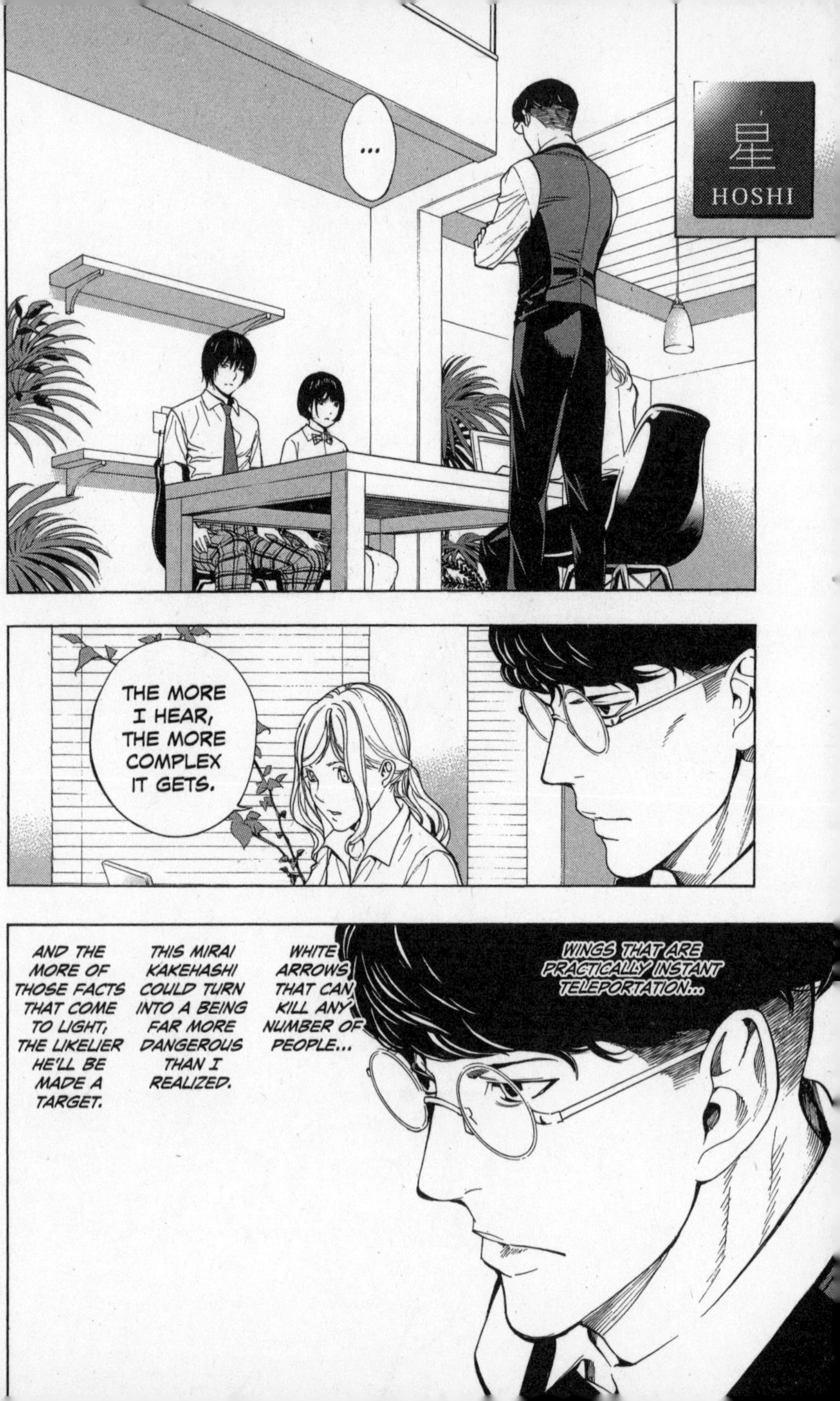
星 HOSHI
...
THE MORE I HEAR, THE MORE COMPLEX IT GETS.
WINGS THAT ARE PRACTICALLY INSTANT TELEPORTATION...
WHITE ARROWS THAT CAN KILL ANY NUMBER OF PEOPLE...
THIS MIRAI KAKEHASHI COULD TURN INTO A BEING FAR MORE DANGEROUS THAN I REALIZED.
AND THE MORE OF THOSE FACTS THAT COME TO LIGHT, THE LIKELIER HE'LL BE MADE A TARGET.

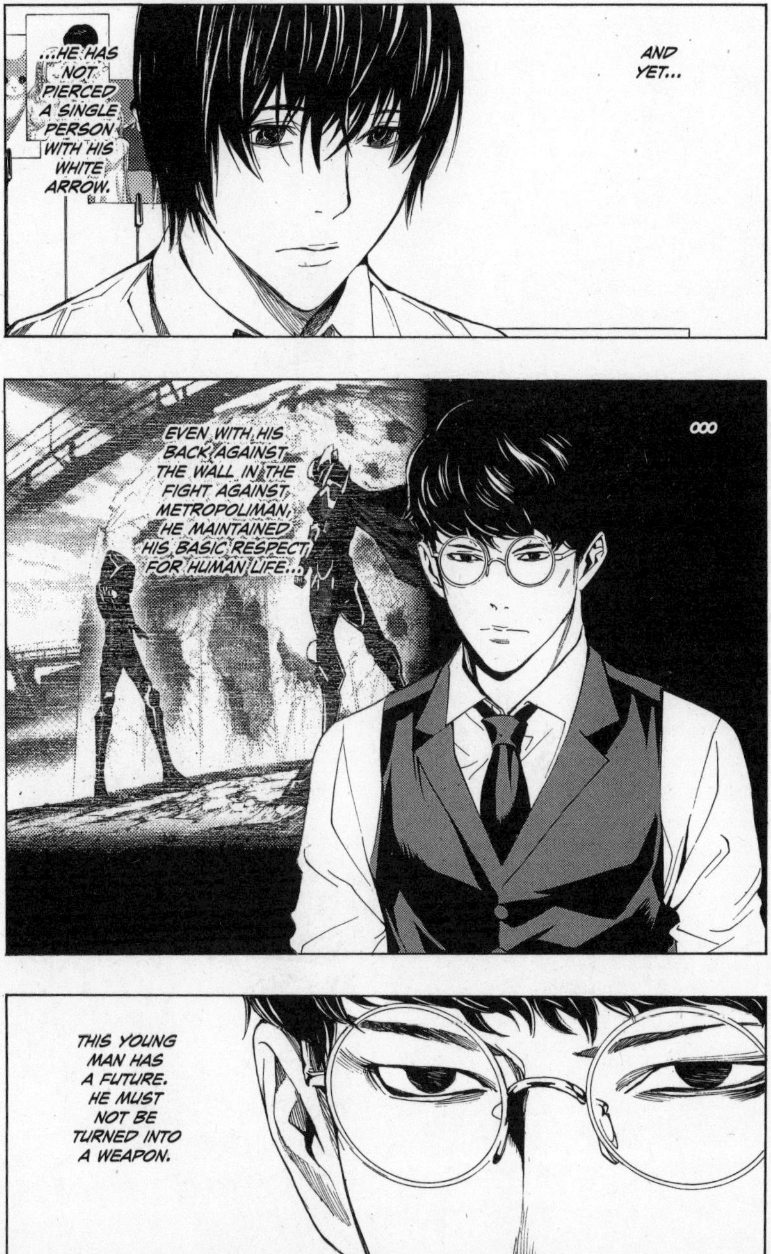
AND YET...
...HE HAS NOT PIERCED A SINGLE PERSON WITH HIS WHITE ARROW.
ooo
EVEN WITH HIS BACK AGAINST THE WALL IN THE FIGHT AGAINST METROPOLIMAN, HE MAINTAINED HIS BASIC RESPECT FOR HUMAN LIFE...
THIS YOUNG MAN HAS A FUTURE. HE MUST NOT BE TURNED INTO A WEAPON.

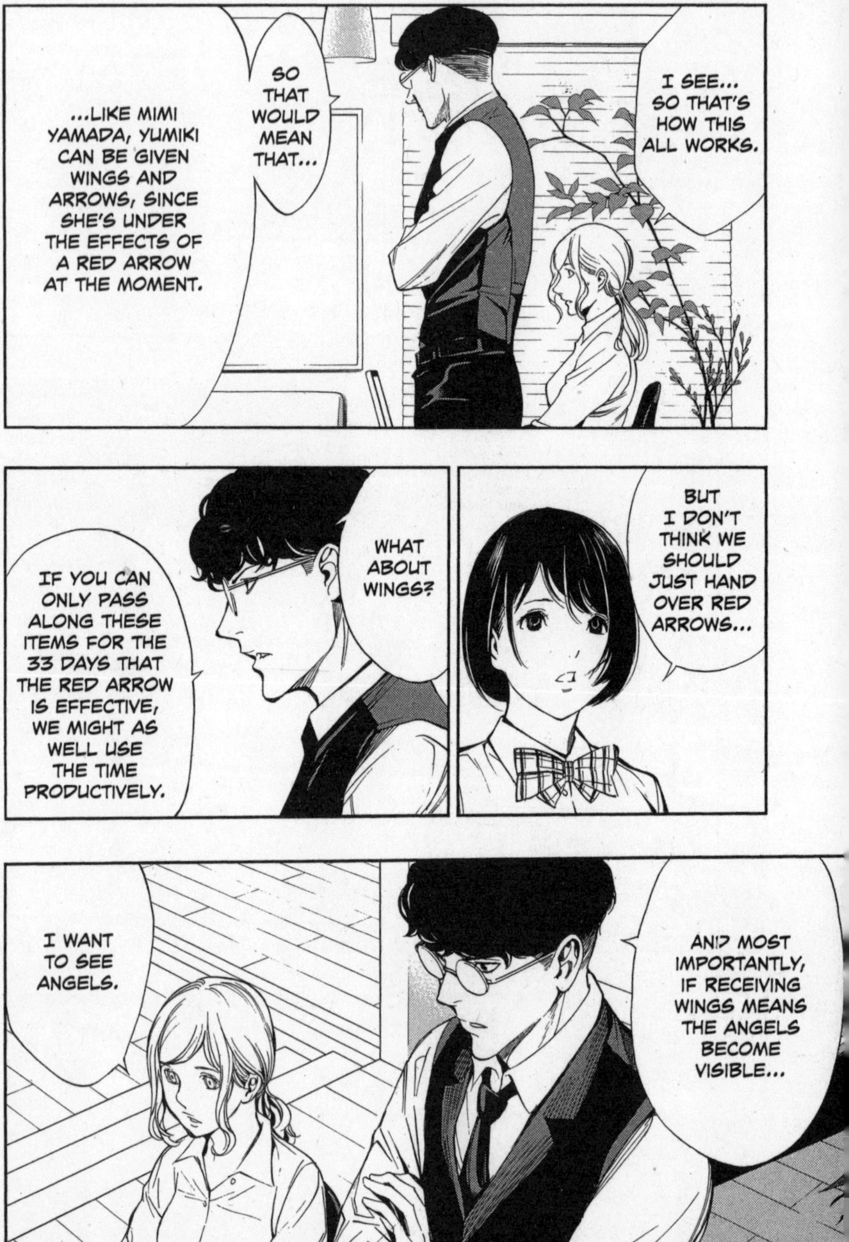
I SEE... SO THAT'S HOW THIS ALL WORKS.
SO THAT WOULD MEAN THAT...
...LIKE MIMI YAMADA, YUMIKI CAN BE GIVEN WINGS AND ARROWS, SINCE SHE'S UNDER THE EFFECTS OF A RED ARROW AT THE MOMENT.
BUT I DON'T THINK WE SHOULD JUST HAND OVER RED ARROWS...
WHAT ABOUT WINGS?
IF YOU CAN ONLY PASS ALONG THESE ITEMS FOR THE 33 DAYS THAT THE RED ARROW IS EFFECTIVE, WE MIGHT AS WELL USE THE TIME PRODUCTIVELY.
AND MOST IMPORTANTLY, IF RECEIVING WINGS MEANS THE ANGELS BECOME VISIBLE...
I WANT TO SEE ANGELS.

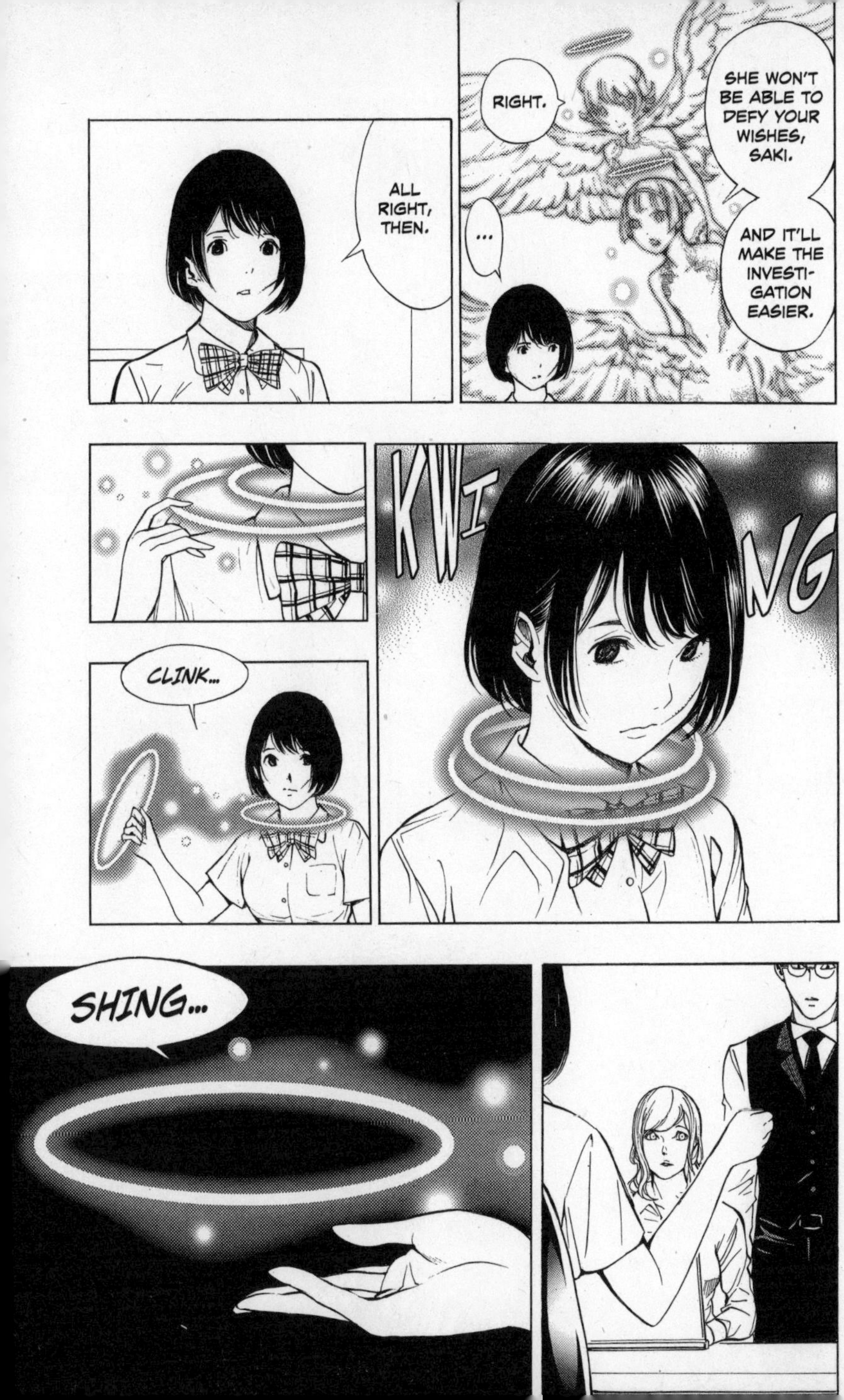
SHE WON'T BE ABLE TO DEFY YOUR WISHES, SAKI.
RIGHT.
AND IT'LL MAKE THE INVESTIGATION EASIER.
...
ALL RIGHT, THEN.
KWIING
CLINK...
SHING...

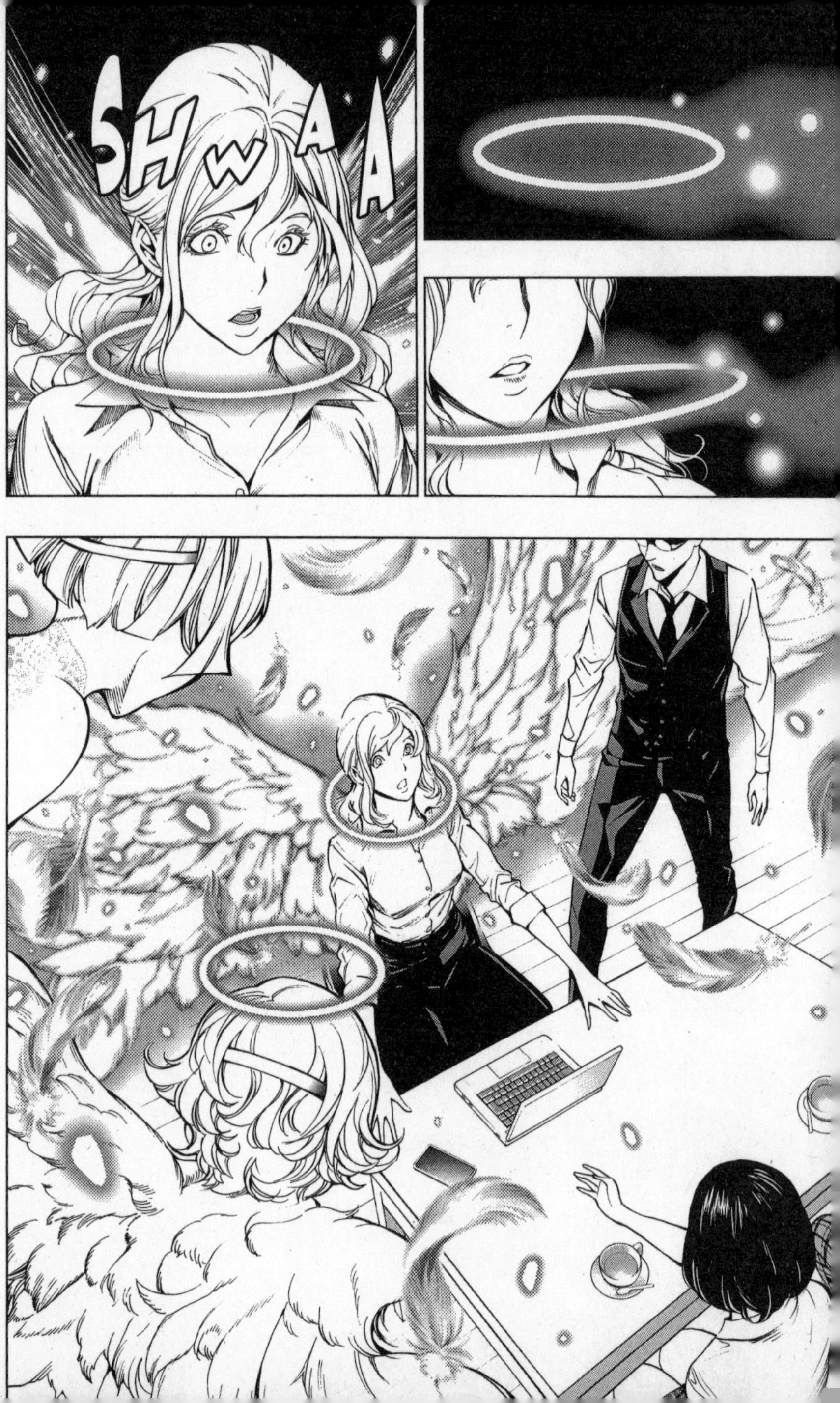
SHWAA

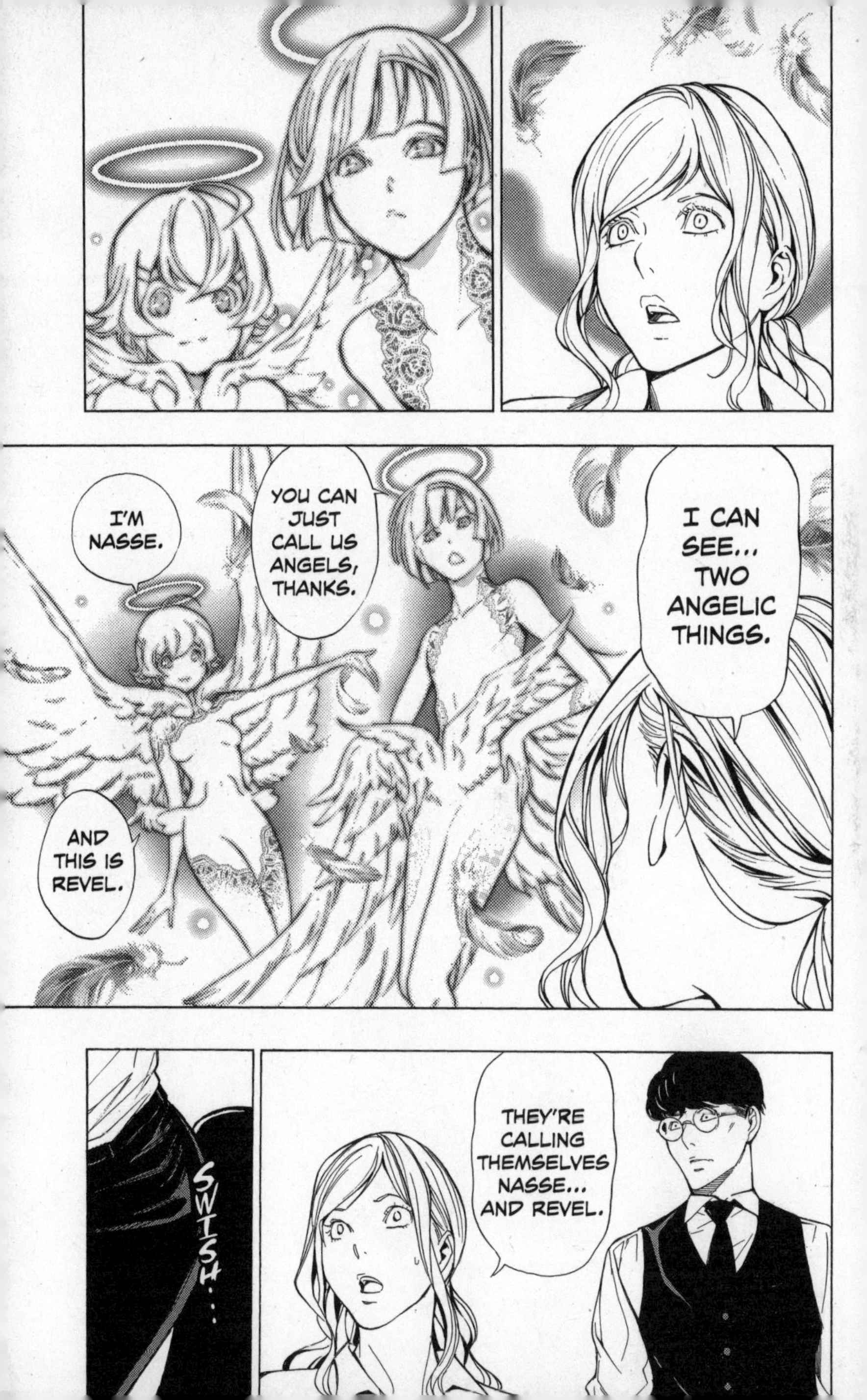
I CAN SEE... TWO ANGELIC THINGS.
YOU CAN JUST CALL US ANGELS, THANKS.
I'M NASSE.
AND THIS IS REVEL.
THEY'RE CALLING THEMSELVES NASSE... AND REVEL.
SWISH...

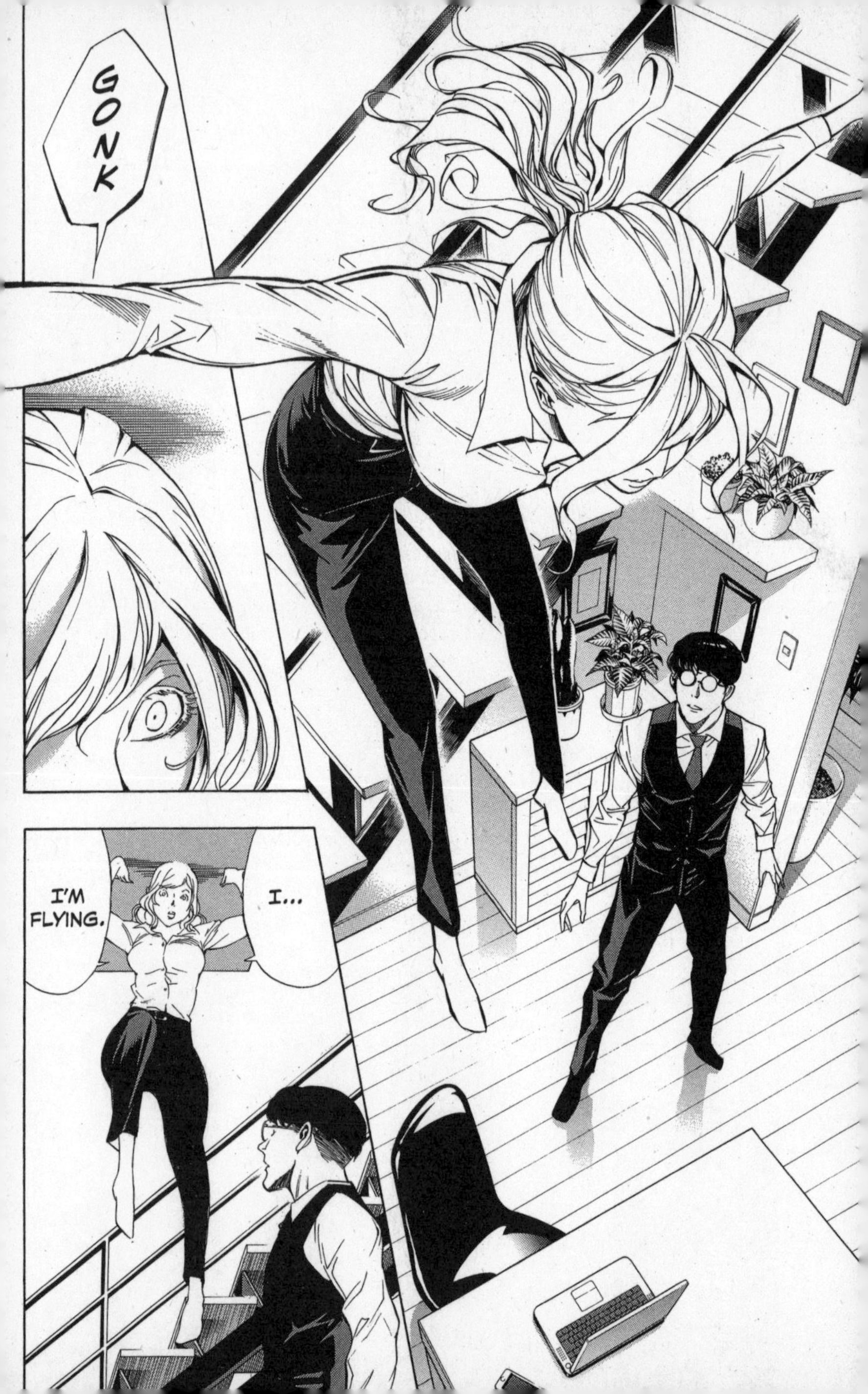
GONK
I...
I'M FLYING.

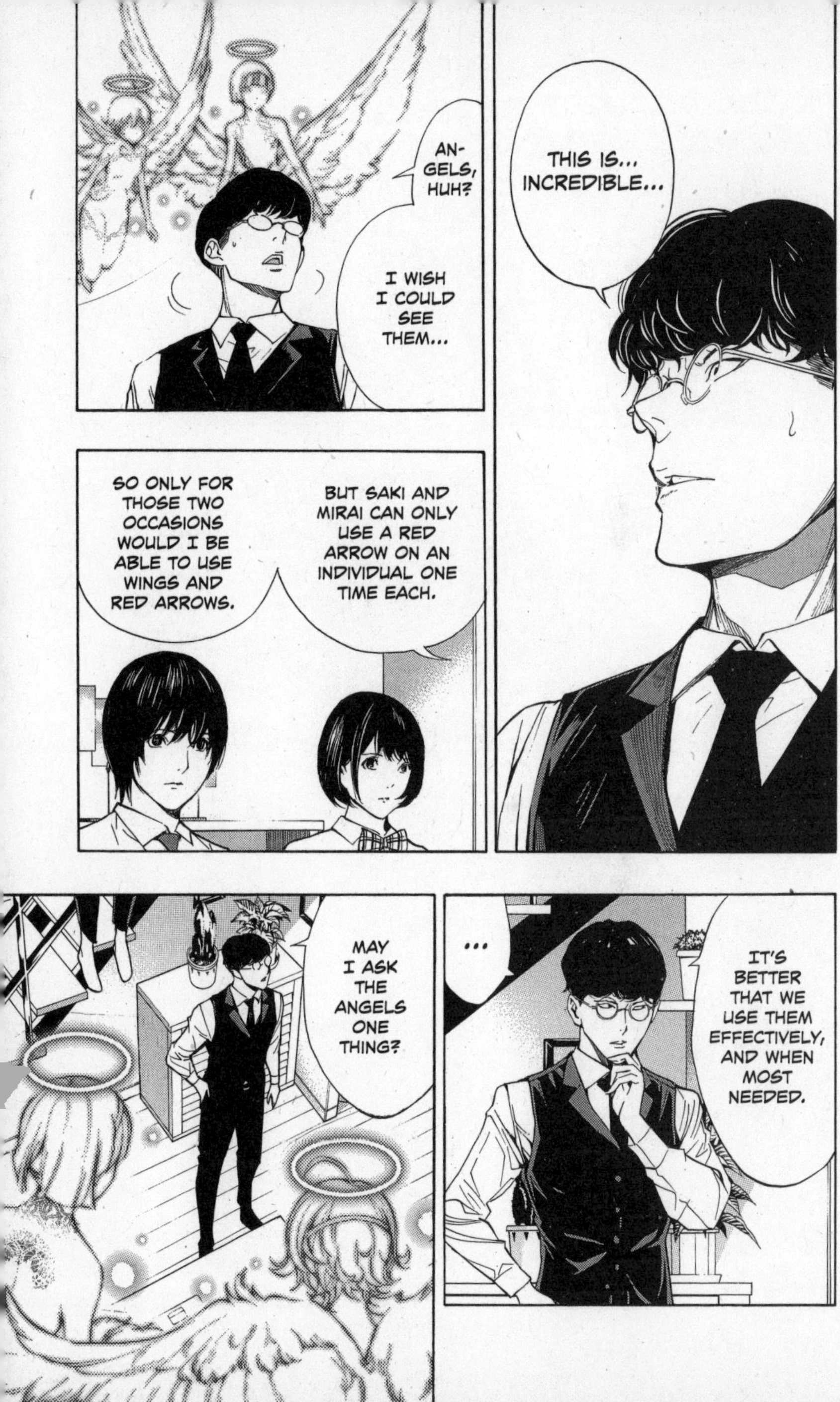
THIS IS... INCREDIBLE...
AN-GELS, HUH?
I WISH I COULD SEE THEM...
BUT SAKI AND MIRAI CAN ONLY USE A RED ARROW ON AN INDIVIDUAL ONE TIME EACH.
SO ONLY FOR THOSE TWO OCCASIONS WOULD I BE ABLE TO USE WINGS AND RED ARROWS.
IT'S BETTER THAT WE USE THEM EFFECTIVELY, AND WHEN MOST NEEDED.
...
MAY I ASK THE ANGELS ONE THING?

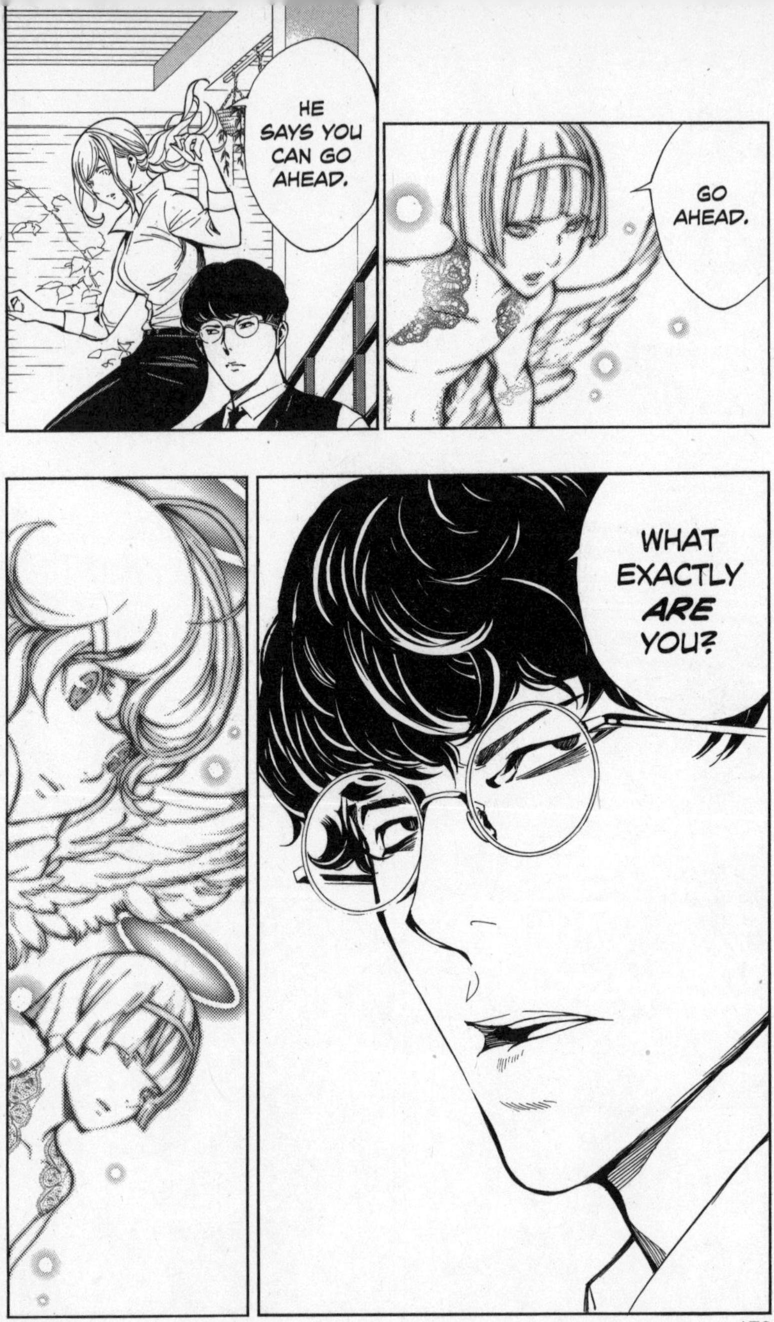
GO AHEAD.
HE SAYS YOU CAN GO AHEAD.
WHAT EXACTLY ***ARE*** YOU?

I CANNOT
SAY WHAT
WE ARE YET.
ANGELS ARE
ANGELS.

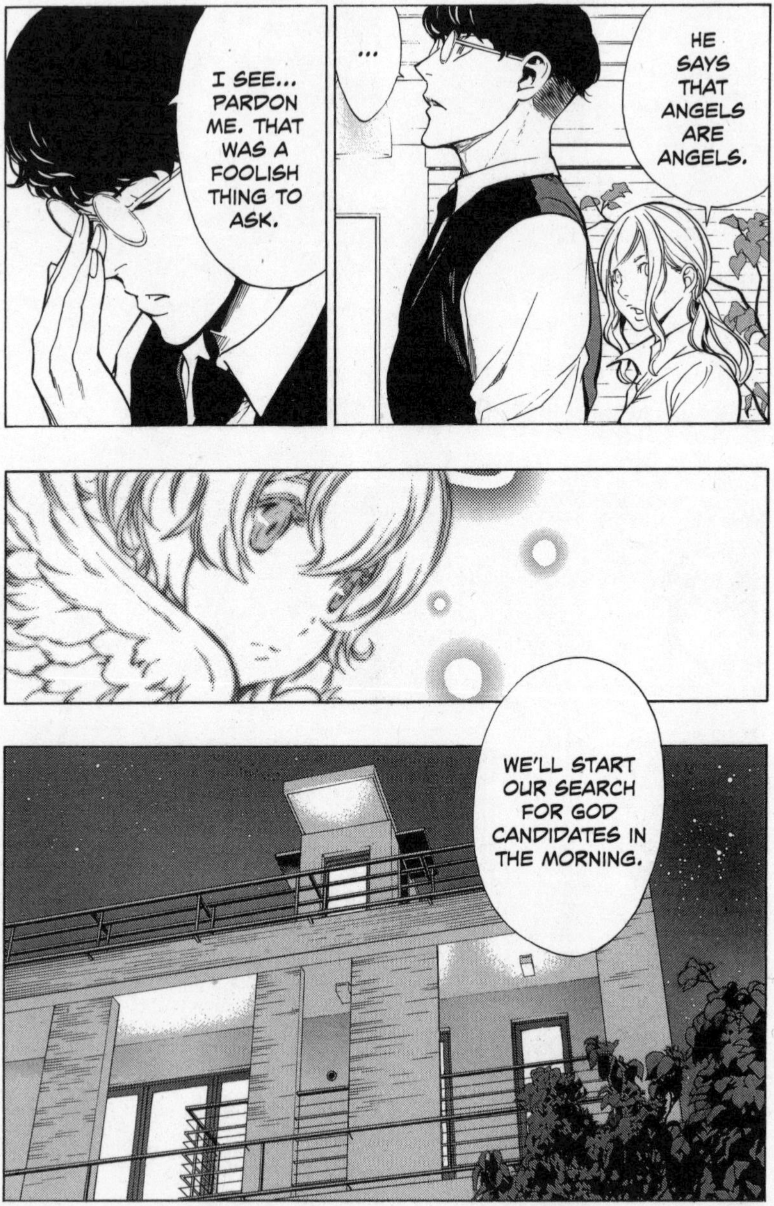
HE SAYS THAT ANGELS ARE ANGELS.
...
I SEE... PARDON ME. THAT WAS A FOOLISH THING TO ASK.
WE'LL START OUR SEARCH FOR GOD CANDIDATES IN THE MORNING.

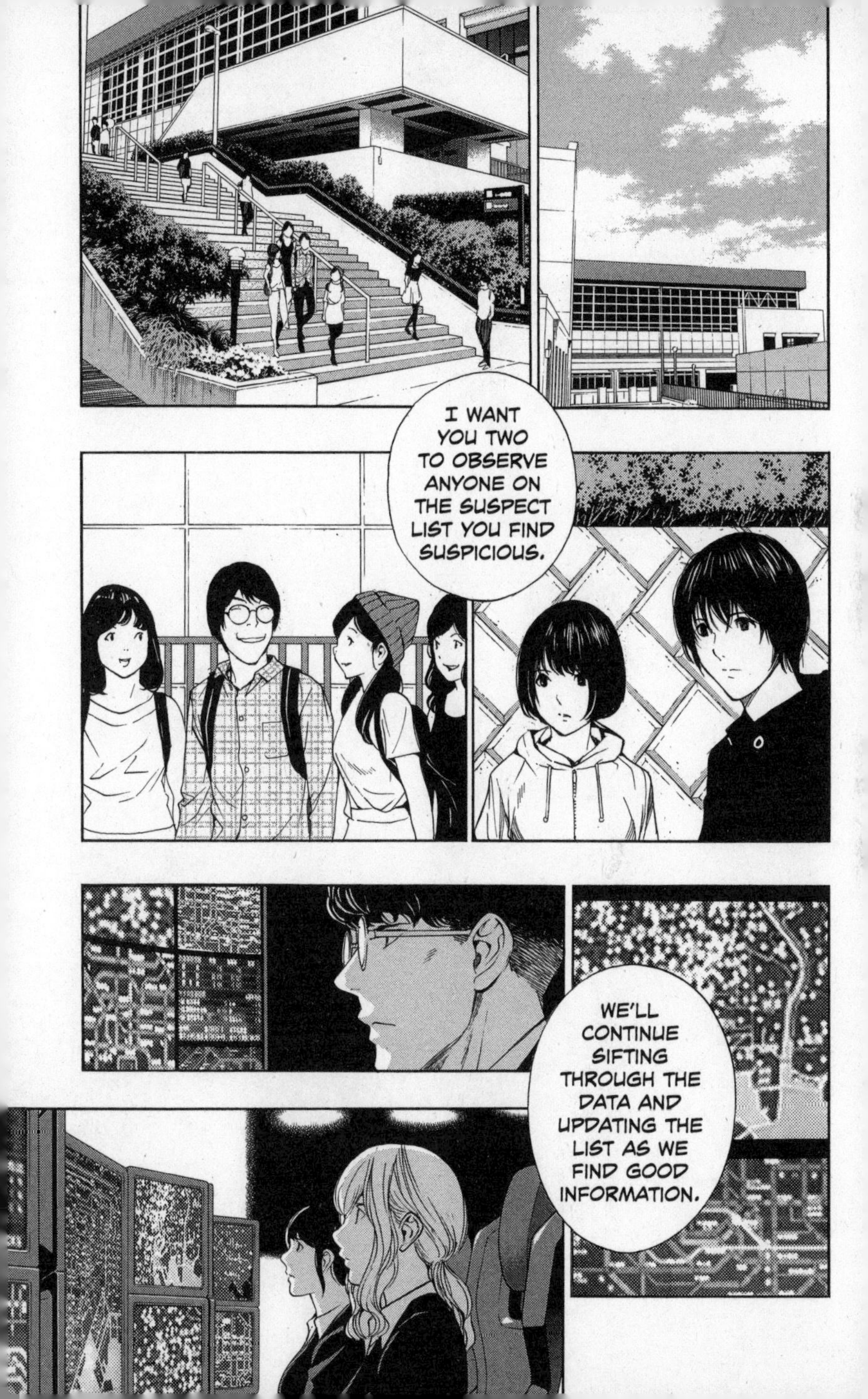
I WANT YOU TWO TO OBSERVE ANYONE ON THE SUSPECT LIST YOU FIND SUSPICIOUS.
WE'LL CONTINUE SIFTING THROUGH THE DATA AND UPDATING THE LIST AS WE FIND GOOD INFORMATION.

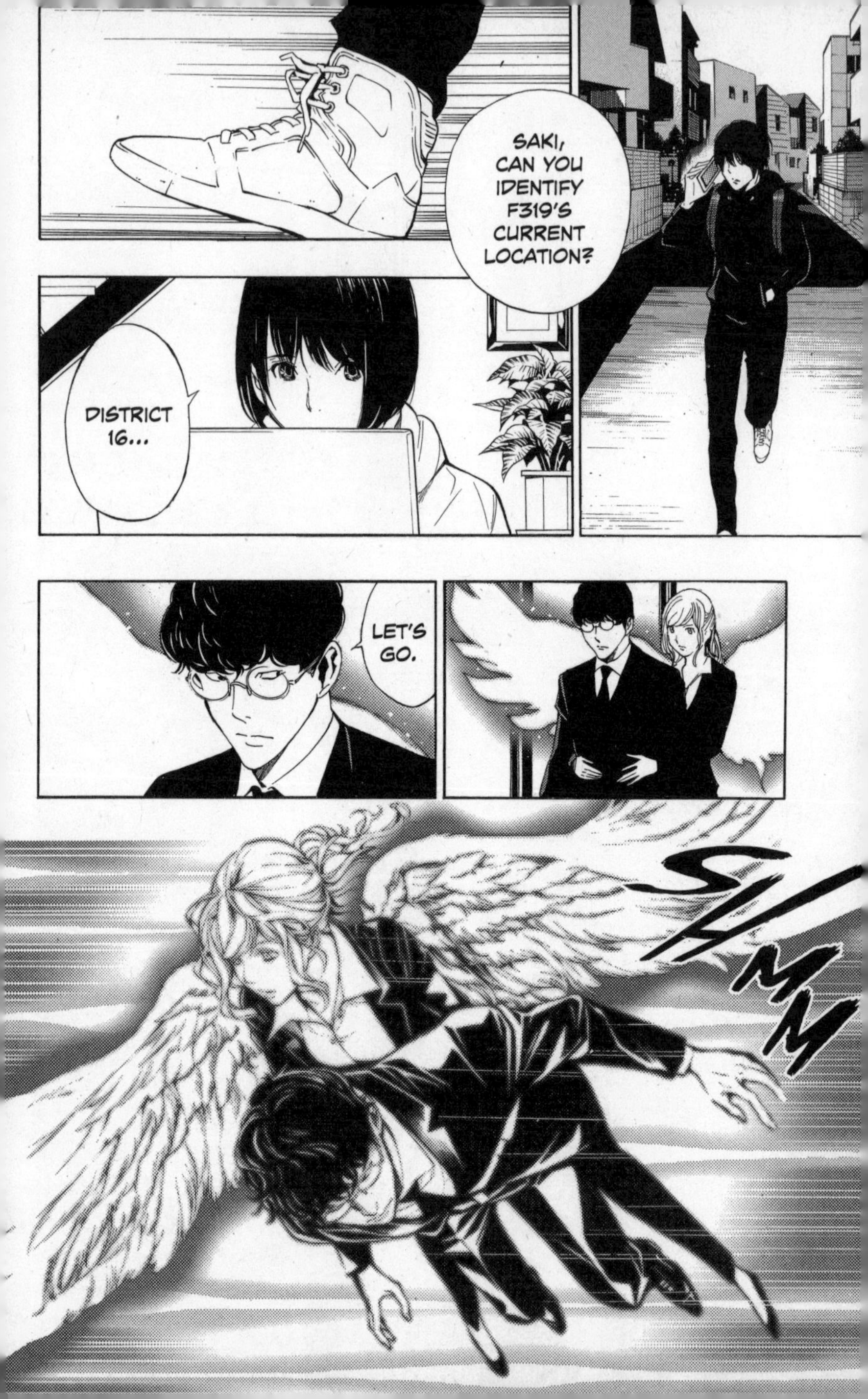
SAKI, CAN YOU IDENTIFY F319'S CURRENT LOCATION?
DISTRICT 16...
LET'S GO.
SHMM

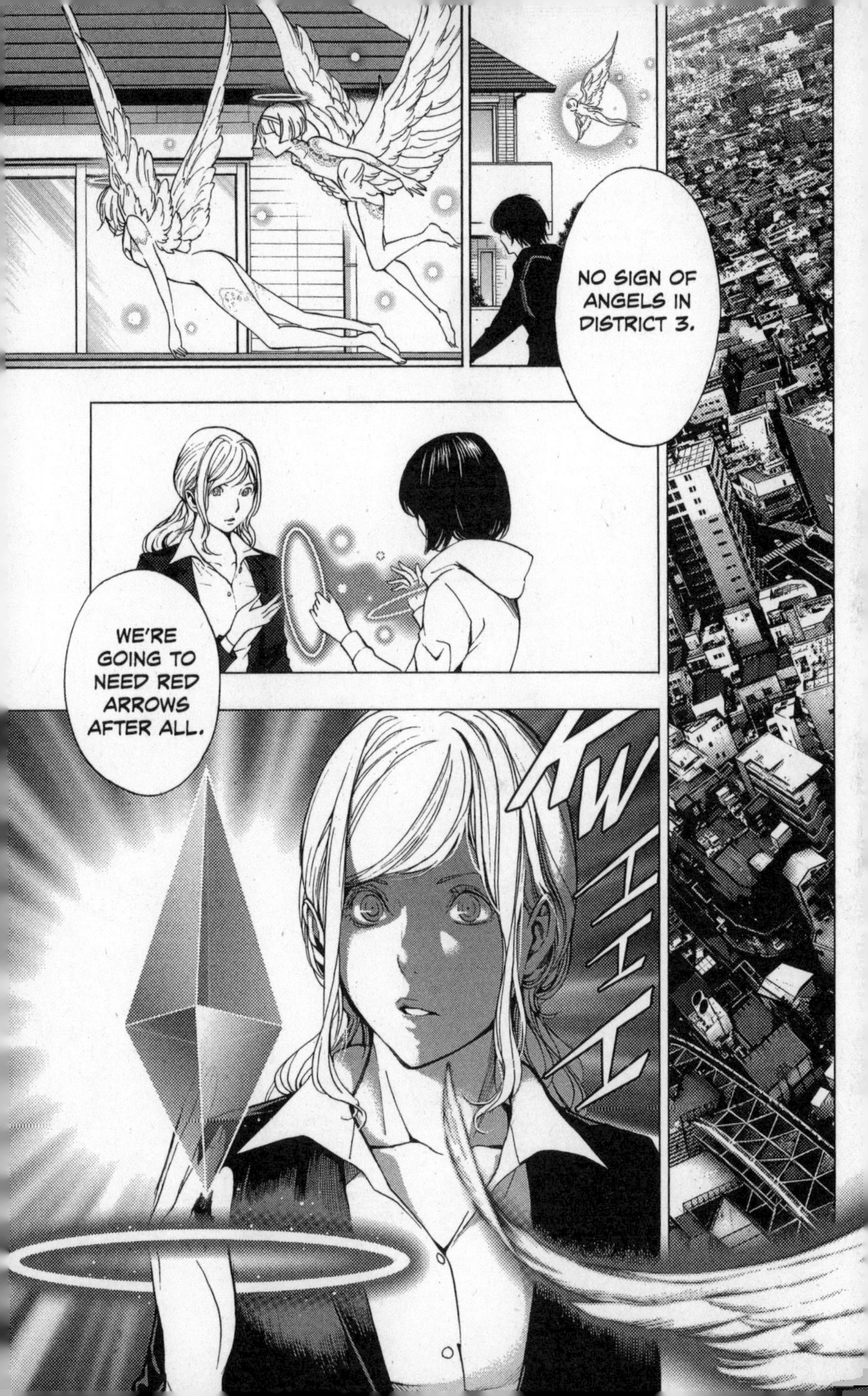
NO SIGN OF ANGELS IN DISTRICT 3.
WE'RE GOING TO NEED RED ARROWS AFTER ALL.
KWHHHH

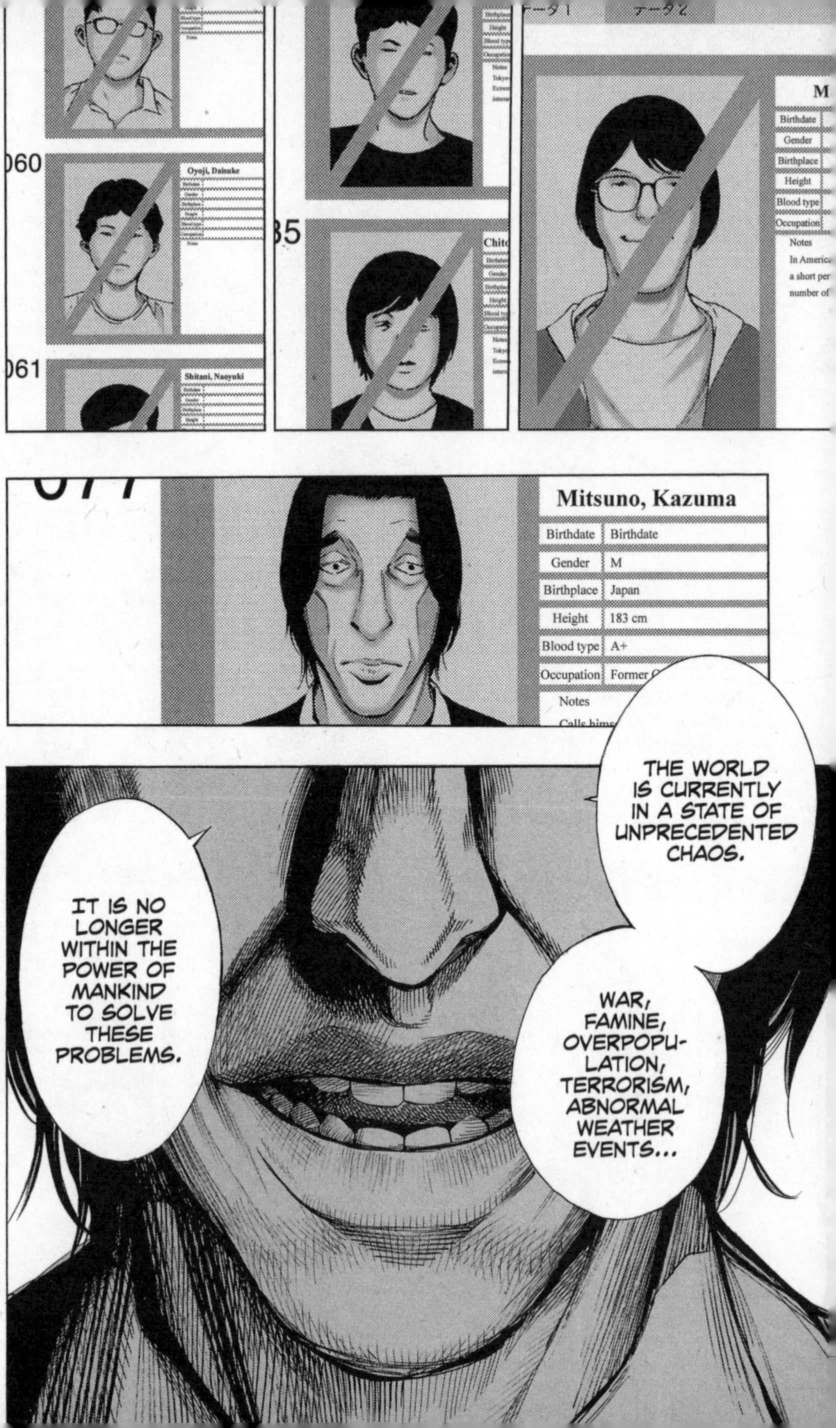

M
Birthdate
Gender
Birthplace
Height
Blood type
Occupation
Notes
Birthdate
Gender
Height
Notes
060
Oyoji, Daisuke
061
Shitani, Naoyuki
Mitsuno, Kazuma
Birthdate Birthdate
Gender M
Birthplace Japan
Height 183 cm
Blood type A+
Occupation
Notes
THE WORLD IS CURRENTLY IN A STATE OF UNPRECEDENTED CHAOS.
WAR, FAMINE, OVERPOPU-LATION, TERRORISM, ABNORMAL WEATHER EVENTS...
IT IS NO LONGER WITHIN THE POWER OF MANKIND TO SOLVE THESE PROBLEMS.

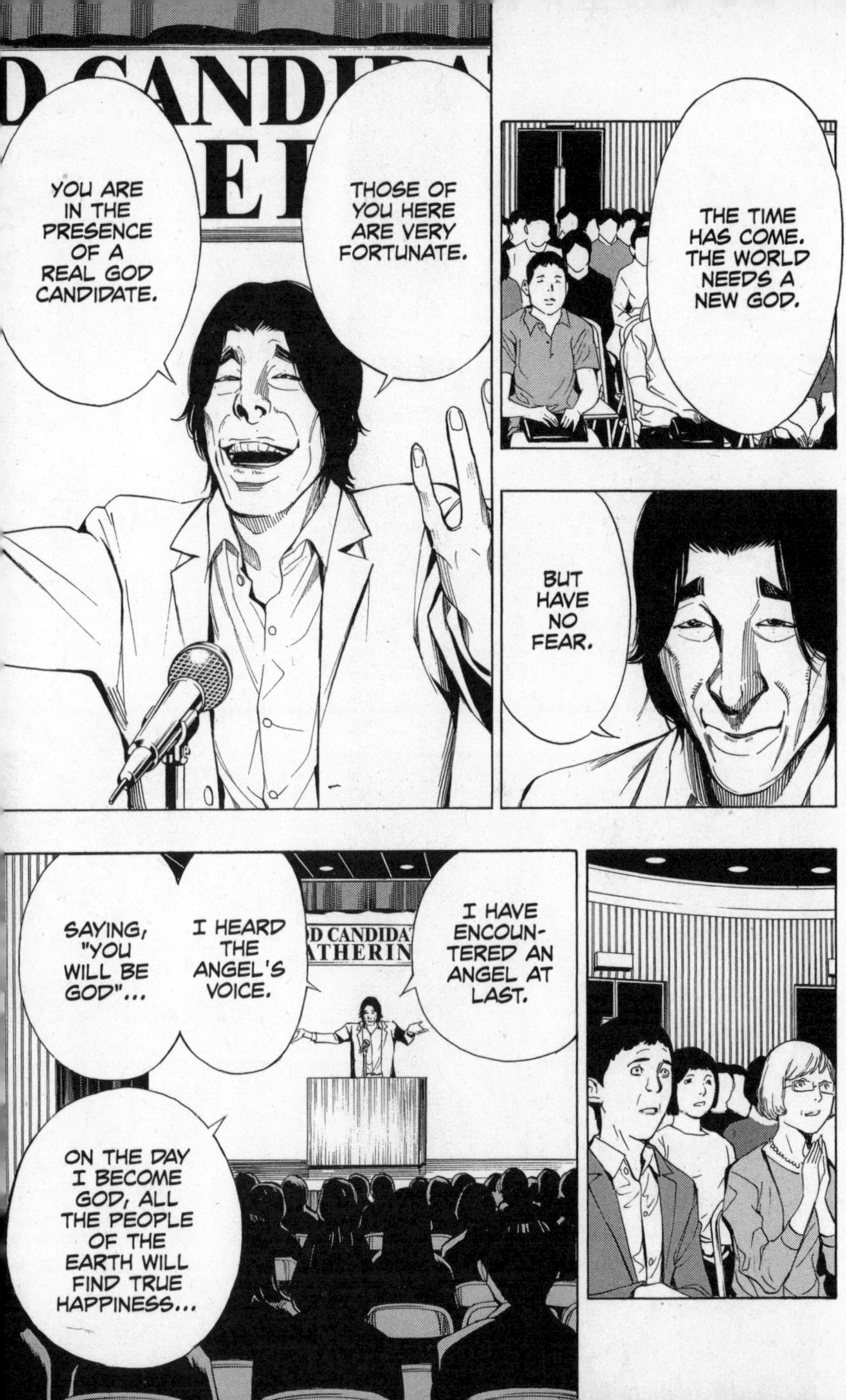
THE TIME HAS COME. THE WORLD NEEDS A NEW GOD.
BUT HAVE NO FEAR.
THOSE OF YOU HERE ARE VERY FORTUNATE.
YOU ARE IN THE PRESENCE OF A REAL GOD CANDIDATE.
I HAVE ENCOUN-TERED AN ANGEL AT LAST.
I HEARD THE ANGEL'S VOICE.
SAYING, "YOU WILL BE GOD"...
ON THE DAY I BECOME GOD, ALL THE PEOPLE OF THE EARTH WILL FIND TRUE HAPPINESS...

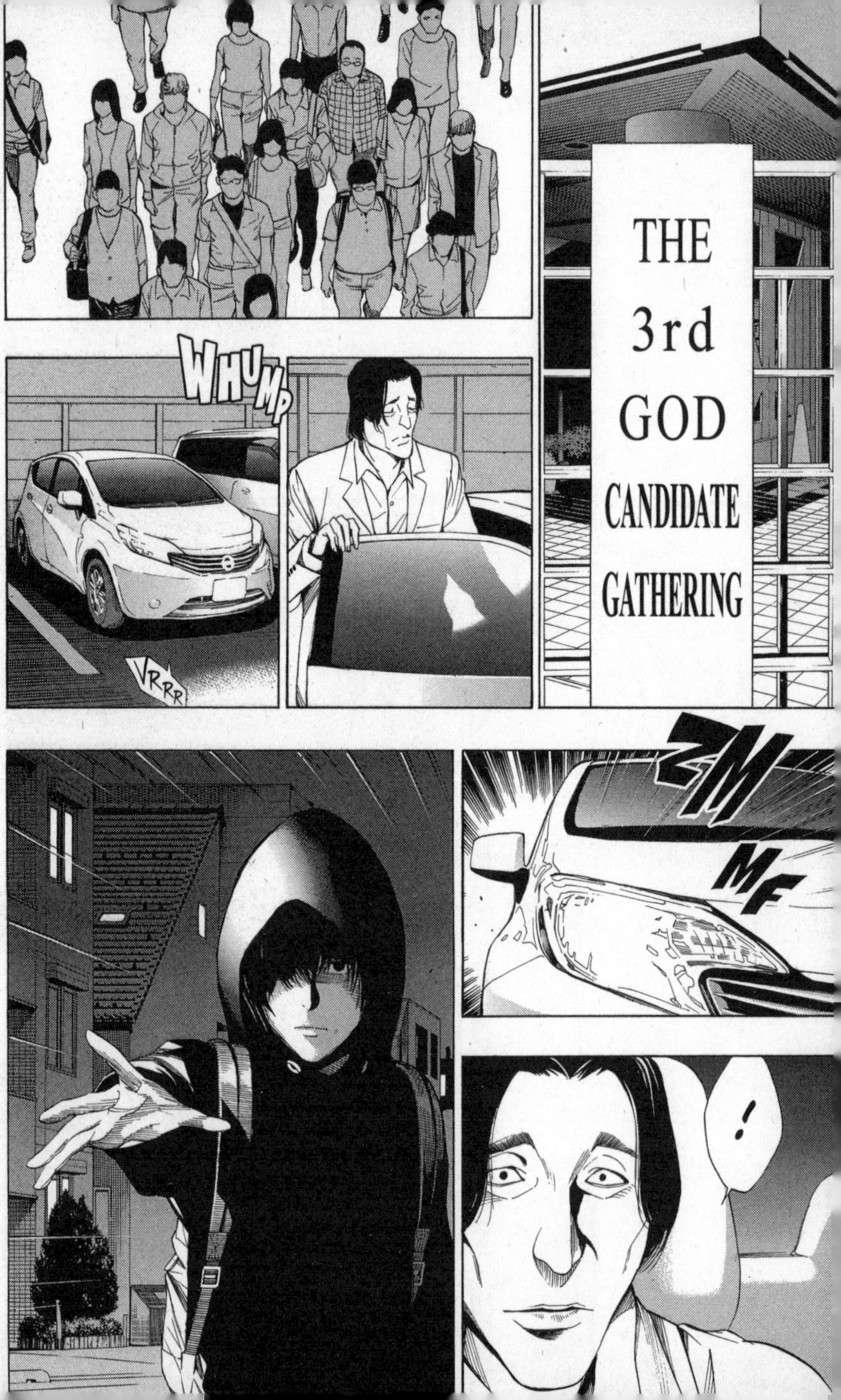
THE 3rd GOD CANDIDATE GATHERING
WHUMP
VRRR
ZMMF
!

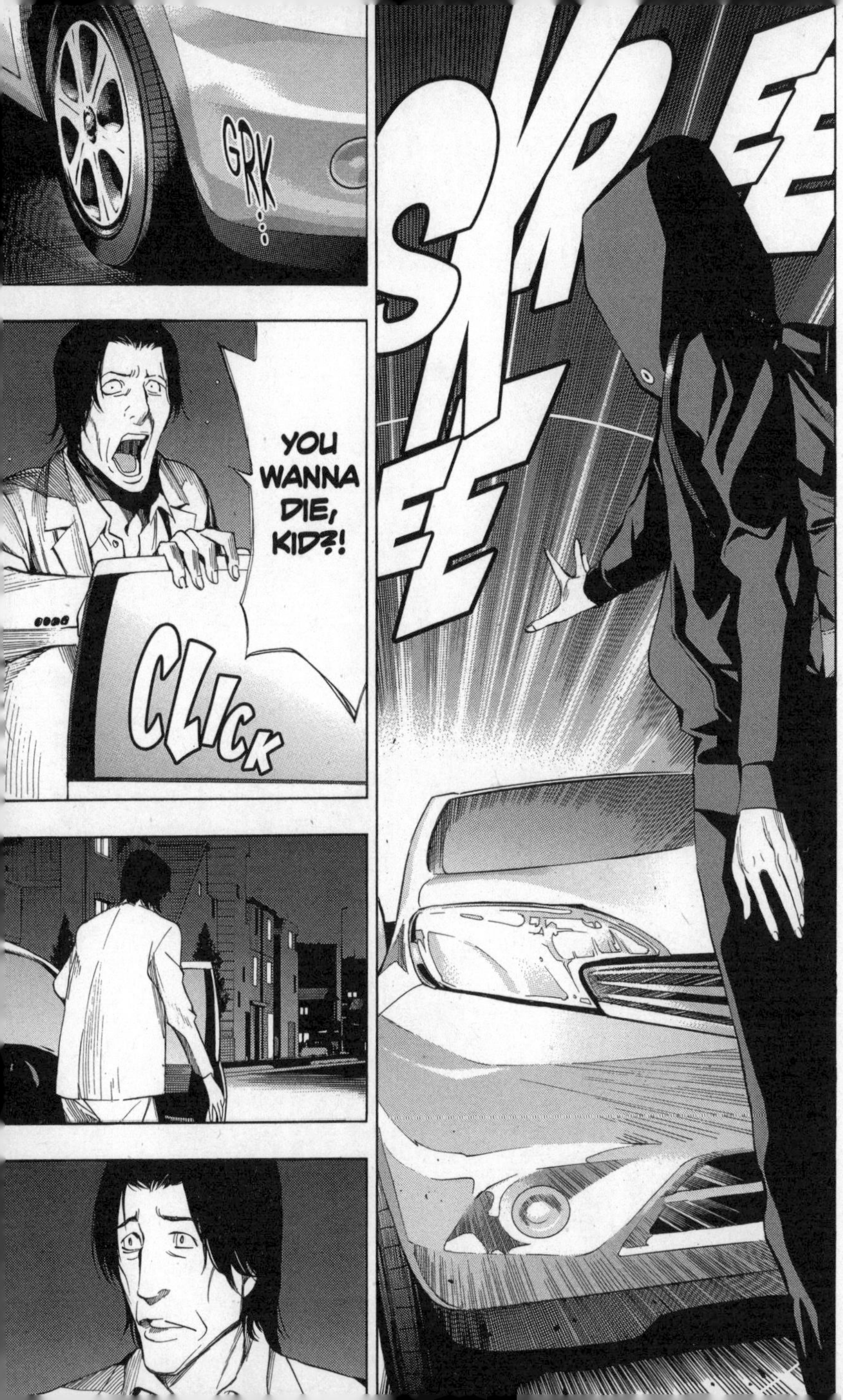
SKREEE
GRK...
YOU WANNA DIE, KID?!
CLICK

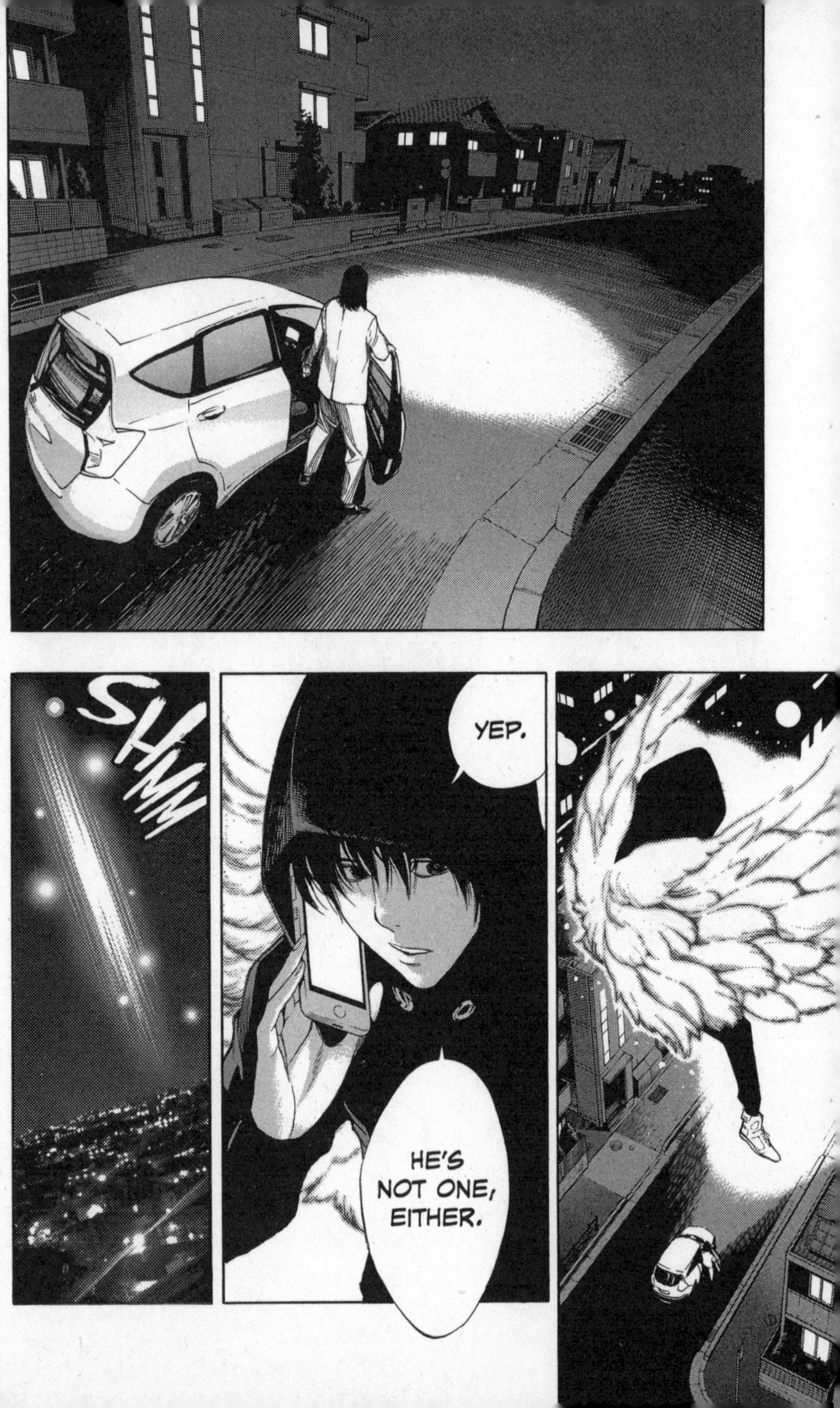
YEP.
HE'S NOT ONE, EITHER.
SHMM

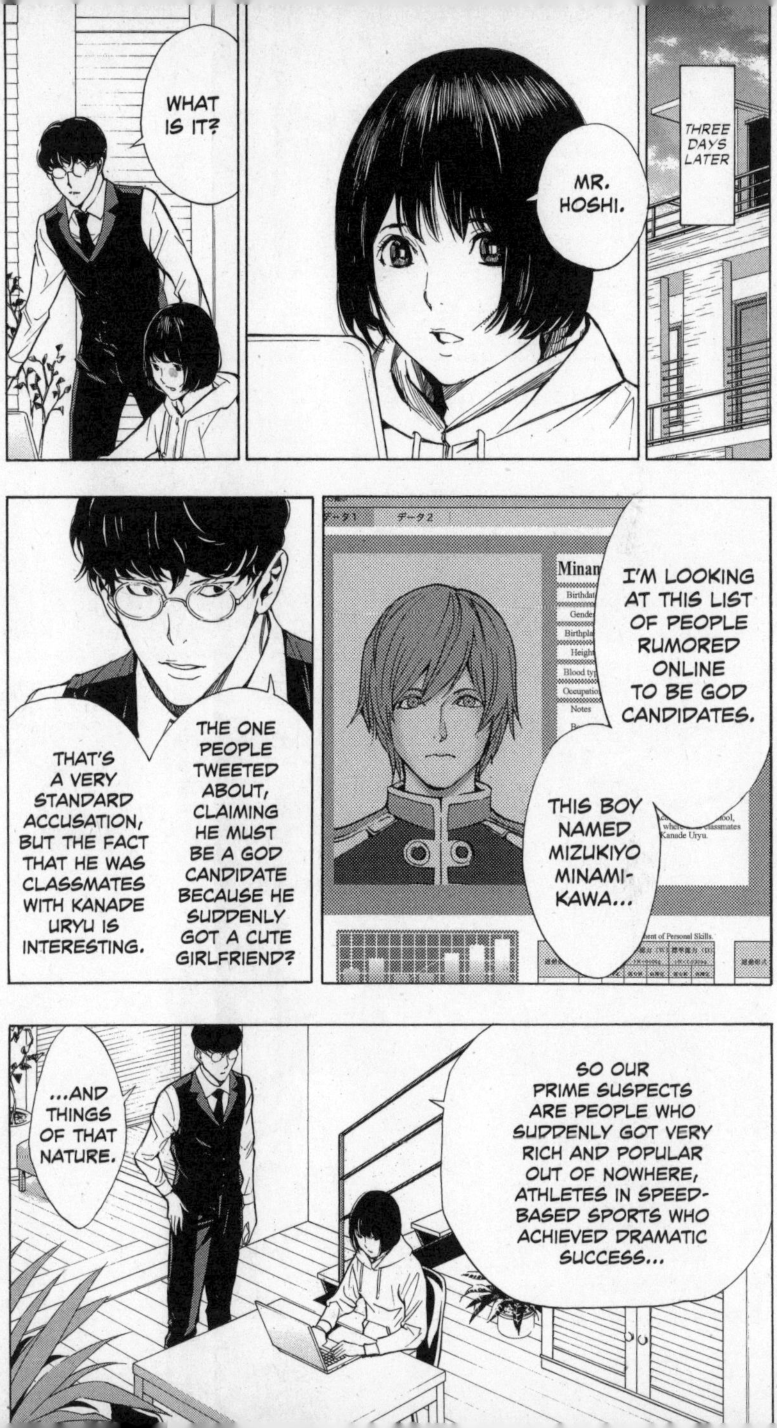
THREE DAYS LATER
MR. HOSHI.
WHAT IS IT?
I'M LOOKING AT THIS LIST OF PEOPLE RUMORED ONLINE TO BE GOD CANDIDATES.
THIS BOY NAMED MIZUKIYO MINAMI-KAWA...
THE ONE PEOPLE TWEETED ABOUT, CLAIMING HE MUST BE A GOD CANDIDATE BECAUSE HE SUDDENLY GOT A CUTE GIRLFRIEND?
THAT'S A VERY STANDARD ACCUSATION, BUT THE FACT THAT HE WAS CLASSMATES WITH KANADE URYU IS INTERESTING.
SO OUR PRIME SUSPECTS ARE PEOPLE WHO SUDDENLY GOT VERY RICH AND POPULAR OUT OF NOWHERE, ATHLETES IN SPEED-BASED SPORTS WHO ACHIEVED DRAMATIC SUCCESS...
...AND THINGS OF THAT NATURE.

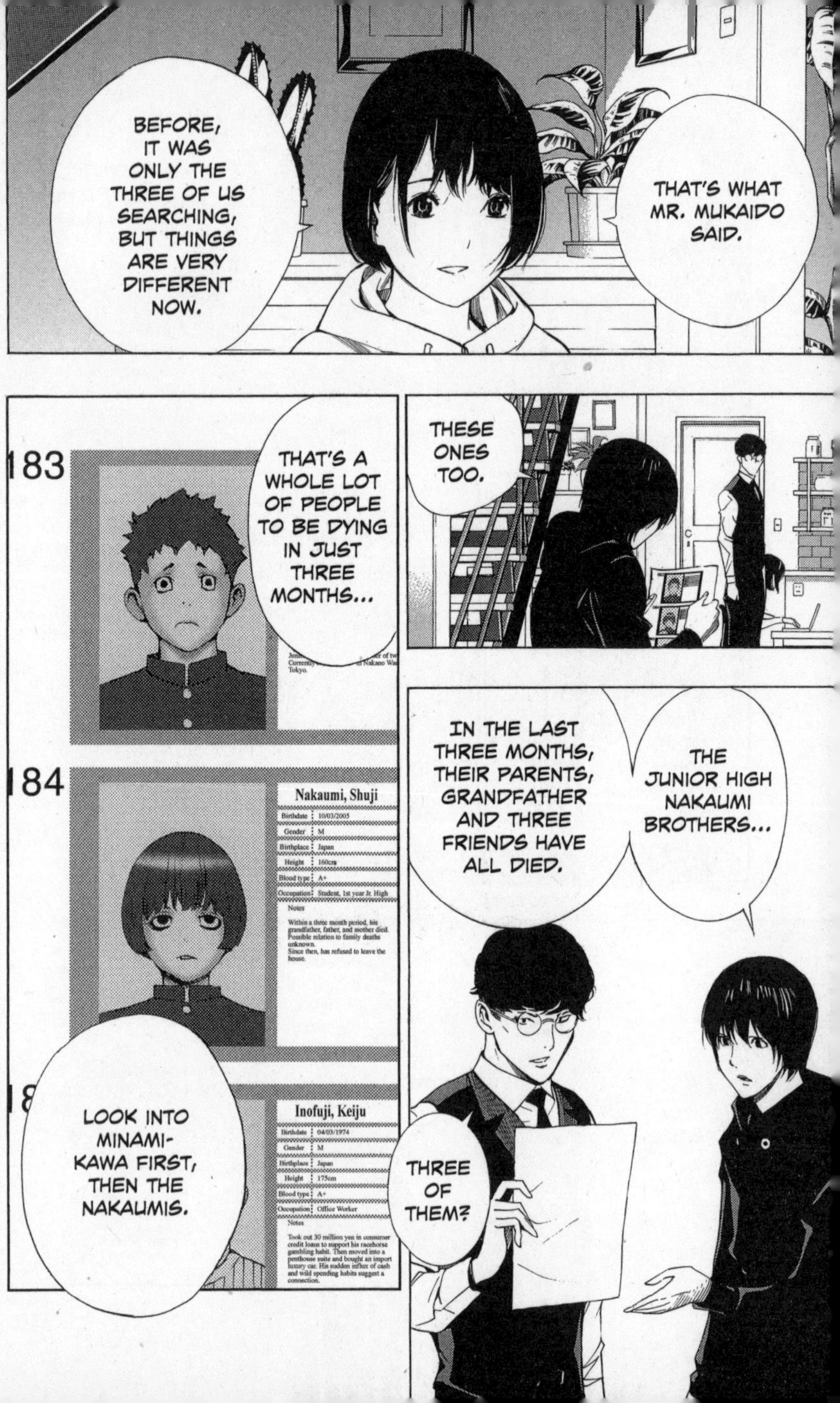
BEFORE, IT WAS ONLY THE THREE OF US SEARCHING, BUT THINGS ARE VERY DIFFERENT NOW.
THAT'S WHAT MR. MUKAIDO SAID.
THESE ONES TOO.
THE JUNIOR HIGH NAKAUMI BROTHERS...
IN THE LAST THREE MONTHS, THEIR PARENTS, GRANDFATHER AND THREE FRIENDS HAVE ALL DIED.
THREE OF THEM?
183
THAT'S A WHOLE LOT OF PEOPLE TO BE DYING IN JUST THREE MONTHS...
184
Nakaumi, Shuji
Birthdate 10/03/2005
Gender M
Birthplace Japan
Height 160cm
Blood type A+
Occupation Student, 1st year Jr. High
Notes
Within a three month period, his grandfather, father, and mother died. Possible relation to family deaths unknown. Since then, has refused to leave the house.
Inofuji, Keiju
Birthdate 04/03/1974
Gender M
Birthplace Japan
Height 175cm
Blood type A+
Occupation Office Worker
Notes
Took out 30 million yen in consumer credit loans to support his racehorse gambling habit. Then moved into a penthouse suite and bought an import luxury car. His sudden influx of cash and wild spending habits suggest a connection.
LOOK INTO MINAMI-KAWA FIRST, THEN THE NAKAUMIS.

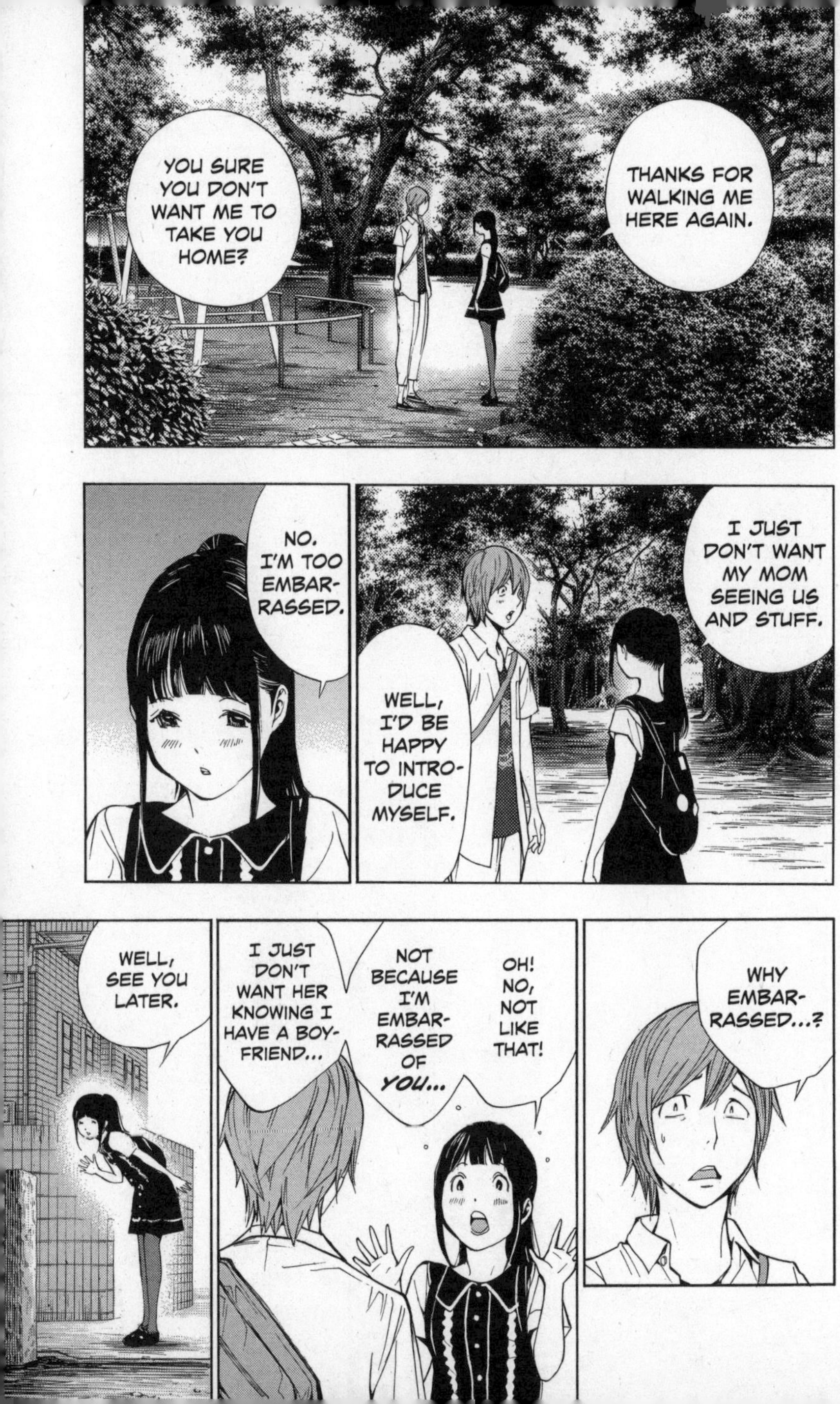
THANKS FOR WALKING ME HERE AGAIN.
YOU SURE YOU DON'T WANT ME TO TAKE YOU HOME?
I JUST DON'T WANT MY MOM SEEING US AND STUFF.
WELL, I'D BE HAPPY TO INTRODUCE MYSELF.
NO. I'M TOO EMBARRASSED.
WHY EMBARRASSED...?
OH! NO, NOT LIKE THAT!
NOT BECAUSE I'M EMBARRASSED OF *YOU*...
I JUST DON'T WANT HER KNOWING I HAVE A BOYFRIEND...
WELL, SEE YOU LATER.

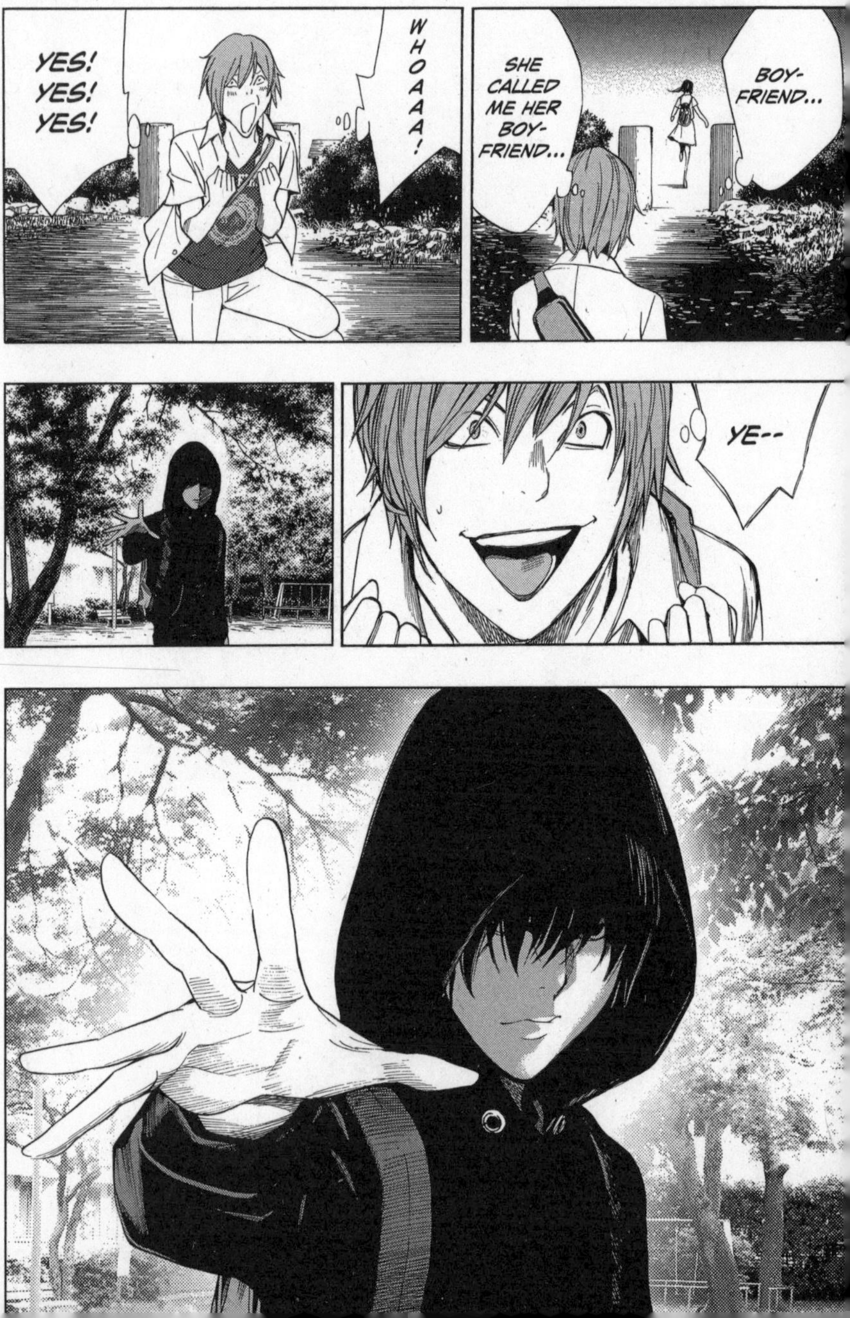
BOY-FRIEND...
SHE CALLED ME HER BOY-FRIEND...
WHOAAAA!
YES! YES! YES!
YE--

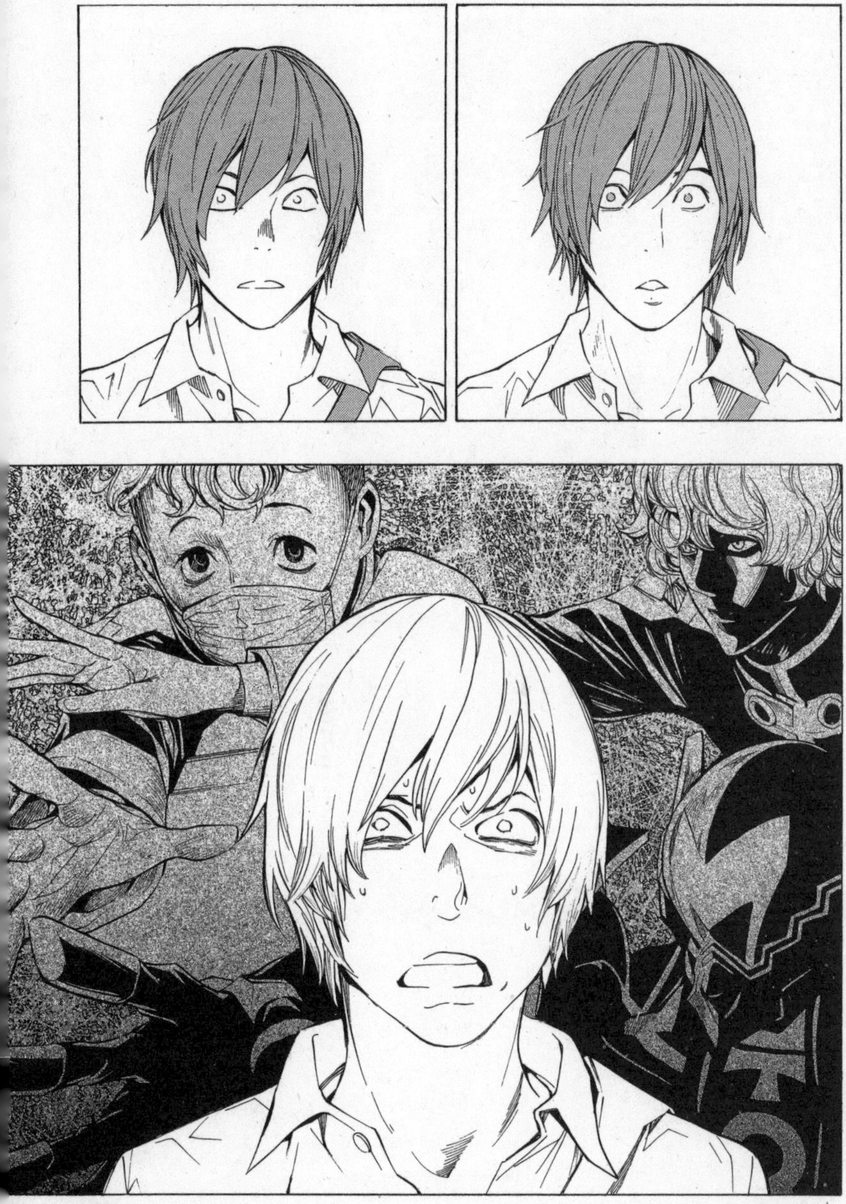

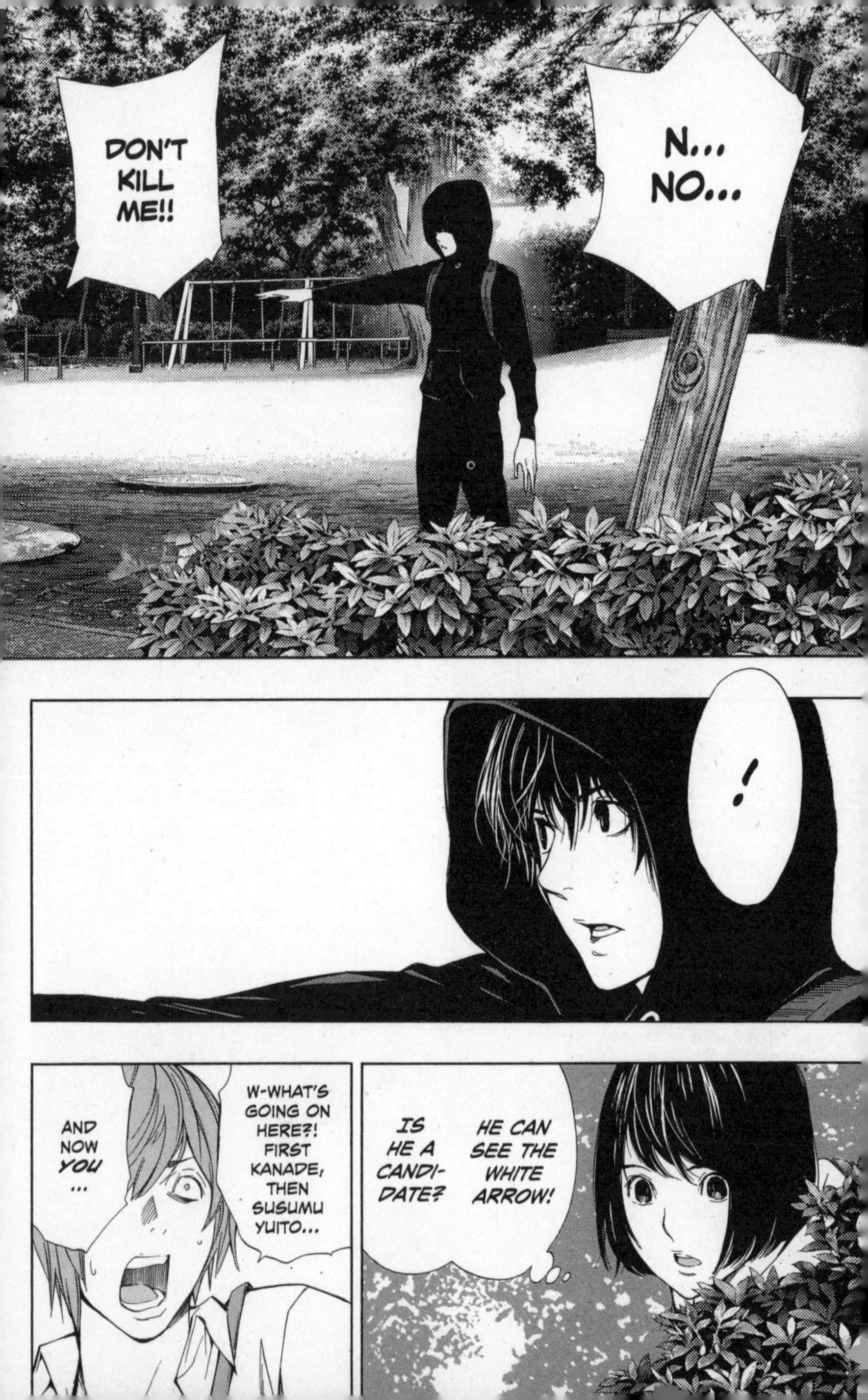
N... NO...
DON'T KILL ME!!
!
HE CAN SEE THE WHITE ARROW!
IS HE A CANDI-DATE?
W-WHAT'S GOING ON HERE?! FIRST KANADE, THEN SUSUMU YUITO...
AND NOW *YOU* ...

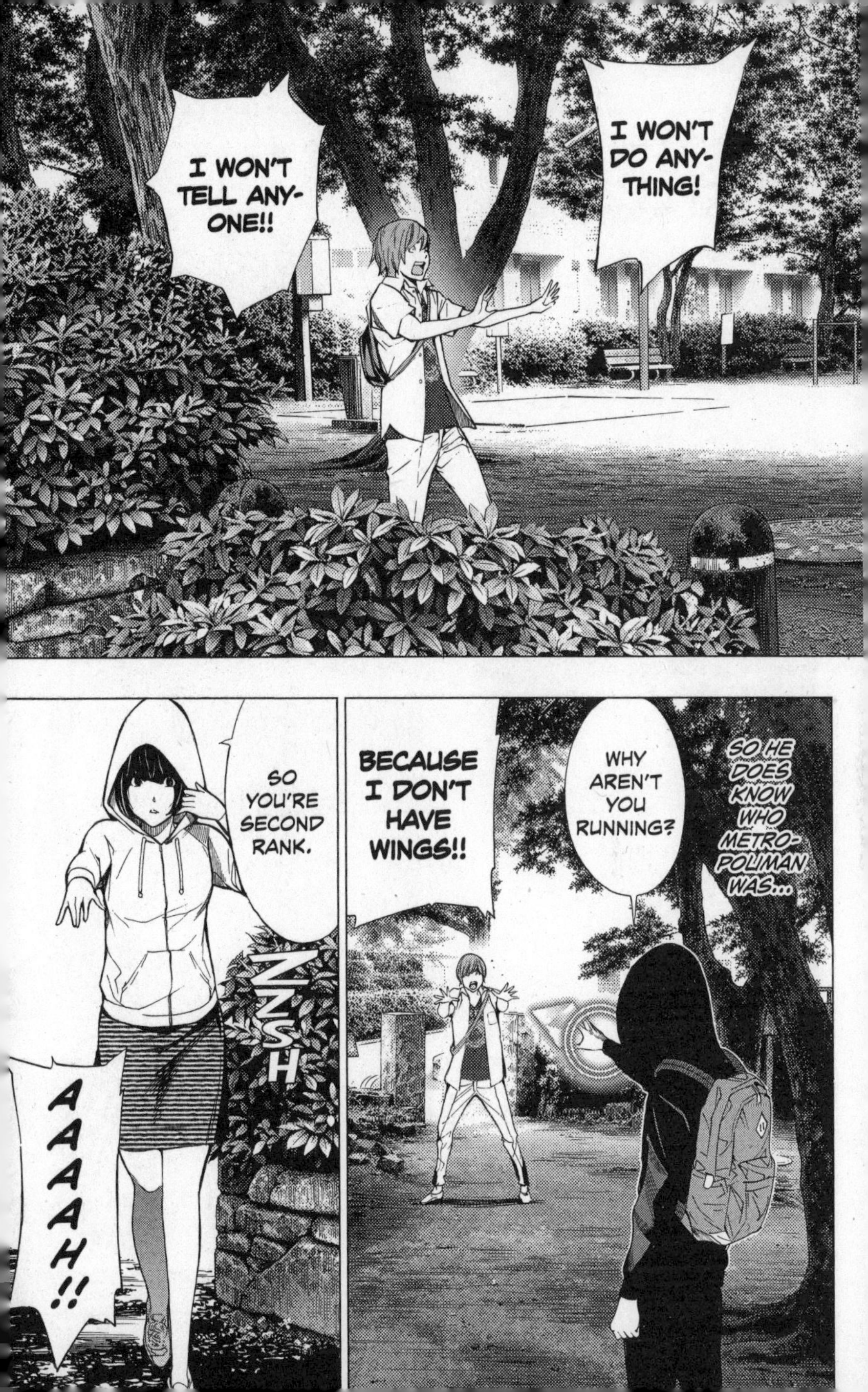
I WON'T DO ANYTHING!
I WON'T TELL ANYONE!!
SO HE DOES KNOW WHO METROPOLIMAN WAS...
WHY AREN'T YOU RUNNING?
BECAUSE I DON'T HAVE WINGS!!
SO YOU'RE SECOND RANK.
ZZSH
AAAAAH!!

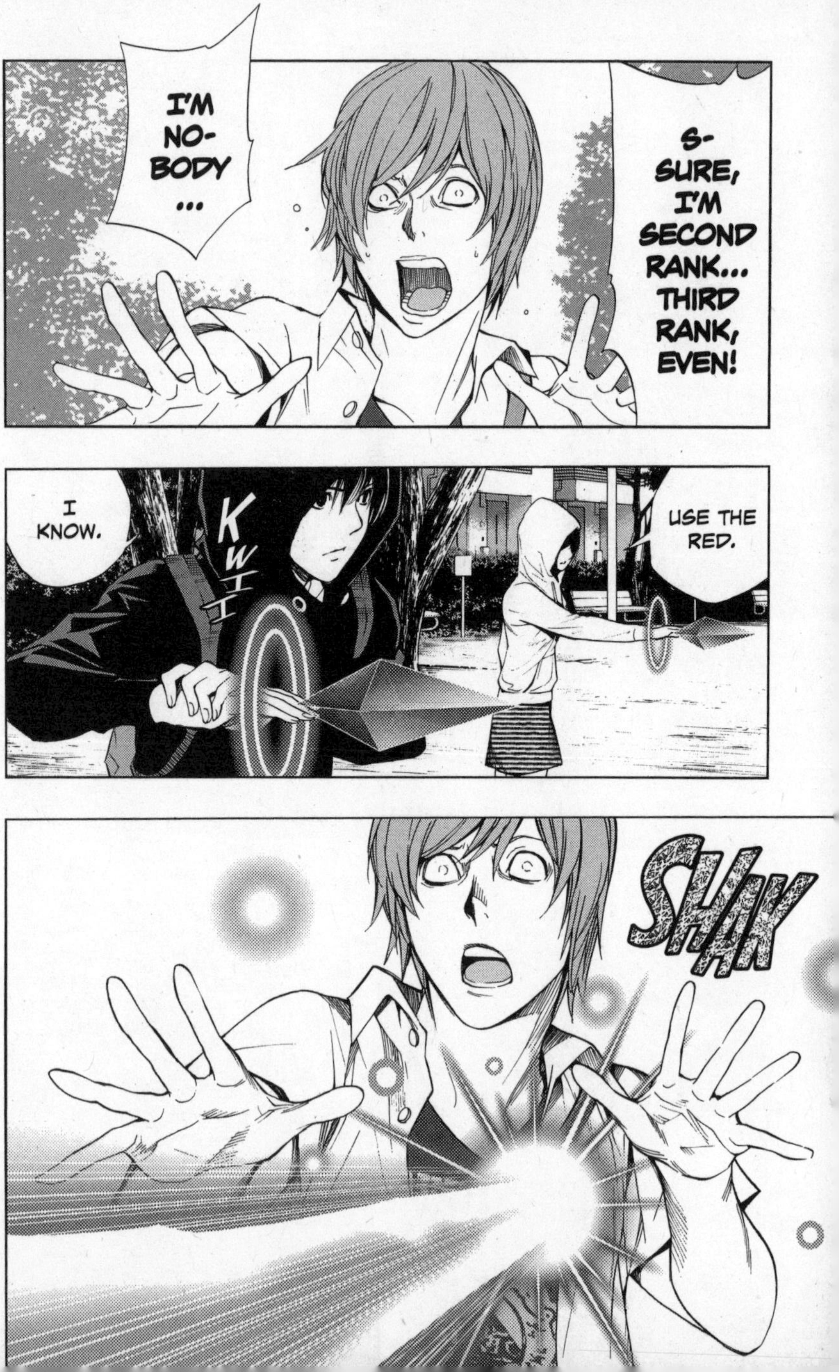
S-SURE, I'M SECOND RANK... THIRD RANK, EVEN!
I'M NO-BODY ...
USE THE RED.
KWIII
I KNOW.
SHAK

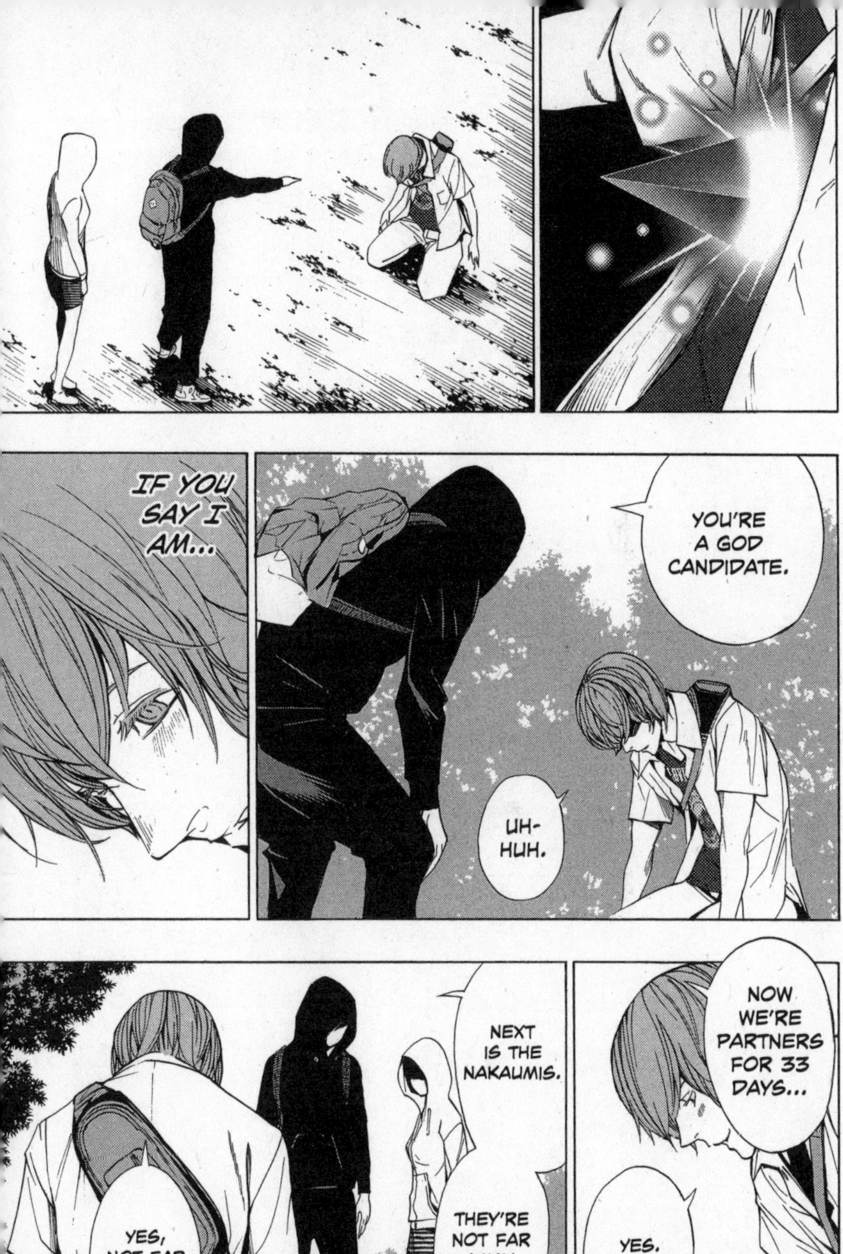
YOU'RE A GOD CANDIDATE.
UH-HUH.
IF YOU SAY I AM...
NOW WE'RE PARTNERS FOR 33 DAYS...
YES. PARTNERS.
NEXT IS THE NAKAUMIS.
THEY'RE NOT FAR AWAY.
YES, NOT FAR AWAY.

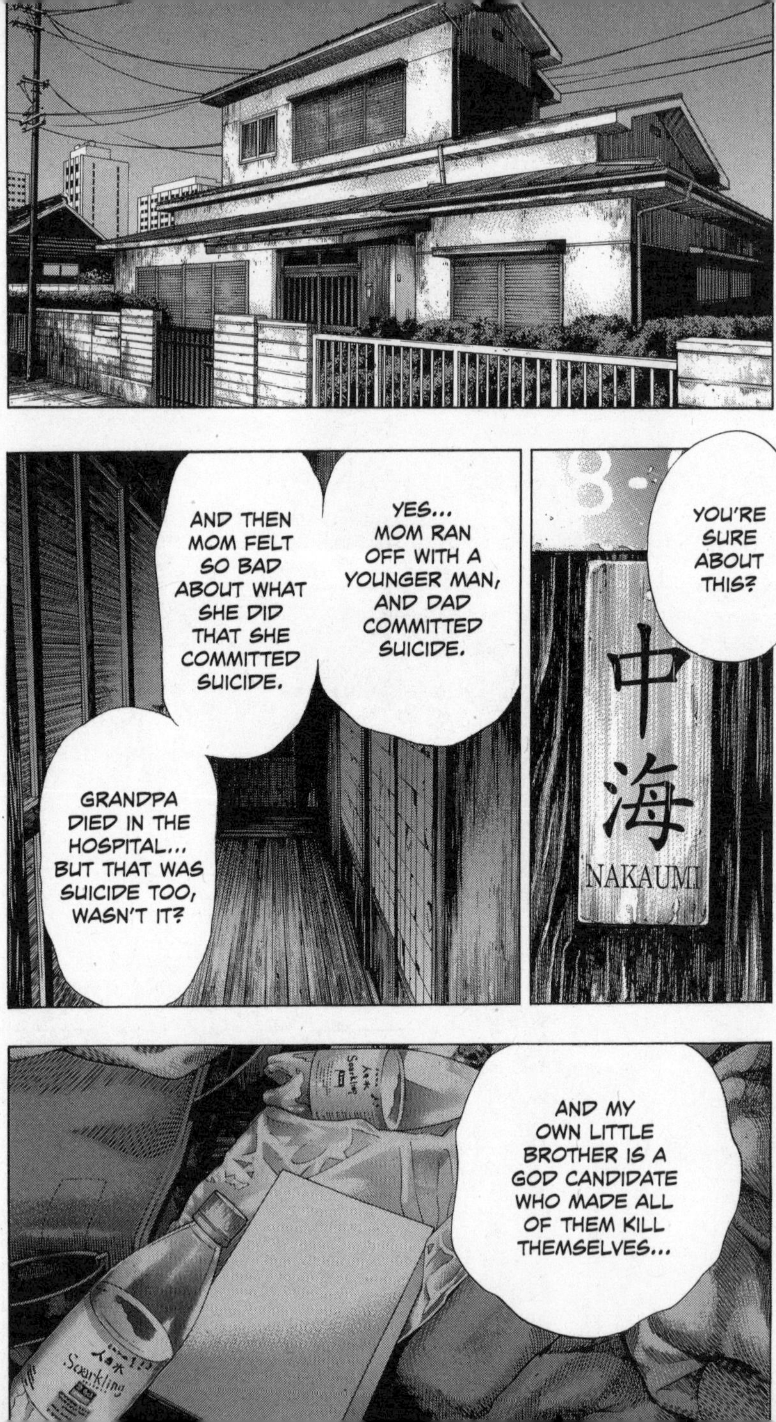

YOU'RE SURE ABOUT THIS?
中海
NAKAUMI
YES... MOM RAN OFF WITH A YOUNGER MAN, AND DAD COMMITTED SUICIDE.
AND THEN MOM FELT SO BAD ABOUT WHAT SHE DID THAT SHE COMMITTED SUICIDE.
GRANDPA DIED IN THE HOSPITAL... BUT THAT WAS SUICIDE TOO, WASN'T IT?
AND MY OWN LITTLE BROTHER IS A GOD CANDIDATE WHO MADE ALL OF THEM KILL THEMSELVES...

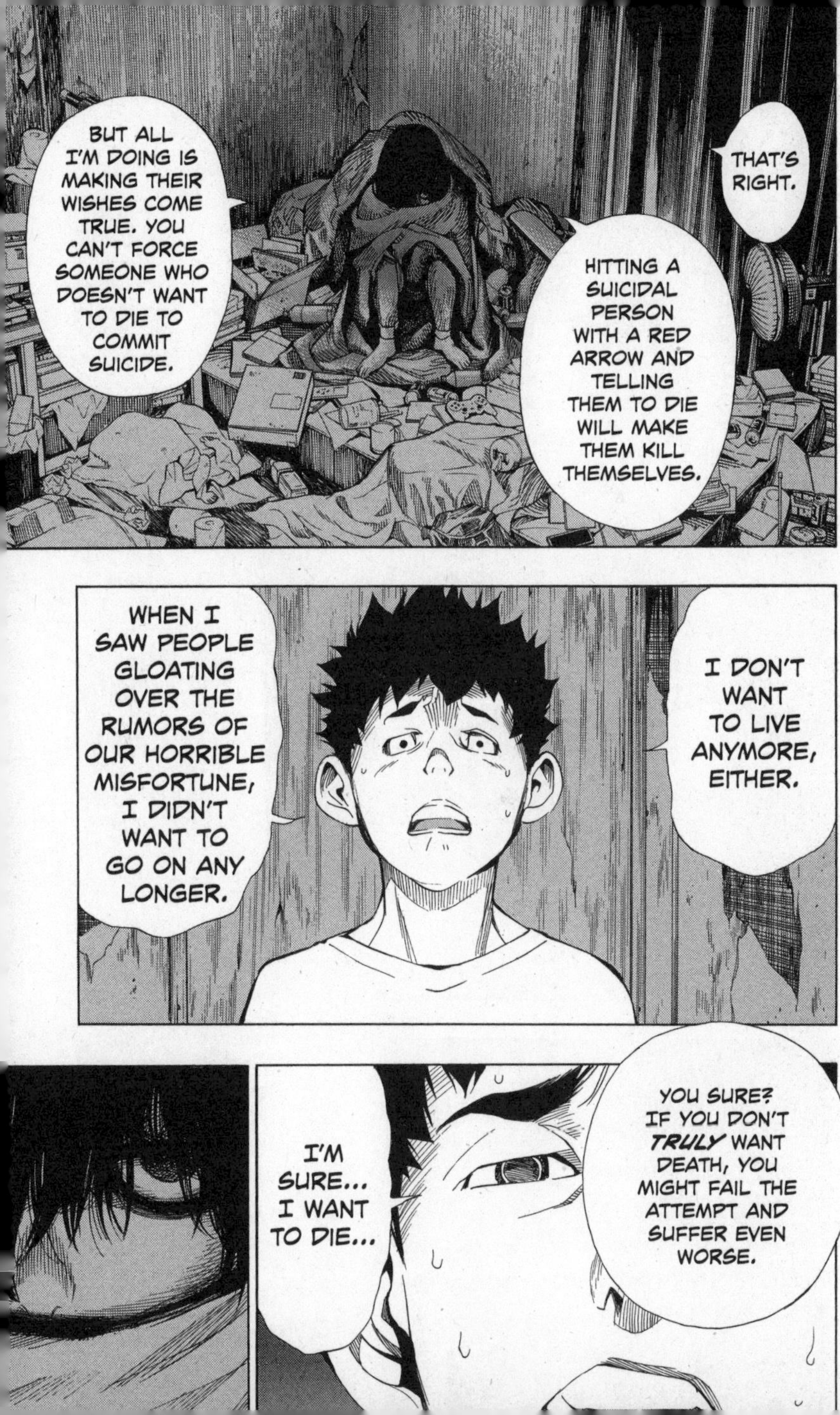
THAT'S RIGHT.
HITTING A SUICIDAL PERSON WITH A RED ARROW AND TELLING THEM TO DIE WILL MAKE THEM KILL THEMSELVES.
BUT ALL I'M DOING IS MAKING THEIR WISHES COME TRUE. YOU CAN'T FORCE SOMEONE WHO DOESN'T WANT TO DIE TO COMMIT SUICIDE.
I DON'T WANT TO LIVE ANYMORE, EITHER.
WHEN I SAW PEOPLE GLOATING OVER THE RUMORS OF OUR HORRIBLE MISFORTUNE, I DIDN'T WANT TO GO ON ANY LONGER.
YOU SURE? IF YOU DON'T *TRULY* WANT DEATH, YOU MIGHT FAIL THE ATTEMPT AND SUFFER EVEN WORSE.
I'M SURE... I WANT TO DIE...

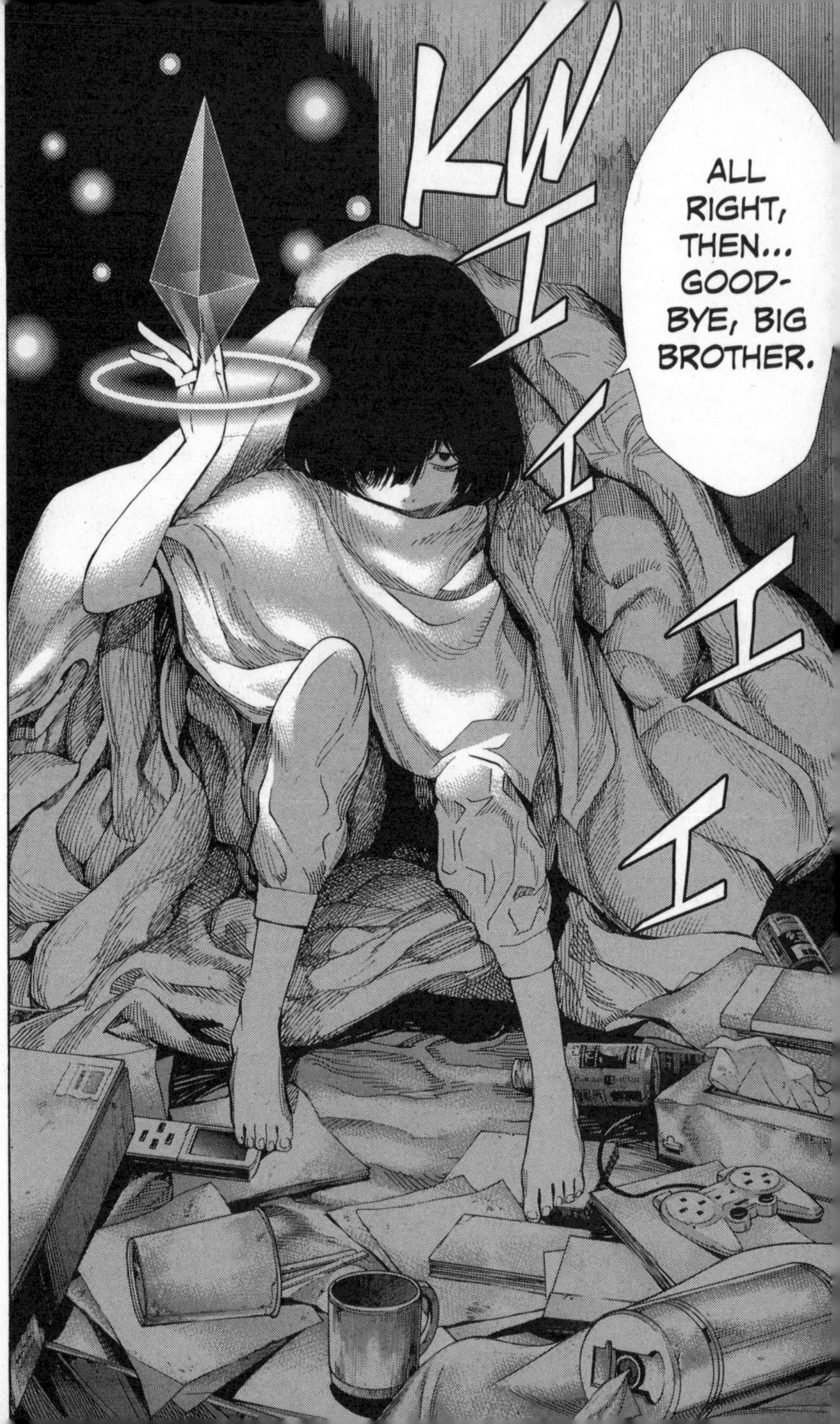
ALL RIGHT, THEN... GOOD-BYE, BIG BROTHER.
KWIIIIII

The tools an angel can give to a person depend on the angel's rank.
Special rank: Wings, red arrows, white arrows
First rank: Wings, red arrows
Second rank: Wings or red arrows

God candidates are chosen from among people who have lost their reason or will to live.

God is determined from among thirteen human beings selected by thirteen angels. The process shall take no more than 999 days.

The angel tools of deceased god candidates can be claimed and used by other candidates.

Angels shall not use their own arrows and wings to directly affect God candidates.

Angel tools from deceased god candidates can also be given to other human beings.

If angel tools are returned before a god is determined, the person who returned them shall die.

When a god is determined, the angel tools of the other candidates are forfeited.

Angel wings can fly faster than the human eye can follow.

Non-candidate human beings cannot see angel tools.

Wings can fly faster than arrows.

The speed of the wings is not affected by any amount of weight the user can carry unassisted. However, they cannot lift more than one extra person.

Angel arrows can strike any target with perfect accuracy, but only if the shooter can see the target.

Arrows cannot be fired while utilizing faster-than-sight wing flight.

Red arrows can pierce up to fourteen people at one time.

Any person pierced by a red arrow will fall in love with the user for 33 days before the effect wears off. The effect will only work on a specific person once.

When a person is under the effect of a red arrow, they cannot be pierced by other red arrows.

If the pierced person dies, that red arrow will be returned to its owner.

Any person pierced by a white arrow will die without fail.

Even a person under the effects of a red arrow may be unable to perform certain actions if lacking an adequate reason or intent to do them.

When a red arrow is used on another person possessing red arrows, they may be ordered to use those red arrows on the original shooter. In this case, the effect of the second arrow overrides the first.

Tsugumi Ohba

Born in Tokyo, Tsugumi Ohba is the author of the hit series *Death Note* and *Bakuman。*.

Takeshi Obata

Takeshi Obata was born in 1969 in Niigata, Japan, and first achieved international recognition as the artist of the wildly popular *Shonen Jump* title *Hikaru no Go*, which won the 2003 Tezuka Osamu Cultural Prize: Shinsei "New Hope" Award and the 2000 Shogakukan Manga Award. He went on to illustrate the smash hit *Death Note* as well as the hugely successful manga *Bakuman。* and *All You Need Is Kill*.